If You Love

The Story of Anna Dengel

Miriam Therese Winter

authorHOUSE®

AuthorHouse™
1663 Liberty Drive
Bloomington, IN 47403
www.authorhouse.com
Phone: 1 (800) 839-8640

Published by AuthorHouse 10/07/2016

ISBN: 978-1-5246-2281-7 (sc)
ISBN: 978-1-5246-2280-0 (e)

Library of Congress Control Number: 2016912602

Medical Mission Sisters Generalate
41 Chatsworth Gardens
Acton, London W3 9LP
United Kingdom

Medical Mission Sisters North America
8400 Pine Road
Philadelphia, PA 19111
United States of America

Acknowledgments

Primary sources, namely, original documents, letters, articles, reports, chronicles, journals and books in the General Archives of the Society of Catholic Medical Missionaries (Medical Mission Sisters) in London, the Society's North American Archives in Philadelphia, and the private collections of individual Medical Mission Sisters around the world were core to the writing of this book. Most important among these were the letters, diaries, talks, notes, reports, and publications of Anna Dengel; the correspondence between Anna Dengel and Michael Mathis; letters and official documents issued by ecclesiastical authorities in the USA and in Rome; relevant source material from the archives of the Congregation of the Holy Cross; reports and minutes of the Society's first four General Chapters; the Dengel genealogy compiled by Rev. Baumgartner, parish priest in Steeg; *The Medical Missionary* Magazine, volumes I – XVII [1927-1943]; the journal of Sister Agnes Marie Ulbrich; the 26-page document by Dr. Josef Faistenberger, husband of Anna's sister, Ida; and *History of the Society of Catholic Medical Missionaries: Pre-Foundation to 1968*. Foundations graphic: Eunice Cudzewicz.

A WORD OF THANKS

Special thanks to the following individuals for their gracious hospitality during the author's fact-finding pilgrimage to Innsbruck, Hall, Salzburg, and Steeg in the Austrian Tirol: Elisabeth Dengel, daughter of Edmund, son of Edmund and Amalie, and Ellie Seidl, daughter of Anna's brother Hans; Professor Hans-Peter Rhomberg, M.D.; Reinhard Heiserer; Josef and Karla Kerner, caretakers of the Dengel estate; Father Baumgartner, pastor of Saint Oswald parish; and the village women of Steeg. The Society is grateful to all who so generously assisted our Founder in bringing her dream to fruition, especially: Franciscan Missionaries of Mary; priests and seminarians of the Congregation of the Holy Cross and Sisters of the Holy Cross in South Bend, Indiana; Ursuline Sisters in Louisville; Religious Sisters of the Sacred Heart in Philadelphia. The author is indebted to Medical Mission Sisters, especially, past and present Society Leadership Teams and the General Archivist in London; Sister Maria Hornung and the Leadership Team of North America; Jane Blewett, Sister Eunice Cudzewicz, and Monica McGinley, who have provided a network of support since the project's inception; Sisters and Associates in the USA and Germany who contributed resources or attended sessions to evaluate work-in-progress, especially, Sister Mary Elizabeth Johnson. M.E. – I could not have done this without you!

INTRODUCTION

Eighteen years after Anna Dengel's death, I was part of an editorial team that published *Fire and Flame: The Legacy of Anna Dengel*, a collection of essays and reflections by individual members of her community. It was a major undertaking that involved those who had known her and had experienced first-hand her passion for the Society's healing charism as expressed through medical missions and related ministries. I rejoice to have been part of that multifaceted effort to lift our Founder out of the shadows and present her to a wider world. However, as time went on, I came to realize that we had not gone far enough. We needed to know more about her. We needed to know her story – her full story. What was known internationally, by and large, centered on the years following the founding of the Medical Mission Sisters. Anna Dengel was 33 years old when her Society came into existence. A lot of years preceded that, and there were many more that followed, years during which her personal story had been subsumed within the developmental narrative of her "holy experiment." I wanted to know, not only the facts, but if at all possible, her feelings. What was the hidden backstory waiting to come to light? I wanted to write a more detailed account of her remarkable life.

The impetus to research and write this book began with a very strange dream, one that took time to interpret. I was being pulled deep into the earth and eventually emerged into an open space excavated out of the mud. Clearly, this was a tomb. I felt but never saw Anna Dengel's presence, and I heard a voice that was hers say: "Down ... come down ... down deep ... deeper." Abruptly, I awoke. I knew then that all that had been written about her and all that was known of her in general had not gone deep enough. I felt she was commissioning me to tell her story, or more accurately, transmit her story by going deeper into the archival materials she had amassed. Indeed, she would entrust to me far more than I could convey. Time and again I would turn to her for guidance as I wrestled with what to include in the manuscript and what to set aside. In this way I gave her the opportunity to tell her story through me. In order to do this I had to approach her as an equal, not as my Superior General, not as the Founder of a new initiative in the Roman Catholic Church, not as "Mother" but simply as Anna – a woman of her times, yet in spirit, way ahead of her times; a feminist who was inclusive; a pioneer who cherished tradition; a practitioner who was a scholar; a brilliant and cosmopolitan individual who was at home among the mundane and comfortable with ecclesiastics; a global citizen who refused to relinquish her Alpine roots. Her compassion for the suffering of women and children is legendary. Her love for all God's creation is her lasting legacy.

As I embraced the challenge of bringing her to life for future generations, I was drawn down deep into that which most historians say is the past, but for me, has been a living present pulsating with energy awaiting release. May this rendition of Anna Dengel's story be a blessing for us all.

It takes a village to raise a child,
or so the saying goes.
It took two women to raise awareness
to what village women and children need in order to survive:
full access to medical resources administered by women,
qualified women with canonical vows,
approval of the Vatican,
a change in Canon Law.
While many worldwide voiced their support,
at the heart of this hope were
Agnes McLaren, physician and advocate,
who set the systemic shift in motion,
and
Anna Dengel, physician and pioneer,
who brought the dream to fulfillment
by founding the international
Society of Catholic Medical Missionaries
~ Medical Mission Sisters ~
in 1925.
This is Anna's story.

PROLOGUE

The Alpine range that encompasses the Tirol in western Austria is breathtakingly beautiful. Long before its snow covered peaks became a destination for tourists eager to ski perilous slopes or hike labyrinthan canyons, families migrated into the mountains for a chance to begin again. Valleys gave rise to villages that defined a way of life for those who opted to settle there, once upon a time. Subsequent generations sank deep roots, transcending the stress of centuries marked by brutal winters that cut off all interaction with the world beyond. During those months of isolation, villagers had to depend on their own ingenuity and on one another in order to survive. Why endure such harsh deprivation? Because of the bountiful blessings that arrived with the first signs of spring. Because of the largesse of late summer harvests. Because there is no place like home.

Members of the Dengel clan were among those early pioneers who crossed the mountains of the Tirol to settle in the Lechtal Valley in the little village of Steeg. The family name, "Dengil," comes from *tangil* or *tangol*, which was the word for "hammer" in the High German language of the past. *Dengeln,* the word in use today, still means "to hammer." It is a name signifying strength and it appears for the first time in 1312 in Pettneu in the region of Arlberg. In 1427 the names of the "Tengl" family were already on record in Pettneu and also in Steeg, a five-hour journey away.

In 1652, or it may have been 1653, Georg Dengel married Anna Rainer and took her to his home in Dickenau, which consisted of several houses on the opposite bank of the river Lech that flows through the center of Steeg and defines this Alpine village. Georg Dengel was the great great great great great great grandfather of Anna Maria Dengel. His wife, Anna, gave birth to three daughters and a son, Johann.

Johann Dengel was 44 years old in 1699 when he married Eva Klotz in the little hamlet of Welzau, which is just east of Steeg. Their third child, a boy, was baptized in April of 1704. They named him Georg. In August of 1705, Johann, who was a trader, died while in a foreign country, leaving behind a wife and three children under the age of five.

Georg Dengel married Katharina Maldoner in 1730 and took her to Dickenau 25, on the other side of the river, to live in the home of Emanuel Dengel, the music director of the parish church in Steeg. Emanuel was related to Anna Dengel, the subject of this biography, through her mother's side of the family on a separate branch of the family tree. Katharina gave birth to four children. Their third child, a son, was born in Hinterellenbogen, a hamlet of Steeg. They named the boy Christian.

Christian Dengel married Anna Maria Klotz in 1763. They named the first of their three boys Josef Anton, born in 1764. Christian, a trader and merchant who dealt in manufactured goods in the Netherlands, was away from home for extended periods of time, which may have been why in 1780 he decided to retire and leave the business to his sons. Back at the family homestead - house No.15 in Dickenau - his interest centered on agriculture until his death in 1802, eight years after the death of his wife, Anna Maria.

Josef Anton Dengel was a farmer and a merchant like his father. In January of 1792 he married Anna Maria Huber, who was born in Steeg four years before he was. Nine months later, a son, Christian Eugen, their only child, arrived. Years later, husband and wife both died in the family home, No. 13 in Steeg, she in 1820, he in 1836.

Christian Eugen Dengel, following in the footsteps of his father and grandfather, also became both a merchant and a farmer. In January of 1819 he married Maria Johanna Spoettel, a native of Steeg. Both were 27. The eldest of their five children, Johann Baptist Nikolaus, was born in September of that same year. On December 17, 1831, Christian Eugen purchased house No. 7 in Steeg from his uncle, Johann Baptist Dengel, who had no children. The sale included all the furnishings. The price: 4000 florins. Christian Eugen moved his family into the new house and lived there until his death in 1856. Maria Johanna died in 1869.

Johann Baptist Nikolaus Dengel married Anna Maria Klotz in 1846. She was born in Hägerau in 1829. He was 27. She was 17. Johann

Baptist was not only a farmer and a merchant committed to continuing the family business according to tradition. He was also the mayor of Steeg, a position he held for a very long time. Johann Baptist and Anna Maria had ten children. Two baby boys died soon after birth. Edmund Wilhelm entered the world on June 25 in 1857. When he came of age he attended a technical school in Kempten in the Bavarian Allgäu to prepare himself to make a living in commerce and merchandise exchange, just like the men of the Dengel family who preceded him. He also learned how to establish and manage a business of his own. In May of 1889, Johann Baptist handed over his property at No. 7 in Steeg to his son, Edmund Wilhelm, and moved to Hägerau. Now, in addition to being a tradesman, Edmund also had responsibilities related to the family farm and homestead he had inherited. His father died the following year, two years before the birth of his granddaughter, Anna Maria Dengel.

~ ~ ~ ~ ~

The Dengel genealogy is a testament to family ties and traditions that have held fast for generations, yielding a sense of belonging and an element of permanence. It also bears witness to the patriarchal orientation of society. The birth dates of the boys who grew up to be men were carefully recorded, while the birth dates of the women those men would marry are often not to be found. Instead, the date of a baby girl's baptism was far more prevalent. Still, there are hints of the strength, influence, and creativity of a long line of women of spirit within the Dengel lineage, right up to the present time.

Dengel families were people of faith, one that was shaped by the sacramental rhythms of the Roman Catholic Tradition and the blessings of God's creation revealed through nature day after day. The mountain, for example, was metaphor for Divine mercy, and consequently, sacramental. Psalm 121 helped to sustain them through bone-chilling winters that pushed faith to the limits. "I lift up my eyes to the mountains—from where does my help come? From the Maker of heaven and earth." In more recent times, one of their members took the groundbreaking determination of her cultural heritage beyond the Alpine ranges and ravines and out into the wider world in order to share with the disadvantaged the wisdom generated there. This book is a tribute to Anna Dengel's pioneering spirit, her selfless and inclusive compassion, her unwavering, healing love.

If we see God's Providence

and God's love

and God's Mercy,

as well as God's Justice, ruling the world,

a lot is "Mystery" but nothing is hopeless or useless.

Anna Dengel

PART ONE

CHAPTER ONE

Steeg, a village in the northwest mountain region of the Tirol, is where this biography begins. Its name means "bridge," a point to remember as the story unfolds.

Three villages – Steeg, Hägerau, and Lechleiten – together with several hamlets constituted the Reutte political district of the upper Lech valley in the late 19th century. The village of Steeg, 1110 meters above sea level, was distinguished by a line of estate houses along the left bank of the Lech, the river that runs through the region and beyond. The hamlet of Dickenau, a small enclave of houses on the other side of the river, was considered part of Steeg. Adjacent to this was the parish church dedicated to Saint Oswald and built on an elevation of solid rock that overlooked the valley, a presence visible to all.

The river and the only road through the village ran parallel to one another in close proximity as they wound through the valley, their destinies entwined. Green fields and family farms lay directly behind those stately homes to the left of the river, where flocks grazed and gardens were cultivated to meet a household's needs. Further back were the smaller hamlets, tucked into the hollows and hills. Hovering over the valley and all within it were the mountain peaks of the Alps: the *Biberkopf* and the *Hohe Licht* and the *Mädelegabel*, a ridge marking the geographical boundary with Bavaria. For the residents of Steeg, however, it was and always would be the distinctive cone of Pimig, the peak rising 2409 meters southwest of the village that signified they were home.

In 1891 Edmund Dengel was ready for a change. He had been a successful tradesman. He was also the sole proprietor of the Dengel estate he had inherited two years earlier and was living in its large house on the edge of the road into Steeg. Like many other men from the upper

Lech valley, where labor is focused on dairy farming and breeding cattle and the soil is simply not able to supply food sufficient for all, Edmund made a living by traveling to areas beyond the mountain ranges that encircled Steeg. Trade for and in manufactured goods in Switzerland, Germany, and especially Holland had been a way of life for his ancestors, and so it was for him. Brothers Johan, Anton, and Christian Dengel had become significantly wealthy and embellished their residences with elements of affluence. Commerce had sustained Edmund's family for centuries, and in one way or another, it would continue on.

On April 6, 1891 Edmund Wilhelm Dengel married Maria Gertrud Scheidle from the village of Hägerau, about a mile away, and brought her to her new home in Steeg. Gertrud, born on November 16 in 1869, was 22 when she married Edmund. He was 34. Theirs was the challenge of blending two different styles into one. Edmund was more conservative, taciturn, some say authoritarian. He had been raised to reflect the old Tirolian spirit: "For God, the Kaiser, and the Fatherland!" As the head of his household, he expected to do the same. Gertrud, on the other hand, exhibited family traits that differed from those of the Dengel clan: qualities of gentleness, an easy going manner, an inclination to be less strict and a lot more flexible. She was, in fact, quite creative, as were other members of her family. Her father, Johann, a stucco worker from the town of Bach, had participated in the artistic decoration of the legendary Neuschwanstein Castle in Bavaria. Their family even carried a second name indicating they were "painters." Because Gertrud was a talented seamstress specializing in vestments, it should come as no surprise that soon after the wedding, Edmund and Gertrud Dengel opened a small business for embroidered church linens in house No. 7 in Steeg. This was in addition to the business for manufactured goods that had long been associated with the Dengel family. The embroidery centered on the skills of Gertrud and was carried out in their home.

On March 16, 1892, at 11:30 a.m., with the help of midwife Anna Singer who had come to her home to assist her, Gertrud gave birth to a baby girl who was given the name, Anna Maria. It was a very prestigious name, honoring her paternal grandmother and those other matriarchs through several generations of the Dengel genealogy.

Anna was baptized that same day, carried in the arms of her uncle Otto, Edmund's brother, across the road, over the bridge, up the little hill, and into the church. Otto would be Anna Maria's Godparent.

The priest, Father Eduard Blaas, baptized her *"In nomine Patris et Filii et Spiritus Sancti."* To this was added a resounding *"Amen."* There is no indication of who else might have been in attendance, only a note that family members arrived later that day. One can only imagine the celebratory spirit in house No. 7 that afternoon and evening, as grandmothers and a grandfather, cousins and aunts and uncles arrived from the neighboring villages to celebrate this joyous event. For the record the family name in the baptismal registry was listed as "Dengl." Later on it was amended, "for official reasons," a common occurrence in Austria at that time. Meanwhile, baby Anna, snug in the wooden cradle that would rock all of the Dengel children in turn, joined a loving family circle on the first day of what would become a most amazing life.

The house Anna would grow to love was spacious and quite functional. Wide stone steps led up to a large, heavy wooden door that opened into a gigantic hall where relatives and guests could gather and mingle and where the family would come and go and do what needed doing. To the left there was a sitting room, with an eating area and a prayer corner, warmed by a wood-fed stove. Beyond that were two bedrooms: one for the parents and the other for the youngest children who would require a watchful eye. Off the main hall was a room for the grandmother, a place for preparing food, and also the stable that was attached to the house, where they kept four horses, and a cow, and most likely several chickens, as well as their horse-drawn carriage. A wooden staircase leading up to the second level opened onto a long wide hall that was big enough to play in and adorned with cabinets and artifacts acquired through the years. It opened onto two big and bright bedrooms that featured large windows with views of the mountains and the river racing by. There was a laundry and drying room large enough to hang not only wet clothing but wide swaths of material for commercial use. There was also an additional space that had been refurbished and ran the length of the house. This was the sewing room and workroom for the production of vestments and church linens. Under each of the four windows along the outer wall was a station for a seamstress, who sewed or embroidered according to Gertrud's instructions and artistic designs. This workplace was an ideal setting for an entrepreneurial mom. Finally, off to the side was a balcony with a view of the village cemetery that began just behind the house. It had been placed there a long time ago when this area marked the middle of Steeg. Gottesacker: God's acre.

That's how it was referred to then. It was – and still is – a patch of serenity in that corner of the world.

The interior of house No. 7 reflected the social status of the Dengel ancestry, with its spaciousness and its solid wood furnishings of artistically carved design. The furniture had its own tale to tell. Each year a local official would arrive and ask the head of the household how much lumber would be needed for the coming year. This meant anticipating how many tables and chairs had to be constructed or replaced. Were the stable stalls adequate? What else might be of use to a rapidly growing family? That information was recorded, along with an estimate of how many trees had to be cut that year in order to meet those needs. That amount became part of the official record, and if the limit were exceeded, there would be a penalty to pay. This ecological framework ensured preservation of the forested areas surrounding the village and the valley. Inherited pieces of furniture that had lasted through generations would rarely need replacing, a boon to a man with a growing family to provide for and a fledgling business to run.

Gertrud, a hardworking woman, was an ongoing support to her husband. His sales of her high quality vestments earned him respect within church circles and a growing reputation as one whom they could trust. Before long she would also prove to be a devoted mother, for she would give birth to five children in seven-and-a-half years. The first three came one after the other: Anna Maria on March 16 in 1892; Ida Rosa Angela on May 31 in 1893; and Johann Baptist on June 24 in 1894.

In the large ancestral manor originally built in 1804 and now home to yet another generation of the Dengel family, Anna had all the room in the world to run and play, inside and out, upstairs and downstairs, with or without her siblings, even when the weather kept her indoors. During the sun-drenched days of summer, she spent as much time as possible out in the midst of God's creation. She would play with Ida and Hans on the sides of the house and in the back of the house but not in the front of it, for it was much too close to the river, where they were forbidden to go. The cautionary tale that they were told was about the legendary *"Blutschink,"* an evil spirit who lived in the streams. He would come out of the Lech, they were warned, and lure little children like themselves into the depths of the river, never to be seen again. Reason enough to mind Mama's words and stay behind the house, where there happened to be eight cherry trees with an attraction of their own. In a flash Anna would be up in a tree and out on a limb, reaching for a ripe red cherry, picking – and eating – the succulent fruit, keeping the family pantry supplied until the season was over. During the summer there was plenty of time to participate in family outings – picnics and picking flowers and losing oneself in a seemingly endless expanse of Queen Anne's Lace, Anna's favorite flower. So many species of wildflowers grace the Tirol, among them the red alpine rose, the deep blue alpine forget-me-not, the wild orchid in the higher wooded areas, the yellow and red or purple *Frauenschuh* (ladyslipper), and the precious edelweise. These and a fistful of fragrant herbs for medicinal or culinary purposes were always a much appreciated gift for the woman of the house.

Summer was also the season to visit relatives and be visited by them. Church-related feasts and festivals were the main events. They brought extended families together because nearly all who lived in the area at that time were Catholic. These joyous occasions featured good food and drink and spirited music, with a chance to catch up on the latest news and reconnect with one another. On the feast of Saint Oswald, August 5, Anna's relatives from Holzgau and Hägerau came to Steeg to celebrate the village's patron saint. On August 15, feast of the Assumption, everyone went to Holzgau for the opening of their annual fair and were greeted by houses lavishly decorated for the event. The three Dengel children loved going there because they received so much attention from several of their favorite aunts. On August 17, feast of St. Roch, who is celebrated as Patron Against Pestilence, they would go to Hägerau to visit Gertrud's married sister and their paternal grandmother, Anna Maria Dengel, until she died on April 2nd in 1898. Two months later, on June 10, Gertrud gave birth to a little girl, Dominika Maria Margareta.

There were sights to see all along the only road through the valley as it wound through village after village and brushed against farm after farm. The wayside shrines, for instance. Each homestead had its own, a visible sign of gratitude for benefits received and a plea for ongoing favor. At Holzgau were the Falls to the far right of the river, its spectacular display in early spring featured a wall of water cascading down a high cliff of gray granite rock and spilling into the Lech.

During the short summer months in the valley, the cattle were driven into the meadows in a daily ritual that followed a strict routine.

At six o'clock every morning, the goatherd would blow his horn and the cowherd would crack his whip at the edges of the village. Stalls would open and all at once neck bells would jingle and clang as goats and cattle emerged to form a long procession through the village, plodding over the bridge and up the hill into the Scheibiger forest and the pastures that lay beyond it, teeming with sweet-smelling hay.

Throughout the summer the hills were indeed alive with the sound of music. Bells tinkled with the slightest movement of each of the many animals, a very efficient way of keeping close tabs on them. Church bells chimed the Angelus three times daily, and on Sunday were a persistent reminder that it was time for Mass. Melodious birdsong from dawn to dusk, rhythmic medleys of the river Lech, choirs of insects serenading one another after the setting of the sun were magnified by the surrounding hills and echoed through the valley. This may be where, and how, Anna first heard the music that she would be so appreciative of her whole life long.

As autumn drew near everyone, including the children, pitched in to help prepare for the winter that lay ahead. Neighbors assisted one another in what was inevitably a race against time. Steeg was nearly deserted during haying season as most of the villagers remained in the fields up on the mountain, either in the Kraback valley or in the Birchetsgump. It was imperative to stay ahead of the rain and to get the hay inside before the weather changed. Anna helped by picking berries and bringing the flowers and the herbs indoors, and one might surmise, by minding her little sister and brother. In late autumn Edmund took his children up into the hills where hazel bushes grew along the edges of the fields. He would strike the bushes with his walking stick and the little ones would gather the hazelnuts, collecting a supply for the winter months, and sampling them as they went along.

Alpine winters come early and they last for a very long time. Snow fell hard and heavy in Steeg, cutting off passage in and out of the village. So much snow accumulated and was piled so high along the side of the road that children trudging to and from school were completely hidden from view. And when the snow melted, the Lech overflowed, spilling onto the road. Because Steeg's peak, the Pimig, had no tree cover on its upper half and no shrub roots to anchor it, thundering avalanches occurred with such magnitude that the Lech became clogged and was often driven to create an alternate path. A lot of life took place indoors during those winter evenings. That may have been when Anna first learned how to read, heard all about her ancestors and the many places her Papa had seen, introducing her to a way of life beyond the mountain range that encircled the only world she knew. She may have learned to embroider then, and to help out with the baking, may have learned the prayers of her Catholic Faith – the Lord's Prayer and the rosary – and sat in her family circle savoring the stories of the saints. In many ways, surely, she was Mama's little helper.

In the fall of 1898, when the latest addition to the family was only a few months old, big sister Anna started school. It was not an easy transition. She shed "copious tears," as she later described it, especially when Papa, who accompanied her, left her there on her own. The school was just a few houses away in the home of the village teacher, Roman Grassle. All public school students in Steeg came together in this one-room schoolhouse, where assignments were displayed on a large board at the front of the room and arranged in columns according to classes, from grade one through grade eight. The instructor would move from column to column and teach accordingly those students to whom it applied. Because Anna was such a bright little girl, one can imagine she learned a lot more that year than what had been the intent of an introductory curriculum.

In May of 1899, at the end of Anna's first year of school, the family moved from Steeg to Hall, not very far from Innsbruck. Edmund Dengel was determined to relocate to an area more conducive to growing his business and expanding his customer base, a location with much better educational opportunities for his children. Anna's childhood in Steeg had been a happy one. Now everything was about to change.

Be optimistic, no matter what comes.

We don't have to be afraid.

We are in God's hands.

Anna Dengel

CHAPTER TWO

When winter was finally over and treacherous mountain passes were once again safe for travel, the Dengel family said their goodbyes and boarded a stagecoach in Steeg. One can only imagine what that arduous journey was like. Gertrud was four months pregnant, her youngest was less than a year old, her eldest had just turned seven, and there were two siblings in between.

The picturesque route took them north, through the valley and to the city of Reutte, where they stayed overnight at the Glocke Inn in the company of distant relatives. Continuing on the following day, Anna may have felt she was on a magic carpet ride as a whole new world drifted by beyond the stagecoach window. That world, new to her, was as old as the hills and the fairy tales Mama sometimes recited to her and Hans and Ida. Surely she had many questions, about castle ruins, dense forests, pristine lakes, and ancient cities as they made their way toward their new home, stopping briefly in Nassereith before boarding the train in Imst. The next stop was, for the Dengel family, their final destination.

The old salt-city of Hall was situated just east of the capital of Innsbruck, roughly ten kilometers away. On arrival in Hall the family moved into a large Gothic-style house in the old section of the city. House No. 4 on Ritter-Waldauf Lane had a big entrance area similar to the one in Steeg, with three levels featuring large rooms where windows revealed mountains on one side and gardens on the other. There was ample space on ground level for the horses and the carriage. These would continue to provide an essential mode of transportation, especially since Edmund would be traveling on business into Innsbruck and beyond.

No doubt there was a feeling of relief in reaching their destination. Not that everything was settled. There was much to be done before the family could begin to feel at home, for a household and a business needed to be reorganized. They also had to find a suitable school for Anna. Although everything was unfamiliar, and more than a little chaotic, there must have been some sense of excitement and anticipation about beginning again, especially since leaving Steeg did not mean never going back. Papa had insisted their country estate would always remain in the family and that they would return from time to time to visit their relatives, attend to essential maintenance concerns, or just to take time for rest and renewal in a place far away from the city, in their ancestral home. Most likely Edmund returned that summer to check on his estate and to prepare his house and property to survive another winter unscathed. Perhaps that is how a small picture card made its way from Steeg to Hall to find a permanent place among Anna's favorite things. Hand-written in German on the back of the card were the words, "July 8, 1899: For Ana M. Dengel, Hall. Class One" – a sensitive teacher assuring a little girl that she was not forgotten.

During her first year in Hall, Anna attended a public school that was under the direction of the Tertian Sisters. She was an excellent student and apparently an avid reader, for it was said that she had to be told repeatedly to refrain from overusing her eyes, which showed a chronic weakness. On October 17 Gertrud gave birth to Karl Theodore Heinrich. It would be a challenging year for the mother of five young children. Anna, the eldest, was only seven and still adjusting to many new changes at home and beyond. After establishing a new household and then giving birth, Gertrud did all that any other mother has to do, and a whole lot more. In addition to feeding her family and breastfeeding her baby, carrying out the rituals of bath and bedtime and the usual household chores while supporting a husband who at times could be somewhat demanding, she was also a responsible business woman. Intent on returning to the design and production of vestments and ecclesiastical linens, she proceeded to set up her workspace and to look for women to embroider the selections for her new production line. After all, expanding this creative enterprise was the reason why her husband had moved their family to Hall.

Anna returned to the Tertiary School for a second year in the fall of 1900. Life had settled into an acceptable routine when the unimaginable happened. On October 24, just one week after Baby Karl's first birthday, suddenly and unexpectedly, Gertrud Scheidle Dengel died at the age of 31. They said it was from lung disease. Consumption is what was recorded. She was laid to rest in Hall.

The loss of a beloved wife and mother was devastating to the family. Anna would remember her mother years later as "a most remarkable woman, business-like, intelligent, holy" – and she would refer to herself ever after as living with a hole in her heart. Indeed as the grace of God would have it, this great sorrow would one day be seen as the source of Anna's compassion for suffering women and children and her insatiable desire to help them. Now, however, she was just a little girl lost in an overwhelming grief that affected her sleep and left her listless and dangerously anemic.

A family member recalls that "the doctors examined Anna and said it was a hopeless case, so her father took her to the mountains, to her beloved childhood home, where she slept and slept and slept. Papa would wake her at 11:00 and send her outdoors, but she was so tired that she lay down under the first tree she encountered and fell asleep again. After some time Papa took her back to see the doctor. She was proclaimed worse than before, so he took her home to die. A maid, who was hired to look after Anna, was overheard saying: 'I hope this *Zader* won't recover.' In the local dialect, *Zader* is an expression of contempt that means 'frail weakling.' The maid wanted the child to die so she would not have to tend to her. Papa then took care of Anna, tenderly and lovingly, and did the same for all his children, so they would not be deprived of the loving care of their mother." In time the sickness passed, and one day Anna returned to normal, regaining her energy and the will to carry on. The hurt that had crippled a motherless child and affected all in the family slowly yet persistently gave way to a new beginning. Then several months later a strange thing occurred.

On March 16 in 1901, Anna's ninth birthday, she was whacked six times on the palm of her hand by Sister Eugenia, because she was always wiping the blackboard clean with her sleeve. One can only imagine the effect that this had on Anna, a responsible little girl who had been through so much and had probably never been punished before. She buried the shame of that painful incident down deep within her, where it remained as a permanent scar.

Two weeks later on Good Friday, March 29, Anna made her First Holy Communion in her parish church, St. Nicholas, in Hall. The celebrant was dean and pastor Rev. Mathew Knöpfler. She was given a certificate with a picture of the Sacred Heart of Jesus and the saying: "I am humble and gentle of heart." The context of that biblical quotation taken from the Gospel according to Matthew (11:29) is a passage in which Jesus is quoted as saying: "Take my yoke upon you and learn from me, for I am gentle and humble of heart, and you will find rest for your souls." Surely this was more than coincidence that a little girl suffering the death of a loved one would receive her First Communion on the day that Jesus died and be given a verse from the Bible to remind her that in Jesus she would find comfort for her soul. Indeed, it would mark the beginning of Anna's lifelong devotion to the Sacred Heart. Later that year she received the Sacrament of Confirmation from Bishop Simon Aichner of Bixen. Her sponsor was Edmund's niece, Mrs. Coleta Geisler from Volders, a kind and compassionate woman who frequently helped out at the Dengel household during the difficult period following Gertrud's death. She also took the children home with her from time to time, thereby endearing herself to them. One can assume she had also helped prepare Anna to receive the sacraments. In the fall Anna returned for a third year of study at the school run by the Tertian Sisters.

The following year, in the fall of 1902, Edmund decided to send Anna to a boarding school, along with her sister Ida. He felt he could no longer manage the increasing demands of his business with so many children still at home. He also felt it would be best for the girls. It would give them structure, a good education, and release them from household duties and concern for the little ones. Anna was ten and Ida nine when they were admitted to Thurnfeld, the monastery school of the Visitation Sisters in Hall. The school was within walking distance of their home on Ritter-Waldauf Lane. No doubt they went there often while adjusting to a new routine. At the same time, they must have relished the new-found freedom that came with being out on their own. The brisk walk, uphill and down, hinted of other Alpine treks, except for the change in scenery. Here they were in the city, walking past the old town hall, the town square, the church and its inviting wayside chapel. As time went by the girls explored more and more of Hall with its array of shops and profusion of merchandise. They especially liked that section of town where wood carvers spilled into alleys to mesmerize onlookers with the skill of their craft as Magi and Nativity scenes emerged from their blocks of wood. They also loved to watch the world famous Tirolean woodcarver, Brunecker Bachlechner, embellish gothic altars and crèches with painstaking intricacy.

While his two eldest daughters were adapting to a more independent way of life, Edmund had been actively seeking to expand his business and ensure greater stability for his family. It is not certain exactly when he opened a retail shop in downtown Innsbruck, but we do know that on November 16, 1903, a year after his two daughters had enrolled in boarding school, Edmund remarried. His new wife, Amalie Rohrmaier from Anwalding in Bavaria, was well known to the family. She was one of Edmund's employees. She did embroidery. Those who knew her described her as very, very nice, very friendly, and very religious - but religious in a nice way. They say she wanted to go to a monastery, but Edmund said, "Your duty is now and it is here. You have to look after these children. You have to marry me." And she did.

Anna stayed four years at Thurnfeld, arriving in 1902 and remaining until the summer of 1906. She grew up there, in an environment that was influenced by the structured ethos of a disciplined convent life. The institution's primary focus was to provide a good education and students were held to a high standard from the moment they arrived. They learned about health and manners, and above all, discipline. Anna and her classmates studied both French and Italian, not only the basics of grammar, but also, through diligent practice, how to converse in a language different from their own. French was spoken on one day of the week and Italian on another. Conversation in German, her native tongue, was permissible only on Sunday. One of her early progress reports notes that there were ten female pupils in Anna's class. That number included Anna. She was ranked #1 with regard to the subject of religion, receiving a grade of "excellent." In Geography, History, Nature, and Diligence, her grades were "very good." In Mathematics (with Geometry and Calculation), German Language, French, Writing–Calligraphy, Geometric Painting, Freehand Painting, Singing, Gym, Female Handcraft, and Keeping Order, the grades she received were "good." However, in those areas listed as Integrity and Behavior According to Regulations, she was graded "not so good," and in the category of Good Behavior, her grade was "less sufficient." There is no indication of what those evaluative comments meant. One can only surmise that this spirited child, accustomed to being affirmed and to taking initiative in a familial setting, struggled with having to conform to new and more rigid expectations, whether she agreed with them or not. In time Anna began to excel at what was expected of her and grew to love the school and its dedicated teachers. A letter written to her parents soon after she turned thirteen tells how she felt about life at Thurnfeld. It is an enthusiastic report on all that she was learning.

"Since Friday the 14th of this month we are on holiday. How are you, dear parents? How are the embroiderers and Dominika and Karl? I hope you are all well and all happy celebrating Easter! We would love to be with you during the Easter break, but we are also happy to stay here in Thurnfeld, as it should be quite nice during the holidays. We are only twelve children; we have chosen the apostles. I was Andrew, Ida [was] Peter, brothers as we are sisters in real life. Until now everyone including us is very happy and having fun. Tomorrow we will have painting and probably handcraft. I will start nice pieces of work. I already looked at them with my handcraft teacher. The writing 'God protects you' I will put right above the fresco, and stitches inside with beautiful adornments.

"Today I want to tell you a lot about what I have learned. I would like to start with my most favorite subject, which is history. We learn about individuals and the most important battles. Bonne Marie Seraphine is our teacher; she also does geography. We learn about the most common soil conditions, size, frontiers, and most important cities. Our confessor is very good. This year we have the big catechism and we already finished it, the last lesson before Easter. After Easter, he said, we will learn the Bible diligently.

"In French, we have a French woman as teacher. We have three hours per week: Monday, Tuesday, and Wednesday. On Mondays we normally do reading and exercises, and on Wednesday grammar and another exercise. Thursdays, Fridays, and Saturdays we have to speak French. It is a French woman called Marie Antoinette in Thurnfeld. I always speak French with her. I do like her a lot. The first few days in the week we speak Italian. French I like more than Italian, although the first mentioned is very difficult to learn. The spelling in French is very difficult whereas in Italian it is very simple as you just write as you speak. When you read, it is the same. In German I have a lady from Salzburg, she is very tough. But we do learn a lot. Every day except Monday we have German classes. We learn a lot of grammar and often do very boring analyses. Talking exercises and analyses we do very often.

"Mathematics I like a lot, but sometimes our exercises are very difficult, then we have to study hard. The simple mathematic rules we already have learned. In nature studies Bonne Marie Seraphine is our teacher as well. In history of nature we have learned about the different 'kingdoms' and we had to describe and enumerate different animals, plants, and minerals. The mineral kingdom we already finished. Just imagine, we could look at many stones and minerals which belong to Thurnfeld, an amazing and very precious collection of minerals, machines to electrify, and padded birds and many other items, which were very beautiful.

"Physics I don't like that much, because I find it very boring. Gym we have twice a week, writing we have every day except Wednesdays, after recreation. Twice we have grammar and twice writing. Mondays, Tuesdays, and Wednesdays we normally have painting for one hour. During the holidays we have one hour of painting and handcraft. The little ones have singing for one hour and I join them. On Sunday there is one hour of geometry. In the evenings all pupils have one hour in order to study.

"What is the weather like with you? In Hall it is more or less nice, but today and yesterday it has been foggy and we had a little bit of rain. Our garden is very beautiful, the trees are lovely and green and violets, daisies, pansies and daffodils are already there. On Sunday we were in Absam and there we have been praying a lot for you, dear parents. I hope we are going to go there again soon.

"We feel very sorry that you cannot come to Hall this year again. I do ask you, dear father, to visit us again if you can. Most of all, I do wish you, dear parents, a happy happy Easter.

"With all the best wishes of your grateful daughter, Anna."

Thurnfeld, 18ᵗʰ of April 1905

That summer, while the two eldest girls were in school, Amalie gave birth to a son, Edmund, in the village of Steeg, where family members could help care for the children.

During the years she was living at Thurnfeld, Anna met Josephine Epp, the daughter of a manufacturer in neighboring Innsbruck. They would remain close friends for life. The two girls would have had much in common and shared in ways that young girls do as they grow up together, providing companionship for one another in their home away from home. Anna would have told her friend about her interest in the missions, a topic often discussed at school, for the Visitation Sisters encouraged their students to cultivate a global perspective. For a while Anna zealously promoted and even sold a popular pamphlet, *Das Negerkind* [The Negro Child], because faraway lands fascinated her and the dire need of women and children already had a hold on her heart.

Anna was 14 years old when she completed her studies at Thurnfeld in the summer of 1906 and went to live with her family. She had barely settled in when the Visitation Sisters asked her to return to help out in the school. She agreed, even though this was not among the goals she had wanted to accomplish. Instead of choosing between two options, she decided to do both, to accept the position at Thurnfeld while remaining committed to implementing her plans for the coming year. The position at the school meant she would live on campus during the week and be at home on weekends, where she quickly established a very different yet satisfying routine.

At the top of Anna's to-do list was her determination to help her father with his work. One can assume that he introduced her to all aspects of the business – inventory, marketing, clientele, proper procedures for soliciting sales, how to keep financial records, how to handle supply and demand. She would have been coached on how to sell what their business had to offer, learning firsthand how her ancestors had been so successful in commerce. On her own initiative she also took up sewing because she wanted to actively participate in that aspect of the family business. She learned to excel at embroidery, reproducing intricate patterns most likely designed by her mother. One can only imagine what a comfort this would have been for Anna, to do what her beloved mother had done and be one with her in spirit. No matter how full her schedule, Anna was still very much a student and remained an avid reader. While her range of interests was broad, her primary focus was language fluency. She worked diligently to increase her knowledge of French, and at the same time, she began to study English. She dreamed of going to France and England, perhaps as a governess in order to achieve language facility through practical application. Before she could take that step, however, she had to pass some very stiff qualifying exams. This she was determined to do.

For the two years following the completion of her student days at Thurnfeld, Anna's life was full. In 1908 another child was added to the family in Hall when Amalie gave birth to a little girl and named her Hildegard. They would call her Hilde. Then something significant happened that would alter the course of Anna's life. A request came to Thurnfeld from a school in Lyon, France, asking the Visitation Sisters to recommend someone who would help them teach German to their students. "They asked me if I were willing to do this," Anna would later explain. "It being a tempting opportunity to perfect my French, I accepted." She was 16 years old at the time. Her work in Lyon would not begin until the following fall. During that period in between, when Hilde was barely a year old and Anna was preparing to go abroad, Amalie gave birth again. They named the little boy Josef.

In August of 1909, Anna went with her father to the Wörishofen cold-water spa in Bavaria. Edmund was there to undergo treatments introduced by the world famous Pastor Sebastian Kneip. His daughter would benefit from a much needed period of rest and relaxation before moving on to Lyon. Afterwards, while in the area, they may have visited churches and monasteries to solicit orders for vestments, since Anna did not have to begin work before the end of October. Back in Hall farewell meals and family celebrations would have reflected a sense of pride as departure day was approaching, as well as some trepidation, for 17-year-old Anna had never gone so far away from home before.

Anna traveled through Switzerland on her way to Lyon in France. On arrival she took up her new position with the *Association familiale des Chartreux* ("Family Association of the Carthusians") as a teacher of German. The school was run by women who were once members of a religious order that was secularized at the turn of the century. At 17, Anna was the youngest member of the faculty and had 100-160 students under her tutelage. Once she had adjusted to her new environment, she excelled in her multifaceted role and loved what she was doing. "You cannot imagine how much I love the children," she writes in a letter to her family. "I am so happy that I can work for them. I am trying to return next year to this topsy-turvy house, where everything is alive and where everyone looks forward eagerly to the future, as I do myself." And in a subsequent letter home: "I live here entirely for the children. I love them immensely. I share in their accomplishments, in their funny ideas, and it really grieves me when they aren't good, even though they are just noisy kids."

Sometime during the winter session, Anna received a letter from her aunt, Philomena Rohrmaier, Amalie's sister, who was a member of the Order of the Angels in Augsburg. On February 23 – it was 1910 – in a letter to her family back home, Anna told them what her aunt had said.

> "Aunt Philomena has written she would like it very much if I would come to her to become a sister. I would like very much to give her this pleasure if my heart were only in it. I believe I must not get her hopes up. But I admire Aunt Cassiana, and if I were actually to go into the convent I would like to be associated with her."

Anna felt close to her stepmother's other sister, her Aunt Cassiana Rohrmeier, O.P., who was a missionary in South Africa. They would write to each other now and then. A letter from Cassiana around this time indicates that Anna did address the issue of vocation with her.

> "Your nice little letter pleased me very much, especially as I learned by it that you are getting on well. You have made great progress in your English since you wrote last,

in spite of devoting your time principally to the French language. I suppose you know that perfectly now.

"You are quite right that musical knowledge is very useful in Missions. In fact, everything, the more the better. Your French will be useful too.

"What shall I say about your doubts concerning your vocation? That is really God's work. If He wishes you to become His Spouse He will arrange things as will best suit His purpose. Keep on praying that you may know God's holy will, offer up Holy Communion for that intention and often ask our good Mother Mary and St. Joseph to pray for you and show you the right way. But once you know the will of God in the matter, you must act courageously, no matter what it costs. Our Lord is a good Master and does the greater part of the work Himself.

"Be sure, dear child, I pray my very best for you in this important business. Have confidence! All will come right, if you really mean to do God's will.

"I wonder what your good papa would say to that step! I feel certain that he would not prevent you from following our Lord in the Religious life. You speak about not being fit for it. But, my dear child, who is fit? We must only do our best and humbly ask our Lord to supply for the rest.

"I should certainly thank God with all my heart if He gives this holy vocation to you or anyone of our Relations, but at the same time I pray that none shall come without a real vocation. Now I have said enough about this."

During the spring holidays Anna remained in Lyon to do some sight-seeing and to become more familiar with the area's rich history. She visited a number of famous shrines, including St. Etienne, the Shrine of Our Lady of Benoit-Vaux.

In October of 1910, Anna passed the French state exam in Innsbruck, qualifying her to teach the language in any Elementary [Secondary] School in Austria – a significant accomplishment - and then returned to Lyon for a second year of service. In the spring of 1911 she translated a surgical paper from German into French and for the first time was directly exposed to the field of medicine. She also did some traveling. In April she chaperoned five students from school on a trip to Marseille, where she saw the Mediterranean Sea. In June she visited Ars, where Father Jean-Baptiste Marie Vianney, beatified in 1904, had labored from 1818 until his death in 1859. The following week she went to pray at the grave of Blessed Margaret Mary Alacoque, who died in 1690. She was a member of the Order of the Visitation of Mary, where devotion to the Sacred Heart of Jesus had first been introduced.

Although the work in Lyon had been satisfying, and she was grateful to have had that cross-cultural experience, Anna did not stay. "I remained at that school for two years," she said, "then I returned home, since I saw no future for me there." Back home after a two-year absence, Anna, at the age of 19, was at a crossroads and ambivalent about her future. She had tried to find a position in England or some other foreign country, but had been unsuccessful. It was summertime, so she decided to go to Steeg.

After a five-week period of rest and renewal in her childhood home, Anna went to work for her father. There had been another addition to the family with the birth of Amalie in 1911. "My father was very well liked; he was very good to the poor and he would never let a beggar go. He would give them a little because he had to look after so many children." With the majority of his nine children in school and the youngest in a cradle, the patriarch of the family was grateful for the skilled assistance of his eldest daughter. The experience she had already acquired prepared Anna to take an active role in expanding their current client base and soliciting consignments. She was often on the road. Her business trips took her through the Tirol, into Vorarlberg and over into Liechtenstein, where she visited rectories, monasteries, and convents seeking orders for vestments and other church accessories. Her itinerary for the fall of 1911 indicates she was at St. Gallenkirch in Montafon in October and in Mayrhofen in the Ziller Valley in November. In the spring of 1912, she solicited orders in Schaan in Liechtenstein in April and in Pritz in the uppermost Inn valley in May. In September she was in Hohenems in the Rhine Valley. Working for her father provided a satisfying interlude for Anna, but it was only temporary. She was not destined to be the one to manage the family business. That role would be shared by Karl and Edmund when the time arrived.

Anna was twenty years old and she was growing restless. The years she had spent away from home had given her a taste for travel and a sense of a much larger world beyond her Alpine horizon. Anything less would never satisfy. There was also a feeling deep within that she could no longer ignore. It had to do with the persistent question of vocation. What were her plans for the future? She didn't really have a plan or even a sense of direction. That she would live a dedicated life was for Anna a foregone conclusion. That the form such a dedication would take would be the consecrated life of a nun was an entirely different matter. Put simply, her choice seemed to be either the missions or a monastery. The pull toward the latter had a firm foundation. The semi-cloistered context of Thurnfeld, where she encountered the sacred at every turn, where discipline had been mandatory and being good was taken for granted, had left its imprint on her. Those halcyon days when having fun meant painting holy pictures, or watching Palm Sunday and Corpus Christi processions wind their way through the center of town, made life on her own less attractive. She had loved learning the Bible, singing hymns, attending High Mass on major feasts, when the sanctuary had been transformed into a paradise of artifacts and a stunning array of flowers; and she had been drawn to the Eucharist. One of the lasting effects of spending her formative years with the Visitation Sisters had been the desire to receive the sacrament of Holy Communion more frequently, and she managed to accomplish that. What about the missions? All she had there was a tug on her heart and a childhood memory of enthusiasm for a cause. There was no blueprint indicating how she might participate, but that was about to change.

"While on a business trip for my father to Vorarlberg," she recalled, "something happened that was to be of great consequence for my future life." She met a Sister of Charity, who was very interested in the missions and concerned about the poor.

> "She had little bits of lace and she would ask my father to buy it from her – my father's business was church vestments. That place was quite far from home. As I walked in, two Franciscan Missionaries of Mary walked out. I went to see this Sister Matthia. She asked, would

I buy the lace. I knew my father would. She had, I don't know how many yards of this lace. She measured it out. She had nothing to write on except this little leaflet. When I was going home on the train – it was hours and hours – I read this pamphlet of the Franciscan Missionaries of Mary, which spoke of a school in Lyon where girls were being trained for nursing in mission countries. My interest flared up and I wrote to my friend Victoire asking her to please get me more information about this school."

That was the beginning of a series of events that would redirect Anna's future and determine the rest of her life.

Victoire L'Abbeye had been a teacher at the school in Lyon when Anna first arrived. When she saw that the newcomer was very inexperienced, she took Anna under her wing, and the two became friends. "Anna occupied the room neighboring mine – I pitied her: so young, so courageous, so isolated, in a society of which she did not even know the language. The more I watched this young girl, the more I loved her. She repaid me by her friendship." After Anna returned to Austria, they kept in touch with one another. "I was surprised, however, to receive a letter from her," Victoire recalls, "telling me that she wanted to devote herself to the missions in South Africa, the religious of the Visitation who had educated her having missions there." Anna's aunt Cassiana was also in mission there. Anna told Victoire that she wanted to study nursing in France. "You asked me to find an inexpensive boarding house," Victoire recalls. "How many flights of stairs I went up to find this boarding house! which I did not find, to my deepest regret. 'Why not,' I said to myself, 'why not throw my little Anna in Miss McLaren's plan?'" That was the turning point. Victoire would be the bridge connecting the worlds of Agnes and Anna, who recalls that defining moment as if it were yesterday.

"Victoire answered by return mail that she had not been able to find this school, but she had other information for me, namely that her confessor knew a Scottish woman doctor who was looking for women doctors for India. What was more, she was willing to help any girl interested in studying medicine for that purpose.

She gave me the name and address of this doctor in France ... Dr. Agnes McLaren."

Anna's immediate response had been:

"I was fire and flame and wrote to Dr. McLaren immediately, telling her of my interest. This was the answer to my subconscious desires and aspirations, to be a Missionary with a definite goal in view, filling an unfulfilled need which only women could fill, to be a Missionary to which I had aspired since my childhood."

Although Anna had never heard of Dr. McLaren, she knew with absolute certainty that this was the path for her. "The decision to offer myself was so simple and clear to me that I did not feel the need to seek advice." From that moment on the lives of those two women would be forever intertwined.

God is in us, around us, with us.

Love wants to give, does not count the cost.

Nothing is too much for love.

Anna Dengel

CHAPTER THREE

Agnes McLaren was born in Scotland on July 4 in 1837. Daughter of a prominent citizen of Edinburgh, she grew up in a Protestant household that was prone to progressive ideas and was actively concerned for the poor. When she was in her twenties, Agnes became involved in organizational aspects of the Women's Suffrage Movement and remained dedicated to the cause of women's rights for approximately nine years. She and six other women lobbied for a chance to study medicine at the University of Edinburgh at a time when it was difficult for a woman to obtain a medical degree. Convinced that the practice of medicine was the best way to respond to Christ's call to her to serve the suffering and the poor, she enrolled in the medical school of the University of Montpellier in France, the first woman ever to do so, and received her medical degree at the age of 42. She took up the practice of medicine, and at the age of 60, she became a Catholic. Her passion from then on was to promote the study of medicine for women who would work with women, especially in the missions. She had a particular concern for the women of India, where religious beliefs and social customs prevented women from seeking medical care from male physicians.

Dr. McLaren was 72 years old when she traveled to northern India in 1909 in order to assess the viability of a proposed hospital for women and children in Rawalpindi. Over the years she had discovered that Protestant hospitals had sufficient female physicians and nurse midwives trained to assist women in childbirth and in postnatal care, but Catholic hospitals did not. There were very few Catholic female physicians at that time and few trained nurses in the mission field. The call to serve in a foreign land is a specific vocation. Catholic women opting for a dedicated life were more likely to enter a convent or monastery than become a missionary. In cloistered settings one could find the degree of dedication required to meet the devastating need, but Canon Law forbid such participation by those who professed religious vows. What Agnes saw in India convinced her to take her case for Sister-doctors directly to Rome. She would make five trips to the Vatican to ask that women with canonical vows be allowed to practice medicine without restrictions. There would be no change in the law, at least not during her lifetime, but that did not dampen her fervor. In 1905 she had received a papal blessing from Pope Pius X, who encouraged her in her quest. She would continue to do all in her power to raise awareness to the need.

In 1909, working with the Executive Committee of the Catholic Medical Mission to Indian Women and Children – the London Committee – Dr. McLaren labored diligently to lay the groundwork for founding St. Catherine's Hospital in Rawalpindi. The London Committee's mission was to promote the cause of medical care for women and children in Rawalpindi, a responsibility that included administrative oversight and raising the funds that would be needed to financially support it. In 1911 Dr. McLaren, in collaboration with Msgr. Dominic Wagner, Prefect Apostolic of Kashmir and Kafristan in northwestern India, declared St. Catherine's Hospital in Rawalpindi officially open. It was a modest initiative that consisted of a single bungalow on the outskirts of the city that was staffed by several lay workers and a physician, the experienced Dr. Bielby, who had worked many years as a Protestant missionary in India before converting to Catholicism. Within months it was evident that she was not the right person for this pioneering role. After she left, it was feared that the project might not survive, but in fact it did. The Franciscan Missionaries of Mary arrived in December of 1912.

After Dr. Bielby left St. Catherine's, Dr. McLaren launched an exhaustive but unsuccessful search for a replacement. It was then that she decided to try a different approach. She would look for a young woman who would commit to earning a degree in medicine in order to fill the vacant position at the Rawalpindi hospital. That individual would be financially supported by the London Committee.

In the summer of 1912, Victoire L'Abbeye, Anna Dengel's colleague and friend in Lyon, responded to Anna's inquiry, saying, "I talked to Father Perra about you." Father Perra was the priest in residence there who would facilitate the overlapping of the lives of three women from three different countries traveling on diverse paths. For years he had been a spiritual director to Victoire and a confessor to Dr. McLaren. He put Victoire in touch with Agnes. God's Spirit did the rest. On July 13, after reading Victoire's enthusiastic recommendation and after seeing a photograph of Anna and her family, Agnes McLaren sent the following reply to Victoire.

"I have received your letter about the young Tyrolean girl. I have a friend who wishes to pay the expenses of studies and examinations of this young lady if *really* upon reflection she will wish to study medicine *to be a missionary*. The conditions will be:

(1) that she pass the preliminary examinations (baccalaureate) and that

(2) every six months she write to my friend to say if she has passed the semester examinations. If she has passed she will immediately be sent the money necessary for the next semester;

(3) that she promise to serve as missionary for five years after having received her diploma. After these five years she will be free to continue her ministry or to quit in order to do something else.

The medical studies last *five* years *after* one has passed the baccalaureate. The scholarship given will pay for the books necessary, in fact, *for the studies*. As to the university to be chosen it will be advantageous, it seems to me, to choose one in England on account of the language. *All* are open to women as well as in Ireland."

Victoire sent the letter on to Anna, who wrote at once to Agnes, enthusiastically accepting her offer and its demanding conditions.

"I wrote to Dr. McLaren and in that way the correspondence started in French because I didn't know English. She used to call me *La Jeune Tyrolienne*."

However, before she could even begin to address medical school requirements, Anna had to complete her high school education. "I was determined to study medicine and become a Mission doctor," she had insisted, even though she was already twenty-one years old and a very long way from the finish line. What a leap of faith indeed, even for an individual accustomed to having one more mountain to climb. Because completing her secondary education could be done in her country of origin, Anna immediately applied for admission to the Reform-Real Gymnasium, the prestigious school of the Ursuline Sisters in Innsbruck, and arranged to begin her studies there in the fall of 1912.

From the end of July through the following March, the two women, Agnes and Anna, exchanged a series of letters with regard to the offer made by the Scottish physician to the young Austrian woman aspiring to follow in her footsteps. Options for moving forward were thoroughly examined and eventually gave rise to a plan.

Once she had completed her high school education, Anna would face two significant challenges. She would have to enroll in baccalaureate studies, and after completing the work, pass the baccalaureate exam. If successful, she would then have to demonstrate fluency in the language in which she would be studying for her degree in medicine. This meant making a decision soon about which medical school to attend, for that would determine which language she would have to master. Anna was already fluent in German and in French and was comfortable with Italian. For years she had intended to achieve fluency in English but had not yet had an opportunity to do so. Dr. McLaren made a number of suggestions regarding a school of medicine: Geneva, Zurich, Fribourg, Rome, Beirut, Glasgow, Dublin, London – even some places in India, and also, Austria, where language would not be a concern. All were open to women. The choice, she said, was Anna's. In the end, the decision was mutual. Dr. McLaren kept coming back to Cork in Ireland. She knew the president of the school personally. "Sir Bertrand Windle had shown interest in Dr. McLaren's efforts to provide medical care for the women of India," Anna would explain to family and friends. "Other reasons for my choice were the *sine qua non* of a British degree." It would also be advantageous to prepare for a life in mission at an institution that understood the missions and could provide a Catholic context.

In subsequent correspondence Dr. McLaren made sure that Anna understood the conditions of their agreement, especially with regard to finances.

"I don't think that my friend will start paying for your studies until *after* you have passed the Baccalaureate in order to have the certitude that you will succeed."

She gave an estimate of anticipated cost. "It will be impossible, either in England or in Ireland, to have room and board *less* than 15 francs a week. Generally it is 25 francs." When Anna proposed working while studying in order to pay for her living expenses, Dr. McLaren responded:

"I have consulted several authorities and *all* say it is impossible for you to *do any work* beyond your studies – or you will miss your Examinations which are very difficult – all time *must* be given to them and to rest and exercise in open air."

And in a subsequent letter:

"Everybody says that it is *impossible* for you to give lessons. I will do all in my power to secure an increase to the Burse but I fear I will not succeed."

Dr. McLaren asked Anna to find out how much time it would take if she went on for her Baccalaureate in Ireland instead of in Austria. This would give Anna the advantage of an extensive immersion in the language foundational to the medical degree. "It is the English examination that I fear for you," she wrote. Anna took those words to heart. English was her weakest language, and if she were going to earn a medical degree in English, she had to be fluent in it. Doing her baccalaureate studies in English made a whole lot of sense. In January 1913, Dr. McLaren wrote to Anna:

"I am very happy that you like your studies and that everything goes fine and that you do not regret having chosen this work. Anyway, dear Miss, you always have the liberty of changing without anybody blaming you. Studies are always good and always useful – useful for the science that we learn and useful in forming character. I believe that your family will be glad to see you with a diploma."

Toward the end of March, Agnes wrote again:

> "You have succeeded very well in your studies and I congratulate you. Hope you will succeed as much in the future as you did in the past."

Those may have been her last words to Anna. On April 17, 1913, Dr. Agnes McLaren died.

Although Anna never met her mentor face to face, she would carry her spirit within her always. Like an eternal flame. Like the spark that gave rise to her own "fire and flame." Like the blaze that ignited her calling. At the end of the 1912-1913 school year in Innsbruck, Anna's transcript indicates that she had received very good marks in her studies. It also states that she left the Ursuline school in Innsbruck on September 27. She had one more year to go in order to complete her high school education. However, she decided not to remain in Austria but to transfer to an Ursuline school in Ireland, where she would complete her program of study and at the same time work toward achieving fluency in English. This would be Anna's definitive first step on her way to becoming a doctor, a concrete attempt to follow in the footsteps of Agnes McLaren.

Once she had made the decision, Anna moved quickly and decisively, taking leave of family and friends and completing final preparations for the journey. Although she had left home before, she knew that this time much more was at stake. God willing, she would not be coming home again until her dream of being a doctor had become a reality. Her father and stepmother, Amalie, accompanied her as far as Zurich. When she arrived in Paris, she was met by Pauline Willis, who traveled with her to London. Miss Willis, secretary of the London Committee founded by Agnes McLaren, had promised to donate 50 pounds annually for a period of five years to help the Committee meet its financial obligation to Anna during her medical studies. Miss Willis also made arrangements for where Anna would live in Cork while completing her preliminary studies.

Cork, a small city in the south of Ireland, was under the British Crown at the time. The overall environment was Catholic, and Anna was warmly received on her arrival at the Ursuline Convent School [College] in Blackrock, which was situated in the southern part of the city. She remained there for two years as she worked to complete her high school studies and improve her mastery of English. "The Sisters were very helpful to me, giving me special attention with English," she would recall, and she remained forever grateful for their kindness to her.

> "I went in October. I was supposed to start medical class in June. I tell you I had to step on the gas. I went to Mother Berchmans about my English. She asked one of the Mothers, Mother Michael, who was an old, old nun on the shelf, who had been a successful teacher. I really learned English through the medium of French. Mother Michael was rheumatic. I would lead her by the arm - get her and take her back. She gave me a class every day by myself. I was very fond of her. She was so wonderful; even when she had a lot of rheumatic pains she would never fail to come, and was glad to help me. I owe a lot to her."

One aspect of the language was especially challenging.

> "I couldn't see the jokes for a long time. I had a hard time to understand the plain, simple language, and they were so sorry for me. That was the saddest thing for them. But I am always glad I had this experience because I think it is no obstacle at all for any missionary to have to start out any place without knowing the language. I know what it was, and I went through it. That is only a minor thing. It is hard work, but it can be done."

During her stay with the Sisters, Anna was often hungry. The food was so very different. "I was starved," was how she would remember those days. "I didn't say anything though. After a while I got accustomed to it."

In June of 1914, Anna received her high school diploma. Immediately following that achievement, she took the university entrance exams, and passed.

At the end of July in 1914, Anna was about to embark on her medical studies when an event of global proportions occurred that would radically alter the landscape of her life in Ireland. The Great War – World War I – broke out in Europe, involving the world's military forces in two opposing alliances: Allies, consisting of Russia,

England, and France; and Central Powers, which were Germany and Austria-Hungary. Austria had set this in motion. Suddenly, Anna was the enemy, cut off from all means of support, both emotional and financial, from family and friends back home. Nevertheless, life went on, and she was determined to make the best of it.

In the fall Anna registered at the University of Cork and began her baccalaureate studies. The Registrar of the Branch Medical Council for Ireland states: "I hereby certify that the name of Anna Dengel was entered on the 27th day of October 1914 in the Register of Medical Students for Ireland." Anna moved in with the Daniels family, where she would remain for the next two years as she worked to achieve baccalaureate equivalency through her university studies. "I was the only foreign student in the class," she recalls. "These times were very hard for me as no mail and no financial help could come from home any longer. I did various things to make ends meet." One of the things she did in order to pay for food and lodging was to offer her services to a gardener. She would get up early every morning to clean and arrange vegetables for display in the market, and then she would take the gardener's children to school. She also gave German language lessons when she was asked to do so.

Anna was repeatedly interrogated as an alien and considered an enemy but never threatened with deportation because time and again individual supporters intervened on her behalf. One incident significantly impacted how she was perceived. On May 7, 1915, the *RMS Lusitania,* on its final voyage from New York to Liverpool, was blown up by a German submarine and sank off the west coast of Cork, killing 1,198. Outrage turned many against Germany. Prejudice against German-speaking individuals intensified, yet Anna was allowed to remain in Cork and continue on with her studies. No doubt the president of the University of Cork, friend of Agnes McLaren, had something to do with that. In October Anna received a letter of Exemption from Deportation from the Home Office in London that stated:

> "I am directed by the Secretary of State to say that he has had under consideration your application for exemption from deportation as an alien enemy, and after consulting the Advisory Committee has decided that you may remain in the United Kingdom. This

decision has not the effect of releasing you from any of the provisions of the Aliens Restriction Orders applicable to your case, and is liable at any time to revocation."

Anna continued to live under the shadow of official scrutiny. Recorded in her Identity Book was the following information:

Present residence	University College, Cork
Whether houseowner	Lodger

Personal Description – to be filled in by Police, not applicant

Height	5 feet, 4 inches
Build	Slight
Hair	Dark
Nationality at birth	Austrian

"Any male relatives in arms for or against Great Britain and Allies during the present war?" Yes.

"Name"	Johann Dengel
"Relationship"	Brother
"For or Against"	Against

Every move she made from one place to another had to be reported to the police and recorded in that official document. For example:

Blarney.	"Alien reported here. Leaving for Cork at 12:30 pm on this date."
College Rd.	"Alien reported here at this place on this date." *Official stamp:* CORK SOUTH

Meanwhile, Anna had no time at all to worry about a perennial threat of deportation as she struggled to earn enough to support herself while at the same time maintain grades that would allow her to continue her education. In the very little free time she had for herself, she went for long walks with a friend from school, Moreen Whelton, who also wanted to be a doctor. Then one day, Anna finally received news of her family through her brother, Hans. She learned that he was a prisoner of war in Italy. He had managed to get word to Anna through the Red Cross, and she was relieved to learn that all were well and were managing back home.

In the fall of 1916, Anna changed her living arrangements and moved in with two women, the Misses O'Connell, at 1 Altona College Road in Cork. She remained with them for the next two years while she took courses focused on various aspects of the medical profession. She was an excellent student, and because the Professor of Anatomy knew she was hard-pressed for funds, he hired her as an assistant Laboratory Instructor, which helped her to manage financially.

During her first year of medical studies at the University in Cork, transcripts from the year 1916-1917 indicate that Anna had successfully completed courses in Midwifery, Materia Medica Pharmacy, Pathology, Practical Pathology, Hygiene and Public Health, Forensic Medicine and Toxicology, and Therapeutics, and had attended 253 lectures in those subjects.

She also had practical experience supplemented by lectures at two local hospitals. At Cork District Hospital, she took a four-month course in Medical Surgical Practice and attended their Clinical Lectures; filled the role of Surgical Dresser for a three-month period and attended the Fever Wards for an additional three months, where she had personal charge of ten fever cases. She finished the year by spending six months at Mercy Hospital, where she attended Clinical Practice for three months and acted as Surgical Dresser for the remaining three months.

Transcripts from her second year of medical studies (1917-1918) indicate that Anna successfully completed courses in Medicine, Surgery, and Ophthalmology and attended 134 lectures. Certification from Cork Hospital verifies that Anna attended the Medical and Surgical Practice and Clinical Lectures delivered in that hospital over a period of five months; regularly acted as Gynaecological Clerk for three months and had charge of six cases; and studied the practice and principles of Vaccination, thereby acquiring the knowledge and capacity to be a skillful and well-informed Public Vaccinator. Mercy Hospital certifies that Anna Dengel attended the Clinical Practice there for a three-month period ending June 30th, 1918.

Anna's third year of medical school (1918-1919) was spent in local hospitals, where lectures and the supervised practice of medicine took place. The following certifications were recorded on Anna's transcripts.

Clinical Clerkship, Cork District Hospital, for six months, October 1917 – April 1918

The practice of this Hospital and Clinical Lectures therein delivered, Cork Lying-In Hospital, from July through December 1918

Medical and Surgical Practice and the Clinical Lectures delivered in the North Charitable Infirmary, South Charitable Infirmary, District Hospital, for six months, October through March 1919

Medical and Surgical Practice and the Clinical Lectures delivered in the North Charitable Infirmary, South Charitable Infirmary, District Hospital, for three months, April through June 1919

Eye, Ear, and Throat Hospital of 35 Beds, in attendance, plus a course of instruction in "Errors of Refraction" for a period of three months ending June 30, 1919

Mercy Hospital in Cork, a Course of Lectures on the "Administraton of Anesthetics" ending June 30, 1919

Attended six complete Postmortem Exams during 1917 – 1918 – 1919. Letterhead Certification, TOWERVILLE, BEACHROCK, CO. CORK, July 20, 1919

Completed a course in Clinical Pathology in the Pathology Department of the University College during summer session of 1919

It is hard to imagine how Anna could do all she did academically and in the actual practice of medicine under the circumstances. She had spent her time at the university as an "alien enemy," earning her degree in a language she had only recently mastered, never knowing for certain if she would have enough money to put a meal on the table and keep a roof over her head, or if she would one day be deported. Cut off from family and homeland, she was a woman breaking ground in a world dominated by men, an angel of mercy preparing for a life among the sick and suffering, a harbinger of peace in a world at war. Until the University said the final word, she would not know for certain if she had worked hard enough to make her dream a reality. All she could do in those days of late summer was hold fast to hope and lean on those who had supported her. The final examinations would determine whether or not she had earned a degree in medicine. Word came in the form of the following decree.

THE NATIONAL UNIVERSITY OF IRELAND
Dublin, 25ᵗʰ October 1919

"I hereby certify that Anna Dengel born at Steeg, Lechtal, Austria on the 16ᵗʰ day of March 1892 has passed a qualifying Examination in Medicine, Surgery, and Midwifery, in this University, as required by the Medical Amendment Act, 1886." *Signed: Mofatt, Registrar*

Not only did Anna graduate, she did so with honors. And she had earned *two* degrees: a Baccalaureate for Medicine, Surgery and Obstetrics; and a Bachelor of Science in Anatomy and Pathology (including Bacteriology). Not only had she taken top honors in her senior year, but she was also awarded a Gold Medal for the best paper of 1918-1919. Her topic: "The Wide Wide World." "In 1919 I graduated with honors," she would recall decades later, still amazed at such an unexpected outcome. "The examination fee was graciously lent to me by Miss Mary Ryan, a professor at the University. She was the sister of Archbishop Ryan of Trinidad. This was the only debt I incurred and it was repaid with my first salary." There were four other women in Anna's graduating class. Her friend, Moreen Whelton, was one of them.

Ordinarily graduates ask a professor or two for a letter of recommendation for their portfolio as they set out to look for a job. Anna was deluged with testimonial letters on her behalf. Here's a sampling of what she received.

~ ~ ~

"I have much pleasure in stating that Miss Anna Dengel has been a student here since 1914. During her college course she obtained Honors in her 2ⁿᵈ and 3ʳᵈ Medical Examinations and secured First Class Honors in her Final Examination. For two years she was Demonstrator of Anatomy. She is a lady of very good abilities and her conduct has been most exemplary during the whole of her time in College."

University College, Cork - Sir Bertram Windle, President –
MA, DSc, LLD, FRS, FSA, MRIA, MD, YSG

~ ~ ~

"I have pleasure in testifying that Miss A. Dengel attended my lectures in Medicine at University College Cork and my clinical teaching at the Cork District Hospital (1000 beds) and also acted as clinical assistant in the women and children's Entries of the Victoria Hospital Cork. Miss Dengel showed herself assiduous and painstaking. She worked steadily and hard during her whole student career and passed with first-class honors in the final degrees of the National University of Ireland. I can with confidence recommend her for any medical practice for which she may become a candidate."

W. Ashley Cummins, M.D., Professor of Medicine, University College Cork; Examiner I Medicine, National University Ireland; Senior Medical Officer Cork District Hospital; Senior Surgeon, Victoria Hospital Cork.

~ ~ ~

"It gives me much pleasure to state that during the period that Miss Dengel has been a student at University College, Cork, she has pursued her medical studies most industriously and in a most commendable manner. Her attendance at classes was regular and her conduct and attention were all that could be desired. During her studentship she won a scholarship and at the recent final Examinations in Medicine she obtained the degrees of M.B., B.Ch. and B.A.O. with First Class honors. I believe Miss Dengel to be steady, earnest, and trustworthy and can therefore confidently recommend her for a medical appointment."

C. Pearson, MD, MCh., FACS, Professor of Surgery University Colleges, Cork, Senior Surgeon to the North Charitable Infirmary, Senator of the National University of Ireland, Hon. Surgeon to the King in Ireland

~ ~ ~

"Miss Anna Dengel was a very distinguished student at University College, Cork. In the earlier years of her studies she became so proficient in Anatomy she was appointed Demonstrator in that subject. She won scholarships, got second class honors at the second university examination and also at the third and at the final obtained first class honors. It will afford me much pleasure to hear of her success in her profession which she so richly deserves."

> *Henry Corby, BA__,__, Professor of Obstetrics and Gynecology, University College, Cork, Consulting Physician, Cork Fraternity; Surgeon, Cork South Infirmary and County Hospital*

~ ~ ~

"I have known Dr. Anna Dengel during her whole undergraduate career in this college. Dr. Dengel was a keen and hardworking student. She has acquired a good knowledge of Pathology and Bacteriology, as well as of the Practice of her Profession generally and will, I am confident, carry on the duties of any position to which she may be called, to the satisfaction of everyone concerned."

> *A.E. Moore, Dean of the Medical Faculty & Professor of Pathology, U.C.C.*

~ ~ ~

"I have very great pleasure in testifying to the highly distinguished undergraduate career of Dr. A. Dengel. Her course in medicine was one of continual success. For one session she acted as Demonstrator in Anatomy to the women and students and proved herself an energetic and competent teacher. This autumn she got her M.B. and B.Sc. degrees with honors – a very unusual success here. Dr. Dengel may safely be entrusted with any post requiring energetic attention and conscientious discharge of duty. She has my best wishes for her success."

> *D.P. Fitzgerald, BA, MB, Professor of Anatomy*

~ ~ ~

Other comments from distinguished faculty: "… an exceptionally brilliant student" …"tactful and practical and sympathetic and possesses a sweet charm of manner" … "I have the highest opinion of her character and skill … she has had a most outstanding career at the University" …

"At the Mercy we all had the greatest respect for your devotion to your work as well as for your willingness to help... your success at the College was very great and you richly deserve all the Honors you got."

~ ~ ~

For male faculty members to bestow such praise on a female, a foreigner, one who had been labeled a political enemy meant that Anna had been an outstanding student, both academically and in her interactions with others. Coinciding with Anna's personal success was good news of global proportions. World War I had ended in November of the previous year. Although it would take unprecedented effort to address and repair the wounds of the world, there was relief in the realization that the overt carnage was over.

Once she had her diploma in hand, Anna had to think about what would happen next.

"Miss Willis wrote to me. There was, on account of the war there, this law that for five years no Germans or Austrians could go to India. Can you imagine! There I had been preparing all those years and when I was finished I got this news that for five years I couldn't go. I knew I had to do something. I looked around for a position that would help me prepare for India."

Anna soon discovered that there were already more than enough doctors in Ireland, so she turned her sights further afield. A notice in the British Medical Journal caught her attention. A position was available in Clay Cross in England, in the region of Nottingham, so she applied and got the job. She would be working for a group of doctors, and since this was her first assignment, she would be an assistant to a Dr. Wilson and under his direct supervision. She was eager to begin. She wanted to learn everything she could from her peers before moving on to the mission field and functioning on her own. Her medical license was issued on October 30th from the Branch Medical Council in Dublin. Certificate Number 12882 would be published in the Medical Register for 1920. It confirmed her Medical Registration in the United Kingdom of Great Britain and Ireland.

After six years in Ireland, Anna left Cork with many good memories and even more stories to tell. She was now a certified physician who, in her own estimation, had a whole lot to learn before she fully embraced the challenge offered to her by Dr. McLaren. She arrived in England near the end of December and celebrated Christmas with a circle of very dear friends in St. Margaret's on Bethell Avenue in a section of London known as Canningtown. Several days later, she went on to Clay Cross, a small town in Derbyshire, and began her work as a doctor. Eager to gain experience, she applied herself diligently, and before long she was working entirely on her own, even making night calls to patients in need when necessary.

Anna was looking forward to gaining significant practical experience and anticipated remaining in England for several years when, after only a few months, she received word that her visa for India had been granted. "Miss Willis and the London Committee had worked tenaciously for it," was how she explained it to her colleagues at work. "They knew how desperately St. Catherine's Hospital in Rawalpindi needed a doctor." Indeed they had been waiting seven years for Dr. Anna Dengel. Nevertheless, "it was a real shock to me not to have more time for professional preparation prior to going out to India. Instead of having to wait five years I was able to leave almost at once." Her colleagues tried their best to dissuade her. "It is very foolish," they said. But Anna simply responded that it was her vocation.

There was a lot to do to get ready. Because she did not have an Austrian passport, Anna had to apply to the Aliens Branch Home Office in Whitehall for a permit for the journey to India. Then she had to forward that permit to the India Office in Whitehall where arrangements would be made to grant the necessary visa to allow her to proceed to India to take up her missionary work. Amid the flurry of preparations, Anna scheduled a visit home. One can only imagine the euphoria of that return after seven long years – most of them war-weary years – in a foreign land. Everyone was there, even Hans, who had been a prisoner of war. Friends and relatives in Hall, friends and relatives in Steeg celebrated Anna's achievement and her triumphant return. But it would not be for long. She still had much to do in England before moving on again. And home was not like she had left it. So much had changed. The fabric of life was in tatters. The currency had lost its purchasing power. Economic conditions were disastrous. There was a devastating shortage of food. Politically, nothing was the same. Yet all family members were in relatively good health, and for that Anna was grateful.

Back in England, on October 15, 1920, Anna boarded the ship *"Kaiser I Kind"* to travel to India. She arrived in Rawalpindi on November 10, 1920. The missionary service she had dreamed of was now about to begin.

God doesn't expect the most heroic,

but reasonable, conscientious and good service,

so that we can let our light shine

and in that way serve,

so that we can let our light shine

and in that way glorify God.

Anna Dengel

CHAPTER FOUR

Rawalpindi – or Pindi – is situated in the Northwest Punjab region in what was the nation of India when Anna Dengel arrived in 1920. The climate was subtropical and humid, with long and very hot summers and short, wet winters. To compensate the area boasted scenic vistas of tree-covered mountains that offered an occasional glimpse of the peaks of Kashmir in the distance. The city was the site of a British cantonment, or permanent military station, which meant that its residents lived in designated areas separate from the indigenous populations.

Doctor Anna Dengel reached Rawalpindi from the port city of Bombay on November 10 and went directly to Saint Catherine of Genoa Hospital for Native Women and Children on Clyde Road. This was the moment for which so many had been waiting, working, and praying for years. A female physician, skillfully trained, was now permanently in charge of this pioneering institution. She recalls:

> "I got to Pindi. The Franciscan Missionaries of Mary were there. I was introduced to the parish priest five minutes after my arrival. I was in my room off the front hall. Mother called me out. Father was very keen of singing. He composed Masses; he liked a beautiful choir. He was emaciated down to the bone. I can still see his eyes. He was like a ghost, honestly! Without introductory questions about my passage, he asked bluntly' 'Can you sing?' 'No, Father,' was my reply. 'Go home,' he exclaimed and left. I went back into my room. That was the reception I got after nine years of preparation."

Doctor Dengel went to work the very next day, and within twenty-four hours of her arrival, sent the London Committee this report.

> "I arrived yesterday at 6 p.m. and was met by the Rev. Mother and another nun. The Convent is at one side of the street and the hospital at the other. I saw the latter only this morning; it is very strange and simple, containing several white-washed wards. Quite well enough for any amount of good work, all sorts of medical cases, labor cases, minor and gynecological operations. The operating room is really the best part, quite good instruments too, some antiquated and some of course conspicuous by their absence. The Dispensary is large, with benches for the patients. One of the nuns is in the Drug Room, which is fairly well stocked. Today, my first day, we had 51 patients and in the afternoon a little operation."

Statistically, a lot had occurred at St. Catherine's prior to Anna's arrival. The London Committee's Annual Report for 1920 listed 11,434 as the total number of cases treated that year. Of these 190 were indoor patients. There were 140 operations performed and 22 labor cases attended. The Report added this note.

> "We hope with the arrival of Dr. Dengel, who has taken up her life's career solely for this missionary service, in the future a very high professional efficiency will be shown at this hospital."

This is precisely what Anna intended to bring about. She would work diligently, with a dedicated expertise, to address the overwhelming need. With a newcomer's enthusiasm, Anna began her tenure as physician-in-residence even before her bags were unpacked.

> "With the help of a Sister, who acted as an interpreter, I started work at once. It was quite obvious that the first thing I would have to concentrate on was Hindustani. I took a *munshi* (teacher) who, I soon discovered, was more fond of discussing comparative religions and

Hindu customs and traditions (he was a Brahmin) and of reciting Persian poetry than of drilling vocabulary and verbs. Sometimes a whole hour passed without any allusion to grammar. Perhaps I was more to blame than he – for I found it all very interesting, and, what is more, in due course it helped me greatly to understand the mental attitude and religious and social practices of my patients. As far as the language is concerned, I learned a great deal from a little Mohammedan girl who hovered around me like a guardian angel. Of the six main languages and 220 or so dialects of India, Hindustani is the most widely spoken – being the mother-tongue of about seventy million people. This highly developed, rich and beautiful language of Sanskrit origin and Arabic script is not very difficult to learn – at least for practical purposes."

At St. Catherine's Anna had to face a number of challenges right from the start. Some she had anticipated, others she had not.

"When we had these difficult cases, I had to give chloroform; I had to use forceps. I had no assistance! Mrs. Donahue sometimes was there; other times she wasn't there. The nuns, when I wanted anything; they just opened the door, about that much, and handed it in that way."

A new language, a variety of new cultures, primitive medical and surgical conditions: these were to be expected. Equally challenging, however, was the realization that she would be living, as well as working, in the midst of a community of nuns. Although she had her own room set apart from the Sisters, she would have to depend on them for many things beyond their professional assistance, such as, activities that were not work-related, companionship, and casual conversation. While a cloistered community context was a familiar way of life for the four Franciscan Missionaries of Mary whose Motherhouse was in France, it was not the same for Anna. In reality, however, they were the only community she had and she did her best to fit in.

The challenge of collaborating with members of a religious order under allegiance to Rome was not only personal, but professional. The Franciscan Missionaries of Mary [FMM's] who had been asked to take charge of the hospital were not trained nurses. While they were dedicated and competent in what they were allowed to do, they were severely limited because of Rome's restrictions regarding women with religious vows. Exposure to the naked human body was canonically forbidden. Consequently, they could not be present during childbirth, were not allowed to provide post-partum care, and were banned from the operating room during certain surgical procedures, which meant that, during surgery, they had to stand outside the O.R. and pass surgical instruments to Dr. Dengel through an open door. When an emergency arose at night, the Sisters had to obey the rule mandating that they be in bed at the designated hour. Because of these restrictions, the Sisters had added a lay woman to the hospital staff. Mrs. Donahue was an Anglo-Indian, a nurse, and a midwife. She was a valuable addition, when she was on duty, which wasn't all the time. Consequently, Anna had to respond to after-hour medical emergencies on her own.

One month after arriving, Anna sent a congratulatory note to the FMM's Superior General in Rome, for Mother Michel had just been elected to office.

> "I wish you could have stood at the dispensary door to watch the rejoicing when the good news of your election came! The patients who were watching the proceedings asked: 'What has happened that the Mothers are so extraordinarily pleased?' I must say that I am so glad too that the choice has fallen on somebody who knows the Pindi hospital, its work, its satisfaction and its difficulties."

She added this personal note.

> "I am only here since the 10ᵗʰ of November and I have not had much time yet to gain experience. The Eastern mind seems so different from ours. The nuns tell me that I have to learn a lot yet and that I will mind it less by degrees. We are all of a different nationality – but as English, French, and Hindustani are the common

current languages – we all seem to belong to the same place."

Anna's introduction to the practice of medicine in her new surroundings began in the hospital, which had only 15 beds. Ordinarily, she would spend most of the morning attending to those who had been admitted and then move into the large outdoor dispensary for the rest of the day. There she could expect up to 100 patients daily, and sometimes, even more. Surgery was performed when necessary, on a daily basis, and when it was possible to do so, she would also make house calls, if the patient lived nearby, and on occasion, even at a distance. Anna wrote to the London Committee in early January.

> "I am trying to get a little Government Grant; everything here is so expensive that we must pull all possible strings. On the 8ᵗʰ of December it was nine years since the Nuns took over the charge of the Hospital and much good work they have done in this time. They are like good angels, full of patience and endurance, and that is required more than anything else. We get all sorts of diseases every day. Really the work is well worth the interest and the trouble the Committee, the Nuns and all benefactors are taking."

The London Committee had lobbied long and hard for this pioneering hospital in the Punjab, persistently asking why "Catholics alone of all the Christian Missions in India have opened no hospitals exclusively to meet the medical needs of women, and have no women doctors to visit the women in their zenanas." A zenana is an area in the home set aside exclusively for the women. The Committee clearly stated their terms for providing financial support for such an institution. It would be "on condition maternity patients should be treated with the same respect as other patients and in all respects be on an equal footing with them." It is hard to imagine today that such a statement would have been necessary, but at that time it was. This first Catholic medical mission in a heavily populated region of India also had to ensure that "the Hospital and Dispensary will be open to native women and children of all creeds" and that their "religious and 'caste' feelings will be respected in every way possible." Although St. Catherine's Hospital was established to serve native (indigenous) women and their children, all women and children were welcome from the very beginning. Residents of the cantonment regularly sought medical attention in the hospital and its open-air dispensary, because at that time there was no other hospital like it anywhere near.

Anna was delighted to report that "among the women and children who came to the hospital and dispensary, there were Hindus, Sikhs, native Christians, some Europeans and Anglo-Indians and many Mohammedans. The latter came shrouded in burkas and were accompanied by relatives." A burka is a cloth that covers the face and had to be worn when in public, because the religious custom of purdah forbid Muslim [Mohammedan] women to be seen by men other than those who were members of their immediate family. At St. Catherine's, in the presence of women, "the women lifted the veil, but the moment a man appeared on the scene they dropped the veil swiftly." Anna enjoyed talking with the women individually and in groups during their visits to the dispensary.

> "Everyone was very friendly and respectful. Practically all the women were illiterate, and when I suggested sending the little girls to school they merely shrugged their shoulders. In the hospital the Hindus could not accept food from anyone who was not of their own caste or at least of a near caste. This necessitated relatives staying with the patient day and night, and also called for separate kitchens for the adherents of different religions. A satisfactory regulation of the diet was out of the question on account of the caste rules. To give only one example – to a Hindu woman who was notably undernourished and who, I knew, could not take meat of any kind, I said: 'Eat plenty of eggs.' Her answer was: 'In my caste, once we are married, we are not allowed to eat eggs.' The outcasts, who number sixty million or so, are the lowest on the social scale. Many came to the dispensary."

A trip to the dispensary made it possible for a woman to socialize with other women, to see a woman doctor, and to eavesdrop on the advice the doctor would give to other women, for any concept of confidentiality in an open air dispensary is inconceivable. It also provided an opportunity for hospital staff to share some basic nutritional information or other helpful suggestions with a large number of village women. Here is how Anna describes the dispensary.

"The waiting room and verandah were the most colorful and, I may say, the noisiest places in the hospital – where rich and poor, caste and outcaste, old and young met and discussed the problems of the day – mostly babies, jewels and ailments. As regards the latter – they were many and varied. There are fevers of known and unknown origin and skin diseases – from ulcers covered with cow dung to intractable oriental sores, endless gastro-intestinal complaints, not to mention the still more endless and hopeless pelvic ones. The latter are mostly the result of bad midwifery at the hands of untrained midwives. Tuberculosis – so widespread on account of unsanitary living conditions and malnutrition – is frequently encountered in the dispensary. Eye diseases, particularly every form of conjunctivitis, glaucoma, and cataract abound. The Punjab, where Rawalpindi is situated, is said to have the highest incidence of blindness in the world. Infants and children form a large percentage of the clientele of the dispensary. Many of them are victims of sheer ignorance as regards food, clothing, or protection from sun and mosquitoes, or lack of timely medical care. The high mortality in infancy and childhood is one of the main contributing factors towards keeping the average expectancy of life at the low level of twenty-five years."

While it was deeply satisfying to be able to help so many who would otherwise have gone without, it is easy to see how a health care provider might very quickly become overwhelmed, and eventually burn out, when dealing with limited resources in the face of unending need. Anna was confronted with that realization early on.

"Often I felt the triple inadequacy of knowledge, of diagnostic facilities, and of means for effective treatment.

48

And with only one doctor it is difficult to advance much beyond the stage of a dispensary. From 1 p.m. to 3 p.m. every sensible white person rests in India. At first I was not sensible – but later I saw the wisdom of following this and other precautions to observe in the tropics."

Finally, on September 21, 1921, ten months after arriving in India, Anna received her Certificate of Registration from the Punjab Medical Council recognizing her appointment at St. Catherine's Hospital in Rawalpindi and officially authorizing her to practice medicine in the Punjab.

An aspect of Anna's medical ministry that she found particularly satisfying was to go out to visit a patient in her home whenever possible. She would have loved to do this on a regular basis but could not for the following reason.

"It is difficult to leave one's post if there is only one doctor in charge of a hospital, no matter how small it may be. This is not so much on account of the in-patients as the dispensary patients, many of whom often walk many miles or travel several days to the dispensary and of course are very disappointed if they find a doctor absent."

Home visits brought a variety of services to those who were chronically deprived and would otherwise not visit the hospital. One day Anna was taken to a sweeper's compound to see a woman with puerperal sepsis and was able to bring her some relief. At another time she incised a breast abscess for a woman who was confined to her zenana. For another, who had gone to a male doctor who had felt her pulse and examined her tongue but could do no more for her because she was a woman, she was able to examine her thoroughly, make a diagnosis, and prescribe appropriate medication. As happened so often in these home visits, the female doctor was asked to look at half a dozen or so other members of the household. Anna always did, and usually discovered significant and unrelieved suffering that had been patiently and fatalistically endured. Because she was passionate about raising awareness in the West to both the needs and the inherent goodness of the women of the East, Anna kept notes on some of her more memorable experiences. She liked to tell this story to visitors and friends.

One evening a poor man of the shoemakers' caste, which ranks very low, asked her to come and take a look at his wife, who lived only a short distance away. He took her bag and off they went. When they arrived at a row of mud houses, they entered one of them through a wooden door. The husband remained in the courtyard. An elderly woman in dark clothes, not very clean, hair disheveled, beckoned to Anna to come inside. A small dim lantern dangling from a wire was the only light in the darkness. A woman was lying on a string bed on a quilt that had been clean once upon a time. The woman on the bed was about to give birth. The other woman was the *dhai*, one of thousands of untrained, superstitious, well-meaning but dangerously ignorant midwives. There was no indication that she had washed her hands. She wore no protective covering of any kind and had done nothing at all to prepare for what was about to happen. Eventually the baby was safely delivered. Anna suggested to the *dhai* that she give the baby a bath. Instead of putting the infant on her lap, for she was sitting on the floor, she put it across her feet, so that its little head and feet were touching the mud floor. Only Anna was aware of how wrong this was. The father and mother were jubilant because the woman had given birth to a son, which now, according to their Hindu belief, meant that they could hope to enter heaven. The *dhai* rejoiced, for the fee for a boy was double the amount of that for a girl. Anna also rejoiced, because everyone was delighted. Poor as he was, the shoemaker insisted on making a strong pair of shoes for the Doctor *Memsahiba*.

Here are some more of Anna's village experiences, which she recalls in her own words. "The following short sketches are not a studied selection of types of women and homes, but merely true to life glimpses of a few among the many whom I had the privilege to visit in connection with my work in Rawalpindi and surroundings, and in Kashmir."

~ ~ ~

"One fine autumn day a Mohammedan gentleman arrived in a luxurious car, accompanied by a native doctor, and asked me to see his mother – he was an adopted son - and his wife. At the entrance to the native city, the car stopped before a heavy gate. Servants emerged from a little doorway and opened the gate. The doctor being a man not of the household and therefore not allowed to see the Mohammedan ladies, waited, while I was conducted by the gentleman to the women's quarters. On the way, I stopped in amazement: I beheld not a garden but a field of roses. I was led past a spacious verandah into a large, well-ventilated room, furnished with a few chairs. The mother, a woman of about 45, was suffering from a chronic nervous tremor. She had a kindly expression, was dressed in clean and costly though simple garments, conversed intelligently and with great common sense. Her daughter-in-law was bejeweled and dressed in brighter colors, her speech and her manner were gentle; however, she seemed unnaturally subdued. The two ladies had several servants at their beck and call. Having no children, being illiterate although highly cultured in their own way, and according to Mohammedan custom of the people of their class, confined for years to their home, they were forced to lead a very monotonous life. They had the advantage of a good home, plenty of food, fresh air, and sunshine, even roses by the thousands in all hues to delight their eyes for nine months in the year, but not the stimulating contact with a variety of human beings and human interests. I thought that the best service I could render them would be to invite them to spend an afternoon with me, which would bring them beyond their four walls. They were very pleased at the prospect but it depended of course on the men to allow it. The gentleman assured me that he was very pleased to drive his mother and his wife to my place on a certain definite date. When the date came, he sent an excuse. I renewed the invitation twice. I then realized that it was a polite way of refusing to bring them. However, they managed to send for me every now and then. Besides medical advice, my visit meant a new face, a new voice, a new topic of conversation for them; also an opportunity

51

of arranging a nice basket of roses, which they knew I welcomed for our little chapel."

～ ～ ～

"New Year's Day is a legal holiday in India and all public offices are closed. Our Rawalpindi dispensary came under that category. Legal holidays, however, do not stop doctor's calls, and the day was still young when a *tongawalla* [carriage driver] brought a *chitti* [note] from a native doctor asking me to see a lady in the native city, as he, being a man, could not examine her. I took my bag and mounted the tonga. We stopped at the *Hakim's* [native doctor's] shop. He was a Sikh. He salaamed me and soon was with me in the tonga. On the way to the city he told me that we were going to a rich Mohammedan household, the owner of which possessed two wives. Everything else I had to find out for myself.

"The house was a regular fortress, four stories high. The staircase was narrow and most of the rooms irregular and dark. The gentleman of the house conducted us to a verandah where a woman appeared, who brought me into the zenana quarters. The men remained behind. The room was light and airy and full of women. Although Mohammedan women are extremely reserved with men, even their own relatives, they are not so among women. It does not embarrass them in the least to tell their complaints and be examined in the presence of women, no matter how large the audience. The essence of the trouble was that both wives had no children and they dreaded that a third wife would come into the house. Although recognized by Mohammedan law, polygamy is by no means a desired state of affairs with the women, as a rule. The general health of the two ladies was not good. Being the wives of a rich man, they were obliged to observe purdah (seclusion) very strictly. They never went out for a walk or a drive; their food was cooked for them and their clothes made for them, and as they were not able to read or write, there was plenty of time left for them to ponder over their sad fate. Their gold-embroidered velvet trousers and kurtas were a consolation, but a poor one. They could not even avail themselves of their husband's country house, which was a regular palace surrounded by a beautiful enclosed garden with a Persian wheel well and full of shady trees. 'Why don't you go out for a change of air?' I said. 'Our jewels might be stolen,' was their reply. They never leave their home. Their life is one of physical and mental stagnation. Their bodies suffer from over-rest and over-feeding, their minds and souls from starvation. In their trials and sorrows they can only fall back on Kismet (fate).

"By degrees the onlookers and listeners became lively too, and told me their troubles: one had goiter; another, diabetes and some skin trouble that would not heal; another had bad teeth; another, cataract; another consulted me about her child. I realized that if I were the physician of the household, I would be the busiest person in it. The timidity and shyness disappeared and, as I made signs of leaving, more and more of them besieged me, asking me all sorts of questions about myself and Valayiat (Europe). Most of them had never spoken to a Christian woman before. One thing did not appeal to them about me: I wore no jewels. One of them had a great desire to put some on me to see how it would look. So my forehead and ears were bedecked, also my neck, wrist, and fingers. The nose, toes, and ankle rings had to be imagined. They thought that I looked ever so much better, and it gave them great pleasure to see me thus arrayed. I was glad that I was a woman and a doctor, for only this combination allowed me to bring a little help and cheer among them."

~ ~ ~

"Sometimes I was called to patients quite a distance away. On account of my hospital duties, it was possible only occasionally. I remember one instance of a visit to a Mohammedan woman on the northwest frontier. She was eighteen years old – very beautiful and worried because she had not yet given birth to a child. She was perfectly healthy. Why did she not come to the hospital for consultation? The answer was that she, being the wife of a rich landowner, could not leave her enclosure. Keeping it strictly was a mark of exclusiveness and distinction. After the professional part of my work was completed, I sat for a while with the hostess and her women servants in the enclosure and chatted on sundry topics. The woman cook was about her business at one end of the compound. As her cough sounded very suspicious to me, I suggested an examination, which revealed tuberculosis in an advanced degree. She was a deadly menace to all the women of the enclosure. Not long ago the first wife of the landowner had died of tuberculosis, and the fate of her successor can be easily guessed had not the cook been removed."

~ ~ ~

"A certain Indian gentleman who spoke English fluently came and told me that his *Malik* (master) wanted him to bring a woman doctor to see his wife. I agreed to go. The train left about 8 p.m. and reached our railway destination about midnight. The *Malik's* manager came to me and solemnly proposed three alternatives. He said: 'You can spend the night here in the railway station, we will give you a *charpoy* and *resai* (string-bed and quilt), or, the *Malik's* servants will carry you in a litter (he pointed to a coffin-shaped box with four projecting sticks), or, if you wish to ride, a horse is ready for you.' I chose the latter. To my great amusement they put a chair beside the horse to make it easier for me to mount. Then we started, the manager and myself on horseback, 14 servants on shank's mare, trotting in front, beside and behind us. The rough path was lit up by the moon and the stars. After an hour's ride – it was one o'clock in the morning – we passed a tank which was surrounded by women. 'These Hindu women worship the moon,' said my companion. After another hour we saw the reflection of the moon in a big pool of water from which rose the melodious refrain of quack, quack. (However, I did not take it as a personal salutation.) It was well after 2 a.m. when we reached the village. I was conducted to an isolated building where I had a few hours' sleep.

"After breakfast of tea and eggs, I went to see my patient. The zenana quarter was a separate building surrounded by a high wall. The queen of this stronghold was Pathani of the renowned Peshawar beauty type, light complexion, Eastern features, dark hair. Her cheeks had a little glow of artificial rouge, her dress was dainty and her jewels not too many. Although she was only 18 years old, her manner was dignified and calm. When my professional work was done, she took me to the sitting room. My patient and I sat on the chairs and a number of women servants were sitting or lying around us. I was asked so many and such varied questions that I was able to sketch for them the life of an ordinary Christian family and the essentials of our religious beliefs, simply and quietly at their own request. Everything I said or did was of interest to them as they had never come in touch with Europeans before. After some time the *Malik* came. When he entered his wife rose respectfully and remained standing as long as he was standing. He offered to show me the place. The mistress of the house could not accompany us.

"From the roof of the guest house we had a splendid view of the *Malik's* dominion, which comprised 18 villages. I said to him, 'What good is all this land when your wife can't even go for a walk?' 'The only time I could take my wife for a walk would be during the night,' he said. 'In families like ours, religion and custom and public opinion are strongly against women appearing in public.' I explained to him that this constant confinement was bad for her health, but he could not see any way out. I also drew his attention to a big pool in the vicinity of the house as an ideal place for breeding mosquitos. 'Oh,' he said, 'that is stored rain water and our only supply. People and buffaloes bathe in it and drink from it; there are no wells in the neighborhood.'

"As I bade farewell, I was asked to come again during the beautiful harvest season, and was presented with a basketful of quails. With the same retinue, I rode through the stillness of the night, reached the train at midnight and my destination at 6 a.m. The fluttering birds in the basket made sure that I did not over-sleep."

In the summer Anna took leave of steamy, teeming Rawalpindi, where she was always either on duty or on call. Her destination was Murree, a fertile hill station where missionaries, and many others, went to get away from the humidity and hectic pace of an urban setting. Anna loved it there. The lush green valley that stretched out toward the foothills of the Himalayan mountains was reminiscent of the Alpine village of her childhood. Although now and then she would be approached for her medical expertise, she also had time to rest and relax, take long walks, read and reflect and write lengthy letters to family and friends back home.

"Every year during the summer I spent a month of vacation in Kashmir. While there I frequently accompanied the sisters on horseback to the villages to visit the sick. No doctor or nurse had ever set foot in these villages before. There I saw perfect examples of the results of disease left to run its natural course – for instance, general anasarca [generalized edema or dropsy] of a degree that I have never seen before or after, a compound fracture so neglected that gangrene had set in and the leg was rotting away, deformity such that the upper arm was united to the side of the thorax, the result of an extensive burn. Osteomalacia, so advanced that the patient was unable to move without agonizing pain."

~ ~ ~

"On a village tour in Kashmir, I was invited to visit a boys' school. I was of course expected to do something or say something. I asked the school master to bring the boys out in the open and line them up in a row. Then I said to the boys, 'Caps off!' In Kashmir men and boys wear a small tight-fitting skull cap. I found what I expected: 75 out of 104 boys had the area of the cap covered with thick scabs, the result of infection carried by the frequent exchange of germ laden caps and the lack of air and light. On that day they received a never-to-be-forgotten lecture on the use of soap and water."

~ ~ ~

"During my holidays in Kashmir, I was frequently asked to see patients as there was no woman doctor in the district. The Head Master of the Mission School called me to see his wife. After a walk of about twenty minutes on a dusty road, we crossed the Jlelum River on a ferry boat which devout sons of Allah run free of cost in loving memory of one of the great prophets. On the far bank of the river was the native city, dilapidated and picturesque. A good number of women were there washing clothes. We reached the patient's house where about fifteen men relatives were awaiting me. To my surprise they followed me up the stairs into an empty room, where the patient cowered in a corner. I requested all the men, except one, to leave; there was quite a competition as to who would stay; finally the mother's choice, which was gratified, fell on a grown up son. The lady was of fine physique, but thinking it necessary to her well-being, had indulged rather heavily in opium to the detriment of her health. She promised, however, to diminish the dose gradually and it was reported to me a year later that she kept her promise with good results. She also had a goiter of moderate size, like most Kashmiri women. As a matter of fact, they take pride in it, provided it is not too large. The little guard of gentlemen had gathered in the courtyard and secured ponies for my companion and me for our journey home on a different route. We were followed by a young man who carried a struggling live cock and another who carried a heaped up plate full of sugar, those being the fee for my services. A number of boys also joined the procession. One cannot live on cocks and sugar only. Perhaps this is one reason why there are so few doctors in certain regions of the world!"

~ ~ ~

"A disease which is very prevalent among the women of India is osteomalacia. It is a softening of the bones brought about mainly by lack of sunlight and improperly balanced food. It occurs among all classes of women. Purdah women, who are confined to their homes, are more often affected. My first case was in Kashmir. I was out with the Sisters when a man approached, salaamed most profoundly, calling down on us all the blessings of heaven, and asked if we would go and see a sick *bibi* (woman) in a house not far away. Off we went and were ushered into a wooden hut with another profound salaam. In a back room, dark and stuffy, with women sitting here and there on string beds, we were introduced to a pitiful figure cowering in a squatting position in a corner. Not without a ring of hope in her voice, she asked, "Is this the Doctor *Memsahiba*?" Then she, and her relatives, women only being present, said that for five or six years she had been suffering from pains in the wrists, spine, hips, knees, ankles, all over, as a matter of fact, and that after the birth of her last baby, she was not able to walk any more. Of late her bones had become so deformed that she could not even lie flat on her back. There she was, helpless and hopeless, a burden to herself and to the household. Nobody knew the cause of her trouble or how to remedy it. I explained. The body needs the health-giving ultra-violet rays of the sun, which are one of the greatest sources of vitamin D, which is also found in cod-liver oil, liver, animal fat and other foods and is a vital necessity for growth and bone formation. The unfortunate woman, living in semi-darkness, and subsisting on a diet of curry and rice, was the victim of vitamin D famine. If vitamin D foods are not available, there is more need to make a fuller use of sunlight in order to supply the deficiency."

Home visits were stimulating for Anna. She loved interacting with women from the many cultural contexts of Indian society and delighted in helping them. Such activities, however, were not a viable substitute for some kind of relaxation where she was free from responsibility, but there was seldom time for that. The demands on her professional expertise continued relentlessly, day after day, week after week, month after month, throughout the first two years of her tenure at St. Catherine's. On the one hand, there was the never-ending stream of human suffering confronting her at every turn; on the other, insufficient resources, together with the realization that no matter how much she did for the people whom she had come to know and love, it would never be enough. Aware that even a minor improvement in the present situation would not happen anytime soon, she simply kept on going. This dedication to duty would eventually take its toll.

> "My days were filled to the brim in the hospital, in the outpatient department, with house visits, with language study, with difficulties from within and from without. Something came over me that I was unable to comprehend or solve. I do not know what 'Night of the Soul' actually means or feels like – but this was the only explanation I was able to put to it."

"Dark Night of the Soul" is often used in Catholic spirituality to describe an individual's feeling of separation from God and the struggle to keep faith when there is no physical or emotional assurance that one is on the right path. The phrase was first used by the 16th century Spanish mystic, Saint John of the Cross.

> "At this time in my life something happened that would begin to point the way to what God wanted of me. This happening was that Father White, my confessor, a Mill Hill Missionary who was stationed in Pindi, had his bicycle stolen. I felt very sorry for him and gave him part of my small salary towards a new one. I can remember the spot where this took place. Father thanked me profusely, and I said spontaneously in my distress: Don't thank me, HELP me! That led to my speaking to Father of the state I was in, which as I said, I could neither understand nor analyze."

The incident involving the stolen bicycle occurred as the year 1922 was drawing to a close. From then until the spring of 1924, Fr. William White was Anna's spiritual director. He sent approximately 30 lengthy letters to her in response to letters she had sent to him during that agonizing period. Anna kept all of his correspondence in her personal archive, which may suggest that she wanted the contents to one day come to light. However, she must have asked him to destroy all her letters to him, and it seems that he complied, for he wrote, "I have done as you have asked," and no letters have been found. Years later Anna reflected:

> "Father immediately came to the conclusion that I was longing to dedicate my life totally to God and he suggested, or told me that I should enter a religious Congregation."

Here are some of Father White's words to the beleaguered Anna who, as he revealed early on, had the same name as his sister, who was also struggling with emotional stress.

~ ~ ~

> "We must do our best to be of glad heart, trusting, forever trusting. There must be no worry whatever. I can safely assert that all worry is a handmaid of the devil.... You left loved ones for God's sake. Perhaps our

Dear Lord wants more – anyway He will show this in due time." January 8, 1923

~ ~ ~

"What you tell me does not surprise me. It is natural for unruly thoughts and shadows to come before you. Fear not. Don't battle or dwell on them, but rather say, 'Lord…what wilt Thou have me to do?' The storm has been with you for long. I hope and pray that you will experience the Peace of security and safety, which you have been seeking. <u>Believe</u> though you do not <u>feel</u>, that all these doubts and forebodings are but evidence of His Love. Take no notice of Feelings. What He wants is the Will. He values more an act of love when we feel cold, than when the feeling of love is with us. 'Fear not!' Let Him lead you where He wills – I doubt not – He will reveal Himself soon." April 2, 1923

~ ~ ~

"All seems dark to you. I feel He will ask, before long, something unusual. In the meantime let us ask and pray, 'Lord, what wilst Thou have me do?'" April 30, 1923

~ ~ ~

Theirs was an intense exchange. Again and again the missionary priest tried to assuage Anna's internal angst, but was unable to do so. She was haunted by fears related to her past that seemed to have little substance except in her own imagination, fears of not having been good enough, of having in some way offended God, an undefined fear that sometimes questioned her eternal salvation. While he listened to her with compassion and tried his best to help her, it is clear from his correspondence that he never got to the heart of what was causing her such distress, emotionally and physically, for she was often ill. Still, he tried to direct her, proceeding as though he somehow knew what God expected of her and what was best for her. He insisted that her inner turmoil was the result of failing to listen to God. Ironically, the priest she had asked to help her find a solution to her problem would become a part of the problem, for he was convinced that God had given him the answer to why she was seldom at peace and was speaking to her through him.

~ ~ ~

"Before commencing this letter, I implored the help of the Divine Spirit for assistance. Perhaps you know the answer already. You have told me many things, which perhaps are known to few others, perhaps to none now on earth. Long ago a holy Priest made a remark that you were marked out for great things. Your life has been a wandering about – seeking for 'The Pearl of great price.' A Holy Nun once passed a remark about 'your seeking religion'; at that time perhaps it was not God's will. When you said you did not feel called to the Religious state, perhaps you do not feel all the inclinations, and yet – it may be that God in His goodness really wants you.

"But perhaps you may say, 'What of my Profession – my medical work? Will not all this be wasted? Cannot I carry on as before, for women with my capabilities are certainly required. This is true, but let us not forget that Prayer does more than Action. Prayers amid humble duties probably account for more blessings than the actions. Someday our eyes will be opened and we shall notice how much the hidden ones of the world, whether they be in the Cloister or in the world but secluded and unknown, it will be revealed to us how they are the great ones. His own was the Hidden Way. We can do wonders even though hidden away.

"You have sought rest and have not found it. Is this not true? Perhaps Our Dear Lord is waiting to give it to you within the Religious Life. And so I would say, 'Enter,' for I feel you will find what you really want, 'Rest' – in the knowledge that God so wills.

"I have written all that I could say. The object is to attain that Peace and surety which seems not to have been yours. These I think you will find, close to the Divine Heart, in His own special Service. There you will be able to give Him everything – there you will have the security of the Vow – there also, I doubt not, you will find that Peace which the world cannot give. It seems but a slight change, for how long you have been in the world, but not of the world. The world seems not to have had the attractions for you which it has for others. How I really long to see you nearer still to the Divine. How I long for that day when He will clasp you to His Sacred Bosom – the Master, the Disciple, the Father, the Daughter.

"It may mean so many breaks, shall I say even a shattering of dreams long cherished. Your dreams will be realities which will appear in all their glory when the Master calls again, saying, 'Come, follow Me.' You followed Me on earth; you gave up your will as I did to My Father. Come, now, and follow Me even to the Home of the Blessed." May 19, 1923

~ ~ ~

"And now we have one beatified whose short life and books after death have astonished the world – the Little Flower of Jesus. Her path on earth was doubtless full of storms – the roses have come after death. I think I can do no better than to commend you to, now, Blessed Thérèse of Lisieux. I decided nothing until the Feast of the Spirit of Peace. Knowing you, perhaps better than others, I was compelled to use Our Lord's words, which are, 'Come, follow me' – 'Leave all and follow me.'

"As to your father, I feel sure, he will come to look upon it as a blessing. As to the Committee – know our Dear Lord is above them. As to the apparent loss to the medical missions – who knows but that God will urge many to follow, for the very reason that you work, as Our Lady, hidden away." May 29, 1923

~ ~ ~

Anna's memory of this moment remained crystal clear.

> "Father White told me that I should enter a religious
> Congregation. What was more natural than to suggest
> the Franciscan Missionaries of Mary, with whom
> I was working. One could but admire their charity
> and heroism, so I took Father's decision, it was <u>HIS</u>. I
> insisted that I could not leave St. Catherine's Hospital
> until a substitute was found for me."

On the first of June, just three days after hearing Father White's decision
regarding the rest of her life, Anna received a letter from Sister Marie
Alberte, Provincial Superior of the FMM's, who had been a member of
the Pindi community. She and Anna were friends.

> "Bravo! I am so <u>awfully</u> happy over the news. You say
> it will be like a bombshell for me – well, it was – and it
> was not. I have long thought that the world would never
> satisfy you: it is too shallow for that – but that the call
> would be so soon. But where does He want you? I would
> not be true if I did not say that of all the orders I know
> ours would seem to be the one for your aspirations – but
> I would not for the world try to influence you – your
> choice must be <u>all</u> your own."

In a subsequent letter on June 21, Marie Alberte wrote:

> "You know my arms and heart are wide open to receive
> you and give you all the help and grace our big family
> can give you through me … and I am glad Father White
> has settled the point for you – nothing would give you
> greater peace than acting by obedience – You are sure of
> not making mistakes... I told you how I became a nun
> only through obedience also – and how I have thanked
> God for it ever since."

On June 25, 1923, Anna made a formal request for admission into the Congregation of the Franciscan Missionaries of Mary. The admissions process included filling out a form with 32 questions, most of them biographically oriented. Among them were the following:

> Since when have you thought of becoming a religious?
> "Since April 1923"
> Is it of your own free will that you wish to enter religion?
> "Yes – through obedience to my confessor"
> What dowry can you bring?
> "Owing to the present conditions of Austria and also being the child of a large family – my younger brothers and sisters still being educated – I cannot ask my parents for a dowry. My own savings will cover traveling expenses and trousseau."

On June 25 Anna sent her application along with a note to Mother Michel, the FMM Superior General in Rome.

> "I had no thought of becoming a nun until recently – as a matter of fact I was so sure of my vocation that I asked my Confessor to allow me to make a vow to work as a medical missionary as I am now – all my life. It is then that he told me to become a nun and to join your order, which he knows very well. My greatest sacrifice is to give up my own ambitions for the medical missions – for which I have a sort of passion – and up to this it seemed my life-work."

Anna was formally accepted into the FMM Congregation, setting in motion a tidal wave of change in her own life and in the lives of those around her. Years later she would recall:

> "Although I could not be fire and flame for Father's decision, yet I acted in obedience when I asked for admission into the Congregation of the Franciscan Missionaries of Mary, which was granted. It was a difficult situation since I could not speak openly about

all this to the London Committee, to which I felt responsible."

The long-awaited letter from Pauline Willis arrived on July 23. "The big piece of news reached me this morning. There is only one thing to be said, God's will and His call must come before anything else." That said, she proceeded to ask Anna: to which vocation is God calling you – the medical or the religious – because Rome has made clear that it is either the one or the other. "The point to find out: <u>which</u> God calls you to, and has He called you to the one and now desires it to be given up?" Indeed, Anna's pursuit of medical studies in order to become a medical missionary was in obedience to the call of the Spirit, which she had never doubted. Miss Willis had gone right to the heart of Anna's dilemma.

By the end of July the inner turmoil that had momentarily abated returned full force and remained with Anna throughout the rest of the year, and beyond it. Father White's letters also continued. His position, and advice, never wavered. "Don't!!! Don't!!! Don't!!! be disturbed about anything. He is calling. The proof of this seems to be the worries with which you are attacked." He insisted:

> "Pray like this: I am not looking back … I have put my hand to the plough. He can get the work done without me, but I cannot carry on without Him. Should all my qualifications, as doctor, be lost, alright. He lived a Hidden Life."

A decision had been made and a course had been set, but something in Anna's DNA seemed to want no part of it, even as she tried to implement, unconditionally, the implications of her consent.

Anna went to the hill region for several weeks in the summer, a place that offered an escape from the complexities of life in the city and a haven for her battered spirit. Toward the end of the summer, Father White wrote the following:

> "May I add a postscript without appearing to be a busybody. This is regarding smoking. Take it reasonably, don't smoke too much, for as you know, this is injurious to the health, but for the time being at least, if a cigarette

seems to work and help, don't you think it would be better to indulge? Please don't think I mean to trespass."

Around this time Anna wrote an article entitled "Medical Missions As Means of Propagation of the Faith." It is dated September 28, 1923, and there is no indication that it was ever published. Its basis may have been her award-winning paper from medical school and its purpose a final reflection on that part of her life that had for years been the primary focus of her concerns and would soon be over. Writing it gave her an opportunity to put aside those feelings that were beyond her control and immerse herself in the rational realm of facts and analysis, where she felt comfortable and in control. Father White had recently chided her on the source of her latest anxiety, saying: "The fear of 'shall I persevere' has assumed the clothes of a giant" – as indeed it had.

The hospital was busy during the Fall. At one point a local doctor came in to lend a hand. Early in November Anna was exhausted and sick with fever. The stress had reached the tipping point. Father White wrote: "I cannot let you kneel for any length of time in your present state. He then recommended that she consult with some priest "more experienced and more endowed with God's illuminating grace." If not, then "it must be one of two things – the convent or as you are at present." She did not seek counsel elsewhere, and sometime after December 10, Anna made a retreat. Father White said this to her: at the end of the retreat, she should come to the confessional, where he would reveal to her God's plan for her, whether to enter the convent or remain as she was. He felt this was the only way that she could truly accept the will of God speaking to her through him. He asked if she would be willing to accept, under Holy Obedience, in the context of the confessional, whatever that decision would be as God's will for her, thereby relieving her of all responsibility for the outcome. She agreed. This point needs further clarification. Anna had already taken steps to enter religious life "under obedience." While it sounds like the same thing, it isn't. She entered the FMM's under obedience to her confessor, insisting that it was his decision, not hers, and that she would obey *his* decision. Now her confessor would reveal to her God's will for her as spoken through God's priestly representative within a sacramental context. Consequently, this would be God's decision and not that of the priest. Anna agreed in advance to accept that decision as God's will for her, whatever the outcome, in "Holy Obedience" to the will of God. Nothing further has been recorded about this, and one had to dig deep into Anna's archives to know this had even occurred. It would soon become apparent that Anna would be leaving Rawalpindi. Until then, nothing seems to have changed.

An entry in the convent Journal for December 23 states that Anna was out getting roses for the chapel for Christmas. On December 30 the Sisters held a party with a Noel tree adorned with presents for poor children, Mass in the grotto, and afterward the distribution of gifts. Many children and benefactors were present and it was a joyous event. Anna was sick in bed with fever. The next day she had to get up because she was needed in the O.R.

On New Year's Day, 1924, Anna remained in bed. Father Stewart came to give her Holy Communion. A letter from Mother Marie Alberte said that Anna would leave only when she had been replaced and that they needed to storm heaven to get a doctor soon. She advised Anna on what she should bring with her to the novitiate and what she could not. "You cannot use your motor scooter in the novitiate." She also added this reassuring word. "I note you speak of bad temper. That will be attended to in one course!" On January 2 Anna got up and went to work for several hours in the hospital. At the end of the week, she left for Murree. She had to get away. She needed time to reflect. So much was happening so fast that Anna had not had a moment to integrate the emerging reality or to deal with her feelings of loss. She could not fail to see the irony in leaving behind what she dearly loved in order to embrace a way of life for which she felt no attraction. In keeping her promise to God, she would be breaking her promise to Dr. McLaren and to those who had sponsored her, who had trusted her to keep her word by fulfilling the terms of her contract. In abandoning the responsibilities of her profession, she was acting irresponsibly. For one whose strength is logic and dedication to duty, this was a heavy cross to carry. Then a letter arrived from Pauline Willis. "How can you think I am disappointed in you or in any way annoyed at your decision! Indeed, I am not. If God calls you, you must go." A visible sign of invisible grace: it would be enough for now.

On February 8, Anna sent the following letter to Mother Marie Alberte, her Mother Provincial and friend.

> "I got the biggest soul-shock of my life today. My poor little unmarried sister told me in confidence and despair that she is going to have a baby."

Anna was devastated. She did not know what to do. Dominika was the fourth child of her birth mother, Gertrud. Big sister Anna had been there for the little girl after the death of their mother. They had grown up together during those difficult years.

"It is so sad – for her – for my poor good old father and for us all. Can't I do something for my poor little sister and my poor father?" She asked if there were a Good Shepherd Convent in Rome or nearby … and if Mother Michel in Rome could help find a place for her sister. She longed to lessen the grief felt by her elderly father and she wanted to stand by her sister, Dominika, during this difficult time.

> "It consoles me now to be able to tell them that I want to give myself wholly and entirely to God and that I shall be able to pray so much for them all."

During the next several months, Anna's family dilemma was overshadowed by conflicting positions regarding her departure date. Letters flew back and forth between those heavily invested in the outcome. Father White insisted that Anna leave immediately. Mother Michel in Rome concurred. The London Committee resisted fiercely, telling Doctor Dengel that they could not release her from her contractual obligations before November. "We want to send another doctor before Anna Dengel leaves" - a reasonable request. Anna herself had said that she would remain until a replacement had arrived and then stay a few more weeks to facilitate the transition of her successor. Father White wrote to Anna:

> "God desires you in Holy Religion. Not after a few months, but at once. In His name and for His honor and glory … I beg you to go and not wait."

Then out of the blue, on April 25, a telegram arrived. It said: the new doctor is arriving tomorrow. The following day, Mother Marie Alberte and Doctor Dengel went to the railway station to meet the new physician, a Parsi woman doctor from Bombay. Two days later, on April 28, Dr. Wadia began work in the hospital and community members began helping Anna prepare for her departure. May 3 was a busy day as Anna continued her packing in between her many visitors, for as the community's journal states: "All the young Indiannes came to see Miss Dengel." May 4 was marked by a monsoon rainfall. "In the afternoon, Miss Dengel had a good rest and we helped her to close the suitcases. At 7 p.m. Father White came to see Miss Dengel. During recreation we spent some time with Miss Dengel because this is her last evening with us." Here is the convent journal entry for May 5, her final day in Pindi.

> "Father White took breakfast with Miss Dengel. Mother Superior went out with Miss Dengel. The room of Miss Dengel is full of Indianne women who have come to say goodbye. Each lady asks for a letter and she, in spite of her shortage of time, gives it with great patience. At 11 a.m. Miss Dengel and Dr. Wadia take lunch. Mother Assistant and Sister Luisa went to the station with the luggage. Mother Superior, Mother Fidele and Dr. Wadia went with Miss Dengel to see her off. Father White and Father Stewart and the family of Mr. Gaylord were also there. Miss Dengel showed generosity and courage. Our doctor left with a good remembrance because of her virtuous attitudes and her missionary spirit with all these Indiannes whom she has loved so much. She wants to give herself totally to God. Maybe one day, these Indiannes who today are crying for her will be happy to see her again with them."

The convent journal for May 6 reads: "The house looks empty. We arranged the room of Miss Dengel for Dr. Wadia." Anna later recalls:

"With a heavy heart and inner feelings which I could never be able to describe, I left Rawalpindi."

It would be many years before she would return.

Serve with love.
Serve God in everybody and everything
with real personal love.

Anna Dengel

CHAPTER FIVE

On May 5 Doctor Anna Dengel took the train from Rawalpindi to the port city of Bombay, where she would board the ship for Europe. While she was there she had hoped to meet with Jesuit Archbishop Goodier, who was passionate about medical missions, and according to Pauline Willis, wise when it came to vocations. Seek a second opinion, she had pleaded with Anna, and although it was much too late for that now, it seemed a reasonable suggestion. As it happened, the Archbishop was away. After leaving Bombay, Anna received a letter from him, saying he was sorry to have missed seeing her.

> "Perhaps God wants it to be quite clear to everyone that I have had nothing to do with your vocation; perhaps later on He is going to send you back here, to work for me and to help me to realize a dream which has been growing already in my mind."

The Archbishop said he had also written to Pauline Willis in response to her concerns, saying that he hoped his words "will not only reconcile her but make her glad that you have done what you have done." Then he added some final words of encouragement for Anna.

> "I trust you will enter on your new life free from all trouble on this front. In any case there is the call of God, and this distinctly tells us that nothing whatsoever should keep us back. May Our Lord accept your oblation, and fill you with joy in His service, and in time send you back to us to work for Him on a still wider sphere."

While in Bombay, Anna stayed with the Franciscan Missionaries of Mary whose Congregation she was about to enter. Once en route, the sea voyage offered long periods of time for some serious introspection. Ordinarily, Anna kept a journal of such peak experiences, but this time she left no notes behind. There may have been too many conflicting emotions associated with what was for her an internal rite of passage with a turbulence equal to that arising from the ocean's watery depths. The final leg of the journey wound through the Suez Canal and into the Mediterranean Sea before reaching Rome. Anna did tell someone that summer that she had visited Egypt. Most likely Alexandria had been her port of call.

Once she had left India, Anna's destination was Grottaferrata, a small hamlet just outside of Rome, where the Franciscan Missionaries of Mary had a major foundation. Their Central Leadership was located there. So was their Novitiate. No date had been fixed for Anna's formal admission to the community, and, as a Postulant, she had no intention of embracing their way of life ahead of time. In order to recover from her arduous journey, she would spend a few days in this serene setting before moving on to deal with all that still needed to be done.

On June 6, the Friday before Pentecost, Anna sent a note to her Mother General. "I had news from home and really things seem to arrange themselves better than I expected." Much to her relief plans were in place for the care and support of her sister, Dominika, for the family had rallied around her. She also adds: "My father does not mention anything about myself – I take it as a sign that he won't raise any objections." Her relief was genuine. She requested permission to remain in Rome for several days of reflection before leaving for home. Permission was granted. Mother General suggested that she stay through Pentecost Sunday and then join her family for an extended period of time. She understood that Anna had places to go and people to see prior to entering into a whole new world and letting go of this one. Mother Michel also told Anna that her entrance into the community would take place sometime during the week of July 21st and that she was to be back in Rome on the 26th at the latest.

On Pentecost Monday, June 9, Anna left for Austria. When the train from Rome arrived at the station in Innsbruck, the returning missionary's spirit soared on seeing her family again. She was warmly welcomed, for she had been away for a very long time. There was a lot of catching up to do. So much had changed, not only in Anna's life, but in the lives of her sisters and brothers, and Papa and Amalie, and in the social and political climate of Austria. Her sister Ida had married Josef Faistenberger in February of 1919. Anna was the godmother of their two little girls, Gertrud Anna Maria and Anna Maria Dominika. Anna and Ida, inseparable for years, would have had a lot to talk about. So would Anna and Dominika. Anna's little sister would have told her what the rest of the family already knew, that after the birth of her baby, she anticipated moving into the family's summer home in Steeg and remain there to raise her child. Anna also had a story to tell. She was now a postulant associated with the Franciscan Missionaries of Mary and would have to explain to her family what she could not explain to herself, her fundamental change in direction, one that was so alien to all she had done to prepare for a life she had really loved and that had made her family proud. She would report the following to Mother Michel:

> "My father is not directly opposing me – but he tells me every now and then that he cannot understand how one can give up one's independence and that I will be lost to my family."

On the 5th of July, the FMM leadership wrote to Anna, saying:

> "Mother General is very glad to hear that things are all right with your little sister. All right too about your coming on the 26th. You will spend the night in Rome and go the next day to Grotta where you will find a hearty welcome."

Meanwhile, Anna had some time on her hands, which was a new experience for one who had lived such a duty-driven life for well over a decade. Soon after arriving in Austria, she received a letter from Miss Willis saying that a Miss Roggen from the Medical Mission Institute in Würzburg in Bavaria was willing to go to Rawalpindi to take her place. As she thought about it, Anna decided that she would like to see if the woman were really suited to the mission there, and at the same time, tell her something about life in the Punjab. She wrote to the director of the Institute, who invited her to come, adding that having Anna there would also be of interest to his students.

The city of Würzburg in Germany was located in Northern Bavaria. In 1922 this notice had appeared in *The Universe:*

> "The German Catholic Association for Medical Missionaries is planning the founding of an institute at Würzburg to train doctors of both sexes for the foreign missions. If this work succeeds the German Catholics will have the privilege to be the pioneers in the sphere of Apostolic activity."

The Catholic Medical Mission Institute in Würzburg was founded that year on December 3, the feast of the Jesuit saint Francis Xavier, by Rev. Msgr. Christopher Becker, a Salvatorian priest with a doctorate in theology and philosophy. He had been Prefect Apostolic of Assam in India. With the support of a large number of missionary societies and congregations in Germany, the institute began its professional training and missionary preparation of Catholic doctors and medical students and was about to offer nursing courses for missionary Sisters and a training program for Missionaries. "I had been in touch with Monsignor Becker, its Founder, and had congratulated him enthusiastically on the foundation of this Institute, which truly rejoiced my heart," Anna recalled. Reason enough to pay him a visit.

> "I decided to go and visit Monsignor Becker, who received me warmly. For several days I participated in the life there, meeting Monsignor, his guests and the students. It was a gay and enthusiastic crowd. Monsignor Becker was very disappointed when he heard of my intention to enter the FMM's. He told me that he had thought of asking me to be of help to him at the Institute, but I felt sincerely that that was not my vocation and I was sorry not to be able to accept his proposition. I admired and honored him greatly and would have liked to help him."

What occurred next can only be attributed to the intervention of the Holy Spirit.

"While visiting at the Institute, something happened that was to be of great consequence to me. Unexpectedly, a friend of the Monsignor, a Mill Hill Father from Rawalpindi whom Monsignor Becker had met when they were in an internment camp in India during the war, entered the room in which we sat. The Monsignor was speechless with surprise and could not even introduce us to one another, but with outstretched arms, pointed to me and then to Father Kuhn, the priest in question. Both of us Missionaries from Pindi. This meeting was not only coincidence, it was Providence. Fr. Kuhn was not able to stay at that time, because of an appointment he had to keep. He said that he was anxious to speak to me and would return, which he did.

"He invited me to come to his parish, which was a short train ride from Würzburg and a two hour walk after that! I went, and Father met me at the station. His was a simple parish home, very conducive for making one feel at ease. My outpouring lasted a long time and Father was a good listener. What a joy it was to be able to speak openly, without hurry, and to feel free and understood. Father knew Pindi and the situation so well, having been there for many years. He took in the whole situation from his side and mine and he knew of the needs and appreciated them. Father advised that I make a retreat before doing anything further – and with that advice and the *resolution* to follow it, I departed after two days of a very helpful and peaceful visit to a Missionary from Pindi, who I think saw into my soul!"

Anna returned to Innsbruck filled with mixed emotions. On the one hand, she felt a deep sense of gratitude and relief at having experienced, at long last, unconditional affirmation of her inner being from a priest of God. On the other hand, she still had an urgent task to do before her time ran out and she moved into an unfamiliar world and another way of life.

"After getting back to Austria, I had to find a way of arranging the retreat and to find a priest who would guide it. It was not unnatural that I would think of the Jesuits. I went to the well-known Jesuit house in the Sillgasse in Innsbruck, where in all simplicity I told the Brother at the door what my wishes were. After leaving my name and address, I awaited an answer at the Sisters of Charity in Innsbruck. It came, and I lost no time in going to the Jesuit house in order to present myself to the Retreatmaster."

Anna was 32 years old and, once again, the trajectory of the rest of her life no longer lay in her hands. She was about to submit herself for a second time to someone else's direction, trusting with all her heart and soul that God would speak directly to her through the wisdom of another.

"A quiet, elderly priest met me: It was Father Rochus Rimml, s.j. who put me at ease right away. I explained the reason for my desire to make a retreat and explained in simple words the circumstances that had brought me to this point, inclusive of the reason why I had studied medicine. Also of my work in India, I spoke. I mentioned, of course, what Father White had asked of me, the meeting with Msgr. Becker and with Father Kuhn who had been in Rawalpindi so long and who had recommended that I make this retreat in order to gain clarity. This led Father Rimml to ask various questions, sounding my inner disposition. Father planned a three-day retreat. Each day we had some discusssions. Father could not understand the advice I had been given in Pindi to enter the FMM's. After a general confession which Father had advised, he asked me if I were willing to follow what he would advise me to do. I said a firm <u>Yes</u> and resolved to do what he would tell me. On the third day Father told me that he had celebrated the Holy Sacrifice of the Mass in honor of the Holy Spirit, and had also spoken about me to the Spiritual Director and asked if I were ready to accept his decision. In all earnestness I gave an affirmative answer, although I did not know what he would ask of me. I was prepared for the one or the other."

Father Rochus Rimml, s.j., met with Anna for the last time on July 22. What followed would shape not only Anna's life but the life of the Church in mission. "Then Father, without any hesitation, pronounced his decision. He said:

> 'You must give up once and for all the thought of entering the Congregation of the Franciscan Missionaries of Mary.'
> 'You must devote yourself to the development of Medical Missions through establishing a Congregation with permission of the Church and under the Church.'
> 'You must always remain in contact with the competent Church Authorities.'
> 'You must never doubt that this is the Will of God for you.'"

And there it was. Simple. Succinct. Profound. Definite.

> "He told me that it was my vocation and duty to start a Medical Mission Society."

Anna knew instinctively that this was God's will for her.

> "Although I had not the slightest idea how, when and where I could do this, I was ready for anything. A heavy burden fell from my heart through this mandate and this decision, since it hit the target like a shot. This decision was fully in harmony with my own desires and feelings. Desires, I cannot really say; it was something more. But I do not know how to express it in any better way. I went back to my home with a light heart."

When sharing with others what had transpired during this decisive turning point in her life, Anna recalled that:

"Father dictated a number of other points which I wrote down, but very unfortunately I lost these. I remembered well that Father insisted on great devotion to Our Lady, on humility in particular, and stressed again that I must never, but never, doubt his advice against entering the FMM's was the Will of God for me. He stressed that very strongly in order to put my mind at ease. He took leave of me, blessed me and put me out to high sea! Where I was going and how things would turn out were a puzzle to me, but I was at peace – and willing!"

Found in Anna's notes describing that transformative experience was the following handwritten prayer, in German, that began with the words, *Liebe Mütter Gottes.*

> Dear Mother of God,
> Under your very special protection
> I put every minute of my remaining life.
> I solicit thy special mercy
> not to waste the precious boon of time
> and to be helpful in salvaging many souls.
> Sweet Heart of Mary,
> be my salvation!
> Holy guardian angels and saint Anna
> remain with me.
> A.D.

One can only imagine the feeling of liberation lifting Anna's spirit, and one can easily predict the jubilant joy of her family. A little while later she received a letter from Father William White dated July 21. It said: "But a few days remain before the Feast of St. Anne, and I fear they will be days of agony. When the cross is hardest, the crown of true Peace is nearest." Little did he realize how true his words would prove to be. July 26 was the Feast of St. Anne, Anna's Feast Day. Ironically, that was also the day when Anna was scheduled to enter the FMM novitiate. Her inner agony leading up to that moment had indeed been replaced with a deep inner peace. However, she would wait a while before telling that to Father White, who was still completely unaware of her change in plans. First, she had to inform Mother Michel. On July 22 she wrote: "Today – practically on the eve of the first day of entry – I have something very startling to tell you, but I am sure that you will see in it also the Holy Will of God and I would like to ask you in the beginning to keep me as your child more than ever and to help me . . . ." Anna told Mother Michel everything, about the advice of the two priests in Würzburg, and shared with her the lengthy process and final outcome of her Jesuit-led retreat.

> "I had to write down all the reasons I had for and against entering the convent – and really apparently more seemed to be for it, so that even he doubted at first. He consulted, with my permission, an old, very experienced priest (S.J.) who is the Confessor of nearly all the Jesuits there and who is reputed for his clear judgment; and the clear decision is: that I shall <u>not</u> go into the Convent, but give myself whole and entire to the cause of the medical missions, for which there is so much need and scope now. The missing thing is an organization – a society – so to say a religious institute for medical missionaries – and my endeavors shall be with much prayer, great humility, great confidence in God - to form such a one in whatever way Our Lord shall show."

She ended her letter by asking Mother Michel to keep its contents a secret for now.

> "I have not written to anybody about it yet, as I just finished my retreat, but I shall tell the same to my confessor in Pindi, through whose order and advice I left my beloved St. Catherine's. I shall also tell dear Mother Provincial in Bombay, who has been more than a mother to me, also to Miss Willis and to Rev. Father Winkley, who is in London."

She wrote to all those mentioned, and many more, and on July 27, she heard from Pauline Willis.

"God's ways are certainly wonderful – how clearly we can see His guidance in all this. Yours is the vocation of Abraham, the willingness for the sacrifice up to the last moment, and then God says that is all He asks."

She offers her own reflection on the outcome.

"In my own heart I am thankful God asks you to work in the world. The religious life would have hampered you, sometimes more and sometimes less. Superiors vary so, it certainly is true we cannot serve two masters, to sacrifice all to a doctor's life would interfere with the religious life in some ways, whereas now we know 'work is prayer' and all of yours can be consecrated as prayer."

Then Miss Willis made this offer.

"What I want you to do is this: come to England as soon as possible, don't linger in London, but come directly through to Winchcombe where I want you to be my guest – for a month. Unfortunately there is no room in the cottage - it is so small, but I shall arrange for a room in The Village, and during those weeks you must get the complete rest you need, and all the work we will do is *talking*. I have two cycles, one old and a better one, so we can ride and discuss future problems by the country side!"

On August 9, Anna finally received a response from Mother Michel, who had been traveling.

"I can only give you my good wishes, dear child, and hope you will never regret your present decision, so different to the one you had taken in India. I am totally convinced of your good intentions, and accept the alteration of those same intentions. It hardly needs to be said that if your desire is to return to Rawalpindi to take up again your activities, we would welcome you with open arms."

Those days spent in the British countryside were restful, refreshing, restorative, and the bond that formed between Anna and Pauline would be one that would last forever. They shared a passion for medical missions and an intuitive sense that, by the grace of God, anything was possible. Anna checked in with the London Committee to make amends for any hard feelings associated with her leaving the Pindi assignment before her contract was up. She need not have worried. All were warmly supportive and assured her that they would be open to hiring her again, if the possibility arose. On August 16, Anna responded to Mother Michel:

> "I see clearly now that my vocation is the medical mission. I told Rev. Monsignor Winkley that I am anxious to return to work at some post or other but I am more anxious to work for the development of medical missions in general. With God's help, I hope to be able to combine the two.
>
> "I left Pindi at the cost of a great sacrifice – giving up so to say my life's dream – because I was told that I should do so, that it was God's will and that I could do more for the medical missions in a hidden life. Of course my confessor followed me closely for the whole time I was in Pindi. He really knows me well – he means well – and I consider him a very holy priest. Besides Rev. Mother Provincial who also means well and who must have experience of vocations also agreed with my confessor. He himself consulted her. I did not, as a matter of fact, I did not suggest myself to become a nun and I didn't make a single step myself toward it on purpose, so that I won't have any responsibility in leaving the medical missions. I simply obeyed gladly. I was even looking forward to the religious life. As a matter of fact, if there were an order for medical missionaries, I would leave no stone unturned to become a member. When I was in Europe I was again advised in the opposite direction, till at last I see and feel myself quite clearly.

"The change seemed so sudden that it is hard to believe it possible. In reality, it was not sudden, for my whole mission life had something to do with it.

"I am staying with Miss Willis for a month – then I'll go to Ireland for at least a month - and then I don't know. It depends on Rev. Monsignor Winkley, whether he approves my taking back with me three or four doctors to the Punjab. If he approves, I must find the means for voyages, support, etc. So I really don't know yet whether I'll return to India this autumn or next spring, more likely the latter.

"I would be very grateful if you asked for prayers for the development of medical missions. Just now, I feel very much alone and isolated, as you can imagine, but not sad or disappointed or unhappy. Just as it was a revolution of my mind and soul to tear myself away from medical missions, *when I saw* such scope in it, just as much it is a revolution to me now, after I had pictured myself leading a quiet, hidden life, learning the spiritual life, to be thrown into a more busy and perhaps more public life than I ever expected. There is really no need to tell these things – but it helps human nature to tell somebody anyhow."

On August 16, Anna also sent a lengthy letter to Monsignor Winkley, Apostolic Prefect of the Punjab region. She had been in England for just a few days. Monsignor Winkley was in London. She told him that while she was enjoying the quiet of the lovely English countryside, she and Miss Willis had already begun making plans for the development of medical missions on a larger scale.

"I know very well that the medical mission will never develop if we wait for the missions to give us the money for voyages, maintenance, running of dispensary, of hospital. The Protestant medical missions with their hundreds of workers, hospitals, medical schools, homes for lepers, the deaf and dumb, blind, etc., would never have spread over the five continents as they did had they

not organized themselves, collected more or less their
own means and simply offered themselves to their own
Church authorities."

What about Catholics?

"Our London Committee is struggling to get the
required amount for Pindi – there are so many demands
on Catholic Charity in England for England, at least as
Miss Willis tells me."

Then she presented the rudiments of a plan.

"Going to America for money for this scheme is more
hopeful, although everybody seems to go there thinking
that there are only rich people there. I have not got that
illusion. However, Americans are charitable, and what
gives me most hope is that such a practical necessary
work as the medical missions will appeal to the masses.
Besides there is a newly formed Medical Mission Board.
They are willing to help out but want a project now and
why shouldn't we be the first? St. Catherine's, as small
and insignificant as it is, is known as the Cradle of
Catholic Medical Missions. In every article on medical
missions it is mentioned. How they got hold of it, I
don't know, but anyhow, I am glad, because we are not
totally unknown.

"Miss Willis approves very much going over. If
possible, she would even go with me. She is an American
and that would guarantee many introductions. She
is already known in certain circles there. Besides she
offered herself to help me financially in the undertaking,
because it costs a lot to go over and travel in America. I
don't believe in wanting the moon, but I think that this
scheme for the development of medical missions in the
Punjab is within reach. It is for you, dear Father, to say:
'yes' or 'no' or to limit it."

Monsignor Winkley's response to Anna:

> "I am of the same mind as you, and it was only because I had not the means, that I did not do more than I have done. You, having been on the spot, know and have seen the difficulties, and therefore, in your zeal, you are anxious to organize and to obtain the means to overcome the difficulties that prevent the extension of this great work, the Medical Mission. It is unnecessary for me to say that I fully approve of your scheme. You know how anxious I am to see the medical work extended and more hospitals and dispensaries opened. It is very praiseworthy of you to make this great effort. I shall remember you every day at the Altar that our good God may bless abundantly your endeavors."

Not only did Monsignor Winkley approve, he immediately wrote a Letter of Introduction "to authorize a zealous missionary helper, Miss Pauline Willis, and Doctor Dengel, a great missionary medical doctor to collect money for a Fund for Medical Mission work in the Punjab, India." Pauline Willis sent the Letter of Introduction to Father Walsh in the USA and also wrote to her friend, Miss Storer, suggesting a plan of action.

> "Here is a big venture to tell you of. Dr. Dengel from Pindi is now here with me and she is going to America this winter to collect funds for the Medical Mission work which we have so deeply at heart. There is just the faintest chance that I may go with her. There is so much to be settled first if I do. The plan is that she reaches New York the first of November and spends two weeks there, then the same time next in Boston, after that the rest of her travels can be arranged. I am sending you a copy of the letter we are sending to Father Walsh to get his advice and to ask him to assist us to get openings for Doctor Dengel to lecture and appeal for funds."

In the twinkling of an eye, what had been an idea became a reality.

Here is what Anna began to tell others as preparations were under way for a major new initiative.

> "Miss Willis, Secretary for the Committee founded by Dr. McLaren, set to work immediately. Letters flew to New York. Letters for Charity's sake were her life. Since she was an American, she had many contacts with Clerics, Convents, and Laity as well as Organizations. Before leaving for the States, I called on Msgr. Winkley, the Apostolic Prefect of Rawalpindi who happened to be at Mill Hill in London at that time. I explained to him the purpose of our voyage to the U.S. and he was fully in accord and gave me letters of introduction, one for myself and one for Miss Willis – and one for the two of us together. As advice for the venture, he said: 'Take two bags with you, a big one for the disappointments and difficulties and a little one for the pleasant things.' In reality I must state here, that the little bag was full to the brim; in any case, both were filled."

After setting her plan in motion, Anna left for Ireland where she visited her many friends and colleagues and former university professors, giving them a vivid eye-witness account of the medical mission apostolate in India and sharing with them the potential for taking this vital ministry to another level. On her return to England, she found a letter from Father White acknowledging her change of direction. He asked if she would visit his sister Annie on her return from Ireland and requested clarification on how to write to her in the future. Should he continue in the role of spiritual guide as he had been in the past, in which she would continue to tell him all, or did she think differently now? He assured her of a remembrance in every Mass and added this with regard to her mission: if this is of God, it cannot be stopped ... "and I really believe it is his will." Reassured, and grateful for the role that this priest of God had played in the way things were evolving, Anna closed the book on a very painful chapter with a grateful and firm, Amen!

In a final note to Mother Michel before leaving Europe, Anna wrote on October 9:

"I am back in England again and staying with Miss Willis until our proposed trip to America to collect funds for the development of Medical Missions in the Punjab."

She pointed out that some of the responses to letters Pauline Willis had sent on ahead of their arrival "are not very encouraging." She said: "I am venturing this visit with only about £100." Miss Willis would not be staying with her for the entire trip. "I dread this venture," she wrote. "But unless we try I won't feel happy. We have plenty of people now, but no funds to develop the medical missions." She also shared with Mother Michel the initial stages of what she had envisioned.

"A little purely religious society for women doctors and nurses dedicated to the Holy Mother of God is in the process of formation so that the work in the future – please God – may be on a solid and stable basis."

She ended her letter with the good news that "The Society has Cardinal Bourne's approval, but he says for the present to keep it absolutely private and confidential."

Monsignor Winkley sent yet another letter prior to their departure, one that Anna Dengel and Pauline Willis would show to Bishops, Priests, Major Superiors of Religious Communities, and Lay Leaders to introduce their medical mission promotional campaign.

The Feast of St. Luke / October 18ᵗʰ. 1924

"These few lines are to make known to the Hierarchy, the Clergy, and the Laity of the United States that Dr. Anna Dengel has been given full ecclesiastical authority to go over to your great country America, that, with your kind approval, she may make better known the great need of extending Catholic Medical Mission Work.

There is absolutely no doubt but that Medical Missions are most useful in every Mission Field, but they are a "sine qua non" aid to make new and difficult Missions a success. Everyone who has been for a length of time working on the Eastern Missions will readily vouch and fully confirm this fact.

Thus I beg of you, Venerable Brethren, to receive kindly this great Medical Mission Worker, and help her to carry out her worthy and noble work, and your generosity, our Eternal loving Father will, I am sure, bless and reward most abundantly."

R.M. Winkley, Prefect Apostolic of Kafristan & Kashmir

To be a good and happy missionary,
one has to go to the missions for the pure love of God.
This love has to be cultivated so that every day
we will grow in love and joy.

Anna Dengel

CHAPTER SIX

Two brave women determined to make a difference in the lives of women on the other side of the planet left London at 10:24 a.m. on October 25 in 1924. Anna Dengel and Pauline Willis, both seasoned travelers who were accustomed to doing things that had never been done before, embarked on an unprecedented voyage into the unknown, heading west in order to do something life-changing for a world that lay to the east. As the shoreline of England slipped away and the picturesque Bishopslight vanished, they set their sights toward what they had envisioned when imagining this adventure and prayed that all they had been hoping for would eventually come to pass.

They had booked passage on a cargo boat. The trip would take ten days. Day one was smooth sailing. The second day was chaotic. "The ship rocked us about like a baby in the cradle, only the baby likes it. We did not." That was the first entry in the journal Anna would keep of her voyage to America and all that would happen to her there. For the next three days, the sea was rough – "fierce and gloomy looking compared to the blue Mediterranean and the Indian Ocean." Both women were quite sea-sick. "The fact that there are no breaks in the journey makes it more monotonous," was how Anna described her Atlantic crossing. On the sixth day, the sea settled down, giving Anna a chance to recover and an opportunity to meet and converse with fellow travelers. "There were only five passengers – Miss Willis and myself the only women. The most numerous passengers were meant for a zoo in the States." The three male passengers en route to America were a Catholic solicitor of Irish descent, a Yorkshire man from Texas, and an elderly, good-natured bachelor who, although not Catholic, volunteered to help Anna by introducing her to his friend, who was connected with the Church.

A stormy final day at sea was prelude to a new day dawning, for not only did the sun rise on November 4. So did a whole new horizon teeming with possibilities, as an emerging New York skyline rose up from the sea. "The Statue of Liberty in her green garb looks as if she were a child of the ocean. The skyscrapers look like large cliffs in the mist ... the great harbor, the ocean of houses ... a very impressive sight." What a blessing to stand on solid ground at last, and what a surprise to see Dr. Paluel Flagg of the Medical Mission Board and Maryknoll Father John Considine waiting there to greet them. "The Board had recommended that we not come to the U.S." Indeed, Monsignor McGlinchey of the Propagation of the Faith did say that, but the two women had come anyway. Anna was extremely relieved to experience a warm and enthusiastic welcome to America. That night she settled into the peaceful atmosphere of the Cenacle Convent for a good night's sleep. The following day, she and Miss Willis returned to the pier to pay customs duty on the glass slides they had brought with them to America.

Their first two weeks were a whirlwind of activity, filled with comings and goings in and around the boroughs of New York, meeting and greeting all manner of people with the hope of raising awareness to and financial support for the cause of medical missions, primarily in the Punjab, and specifically for women and children. Priests, nuns, lay leaders in religious and sacred settings were made aware of the medical mission movement and the need for Catholics to become more involved. For the most part, their message was graciously received, and Anna was moved, time and again, by the genuine kindness shown to her on so many occasions.

They took time out to celebrate the birthday of Pauline Willis on November 9, spending a very pleasant day with the family of Dr. Flagg. Otherwise, Pauline was out and about preparing the way for Anna who would soon be on her own, and Anna was either giving talks when she was invited to do so or setting dates to give talks as soon as they could be scheduled. Parishes, convents, hospitals, colleges, seminaries, diocesan offices and national organizations were approached one by one. Talks were or would be given by Anna at Maryknoll, the Sisters of Charity, St. Vincent's Hospital, the Red Cross, Helpers of the Holy Souls, Sacred Heart Academy, Holy Cross Academy, Holy Child Academy on Riverside Drive, the Long Island Medical Academy, and the Visitation

Convent, where "everything was just like Thurnfeld," the school Anna attended after her family had moved to Hall. One afternoon, as Anna came out of the subway, she asked a woman how she might get to Visitation Convent, and was amazed when "she drove me there." For Anna, this was "God's Providence," with her every step of the way. She found Americans to be very gracious and interested, but at times a bit odd. They have a "funny way of cleaning shoes in New York." During this introductory period, she received a check for $10 from a physician, their first donation for medical missions, and $5 from the Visitation nuns. A start, yes, but if they were going to staff a hospital, they would have to do better than that.

Anna found her initiation into the role of public speaking somewhat intimidating. She was nervous and unsure of herself, but that did not stop her. She adapted her approach to her audience, which differed dramatically from elementary school children to high school or college students, seminarians, parishioners, nurses, or lay leaders of diocesan or parish organizations. After each talk she evaluated the effectiveness of her presentation, noting what went well and what needed improvement. She felt a bit more at ease when speaking to the nurses at the Long Island Medical School. The group was not large, and therefore "it gave me a chance of practicing and seeing my slides and timing myself." She would eventually become more confident. Nervous or not, however, she was out there promoting medical missions enthusiastically and wholeheartedly and clearly was devoted to the women of the East. This aspect of her personality endeared her to many and would be foundational to the future she was laboring so courageously to bring about.

On November 26 the two women left New York for Boston. On arrival they were given hospitality at the Sacred Heart Convent on Commonwealth Avenue for the duration of their stay. For Anna, stepping into the New England culture was a different experience. For Pauline, it meant coming home to familiar faces and so many places she had been part of a long time ago. Because the Catholic Women's League in Boston owed its existence to Miss Pauline Willis, who was instrumental in its founding, Pauline now had access to a long list of female contacts, both friends and associates, whom she could call on to gather groups that would listen to Anna's message and perhaps be moved to support their cause. A talk to the Catholic Women's League took place at the Club of Catholic Women Artists, where Anna and Pauline were also introduced to many influential women. While in the area, Anna spoke to nurses at a local hospital and was interviewed by *The Pilot,* the diocesan paper. She also visited Msgr. McGlinchey of the Propagation of the Faith, who was extremely kind, and met Jesuit Father Keating from Boston College, who was in charge of a local chapter of the League for Nurses. He was very sympathetic, promised to set something up for Anna, and advised her to get in touch with one of his colleagues at Fordham University in New York. Pauline also arranged a meeting with Cardinal O'Connell and, as Anna remembers it, Pauline "in her enthusiasm spoke without a pause of the purpose of our being in the United States. Since I did not wish to interrupt her flow of words, the Cardinal asked Miss Willis whether or not I spoke English!" He gave his blessing to the work and then sent them on their way with a word of caution: "Sow the seed...and don't be in a hurry."

One thing Anna could not resist was slipping into a medical mode at every opportunity. She was, after all, Doctor Dengel, and it helped her immensely to remain connected to that essential aspect of her persona, a reminder that all this promotional work was prelude to her return to India and her medical missionary ministry. When she visited a hospital or interacted with medical personnel, her diary notes on fund-raising options were interspersed with the latest surgical procedures, or how to treat one or another disease more effectively, or recommended dosages of new and effective pharmaceutical products. She was in her element in Boston, where she spent time at the Red Cross offices, the Children's Hospital, the Perkins Institute for the Blind, and the Tuberculosis Asylum, marveling at all the new and effective services now available and the creative techniques being tested, noting what might also work for her in a vastly different context.

A brief visit to Elmhurst College in Providence, Rhode Island, was also on the agenda. This institution of the Religious of the Sacred Heart was where Pauline Willis had been a boarder when a student there, and it was where she, her mother, and her sister had been received into the Church. Just as in Boston, there was genuine interest in what Anna had to say and in the mission to which she and Pauline were committed. They returned to New York and to their rooms at the Cenacle Convent with a joyful heart.

The next day Anna went to the office of the Medical Mission Board to hand in the money they had collected: a check for $794 plus two smaller checks that totaled $45 and was told she had been "trespassing." Word had come from the Director of the Propagation of the Faith in New York that "two lay women were going about giving talks without permission." How could this have happened? Anna had letters of authorization to do what they had done. Dr. Flagg, head of the Medical Mission Board, was well aware of that. Everything had been out in the open. Anna was horrified.

> "I had a talk scheduled for that very day which I could not cancel, therefore I went post haste to the office of the Director, who was an Auxiliary Bishop, in order to explain my predicament. When he heard through his secretary that I had come, I heard him pound on the table and say that we had to stop those talks immediately! I asked the secretary to tell the Bishop that I was on my way to the Religious of the Sacred Heart and could not possibly cancel the talk. No answer was given me whether or not I could give the talk, so I went ahead and gave it!"

Pauline Willis was very upset that she and Anna had been forbidden to carry on their "Good Works," which was a favorite expression of hers. She told Monsignor McMahon, pastor of the nearby Parish of Our Lady of Lourdes, who knew of the London Committee because the mother of his colleague, the Rev. Bede Jarrett, was a member of that Committee. Unfortunately, Pauline was unable to assist in resolving this dilemma because, according to initial plans, she was scheduled to return to London. Hard as it was to do so, Pauline departed, leaving Anna to deal with the situation on her own.

Much to Anna's surprise, Monsignor McMahon invited her to give a talk at his parish – "probably to look me over!" – and Anna agreed. "After the talk, he advised me to ask the Cardinal of New York, Cardinal Hayes, for an audience, which I did, with the remark that Monsignor McMahon had suggested it." The audience was granted. With Pauline gone, Anna had to look for a place to stay.

> "The Cenacle was very expensive. I had to pay out of
> my own savings, so I wanted to stay at a cheaper place.
> I stayed with the Flaggs for a while."

Then Anna moved to St. Joseph's Convent on 81st Street, a low-cost residence for single women, and used this as her permanent address on all her correspondence. It was a small room, which she had to share with a stranger. "Very uncomfortable," she wrote in her diary: "no table" – "room unbearably hot." She met with Dr. Flagg to get his perspective on her current situation with regard to raising funds for medical missions and what might have led up to it, then took time off to write some letters. To the Mother General of the FMM's she sent Christmas and New Year greetings, adding:

> "I hope for myself that I will have a less agitated year
> before me than behind me. I expect to remain in
> America until the spring – then spend one month or
> so in England – two months at home and then return
> to India – not to St. Catherine's – but to the City in
> Rawalpindi."

She also clarified her status so there would be no misunderstanding.

> "As the Committee in London has formally accepted
> my resignation this spring – I will avail of it – as it will
> leave me freer. Monsignor Winkley knows these plans
> and approves of them."

On December 15 Anna went to the Propagation of the Faith office to explain everything and to get an answer from Bishop Dunn with regard to her current status. She was told she would be allowed to lecture at 533 Madison Avenue, where she was already scheduled to speak, but to await instructions before proceeding to add other talks to her schedule. She was pleased with the lectures she gave there. The pupils were very interested and Reverend Mother was very kind. She had tea with several influential women interested in her work, and from them learned about the Catholic Converts League and the NY Archdiocesan Council of the National Conference of Catholic Women, two very important organizations.

December 19 marked a decisive turning point. That was the day when Anna met with His Eminence Cardinal Hayes. Here is her account of what happened.

> "I heard that this Cardinal was called 'the Cardinal of Charity' and indeed I received a very cordial welcome. I mentioned to the Cardinal that I had no permission to give talks, but I told him of the dire need of the women of India and showed him the letter of recommendation Monsignor Winkley had given me. Neither what I said, nor the letter seemed to impress him, until I showed him some photos. Among them was one of the sick twins who had been patients at the Rawalpindi hospital. The Cardinal asked me for the letter of Monsignor Winkley and he actually read it. He asked me where I was staying. Since I was now on my own, I said, I stayed at a cheap home for working girls. Then he asked me to whom he could make out a check. I gave him the address of Monsignor Winkley whose letter he still held in his hand. Then he left and returned shortly after that with joy in his face and radiating goodness. He handed me a check for $1,000.00. I thanked him with my whole heart. He gave me permission to speak in his Archdiocese where and as often as I wanted to. He said I can speak and make the needs known and *'take whatever I can get'* - and he repeated it. Then he gave me his blessing."

Tears streamed down Anna's face as she headed to the office for the Propagation of the Faith to show them the check and the permission the Cardinal had given her to speak in his Archdiocese. The check – and the permission – astonished everyone.

Later that day Anna went over to the Cenacle Convent where she had been staying when Pauline was still with her and to the adjacent Holy Childhood Church. She had to share her joy with those who had supported her on arrival and to spend some time giving prayerful thanks to the God of such bountiful blessings. Then she wrote to Monsignor Winkley, explaining how Cardinal Hayes of New York "was kindness itself when I saw him today...he allowed me to speak and, to use his own words, 'take what I can get for the work.'" She told him about the check for $1,000 "made out in your name" and asked him – twice – to be sure to send a letter of thanks to the Cardinal for his gift. "I wish everybody were like him, but then I am afraid that America would be full of propagandists." In closing, she wrote: "Pray real hard that I may be able to finish this campaign by the end of the spring – and then return to India in the autumn." She enclosed the check with the letter.

Anna made some valuable connections on the days leading up to Christmas. A well-known Jesuit associated with *America* magazine put her in touch with some important people when he learned that she was from Austria. He had been instrumental in helping impoverished Austrian Contemplatives after the War. He gave Anna letters of recommendation for convent schools and organizations "and told me to carry on despite discouraging incidents." She met with Paulist Father McSorley who gave her some valuable advice about dealing with the press and told her to get a few lines in writing from the Cardinal in support of her initiative. He also advised her to get in touch with the group at Graymoor and introduced her to the editor of *Catholic News* and the director of travel for the Propagation of the Faith, who was open to supporting her. Before the end of the week, his office said they would give her a chance to speak on the first Sunday of February before a large audience at which the Bishop would preside. She also met with two priests who had worked in India and she had lunch with several influential women to introduce them to her mission.

In between all the coming and going, Anna studied the Catholic Directory to become more familiar with her locale and to increase the potential for supporting medical missions by knowing what institutions were included there. She also wrote letters, among them a response to the lengthy ones she had received from Father William White, who had opted to continue informally as her spiritual advisor, sending her scripture texts that indicated the right thing to do and the right way to behave, albeit out of a well-meaning pastoral concern. "I am sorry to hear that your home affairs are rather worse than better," he wrote in a recent letter, the only indication we have that Anna continued to carry the concerns of more than one world in her heart.

"Then I met Father Mathis," Anna recalls. "He was in New York with Doctor Flagg. Father Mathis was going to Europe in December. I met him at Doctor Flagg's."

Anna spent Christmas in America with the family of Doctor Flagg. They attended Midnight Mass at Saint Patrick's Cathedral and Anna stayed at their home overnight where she was part of the excitement and anticipation only children can generate at this time of year. "I enjoyed watching the children looking at their gifts in the morning," she wrote, adding: "Dr. Flagg gave me an instrument invented by himself," something only a physician could understand and appreciate. He also shared with her his color scheme for the hospital theater and gave her a mission pamphlet published in 1915 that included Dr. McLaren, which delighted her. "I spent a very quiet, happy, peaceful day and returned home in the evening."

The next day Anna went to see a woman associated with the Lecture Guild, who said that she would support her, and in the afternoon called on a Paulist priest who also was very helpful. He gave her addresses, a paper called *The Missionary* and $5 and said: "Let us hear from you when you are in India." Anna wrote in her journal: "All the Paulist Fathers I met or saw so far are radiating with joy and simplicity." She had appointments every day until the end of the year: Marymount in Tarrytown; Father Barrett's friend, Eugene Walsh, who gave her $20 wrapped up in red tissue paper and a Christmas seal; the home of a potential female benefactor; and Holy Cross Rectory where she made a request to speak. On the 30th she met with several women who were becoming part of an inner circle that would offer her some assistance, and in the evening she lectured to a small audience at the Church of the Annunciation, at which, in her opinion, she did not speak very well. Finally, on the last day of the year, she paid a visit to Graymoor, a spiritual center dedicated to unity in the Church. She met Father Paul Francis and Mother Lorena, visited their chapel with its beautiful Nativity setting, was told that she could write something for their publication, *The Lamp,* and that they would pray for her in the night watch. From there she went on to Maryknoll, where Mother Joseph and Father Walsh took her on a tour of their campus. Before the end of the year, the following PR Letter on Anna's behalf was sent from the Editor of *The Catholic World* to the Editor of *The Commonweal* in New York:

"Dr. Anna Dengel, whom I have urged to call upon you, is doing an exceedingly important work, as no doubt you know, in India. Her visit to this country and her work amongst the American people, has been wholeheartedly approved by the highest authorities, including our own Cardinal Archbishop, who has been the first to assist largely in it. I am not quite certain whether it would be possible for you to introduce Dr. Dengel to some of the metropolitan newspaper men and thereby aid her in getting publicity in the daily papers, but if you can, I know you will."

What a list of accomplishments were annotated in Anna Dengel's journal. She had been in the country barely two months. This is how she would remember those days: *"The Catholic spirit is wonderful."* Such a graced way to bring to a close what had been for Doctor Anna Dengel a roller coaster year.

The race for one world is on.

It is not won yet by far, but the fact that it is in motion,

is the significant factor.

Be in step with the needs of our own lifetime,

into which our responsibility is set

by God's Providence."

Anna Dengel

CHAPTER SEVEN

"January 1. . . Did not stay up to see New Year in – too tired last night. New Year! I wonder! Everything A.M.D.G ." *Ad majorem Dei gloriam* is the Latin motto for the Jesuits and it means "For the greater glory of God." This was Anna's approach to life and would always be her orientation. Her special New Year's resolution, however, was "to leave myself altogether in the hands of God." She spent "a very pleasant day" with Father Barrett at the home of his sister and her family in Brooklyn, where they talked the whole time about India.

The weeks that followed were a mirror image of the previous ones, with Anna walking up and down the sidewalks of New York, moving in and out of churches, rectories, convents, seminaries, schools, and offices of major organizations, meeting with individuals of note, seeking an audience and an opportunity to solicit financial support. There was, however, the realization that donations had to be more substantive, for to date she had received very little. She could not continue this way if she were ever to realize her goal of a well-equipped Catholic hospital for women and children in the Punjab. She had spent significant energy raising awareness to the need. Now she had to address the challenge in a more realistic way. Surely the affirmation and substantial check from the Cardinal were signs that things could change.

Early into the New Year Anna met with several priests associated with the Medical Mission Board. "I told them of my experience of loneliness" and the "idea of an organization." Several days later Dr. Flagg told Anna that members of the Board were willing to let her speak and solicit funds for the missions "under their auspices." Anna was delighted. What that would actually mean was in the process of being decided.

Later that month she summarized their offer in a letter to Monsignor Winkley in Rawalpindi.

> "The American Catholic Mission Board held a meeting a few days ago and they decided to let me speak under their auspices – which means great help to me – as they will help me to get opportunities to speak. Of course – Dr. Flagg told me to work at it as hard as possible myself too. As in U.S.A. everything is a business proposition – they suggested that of the contributions which I get 2/3rd should go to the development of Medical Missions in the Punjab and 1/3rd to the American Medical Mission Board. As I have nobody near to ask, I took it upon myself to agree to it – because I really don't mind how things are – as long as the Medical Mission cause is served. I am very – very – glad that they are taking me under their wing – because alone it is *very* difficult."

And what exactly was the Medical Mission Board? This recent Catholic organization based in New York City had been officially constituted shortly after the Catholic Hospital Association established a Medical Mission Committee at its Seventh Annual Convention in the summer of 1924, thereby signifying formal sponsorship of Catholic Medical Mission activities. The Chairman of the Board was anesthesiologist Dr. Paluel Joseph Flagg, who had worked among lepers in Haiti in 1912. The dozen Board members, all of whom were male and either physicians or clergy, were eager to generate medical mission initiatives within the New York archdiocese, primarily through sending medical supplies to mission stations in other lands. In order to function more effectively, the Board had recently opted to affiliate with the Society for the Propagation of the Faith and had increased its membership to 32, five of whom were now women who belonged to religious communities. Sir Bertram Windle, president of the University of Cork, was also a member of the Board. Anna Dengel had arrived in New York City at an opportune moment. The public relations and fund-raising potential of the charismatic missionary doctor was just what the fledgling Board needed at this transitional time.

Being part of something larger than her own focused agenda gave Anna a modicum of stability in the midst of endless fluctuation. It would also provide opportunities for exposure and solicitation that she was unable to secure on her own. In between her hectic pace, Anna wrote letters keeping her connected to the world she had left behind and also some that might open doors to the world she had recently entered. She also read reports on the latest advances in medicine and in the mission field, and occasionally read something inspirational or of a spiritual nature. She would copy out passages that spoke to her, interspersing these among the more pragmatic notations in her diary. For example,

> "It is a standing lesson to Christian souls that the amount and endurance of their work depends far more upon the character which they have personally formed than on the years of labor that they put into life... Only one who has built carefully one's character may hope one day to build the world – 'nearer to the heart's desire.'"

And also:

> "The discipline of spirituality works in the direction of setting the soul afire. It enables the high of deep thoughts to blossom out into action."

Anna was prone to deal with life from the perspective of facts, not feelings. The following insight, culled from a pamphlet on healing by Board member Dr. James Walsh, was tucked into the pages of her diary:
"The mind can produce all sorts of symptoms; and when it does, only the mind can cure them."

She valued words of wisdom such as these, offering reassurance that a transformative source of healing energy was already there within her.

The New Year had barely begun when Anna received a very troubling letter from Dr. Wadia in Rawalpindi concerning rumors about a new hospital in the city, something Anna had hoped would be kept confidential until funding had been secured and a definite plan was in place. She wrote to Monsignor Winkley to express her frustration regarding the points Dr. Wadia had raised and to clarify her own position.

"I am working heart and soul for a scheme which was thought of and talked of for some time before I left India and for which you secured the ground in the city and for which you have made it possible for me to come to U.S.A.

"Pindi City has 50,000 inhabitants. If the hospital could admit any and every case and have sufficient equipment and staff to do major surgery, only that gives a hospital a real standing. There is none like that in Pindi – or near it – for women. Not an amateur hospital, which closes up in the month of July and where there are no trained nurses and where there is only one doctor. There are already a good number of these amateur places in India. If we really want to develop medical missions, we must go beyond the amateur staff and that is the thing the nuns are afraid of.

"Dr. Wadia thinks that it would be waste to crowd so many women doctors into Pindi. When I was there, I would have found work for 3 – if I could have multiplied myself. Besides 2 in one place can achieve more than 2 independently in different places, because one alone cannot tackle major surgery. For one alone the responsibility is very great, because if one gets ill or has to go away for some reason, the hospital is an amateur hospital again.

"I don't know what Rev. Mother means by saying that I thought differently a short while back. As regards the proposed hospital in Pindi I never thought differently. As regards myself I did. I knew then I would not be in the least necessary to carry out this scheme and now too I know that I am not in the least necessary. As a matter of fact, things have turned out so differently from what I planned that I would not be so surprised if more unexpected things would turn up.

"I thought it is only fair that you should know the sentiments of the nuns – and mine too. It never struck me before that they think of any antagonism as it never entered my head that the new mission center in the City would not be under their charge. As a matter of fact, it would not be a success without them. I like the F.M.M. and I consider them excellent nuns, full of good will, which goes a long way; but nowadays training must go with it. I can say in honesty and truth that I got on very well with them in Pindi, but I had to be on the *qui vive* all the time that they would not boss me and that the hospital did not run on absolute amateur lines. I am telling you these things absolutely confidentially – just that you understand the whole situation.

"I have one consolation and that is, that I need not take anything in India on my conscience. You will advise me and guide me and I shall only be too delighted to carry out your wishes if Our Lord should want me again in India.

"I carry on my work here in America with the same vigor and vim as if I had not received this letter, which seemed to me very strange and really, as you can imagine, hurt me very much."

Monsignor Winkley's immediate response was encouraging and affirming.

"With regard to Dr. Wadia's letter. It is certainly very strange that she has written in the way she has. I can well understand that it hurt you. But the scheme was talked about and the Rev. Mother was pressing me for a long time and telling me that St. Catherine's was too far away, and that it was necessary to have a place in or near the City. I cannot understand what Dr. Wadia says that Rev. Mother agrees with all that she writes. Be assured of this, Dr. Dengel, that our good God will make everything work."

Toward the end of January Pauline Willis sent Anna a letter that she had received from Rev. Christopher Becker in Würzburg. It was just what Anna needed to lift her spirits.

"It was very good of you to go over to America with Miss Dengel. I hope and pray to our Lord that her work there may be successful. She certainly is the very person to succeed. It would be nice if there could be a gathering in Rome for the medical mission work. Perhaps it may be useful to wait until Miss Dengel is back from America, that she might also be present."

To this Pauline added her own comment in her note to Anna:

"Indeed I hope you can be in Rome when such a meeting is held." Anna also received encouragement from Father William White, with whom she had resumed the practice of exchanging weekly letters. He wrote:

"I hope you will go for the Holy Year, surely you could manage it; I am sure it will be worthwhile, and that you will reap huge benefits for your work. To be at the center of things, especially with the Missionary Exhibition, should bring its advantages."

On February 5th Anna met with members of the Medical Mission Board and the Propagation of the Faith to clarify details of their new relationship. From now on all money that she received would be channeled through them. According to Anna the percentage the Board had originally suggested would be theirs had changed. Their final decision: 60% for Rawalpindi and 40% for missions selected by the Board. Anna agreed – she had little choice – saying to the Prefect Apostolic in Pindi to whom she reported: "I don't mind – as long as it serves Medical Mission purposes in any part of the world." Donations had been a disappointment, but Anna was encouraged when "a priest of the Mission Crusade told me, the fact that I was able to get into the swing of things at all looks hopeful." After the meeting, Anna had a photo taken and then boarded the train for Philadelphia. Miss Willis had arranged hospitality for her with the Religious of the Sacred Heart in Overbrook – "a lovely place."

Dennis Cardinal Dougherty, Archbishop of Philadelphia, had sent Anna a very nice letter giving her permission to speak on medical missions in his archdiocese and inviting her to pay him a visit while she was there, which she did. She was with him for 1½ hours. "His

Eminence was very interested – asked many questions – in favor of more women doctors – also in favor of a religious order for women." He asked his Director for the Propagation of the Faith to help Anna and then asked Anna to return the next day with some photos. During their time together, the Cardinal was very gracious and interested in all Anna had to say, listening attentively to her concerns and asking her many questions. He himself had been a missionary bishop among the poor in the Philippines years ago, so he could empathize. The following day Anna returned to New York with a ray of hope in her heart. She now had the support of several members of the hierarchy: Cardinal Hayes of New York, Cardinal Dougherty of Philadelphia, and apparently Archbishop Curley in Baltimore, who was known to have an interest in Medical Missions. Anna wrote in her journal that Archbishop Curley had "told a friend of Miss Willis (Miss Storer, who knew Dr. McLaren and who paved the way for me in Baltimore and Washington) that he will help me when in his diocese."

After a busy week in New York, Anna returned to Philadelphia to lecture at Assumption Academy in Raven Hill. Reverend Mother had known Dr. McLaren, who always stayed in their convent in London whenever she visited there, and she had liked her very much. Cardinal Dougherty, a benefactor of Assumption Convent, was present for Anna's illustrated lecture. He had come specifically for that. "I did not feel nervous," Anna recalled. After the talk, the Cardinal pulled out a check for one hundred dollars, and then he said he would give me five thousand dollars. I thought it would take some time. In a few days, he called me to his office and there was the check. He asked me a few more questions. Said I must talk more slowly. He also said that young speakers usually speak in a monotonous voice – I don't know whether that applies to me too. Probably." The Cardinal said:

> "Money is required and that he would like me to get some in Philadelphia. He told me I didn't know how to go about it at all, so he called the head of all the charities. I was put in his hands. Really, I am so glad. It gives me hope that we will be able to have a really *useful* hospital in Pindi – one in which we can deal with everything."

Anna did a lot of work in Philadelphia. She stayed at the Sacred Heart convent. "They were wonderful to me." The Cardinal instructed the head of Catholic Charities to get church collections for Anna and to help her in every way possible, and he also wrote a letter to be sent to all the churches and religious institutions under his jurisdiction encouraging their support. As a result, what followed was an ad hoc campaign organized by the Cardinal's representatives to promote medical missions. During the remaining weeks of February and into March, Anna was in the Philadelphia archdiocese making the rounds. She met with potential donors; spent time with supporters; was interviewed by the diocesan newspaper, *The Catholic Standard and Times;* spoke with a public relations person who was designing a brochure; lectured at various institutions, including the Women's Medical College; and, beginning on Ash Wednesday, began an intensive effort to acquire church collections. Anna and the Monsignor assigned to assist her visited church after church, asking pastors to give Anna a church collection for medical missions. Nearly all who were approached agreed.

"Monsignor hired a taxi," Anna wrote in her journal, "and took me from rectory to rectory. He did all the explaining and just introduced me. Alone – I would have had no chance at all."

On the final day of February, Anna gave an informal talk to the Nurses Guild and suggested they set up a fund to support one nurse in India. They said they would seriously consider doing that. Later she had dinner with five nurses who had expressed an interest in knowing more. One of them said that she herself might go out as a missionary. Even as her fund-raising efforts in the USA intensified, Anna continued to play a role in shaping the future of the Rawalpindi mission.

> "Miss Willis says something about the Committee wanting a European doctor for St. Catherine's. I think that it would be a great mistake to lose Dr. Wadia, as she seems to get on so nicely and has made up her mind to stay. Also an Indian is in some ways more valuable than a European. I know a little how long it takes to just understand Hindustani and a little of the customs of the people and as long as one does not know how they live and what they eat, etc., one cannot really treat them

successfully. If we want to develop medical missions in the Punjab, we want every doctor available, so it would be a mistake to lose Dr. Wadia, who after all gave up good prospects in Ahmadabad and was recommended to us by Archbishop Goodier. She opposes the city scheme, because she can't see that it will work together with St. Catherine's. The very fact of her opposition makes me think that she is really interested in the good of the Mission. So I do hope that she will stay."

Anna's persistent defense of a woman who had recently wounded her reveals something significant about her sense of integrity. She also told Monsignor Winkley that Cardinal Dougherty wanted to visit India, and that he said "within the next few years, he would send us $50,000 for the medical mission."

The first promotional leaflet describing the cause to which Anna was so passionately committed was printed in Philadelphia and distributed throughout the region in the spring of 1925. It included Cardinal Dougherty's February 18th Letter of Introduction, some mission photos, and this message.

PROTESTANT MEDICAL MISSIONS

✝✝✝ We have nothing but praise for our Protestant friends. Their efforts are successful because they are well organized.

✝✝✝ But what about our work? We have a keen appreciation of spiritual values. Heaven is near and dear to us. But we are inclined to underestimate the enormous value of medical missions as material means to spiritual ends.

✝✝✝ In other words, the application of the parable of the Good Samaritan lies with us. There are wounds to be bound and souls to be saved. Very often one leads to the other and, as in the Gospel narrative – PENCE are necessary

✝✝✝ The countries of Europe provided the missioners and funds, in large measure before the World War. But these sources of revenue have ceased.

✝✝✝ "We are living in times when unenlightened heroism is not enough."

> -- Pope Pius XI at the opening of The Missionary
> Exhibition in Rome.

CATHOLIC MEDICAL MISSIONS

If you seek a Reason:

††† Because a billion human beings know nothing of medicine, surgery and hygiene.

††† Because hundreds of thousands of your fellow creatures not only die but live long lives of suffering from preventable and curable diseases.

††† Because medical missions remove prejudice and make for the rapid spread of Christianity and civilization.

††† Catholic medical missions are Catholic in their burden but their charity is and always has been extended to all.

††† Hundreds of thousands of hands are stretched out to us. What an opportunity for the Catholic in the land of St. Francis Xavier.

††† Building a Catholic Hospital in a pagan community means planting Christianity.

MISSION AT RAWAL PINDI, INDIA

††† This first Catholic Medical Mission in India that was definitely founded by Dr. Agnes McLaren in 1909, a pioneer in this field, of Scotch-Irish ancestry, and a convert, is now being successfully carried on under the charge of the Franciscan Missionaries of Mary at Rawal Pindi.

††† Year by year the work increases. During the last year, 13,380 out-patients were treated, 242 indoor patients, 253 operations were performed, and 35 obstetrical cases attended. The natives are also visited and treated in their homes.

††† A foundling home is attached to the hospital and a branch dispensary was started in Kashmir in an absolutely pioneering medical field.

††† Dr. Anna Dengel, who graduated from Cork University, lives at the Convent, and has the medical supervision of the work. She has also an office for private patients, and visits as well

the people in the native city. Her life is entirely
devoted in this Apostolic work.

✝✝✝ To feed, house and treat one patient per day
costs twenty cents, for a month, $6; to maintain
a bed for a year, $72; to endow a bed, $1,200;
100 bricks for the new hospital, $1; 1,000 bricks,
$10; to build one ward, $1,000; the entire medical
mission will cost $50,000.

✝✝✝ Means are now urgently required to maintain
what has already been started and to extend
the immense field for Medical Mission work in
the East.

✝✝✝ All contributions, church collections and offerings
from organizations and individuals may be
forwarded to Dr. Dengel in care of the Society
for the Propagation of the Faith, 1700 Summer
Street, Philadelphia.

As a result of Cardinal Dougherty's magnanimous response, Anna's
fund-raising focus shifted from New York to Philadelphia and the
surrounding region. Early in March she went to Scranton, where the
local bishop understood the need for medical missions, although he
could not support her financially at that time. Anna made a note that
"later he may have a drive for all medical missions and we get our share."
While in Scranton, she spoke at Marywood College, visited several
institutions, and met with the Catholic Daughters of America, where
she suggested that they "do something definite - support a bed or a
worker," and stayed at St. Mary Keller Memorial Hospital run by the
Franciscan nuns, all of whom were "kindness itself." On March 8th she
returned to Philadelphia and stayed with the Sisters of the Sacred Heart
in Overbrook, where she was and would always be warmly welcomed.
She was able to confirm that church collections would be taken up
at Holy Rosary and Corpus Christi parishes. She was off again the
following morning, this time, for Washington, DC. On the way Anna
stopped in Baltimore to see Archbishop Curley. "His Grace said that he
could see the necessity of medical missions – gave me full permission
to speak – and told me to write to him later. Miss Storer had told him
of our work on her way to Florida."

On arrival in Washington, Anna went to the School of Social
Service to give a lecture to the students and to meet with a local priest
and the Bishop of Cleveland to discuss the merits of training medical

mission workers in a social service context. She spoke at a number of places: Trinity College; Providence Hospital; Immaculata Academy; Holy Cross Academy; Georgetown Visitation Convent; and briefly, at Georgetown University Hospital. In Baltimore, Anna lectured at Notre Dame College and at St. Joseph's Hospital, where she was staying while in the area. In both places she was cordially received. Then the surgeon within her emerged and she took advantage of an opportunity to immerse herself in some aspects of her medical profession. At Johns Hopkins Hospital, she was an observer in surgery and "the whole afternoon watched cystoscopics," journaling the process in detail. The next day she "spent the morning in the operating room, St. Joseph's Hospital, two appendectomies," again recording it in precise detail for future reference. One can only imagine how much Anna missed that aspect of her medical mission calling, for which she had trained so long and so hard and at which she had been so competent.

The following day was the 16th of March. She wrote this entry in her journal.

> "'My birthday.' 33 years old. Life is short – it is made up of time – Don't waste one minute of it. Great resolution for the remainder of my life: not to waste one moment. My God, every moment of the remainder of my life for You!!! – J.M.J."

At the end of the day she wrote in her journal:

> "Spent birthday in Baltimore. Lecture at Visitation. – My nerves very bad. – Broke down. – Must have a rest."

Living out of a suitcase, always on the move, always in the spotlight, always pouring out energy in an effort to get others to see the urgency of the needs that drove her daily to the edge of her endurance – Anna's practical side was often overshadowed by her desire to achieve her goal. As a physician she should have known better, one might be tempted to say, found a way to slow things down and to take care of herself. But like any visionary chasing a dream, the impossible often seems doable and the proverbial pot of gold just around the bend in the road. What is amazing, given her recent history, is just how much inner and outer stamina she seemed to have.

Ironically, on this her 33rd birthday, Anna's resolution for the rest of her life was "not to waste one moment."

Ad majorem Dei gloriam. "For the greater glory of God."

Right from the beginning
it wasn't easy,
but the impossible of today
is the work of tomorrow.

Anna Dengel

CHAPTER EIGHT

There were three centers of opportunity for Anna with regard to medical mission development during her visit to America. The first was New York City, her focal point on arrival. The second, Philadelphia, where doors began to open and possibilities started to emerge. The third, Washington, DC. In each of these three cities, an individual or an organization would play a pivotal role in the evolution of her vision. In New York, it was the Catholic Medical Mission Board. In Philadelphia, Dennis Cardinal Dougherty. In Washington, the one who would join forces with Anna to forge a path into the future was the Rev. Dr. Michael Mathis, c.s.c.

Michael Mathis, a Holy Cross priest, was founder and director of his community's Foreign Mission Seminary in Washington, where he taught Missiology and Theology to seminarians to prepare them for their mission assignments in the Bengal region of India. He was also a founder and a current member of the Medical Mission Board. He had no medical background. His initial contact with Anna was in the spring of 1923. He had sent out a questionnaire to Catholic women involved in medical mission work and she had received a copy. She filled it out immediately and returned it to him in Dacca, where he was staying while visiting the Holy Cross missions. She invited him to come see her in Rawalpindi before returning home, and on March 26th he sent this response.

> "Thanks so much for your kind letter. I had of course heard of you before and was accordingly so glad to receive your note. It will be impossible for me to go to Rawalpindi, in spite of the fact that I looked forward to visiting your hospital even before I left America. I sail

for the U.S.A. from Bombay via Europe on May 1ˢᵗ. Please do send me pictures of your work and especially of yourself, as this will encourage other young women in the States to follow in your footsteps."

There was no further communication between the two of them until after Anna had left India and had come to America. Hoping to finally meet her, Father Mathis wrote to Anna in the Fall of 1924. His letter, sent to New York, was forwarded to her in Boston. She responded:

"I received your letter only now as it had to be forwarded from N.Y. I am very glad that you are going to Rome. I tell you why. I do hope that a little representative International Medical Mission Conference will be held in Rome next year. Col. O'Gorman of London and Monsignor Becker of the Medical Mission Institute of Würzburg, Bavaria are in favor of it. I am very anxious that you should meet Monsignor Becker and actually see the Medical Mission Institute in Bavaria. It would be a revelation to you to see so many earnest young men working there to be medical missionaries – for us Catholics quite a new and wonderful thing. There is also a movement on foot in England to form a religious Society for women medical missionaries. Abbe Totsuka – a Japanese priest – who as far as I can gather from a little article in *The Universe*, has started a little religious Society for Medical Missionaries. My idea is that people interested in medical missions should be in touch with one another to achieve anything at all."

Anna was determined to see Michael Mathis while she was in America and perhaps discuss with him some kind of collaboration that would be of benefit to the Punjab. She concluded her letter by saying: "I shall be disappointed if I don't meet you, as I would have liked to talk over several things with you, chiefly the question of medical missionaries and the possibilities of expansion in India." They met at the home of Doctor Flagg. Anna had been staying there while looking for an inexpensive room to rent. Mathis had come to New York for a meeting with Doctor Flagg. "Father Mathis told me he had sent four lay nurses to India.

I said, 'What a risk!'" It was a brief encounter. A more substantive conversation would have to wait until sometime in the New Year. On December 26 Anna wrote to Mathis who had gone on to Rome for the Holy Year festivities.

> "You are very fortunate to be in Rome for the opening of the Holy Year! I wish you all the possible blessings for 1925. I spent Christmas Day in the Flagg family – so my one Christmas Day in the U.S.A. was a happy one. Next year I hope to be back in the north of India. I hope, dear Father, that you will go to Würzburg to see Monsignor Becker before your return. Your and his interest are the same and I think that it would mean a step forward for the medical missionary cause if you could both meet. Please look at St. Catherine's Hospital in miniature at the Vatican Exhibition."

In March of 1925 Anna arrived in Washington on a promotional tour. She went to see Father Mathis.

> "I shall never forget the first evening when I was in Washington. I was so tired. It was terrible. I went up to the Holy Cross College – up steps and steps and steps. They told me that Father wasn't there, that he was at the Bengalese. They must have seen I was at the end, so they put me in a car and drove me over to the Bengalese. I just couldn't go another step. I met Father. He was very, very kind. He asked me to give a talk."

The next day she spoke at "The Mathis Club," which was a private and select group of friends and financial supporters of Michael Mathis and his outreach projects. "He took up a collection...introduced me to the Mathis Club ladies." In the evening of March 11, she gave a talk at Providence Hospital and made this notation in her journal: "Rev. Michael Mathis was present and he introduced me." A subsequent meeting between Anna and Father Mathis was set for the evening of March 23rd when she would return to Washington. It was then that the two of them were able to discuss medical missions at length, primarily from the perspective of Michael Mathis.

Anna records that they had a "long further discussion about the Laywomen's Medical Mission organization" that Mathis had recently established. "Rev. Father Mathis thinks I should take it on." He had sent four nurses to India without any organizational structure and no specific spiritual preparation. "The very first moment Father Mathis mentioned that to me, I said: 'What a risk!' I could visualize all kinds of difficulties." Within a few months, word had arrived that one of the nurses had fallen in love with a married man. Another, full of zeal and convinced that publicity was a value, began to publish all kinds of things without the Bishop's permission, much to the embarrassment of the local mission. Before long the nurses had returned to the USA. Mathis said to Anna: "What do you think it would take to make it work?" Here is what Anna remembers:

> "I was ready for the question because in my own mind I knew what was needed. I didn't tell Father that I knew it. I said, 'I'll work it out.'"

The following day, March 24, Father Burke, Father Mathis, and Anna met to discuss "the need for organization. Father Mathis put his whole plan before Father Burke. Certain things are clearer to me – not all yet. Can't see yet how lay organization can work."

Anna returned to Philadelphia on the 25th of March, the Feast of the Annunciation. It was, she records, "a beautiful spring day. Day of *Ecce Ancilla Domini*. I kept on saying it." Behold the handmaid of the Lord. Mary's response to the Angel Gabriel when she was told that the Holy Spirit had a plan for her. This was also Anna's response to the Spirit of the living God with regard to her own life and calling. Two days later, on March 27, she sent a lengthy letter to Michael Mathis.

> "First I must thank you very heartily indeed for your kindness to me while in Washington. As regards the proposed Medical Mission Society – I am more interested than I can either express or show. That I must not shirk taking some share in the development of Medical Missions – I know from my own conscience and also as the result of serious deliberation and advice last July. Without an organization of some kind, Medical Missions will not develop – or at least [will

develop] very slowly. Isolated efforts are good, but
not so efficient and permanent. Besides the life of the
isolated medical missionary is too lonely. As I told you,
Monsignor Becker suggested that I should take 3 or 4
German women doctors back with me to India, live
out the life together and then establish a home center.
It is not possible to take Germans to India, especially
in Northern India just now. *One* might be allowed, but
not a whole group. But I liked the spirit of the Medical
Mission Institute very much – and I saw that it works –
for the student years anyhow."

Anna then proceeded to tell Father Mathis about some of the medical
mission organizational initiatives that were already underway and how
she felt about her own participation in what seemed to be emerging.

"In England I got in touch with the *Institutum Deiparae*,
which has so far about five scattered members and aims
at being of a *completely* religious character. The priest
who founded it is a Jesuit and a doctor, but does not
know conditions and requirements of the missions. But
some other priest of his Society could fill that need. I
met Rev. Father Agius myself. He outlined the idea
for me, as I told you, but no details were fixed and
the whole thing had to wait until he could come out
of his tertianship. It appealed to me, but Father King,
S.J. who has charge of this idea until Fr. Agius is free
to take it up, told me to wait. Since then I have had
several months to think about these things. I was not a
bit worried or anxious or in a hurry, though eventually
I was hoping to find some Medical Missionary family
to which I could belong."

She brought the issue closer to home when she reflected on her
recent meeting with the Bishop of Cleveland during her first visit to
Washington.

"I had not the faintest notion why I was asked to stay
at the Social Service school until after my arrival when

I heard that Rev. Father Lynch, C.S.S.R. had spoken there on Medical Missions and that it occurred to them that an organization for this might be a good thing. Then Bishop Shrembs and Rev. Father Burke took the trouble to come over one evening and discussed it at length. I did not want to encourage or discourage them without getting your opinion on the matter, and so it happened that you told me your plans and I told you some of my experiences and ideas. If you really think that I should take a share in the formation of a Medical Missionary organization, I am ready to cooperate with you wholeheartedly and gladly."

Clearly and succinctly, Anna told Michael Mathis what kind of medical mission organization she herself envisioned, a new and much needed reality to which she felt drawn by God.

"To satisfy my soul and my mind, it must be missionary, medical and international. Religious or lay, I don't mind – whatever achieves the aim better. To be Missionary, it must be for God and man [sic] anyhow, so it does not matter much under what name or what garb. The more I think of it, the more difficulties seem to crop up, but after all nothing is started without difficulties and certain risks ….It is my great desire to start a hospital in the city of Rawalpindi, to study conditions in India more and especially the condition of the women in India and other pagan countries and it was and is my hope to bring medical relief (missionary) to the Mohammedan women of Afghanistan. If once the ball is set rolling, I could return. I would be very glad."

She concluded that letter by adding: "I am going to Washington on Friday. On Saturday, I am free. I shall ring you up." After some local appearances in the nation's capital, she planned to return to Philadelphia and then go on to Pittsburgh. She told Father Mathis that she was running out of time and wanted "to get on" with some clear plan for the future because, as she had been saying persistently, "My plan was to stay in the U.S.A. till about June or July, then spend the summer at home and return to India in the autumn." Her final comment: "I enclose a few puzzles. (I never work puzzles as I always have real ones on hand.)"

On March 29 Anna rose at 4:45 a.m. and went to St. Stephen's Church in Philadelphia where she had to take up the collection at the 7:00 a.m. Mass on her own. "Then the others turned up," she noted. "Was not so hard as I expected. Nuns were very kind, gave us lunch and helped to count the money." Afterwards Anna had to rest because she was exhausted. Later that day she went to St. Bonaventure's Church and did not get back to her room until 11:30 p.m. The next morning she turned over the proceeds from the church collection - $686.59 – to the office of the Propagation of the Faith. That evening she wrote to Michael Mathis and enclosed a list of questions.

1) What motives should bring people to the proposed organization?
2) What should be the obligations?
3) What is necessary professionally (missionary and medical) for a medical missionary?
4) What are the hardships of a medical missionary?
5) Should we take the Protestant lay missionaries as a pattern? Can we do it less well – just as well – or better?
6) What is the relationship between members of a religious family?

The following morning she wrote in her journal: "Great longing for religious life"- and then mailed the letter to Father Mathis.

Anna began to think seriously about what kind of an organization would represent what she envisioned. It would have to be one that was rooted in the wisdom of her own experience, one that responded genuinely to need and would satisfy her heart's desire. She knew she would have to do something that had never been done before: found an international society whose members were neither Religious nor lay, yet at the same time, were individually both lay and religious. In a tiny journal that fit in the palm of her hand, she scribbled what appears to be a brain-storming list of items numbered from one to one-hundred under the title "First Plan of the Society." It wasn't actually a plan but a column of words or phrases that she felt were virtues or values essential to a life dedicated to medical missions in the context of a community. Here are her first five entries:

- o Carefully and totally forever (for myself, not for others)
- o To resolve to lead a life of sacrifice out of love
- o In the missions for the sick
- o Never to refuse anybody seeking help
- o With joy

Other phrases could serve as examples for a purpose-driven life.

- o Love one another
- o Work – work – when you don't work, pray
- o Preach by example
- o Learn language
- o Keep highest scientific standard possible
- o Aim more at having efficient places then a number of places

Several entries are surprisingly pragmatic.

- o To be under the authority of priest … not minus reason!
- o Read newspaper
- o Take higher degrees … if they are free
- o Motor-cycle … horse … if provided – or necessary … why not?

On April 5th, Palm Sunday, Anna went to the Foreign Mission Seminary in Washington, DC, which was the home base of Rev. Michael Mathis. After the solemn liturgical rites, the two of them met to discuss a proposed Society and, as Anna records in her journal, "started to write out Constitutions." Father Mathis gave her the Directory and the Rules of his own Holy Cross Congregation. After that meeting she returned to Philadelphia to the Sacred Heart Sisters, who had always made her feel so at home. On Holy Thursday Anna spent nearly the whole day in their convent, keeping vigil before the Repository in their chapel, which was "very beautiful." She "felt very happy" and "wrote a lot of letters." She also received a copy of the provisional Constitutions of a medically oriented religious order that was coming into existence in England. The next day, Good Friday, she wrote to Michael Mathis:

> "I also looked through your rules and Constitutions. Everything is so wise and nothing seems to be forgotten. I really prayed with all my heart yesterday that Our Lord may show us more clearly what He wants and whom he wants to do it."

She spent all of Good Friday in the convent as well, relishing the opportunity to participate in the Stations of the Cross and to hear the touching meditation given by a Jesuit priest.

On Holy Saturday Anna met with Cardinal Dougherty and thanked him again for his generosity and support. "He said that all the money from his Diocese is to go to our mission." This meant that the Archdiocese of Philadelphia, with regard to money collected locally, was overriding the arrangement imposed on Anna by the New York Medical Mission Board and the Propagation of the Faith. Then Anna sought out his perspective on the issue dear to her heart.

> "I asked his advice about the proposed society. He said he would like to see more women doctors in that work. We should form a pious organization. Rome probably will not allow vows. But have rules like a religious order. He said to me why don't you start it? – I said – I can't alone."

Anna told the Cardinal about Father Mathis, and he asked her if she was under an obligation to the Mill Hill Fathers. Anna said she was not. Then he told Anna that "out of loyalty and because I know them I should tell them about it." Easter Sunday in the Convent of the Religious of the Sacred Heart in Overbrook was a day of relaxation and renewal for her.

> "The altar was the most beautifully decorated I have ever seen – all lilies and a few roses. Just what I like. Mass was very solemn. Went for a stroll. Afternoon went out into a field and lay down and read letters of St. Chantal – and smoked. Enjoyed myself immensely."

That evening she wrote a long letter to Father White explaining the planned Society to him.

On Easter Monday Anna spent the whole day with the president of the Guild of Our Lady of the Visitation who took her to the Catholic Sisters Convention, where she spoke briefly to the assembly and extensively to a number of individual women. She was told that they would try to secure a nurse's salary for Pindi. That evening she boarded a sleeper train bound for Pittsburgh, and the next morning went straight to work. She was handed a list of engagements beginning with a talk to the nurses at St. Francis Hospital that evening, then Mercy Hospital where she lectured to a large number of nuns and nurses. A meeting with Bishop Boyle, who gave her a letter of support, then lectures at the Pittsburgh Hospital, and to a large gathering of the National Council of Catholic Women, and to Lynam Hall for Crusaders filled out the week. After that she went on to Wheeling, West Virginia, where she lectured at De Chantal, a beautiful, natural enclosure where "the nuns were all very kind and nice." Next, the Carmelite Convent, where she asked for prayers. "I would love not to have any distractions of the outside world – but I know it is not my vocation – for now anyhow." Then she spoke at Wheeling Hospital, where the Sisters of St. Joseph graciously gave her $25 for her mission, and then to the Catholic Women's Club at St. Joseph Academy, where the Sisters were very interested and all the women very kind. Anna "enjoyed it very much." The President of the group gave a little dinner party for her. She returned to Pittsburgh on April 24th where, during the next two days, she visited the Chancery, gave several talks, received $100 from a Protestant business man who had an interest in medical missions, then boarded the 10:30 p.m. train for Philadelphia. The following day, April 25, Anna went directly to the 7:45 a.m. Mass at St. John's Church and helped the women with the church collection. They received $600 and Monsignor Wartl added $900 more. April 27 – 9 a.m. According to Anna's journal it was "a most glorious spring day."

> "I am out in the field of Overbrook. Too many years the singing of the birds did not seem so melodious. So many patches of wild violets in the field, unseen by anybody – everything bubbling and blowing. I am giving myself this day for correspondence – thinking of M.M.S. – and to be alone with God and nature."

She wrote the following letter to Father Mathis that afternoon.

"I wonder would it be convenient for you if I came to Washington this Friday. I am going to York on Wednesday, I'll be in Harrisburg on Thursday, and on Friday I could go to Washington. I am booked for Louisville for that day, but I can put it off for a day or two. Then I'll be further West – Chicago, etc. – and it will not be easy to come back and, as you say, plans – no matter how provisional – should be made soon. It would be more satisfactory to me too as the summer will be here very soon. I'll have some points ready, so that we could go through the whole thing perhaps in a day. If not, I'll stay Saturday too, because after all it is more important than lecturing in Louisville."

On May 1st Anna left Harrisburg early for Washington and spent the day with Michael Mathis organizing a Medical Mission Society. Progress was made, she reports in her journal. They even consulted with a canon lawyer whose expertise was helpful. Anna went on to Louisville the following day where, for the rest of the week, she was busy organizing events and venues and giving talks that had already been scheduled. On Sunday she went to 10 a.m. Mass and then spent a peaceful day at Saint Mary and Elizabeth Convent/Hospital where she was scheduled to speak in the evening. On Monday she visited Bishop Floersh, who was extremely gracious and suggested she combine all the schools into a single Rally instead of talking at multiple sites. She gave a talk to the Ursulines in the afternoon and spoke at St. Anthony's hospital in the evening. Tuesday, May 5th, was a milestone.

"Just one year today since I left India. How many things have happened? Passed by rapidly. God's visible help."

She went on to Nazareth, Kentucky, where she attended Mass, listened to a lecture, and then gave her own talk at the Rally attended by a large number of students from various diocesan schools. That evening she returned to Louisville with the Ursuline nuns "who are very interested in Missions and very very nice." The next morning she went to Mass at 6:00 a.m. at the Ursuline Chapel and to Benediction at 8:00 a.m., then on to Sacred Heart Academy "beautifully situated in the outskirts of Louisville. Keep that plan in mind!! Octagonal church with passage all around," she noted in her journal. Over the next several days she spoke at a parochial school and met many nuns, all of them very kind and very supportive. She recorded this in her journal:

> "*Wrote the Constitutions roughly* during my stay in Louisville at the Ursuline Convent."

On May 8th Anna wrote the following letter to Michael Mathis.

> "Yesterday and today I was free, so I tried to work at the Constitutions. Provisionally – from my side – they are ready, and as soon as I have them copied out, I shall send them to you for corrections, additions, etc. I am booked for Harrisburg for May the 11th. If you think it advisable that I should come to see you once more in order to settle things more definitely and even see Archbishop Curley, I could come down for a few days."

Anna's journal entry for May 9th reads:

> "Rainy day. Had no appointments. Very providential. Was able to copy out Constitutions and sent them on to Rev. Father Mathis."

Here is the note she enclosed with her initial attempt at producing a Constitution for a Medical Mission Society while she was in Louisville.

> "I am enclosing my attempts. I tried to put in things which are necessary for the beginning and left many things to be worked out later. I am sending it now. Perhaps you would be so kind as to look over it if you have time so that we can discuss the corrections and additions etc. Perhaps I left out some things which are very essential. Some things may be only a personal fancy."

On May 10th Anna went on to Harrisburg. The following day she was back in Washington. On May 17, with the help of Holy Cross Fathers Michael Mathis and Francis McBride, she finished the Constitution.

By the grace of God this happened on the Feast of the Canonization of the Little Flower, Saint Thérèse of Lisieux, the Church's new Patron Saint of Missions and Missionaries. Here are some of the key elements of that initial document.

A.M.D.G. Washington DC. 17.5.25

FIRST CONSTITUTIONS OF THE SOCIETY OF CATHOLIC MEDICAL MISSIONARIES

- ❖ The Society shall be called "Society of Catholic Medical Missionaries"
- ❖ It shall be a Society whose members lead a community life after the manner of religious under proper superiors but without the three usual vows of religious life
- ❖ The Society shall be dedicated to Our Lady under the title "Cause of our Joy"
- ❖ The Society shall be international
- ❖ Only those are members of the Society who are fully qualified or trained and have certificates as members of some branch of the medical profession, including doctors, dentists, nurses, pharmacists, etc. ...those who have taken the pledge of service in the Society
- ❖ The dress shall be that of a lay person
- ❖ After a year of probation the candidate pledges to follow the rules and constitutions of the Society for three years and the directions of superiors and the decisions of the general chapter in all that pertains to the constitutions and rules of the Society. After that she may renew her pledge for another term, or for life. The pledge shall be made in public.
- ❖ As religious who make public vows and who wear the religious habit have certain restrictions as to going out alone and attending obstetric and other cases, the members of the Society of Catholic Medical Missionaries sacrifice the privilege of making public vows in order not to be prevented from engaging in any kind of medical work, so as to be able to help people, especially women, in all their needs. All members must strive to live in the spirit of the evangelical counsels so far as compatible with medical mission work.

❖ The superior decides the dates of the annual holiday for each member which shall not be less than four weeks and not more than six weeks.

These core elements are what Anna had long envisioned but had not been able to put into an organizational framework until now. The full text of the document, however, consisted of 25 "Constitutions" and 106 "Articles." Most of these were canonical elements mandated by the institutional Church and written into the text by theologian Rev. Michael Mathis and canonist Rev. Francis McBride. The result was a finished product with a degree of ambivalence, which, until Canon Law introduced certain substantive changes into its received Tradition, was the best that could be done.

In between travel, talks, and collaborative efforts to give birth to a dream that would have the approval of the institutional Church, Anna managed to publish two articles during the month of May: "Women of the East and Their Needs" in the *Bulletin of the National Council of Catholic Women;* and "Medical Missionary Work in the Vale of Kashmir" in *The Public Health Nurse.* Their thematic substance is summarized in these lines from one of the texts.

> "Can we call ourselves Christian if we let generation after generation pass away without trying to make our gentle, forebearing sisters of the Orient happier in body and soul? In the East, and especially in India, a woman depends on a woman in her hour of suffering and need, and of suffering there is a great deal."

Meanwhile, Michael Mathis had reached the point where he needed the permission of his community before he and Anna could proceed in a more definitive way. In his May 22nd letter to his Provincial Superior, the Rev. Charles O'Donnell, he clearly states his own understanding of this pioneering initiative and of the supportive role both he and the Holy Cross Congregation would play in the development of the charismatic Anna Dengel's Society of Catholic Medical Missionaries. Clearly, it was her Society. As a Holy Cross community member, his role had been to assist her in bringing it about. He writes:

"The second approbation I ask today is for the part our Congregation is to play in the plan for the founding of a new society of Catholic Women Medical Missionaries in the event the society is approved by proper ecclesiastical authority. Thus far I have acted only in the capacity of advisor to the founder, Dr. Anna Dengel, M.D., a young Austrian doctor who made her medical course at the University of Cork in Ireland, during the war, and who for three and a half years served at the first Catholic women's hospital in India, Rawal Pindi in the Punjab. Dr. Dengel is in this country in the interests of her Indian hospital and of Catholic medical missions whose most pressing need at present is the foundation of a society which will train to community life and support on the field its members.

"A practical illustration of the confidence which this woman can inspire in leading members of the American hierarchy is the fact that in her first interview with Cardinal Hayes, His Eminence gave her his personal check for a thousand dollars. Cardinal Doherty [sic] gave his personal check for five thousand dollars, and later assigned to the best money-getter in Philadelphia the task of raising twenty-five thousand dollars for Doctor Dengel's work in India. I have known Doctor Dengel for some three years and consider her one of the best qualified from the spiritual, missionary, and medical point of view to found such a society, and I am interested for the reason that by co-operating with the proposed foundation in Brookland we can secure medical missionaries for our mission, without the care and trouble of governing and providing for them financially. The proposed society is canonically classified as a society of lay women living a community life under superiors, but without making the regular vows of religious. The Canon Law governing such a society has been followed in the constitutions which were completed by Doctor Dengel last Sunday.

"The only connection our congregation would have with the society is as follows:

1st To give the members of the new society the opportunity of attending the classes which we already provide for our Holy Cross Sisters, namely, classes in the Bengali language, mission study, and apologetics;

2nd To give them a spiritual conference once a week and to say Mass for them daily excepting Sundays;

3rd To offer the facilities of the *Bengalese* magazine in the measure in which medical mission work in Bengal is concerned."

The Holy Cross Provincial Superior gave his approval to what Michael Mathis had proposed.

At about that time, Anna received the following letter from Father White in Rawalpindi. It had a very different effect.

"I fear my letter may be a disappointment. I gather from your letter that you feel inclined to join forces with Father Mathis in such a way that you could have all India, instead of one Province, for your objectives. I don't see how you can transfer your work and the money collected without guaranteeing that others will come and the money spent on the Punjab, if the money was collected for the Punjab."

Anna had not anticipated the implications of including the Holy Cross missions in her organizational plan. Cooperating with Father Mathis meant including Bengal. While she had always considered professional medical care for women and children from a global perspective and had hoped some kind of organization would emerge and extend throughout India, and perhaps even beyond, she had been and would continue to be committed first of all to the Punjab. She knew that the money she had been collecting was meant to go to Pindi, and it would. She remained determined to construct a first-rate hospital for women and children in that region and to eventually return as its physician. In a subsequent letter to Monsignor Winkley, the Punjab's Prefect Apostolic to whom she was accountable, she informed him of the organization that she, with the help of Michael Mathis, had designed.

"I do not know yet when I will return. I don't think that it will be very soon. The reasons being two: First – I have very little money for the Pindi hospital and chapel yet. Secondly – I am very interested in leaving something permanent behind – a little society of workers – and with it some auxiliary for financial aid for medical mission work. Whether it is God's Will that the society should come about or not I do not know yet, but I have found a priest here – he belongs to the Holy Cross Fathers who work in Bengal - who is very anxious to see a society of that kind started. Within a month or so it will be decided whether anything is to be done this year or not. I wish often I could ask your advice and also consult Rev. Father White. It is rather hard to have to act so independently. Anyhow, as soon as I know more, I shall let you know and I would also be grateful for your opinion as to the advantages of a Medical Mission Society whose only aim would be to bring more workers (medical) and more means to the mission field for the good of the bodies and souls of people in the East. Financially, I have about $15,000 now. Some of this has to go to the Medical Mission Board according to my agreement."

Anna's dream of a medical missionary organization still needed official recognition from the institutional church. On June 10, Rev. Michael Mathis sent a formal request to Michael J. Curley, Archbishop of Baltimore.

"It is proposed to establish a new society of medical missionaries for foreign missions. The enclosed document contains the constitutions of the projected society, and as it is proposed to establish it in the archdiocese of Baltimore it will be necessary to have Your Grace's approbation which I humbly request. The constitutions of the new society have been modeled upon the requirements set down in canon law for a society of women who lead a community life after the manner of religious under the proper superiors but without the three usual vows of religious life (Canon 673). The founder of the proposed society is Doctor Anna Dengel, an Austrian by birth. I look upon her as a most remarkable woman filled with true apostolic zeal."

The letter of request Father Mathis sent was lengthy and detailed. The response of Archbishop Curley was characteristically brief. Two days later, a surprisingly swift turn-around time, the Archbishop wrote:

> "You may begin the work of the Foundation Medical Missionary Society outlined in your letter of June tenth. However, no financial appeals are to be made for this work in the Archdiocese of Baltimore, and no collections are to be taken up.
> Yours sincerely, + Michael Curley, Archbishop of Baltimore"

The Archbishop's quick and succinct response was totally unexpected. No doubt Anna's stop in Baltimore on her way to Washington in March and the testimony of a number of Bishops, two of whom were Cardinals, plus the advocacy of several notable lay women, contributed to this outcome. Equally unexpected, however, was the imposition of financial restrictions. How were they to manage if they could not solicit support in their own neighborhoods? Mathis was afraid that this would convince Anna to look elsewhere, most likely in Philadelphia, where the Cardinal continued to be exceedingly generous to her, so he sent her a letter explaining that the Archdiocese was prohibiting all collections and financial appeals only temporarily, for a period of three years, in order to implement some much-needed diocesan projects. In an effort to persuade her to stick to their original plan, he cited the benefits of seminary courses and priestly services from his Holy Cross congregation. His concern was unwarranted. Anna had no intention of starting her missionary Society elsewhere and she hastened to reassure him of that.

> "I am really glad and happy that the Archbishop approves, although it will surely bring many difficulties and responsibilities, but through Medical Missions so many souls can be saved and so much suffering lessened,

that it is worth it, and I have full confidence that Our Lord will help. If He wants it, we won't perish for the want of money. Really – the money does not worry me so much – you will probably attribute that to my inexperience and youth, but perhaps it is good not to see all the bugbears ahead, otherwise one would not have the courage. If I had foreseen the war and all its attendant financial and other difficulties it brought me, I would never have taken up medical missions. It would have been worse than insanity on my part, but everything came one by one, and there was always some solution to the question. So, I trust in Providence also for the future."

With immense relief Mathis wrote to Anna:

"I am delighted indeed to see the spirit in which you take the answer of the Archbishop. I am happier than I can say with the tone of your answer and I feel that it augurs well for the success of the Divine adventure upon which you are to launch."

He said as much to the Archbishop in acknowledging the permission granted.

"Your Grace's letter of June 12, authorizing us to begin the work of the foundation of the Society for Catholic Medical Missionaries, was received. I did not acknowledge Your Grace's letter at once for the reason that I did not wish to speak for the founder, Doctor Anna Dengel, M.D., to whom I forwarded your reply. This morning I received from Doctor Dengel a very beautiful expression of her gratitude for Your Grace's authorization and of her trust in Divine Providence for the funds which, according to the letter of authorization, were to be provided in places other than the archdiocese of Baltimore."

Anna's activities in June and July took her out to the Midwest. Everywhere people were very kind to her, but as she explains in her letters and her journal: "Money is hard to get – harder and harder – because *all* appeals come to America." Still she kept on trying.

> "Medical Mission for most Catholics is a 'new cause' and I am often told that for that reason I cannot expect results at once. Only a few days ago, I met the International Catholic Guild of Nurses and the President of the Catholic Hospital Association, who invited me to attend another Conference of nuns – all nurses – delegates from the 600 Catholic Hospitals of the United States and Canada. Rev. Father Moulinaris, the President, told me that the Hospital Association would help medical missions."

She met a few people who said they were seriously thinking of going as trained doctors and nurses to the mission field.

> "So the recruits for a society are not wanting, and by degrees there will be many fields in India, China, Africa, especially if the Society will provide the means for the development of the medical missions. I feel and I am sure now that this is my ideal and my vocation." And then she added: "My health is much better too."

However, introducing the new society would also have significant financial and administrative implications, which Anna outlined in a letter to Monsignor Winkley in Rawalpindi.

> "Now as I would like to have everything clear and satisfactory, I want to put before you a few points that have occurred to me:
> 1) We will have to collect more money: As this will be done when the Society is already functioning, whose shall the money be? The Mill Hill Mission, as the sum so far collected, or the Society's? When I am a member of a Society, I am not free to dispose of it as I like, so what is the right thing in that case? I shall abide

by your decision up to the sum of $50,000, this being the original estimate (this however does not imply a guarantee of that sum).

2) The second question is this: who shall have charge of the Hospital – in other words, who is responsible for its upkeep? If the Franciscan Missionaries of Mary are, they must see to the financial side of the Hospital and give us an allowance; in other words the same relation as I had with them in St. Catherine's; or if they are not willing to undertake that burden, then the relation would be reversed. And we would give them an allowance, for instance as they have in Government Hospitals in Colombo, etc."

Once again Anna explained to Monsignor Winkley the importance of a professional approach to the medical aspect of their mission and the necessity of making it mandatory.

"There is another point in connection with the Nuns. Of course, it is ideal to have them, besides, they have and still are paving the way, and I am sure they like to undertake it, but they must send a few trained people, or if that should be impossible, they must be willing to be trained, otherwise we have only a sort of an amateur – milk and water Hospital. There are plenty of that kind already and we would have no chance of success unless we were really professionally efficient. It is precisely an *efficient* Hospital which is needed in Pindi, where every kind of disease can be treated and where everybody can go. There is none of that kind for women and children in the whole Pindi district. The Nuns must be trained if they have charge of it."

A core concern of Doctor Dengel was: "Amateur work plus good will goes a long way, but *real* hospitals cannot be run by people who have *no* professional training at all." With regard to professional training, Anna had said the same thing many times to her friend, Mother Provincial Marie Alberte, in Pindi. She wrote to her again from America:

"Please forgive me when I say that I often wish that the FMM would train a few nuns as nurses – but not only just a year or so – but the full training where they would be on an actual footing with the nurses. In USA many nuns train with the nurses and it works out quite well."

Anna assured Monsignor Winkley that her fundamental commitment remained firm in the midst of all the unanticipated changes to her original plan of simply coming to America, getting the money they needed, and returning to the Punjab.

"I really don't mind how the whole thing is settled, as long as we can do some real good to the people and help the Missions. You may rely on my loyalty to the Punjab and to Mill Hill, on my submission to your decisions and on my gratitude. Medical Missions and their development is my greatest desire."

She also shared with her mentor something she had learned from her exposure to the American way of life.

"In America people are so different from Europe. Everybody – even priests and nuns – act very rapidly. If one does not step out with them, one is left behind altogether."

This characteristic, along with others that defined a nation consisting of many nationalities, made a whole lot of sense to Anna.

"Now just one word more, and that is, why America appeals to me for the starting point of a society. My idea is that the Society should be international. America is a very cosmopolitan place. The missionary enthusiasm in America is fostered very much and promises good results. And for medical missions, more than others, means are a necessity. In Europe for some time to come, that will be difficult."

During her time in the Midwest, Anna spent several days in Rochester, Minnesota, where she spoke to the nurses at Mayo Clinic and was delighted when they spontaneously promised to adopt the hospital in Rawal Pindi. The following morning she attended surgical operations at the Mayo Clinic and afterward met Dr. William Mayo. "He asked me where I had studied medicine. When I told him Cork, he said that an honorary degree had been conferred on his brother Charles in Cork that very morning." Although she experienced a scattering of graced opportunities, it really was not a good time to be on the road soliciting. "The schools are closed and women's activities adjourned," she wrote in her journal. In St. Paul, Minnesota, Archbishop Downing was very kind to her but could not contribute financial aid. "I made a little start," she said," but I always live in hope." From there she went to the National Council of Nurses gathering in Milwaukee where she gave a brief lecture and then returned to St. Paul before going on to Chicago, where she spent the July 4th weekend at a two-day retreat held at the Cenacle Convent. It was given by a Jesuit, Rev. F. O'Neill, and was on the theme of sanctification and vocation. Anna recorded several thoughts to reflect on during the year.

> "Throw yourself in God's arms."
> "Pray to the Holy Spirit."
> "Learn as you go along."

Anna also met a woman who was interested in medical missions and gave her a copy of the Constitutions. The next day they went to Mass together. "She told me that she liked the idea of the Society." Anna did not know then that Doctor Joanna Lyons would be the first to join her in beginning the new medical mission society.

Rev. Michael Mathis wrote to Anna, saying: "While you are in the Middle West, try to visit the University of Notre Dame and St. Mary's. These are respectively the mother houses of our Congregation and of the Sisters of the Holy Cross." Since Anna had wanted to consider next steps for the new society, and Mathis had to be at Notre Dame for his community's Provincial Chapter, they decided to meet on the campus in South Bend, Indiana. There they agreed to begin the society immediately, even though they had no house, no resources, no candidates, and no clear idea of how or where to begin it. Michael Mathis did not want to delay. There was too much talk going on in religious circles about the need for medical mission initiatives, and if anything was characteristic of him, it was his determination to be first. They already had ecclesiastical permission. All they had to do was do it. Anna scribbled in her journal:

> "Definitely settled to begin in September. Even if there are only two members. Now – I must look – for a house – and a reserve fund. *In Te Domine speravi* shall be my motto for everything!"

Anna concluded her Midwest fund-raising and consciousness-raising tour prepared to undertake the herculean task of bringing into being the new Society to which she was wholeheartedly committed. She soon discovered she would have to lean heavily on her new motto: "In You, O Lord, is my hope." She summarized the situation she was now facing in this letter to Michael Mathis.

> "I arrived in New York at 3 PM yesterday and I went straight to the Mission Board where I met Dr. Flagg and Mr. Keeler. They asked me about the nature of the Society. I explained it to them and Mr. Keeler said it was *exactly* the idea Dr. Lamont had. Both Dr. Flagg and Mr. Keeler agree that the Society is needed but they think that it should be linked up with the Board – so as to be universal! Dr. Flagg thinks that the Society can't grow and be financed without the Board. He has some plans now on a big scale, he said – but he did not tell me what they are. In other words – the Board is ready to make an appeal but wants something tangible to appeal for. I said: 'The Society would be an excuse or an object for the Board to make an appeal.' Mr. Keeler said: 'That's just it.' Dr. Flagg's idea is that the Society should be under the supervision of the Board. I said that we wanted absolute freedom to develop and that we could not have that under the Board, because whoever finances has the power."

Anna was clearly upset by this unexpected turn of events.

> "To sum up – it is Dr. Flagg's idea that the Society can't
> exist without the Board – also that it would be a great
> pity not to use the machinery of the Board, and both
> he and Mr. Keeler wanted to warn me in time so as not
> to make any false steps!! Dr. Flagg thinks that this will
> have to be decided at the Board meeting. He advised
> me to wait in the meantime – as there is no hurry about
> it!! No doubt they see it from their own point of view
> and mean it very well. But they have not been able to
> tell me definitely what the Board proposes and what is
> more, can guarantee for us."

What the Board members did not realize was the innate ability of this determined woman to see to the heart of the matter.

> "It is my own private opinion that the Board could be a
> great help to us, but that it will be easier for the Society
> to exist without the Board, than for the Board without
> the Society. For if the Board does not act and help, what
> is the use of its existence?....But just as we have to prove
> that we can begin and develop without the Board, the
> Board will have to prove that it can do anything in
> the way of financial help. So far they have helped me
> with their prestige and organized a certain number of
> audiences in schools and hospitals. But Dr. Flagg does
> not realize that so far the Medical Mission Board is
> very little known. The Board has helped and I am really
> grateful for that, but they made me pay for their help
> and I am afraid it would be the same in the future and
> as a Society we could not afford to do that....I shall tell
> Dr. Flagg this evening that I am going ahead."

She also told Mathis that "Dr. Flagg thinks that anyway we won't be able to start until after Christmas!" Then Mathis sent a lengthy response to all that Anna had shared.

"I congratulate you upon the way you handled the affair. Concerning the attitude of Doctor Flagg and Mr. Keeler as to the Society, I think they have failed to understand perhaps the most important feature of the new organization, namely, that it is an ecclesiastical society subject to the supervision and control of only one body, the Catholic Church. For this reason it is preposterous in Doctor Flagg's even imagining that the Society of Catholic Medical Missionaries could come under the supervision of the Medical Mission Board in any way other than the relationship which the Board now stands in with regard to every other society approved by the Church. Your Society can be supervised only according to canon law which alone determines the limits of jurisdiction in the relation of the Society of Catholic Medical Missionaries with other bodies. If the Board realizes the purposes for which it was instituted it ought most willingly to foster the new society, and if it discriminates against your society it is violating one of the fundamental agreements on which the Board rests."

Mathis was very upset at the audacity of his colleagues.

"So Dr. Flagg thinks that we will not be able to start the Medical Mission Society until after Christmas. If I may delicately suggest, I would say that he has another think coming. In the most essential matters it is already started."

He offered Anna this piece of advice.

"Have courage to say frankly to Monsignor McGlinchey what the true nature of your society is and make an appeal for finances. That will put him on the defensive at once."

To this Anna responded:

> "You need not be afraid. My stand for independence of
> the Society will be very firm, because I do not see any
> other way for its real development."

Meanwhile, to fulfill the terms of her contract with the Medical Mission
Board and to bring it to a conclusion, Anna submitted a written report
for the period covered by their agreement, which was from January 6th
to July 12th of the current year. During that period of time she had given
104 talks to schools, hospitals, and various guilds and organizations, and
had received a total of $13,394.86, from which she deducted $647.14
in personal expenses. In addition one bed was endowed for $1200 and
she had met and been encouraged by 4 Cardinals, 2 Archbishops, and
7 Bishops. "I did my best to make the Medical Mission Board and the
book *Catholic Medical Missions* known," she concluded." I am grateful
for all the kindness and help extended to me."

On August 6th Dr. Paluel Flagg, Chairman of the Medical Mission
Board, sent a telegram to Michael Mathis.

> REV. MICHAEL MATHIS   FROM NEW YORK
> CONGRATULATIONS ON YOUR NEW MEDICAL SOCIETY.
> DR. FLAGG

He followed that up with a letter to Mathis the following day.

> "Yesterday I saw the announcement of the new Society
> of Medical Missionaries which you have begun with the
> very capable aid of Doctor Dengel. I hastened to send
> you my congratulations which I hope you have received.
> The society or the work which it proposes is of course
> essential and as a matter of fact in a different form it
> was the occasion of our first getting together. We are
> all looking forward to a more detailed account of this
> Society and its plans when we meet on the 29th."

Michael Mathis immediately wrote to Anna Dengel.

"I don't quite understand Dr. Flagg. This morning I received a telegram which reads as follows: 'Congratulations on your new medical society.' These congratulations do not seem to be very sincere unless he has had an overnight conversion. Of course I must acknowledge his apparent good wishes, and they may be the indication of some new understanding you have had with him. I am much surprised to have him say that it is my society when he must know that it is yours. Yet, that may also be his way of trying to be nice."

He also said to Anna:

"Your stand for the independence of the society is splendid. It has often occurred to me that it is plainly a special providence that the Archbishop of Baltimore approved the foundation before he sailed for Europe and that his absence in Rome and elsewhere on the other side of the pond will be prolonged until October. You cannot tell what influences would be brought to bear on him to have him revoke his approbation. Hence, in the words of Saint Theresa, I advise you to begin functioning just as soon as possible."

Michael Mathis then wrote to Doctor Flagg.

"Your letter of August 7 was a gracious confirmation of your thoughtfulness and kindness to wire me congratulations on the occasion of the establishment of the Society of Catholic Medical Missionaries. I am very thankful for this courtesy and kindness on your part, although you probably realize as well as myself that the Society is really the work of Doctor Dengel. I am of course deeply interested and have rendered such help as it was possible for me to give. Looking forward to our Board meeting at the end of the month."

Doctor Flagg seemed to be convinced that Michael Mathis and the Holy Cross Congregation had somehow co-opted Anna, who was in the United States under the aegis of the Medical Mission Board and who had been representing them as well as raising money for her own medical mission project. Mathis told Anna that he would confront his colleagues at the annual meeting when the issue of the new Society would be on the agenda.

> "I presume that our next Board meeting will be an interesting one especially in educating some of its members to the canonical rights of societies approved by the Church and governed by canon law. Yet, I do not wish you to feel that I have not a sufficient sense of humor to see that these men mean very well but are becoming involved in a field in which they are not conversant. Your fine judgment saved you from any serious compromise along this line. Be sure that this is only the beginning of the trials and contradictions with which you will be confronted in organizing this great apostolate. You may be sure also of a daily remembrance at the altar during these strenuous days of foundation."

Anna felt the need to meet with the Board member who had originally told her not to come to America. She wanted to hear his views.

> "I returned from Boston this morning. I saw Monsignor McGlinchey yesterday. Dr. Flagg had not told him anything. He was very guarded and said that the whole thing will crystallize out at the Board Meeting when everybody will give their views. I gave him to understand that as far as our Society is concerned things are settled. He said that he would help us; he told me that we want the good will of everybody, so that we must not antagonize anybody."

Michael Mathis responded.

> "It must also be remembered that my good friend Monsignor McGlinchey was the member on the board

who exacted forty percent of your collection for the board. And there is not the least doubt in my mind but that the true reason for any objection whatsoever against your society has come from your services to the medical mission board and the board's reluctance to part with you."

In some final words of advice to Anna, Mathis wrote:

> "As I said before, the time consumed in discussing these things with the board ought to be measured according to the primary interests of your society for the time being, and these are to line up the recruits and to get the money to run the house. As you have well said, everything else is theory and of secondary importance. It is, however, important enough to make us act wisely so as not to antagonize, as Monsignor McGlinchey says, the blessed medical mission board."

Mathis insisted that Anna now turn her attention to the vitally important task at hand, which was getting the new Society up and running before the end of September.

> "Indeed I would spend little time if I were you in trying to get the Medical Mission Board to endorse the Society of Catholic Medical Missionaries. I would use my time rather in landing the funds which are essential to open up shop. Believe me you cannot start too soon. Therefore besides getting some funds on which to function, try also to line up the recruits. Answering mail of applicants with a view to starting at least in September and begging funds, these are in my humble judgment the things that should claim your mind and heart these days. Everything else is secondary."

The chaotic nature of her evolving relationship with the Board was certainly not how Anna wanted to conclude the initial phase of her sojourn in America, but life is what it is, and one has to deal with it. Fortunately, she already had lots of experience in doing just that.

In the days ahead Anna focused on securing one or more candidates, which meant, first of all, being absolutely clear about what kind of society she was inviting others into. She had met with a priest who had extensive mission experience in Puerto Rico and he tried to convince her to reconsider salaried membership. Anna had rejected that option, which signifies a different kind of commitment and organizational relationship, and she was not persuaded to reopen the question again.

> "Father Lynch thinks that there should be a salary basis. I have discussed this with several people since I saw you, but I feel more and more inclined toward going the whole way and only admit such people who intend at least to take up Medical Mission for life and remain in the Society for life, instead of worrying what they are going to do in a few years and when they are old or sick."

Father Mathis concurred.

> "In fact Father Lynch's notion was one I long cherished until I met you. Your experience and your judgment of the spiritual standards essential for sustained and continuous medical mission work in these faraway lands changed my point of view. Our experience in Dacca today on a salary basis still further confirms me in my judgment. The salary basis makes the whole situation far more insecure, from the point of view of mission work, than would be the case if they were members of a society such as you had planned in the Society of Catholic Medical Missionaries."

Working for a salary, even as a missionary, changes the nature of the affiliation. It is more like filling a position than responding to a call. Mathis continued :

> "There isn't the least doubt that it will be easy to get any number of nurses and medical people to go out to India on a salary basis and that it is going to be difficult, especially in the beginning, to secure many

for the Society of Catholic Medical Missionaries. The important question is this: What is the use of sending missionaries in any number to India on a salary basis when they will not be able to do consistent and sustained missionary work? Give me only a few real missionaries of the type you had in mind when you drew up the constitutions of the new society, and I for one will be satisfied with these above any number about whom I would always have the greatest anxiety. Yet, the three year pledge ought not to be overlooked. I would not demand a life service. It may unduly frighten."

There was then a conversation regarding vows. Anna wrote:

"Several experienced nuns told me that there can't be and won't be any stability without vows."

Mathis responded:

"Perhaps what those experienced nuns told you is true, yet I would not be too lightly stampeded into thinking that 'there can't be and won't be any stability without vows.' I freely admit that with vows the stability would be guaranteed. Yet when we realize that the chief purpose of the society is to do a work which by the reason of vows others cannot do in its full scope, and since this work from your own experience is admirably fitted to achieve great things in the conversion of souls, I for one unhesitatingly cast my lot and my interest with a society that is fitted to do the work in question and which the Church can provide for by its canon law. In a word the vows give the greater and guaranteed stability, but who will say that those societies in which vows are not taken are not stable enough to accomplish the end for which they were established."

It was a convincing argument and one with which Anna inherently agreed.

> "The status of the Society is according to Canon Law, a society of women living in community without taking vows. The main idea is to do the work for God only, with the necessary liberty to do it. As an isolated person, as I was, it is very hard. There is no professional companionship. No guarantee for illness, old age, emergencies, etc. Also, we are expected to be missionaries without any spiritual training, whilst it takes nuns 5½ years of *spiritual* training before they have to stand the hardships of the missions. It is intended to give candidates at least *one* year's special medical *missionary* training."

Anna intensified her recruitment efforts while Father Mathis handled other administrative concerns. She told him about the following experience with a potential recruit.

> "When I was out in the Middle West, I wrote to Dr. Lyons. I had been in correspondence with her before. We agreed to meet in Marshall-Fields. She said she would wear a red scarf. I thought if she is so flashy to wear a red scarf, I am sure she isn't interested. To the corner of Marshall Fields is a restaurant. We had dinner there and talked, and talked, and talked, and talked. All of a sudden we look up and the place was empty. The waiters were around us in a semi-circle. We were completely oblivious to everything."

Anna knew that the woman who had just finished her internship was seriously considering her Society when she was told that a family member wanted to check her out. "Dr. Lyons' youngest brother was a Jesuit. He was most kind and he looked me over from A to Z. He was so terribly concerned about his sister, the apple of his eye. I had to go quite a few times." However, "Dr. Lyons didn't say anything definite at all." Later that summer, Anna had this to report.

"I was in a boarding house in Washington. One fine day, must have been in July, who turned up but Dr. Lyons! I was so amazed to see her walk in. Somebody had given her a graduation present to go to Rome. She heard Archbishop Curley was also in Rome. She went to see him. She asked him about this new idea, whether he approved. He said yes. She told me she was going to join the Society."

Anna needed some names in order to strengthen her recruitment efforts and learned that Father Mathis had made another appeal for nurses to go out to India. "He only chose four, but he had the names of many others who had written." He gave those names to Anna, along with a desk at the Bengalese, "so that I could write to all of them." From that pool of potential candidates, two nurses seemed viable: Marie Ulbrich and Evelyn Flieger. Miss Flieger was at a boarding house in New York. She contacted Doctor Dengel.

"She came to see me. She was very, very young. She had beautiful hair – the most beautiful hair I have ever seen in my life. Later on she cut it and I nearly wept. Father Lynch, of the Medical Mission Board, happened to be there. I was supposed to tell her about this new venture. I painted it very black because we had nothing – not even a house. There was nothing except just invite them to come. All of a sudden Father Lynch pulled me [aside]. 'If you tell her all those things she won't join.' Anyhow she became interested. It just shows how Providence works. She was a graduate of Bellevue Hospital in New York. She had heard so many Protestant Doctors and nurses in Bellevue give talks on India. She heard also through Father Mathis and then she became interested. As a result of that she was the first nurse to join the Society."

Miss Flieger was seeking a salaried position, but after hearing the pros and cons outlined by Doctor Dengel, she changed her mind and opted to enter Anna's Society under the terms she had described.

Anna Dengel reported to Michael Mathis that three women had expressed interest in joining her Society. This meant that they could move ahead and solidify their plans

> "You said the two things that matter now are to line up the recruits and to get the forms. Dr. Lyons is returning on the 21ˢᵗ of August. I shall either see her here or ask her to come to Washington. Miss Flieger is more anxious to join a Society like ours than one on a salary basis after all, when I explained things to her. She has to go in for her State exam on September 21ˢᵗ until 23ʳᵈ – after that she is ready any day to come. Miss Devine from Philadelphia is ready and anxious to come any day. She is a technician – and over 35 (I did not know that before) – but I like her, and I think that she will be an all 'round help. She is willing for that. So with three and myself, we can start. If two more should be anxious to come, I think we could take them, but not more for the present."

Michael Mathis sent words of encouragement.

> "Keep up your courage and focus your efforts on recruits and money. Praying sincerely that God will bless you with both in abundance."

There was another nurse who had expressed interest. She had only one concern. After Anna had told Marie Ulbrich they would be wearing "completely lay dress; whatever anybody had," she asked "whether you could have bobbed hair." Miss Ulbrich was from Iowa and had grown up on a farm. She had attended a rural parochial school and an academy in Milwaukee before completing nurse's training at Mercy Hospital in Dubuque. She had felt a call to religious life and was in the process of discerning what community to enter when she saw the announcement from Father Mathis about nurses needed for India. She applied and heard nothing. When the call for nurses went out again, she wrote a second time, and then went on pilgrimage to the Shrine of Saint Anne in Quebec and asked the saint and the mother of Jesus to "arrange it somehow or at least give me a definite assurance of being sent as a medical missionary before December 8 of that year. I considered two years wait long enough. If not I intended joining the Mercy Sisters in Dubuque on that date." She received a letter from Doctor Dengel before the end of July. A Society was being founded. "I again volunteered and was accepted."

A concrete need of the new Society was having a place to live. Mathis had a lead on a house that belonged to the Holy Cross Fathers and was unoccupied at present. He would need their approval to rent it and that meant waiting until the end of summer break. "Don't take the little house – definitely – please – until I am back," Anna told him, and he agreed to wait. Was Anna concerned that Dr. Flagg would see this as yet another tie to the Holy Cross community? But then she reconsidered. "If Rev. Father Paul should commit to give the little house, I think it is better to take it before the meeting of the Board. After all, if we would find something more suitable we are not obliged to take it." Once she returned to Washington, Anna was completely absorbed in securing a suitable residence for her Society. Its first member was about to arrive. She wrote in her journal:

> "Dr. Lyons had to go back to Chicago. She was the youngest of fourteen children. She stayed with her mother a long time to look after her. That made her a little older, besides all her studies. She is just six months younger than I. She had various things at home, such as linens; she was the last of the family. She decided to come back as soon as she could. I went to the station to meet her in Washington. I saw something walking along. It was all bundles. You couldn't see the person – it was Dr. Lyons."

Meanwhile, Michael Mathis was actively engaged in promoting the new Society in a variety of ways. To Anna he wrote: "I am enclosing a copy of the proof of your leaflet. Tell me what you think of it, though as it is being run off it will be impossible to make any change." In addition to leaflets that were in the process of being printed, Mathis had published an article in the Holy Cross magazine, *The Bengalese*. He also began sending personal letters to individual friends and benefactors requesting their support.

"I am taking the liberty of introducing to you one of my best friends and a woman who has done great things for the Church and one who is now associated with me in organizing a Society of Catholic Medical Missionaries.

"I have already sent to India, as you have probably seen in *The Bengalese*, four nurses last fall, but they need a regular society of lay medical missionaries to take care of them and to prepare others to help them in the field. We have many volunteers. The new society has already been approved by the Archbishop of Baltimore and we shall begin early in September in the City of Washington close to Bengalese headquarters.

"Dr. Anna Dengel was born in Austria, made her medical studies in Ireland, and for three and a half years labored in India as a pioneer medical missionary. Dr. Dengel will organize this new society under our auspices."

The publicity announcing this new endeavor was filled with mixed messages and fundamentally inaccurate. Whether intentional or unintentional, this letter and subsequent public relations initiatives by Michael Mathis began to blur the distinction between whose Society this really was. Hers? His? Theirs? In time the resulting ambiguity would take on a life of its own.

Be optimistic no matter what comes.

We don't have to be afraid.

We are in God's hands.

Anna Dengel

Chapter Nine

The long-awaited Society of Catholic Medical Missionaries came into existence on a Saturday morning in 1925. The house journal that would chronicle the development of this pioneering initiative recorded the milestone moment.

> "September 5th - This morning Dr. Dengel signed a lease of thirteen months upon a house at 1000 Newton St. N.E., Washington, D.C. Late this afternoon Dr. Anna Dengel and Dr. Joanna Lyons together took possession of this house. Cots, tables, and chairs were lent by the Holy Cross Foreign Mission Seminary. The Holy Cross Fathers, Seminarians and Sisters have been most kind to us in our work of finding a house and settling down. The monthly rental of the house is $100. Rent begins on September 15th and payment was made today for the month September 15-October 15."

On the following day Doctor Dengel and Doctor Lyons attended Mass at the Holy Cross Foreign Mission Seminary.

> "Mass was said by Rev. James P. Kehoe, who requested all present to offer their Mass and Holy Communion for the success of the new Catholic Medical Mission Society."

The Holy Cross Sisters, priests, and seminarians helped Anna to get settled.

"Sister Patricia, Superior of the Holy Cross Sisters, was very, very nice, wonderful – she was Irish, very tall, very kind, and capable. There was a Father Kehoe who was also very kind. They helped me to find a house…. It was totally empty; there was only a broom in the basement. By then, of course, Dr. Lyons brought her suitcases. She had suitcases and linens. The Bengalese gave us a card table. Dr. Lyons had gone up to St. Joseph's in Montreal and she brought our statue of St. Joseph, and she put that on the card table. That was really our first possession."

On Monday, Labor Day, Anna and Joanna Lyons again went to Mass at the Holy Cross Seminary, and then spent the rest of the holiday writing. Tuesday, September 8, they visited some people, bought several household items, and celebrated two significant events: "Our first meal in the new house;" and, as they wrote in the journal, "we also started Community life – prayer together." Anna could hardly wait to share the good news of the new foundation with Monsignor Winkley.

"Our little Society is beginning to settle down. By the end of this month, five of us will begin definitely. So far Providence has paved the way for us, and although we are very poor to begin with, we ventured to take a house; and another young doctor from Chicago and myself are very busy settling it for the others. We are starting with five; several more have applied. I myself feel very, very happy that I have found my real vocation, and if Our Lord blesses our work, I shall not mind any difficulties or rebuffs."

On the day that Anna announced the formal beginning of community life in the new Society, she received a letter from Father William White that included the following words of affirmation.

"I sincerely trust that all will go well and that a new era has dawned for The Medical Missions. I am more than grateful to hear the news that you have found a Confessor to guide you, for I think such is necessary. As

150

I said on a former occasion, there is nothing I dare add
to the wise counsels of your directors, for if I end where
they began I shall consider myself blessed."

That first week was a busy one for Anna. She attended the Catholic
Charities Conference at Catholic University; spent time with Mrs.
Muir, one of her earliest supporters, who was in town for the conference;
entertained Father Mathis and Father Goodall one evening as they paid
a formal visit to the new foundation; and then met with Father Mathis
again to plan a fund-raising campaign under the patronage of the Little
Flower. There was correspondence to sort and to answer while visitors
came in and out of the house. A woman donated a sewing machine via
the Holy Cross Sisters; a Doctor Long promised a camera with a cinema
attachment; and a Mr. Simpson wrote about the new foundation in
the *Evening Bulletin*. Meanwhile, Doctor Lyons took care of essential
business and other details, which included getting a license and keeping
the daily journal. On Sunday, September 12, they spent the day at
the Sacred Heart Convent with Father Mathis and Mrs. Muir, where,
Anna said, "the Mothers were most interested and kind and are going
to find friends for us." That evening they went to see a movie at the
Holy Cross Seminary. Afterwards a "big storm came up," impressive
enough to warrant a mention in their journal, along with Anna's sense
of satisfaction for being led at this time to this place.

> "People in the U.S.A. are very kind and generous and as
> far as I can see, it is the best place to start our Society."

Having shared this in a lengthy letter to Monsignor Winkley, Anna
then proceeded to tell him about her most recent interaction with the
Medical Mission Board.

> "On the 29th and 30th of August, the annual Conference
> of the Medical Mission Board was held. Monsignor
> McGlinchey of Boston, Rev. F. Thill of the Students
> Mission Crusade, and Dr. Flagg presided. It was a most
> representative gathering: several Provincials of religious
> orders and missionaries from the field, chiefly China
> and Africa; also from religious communities of Sisters –
> the F.M.M. included. The conclusion that Medical

Missions are very important and even necessary was unanimous, so much so that the affiliation with the Propagation of the Faith was discussed. After quite a lot of talk and consideration, it was decided to put the question up to Monsignor Quinn, national director of the Propagation of the Faith in the U.S.A. He not only consented but became a member of the Executive Board and treasurer. Monsignor Quinn is very much in favor of our little Society and has promised to help us, so I am very glad that this step has been taken."

Anna elaborated on the status of the money that had been designated for the Punjab.

"I asked the Secretary of the Medical Mission Board to settle the accounts and to send you the money as soon as possible. In Philadelphia I received over $10,000 so that will all go to Pindi anyhow, perhaps more. Would that be enough to start a place for the nuns and one or two doctors and a nurse?"

Anna's question led directly to one more matter of concern. What role would her Society play in the Punjab of the future? Where would the proposed new hospital be located? What were the chances that this ongoing dream would be actualized anytime soon? She needed to be able to tell aspiring candidates where in India they might be missioned and approximately when this might occur. Although she had already raised these concerns a number of times before, she now needed some definitive answers.

"Just for the sake of my own satisfaction I would like to tell you my ideas once more: 1) Perhaps you would like to build the hospital in another place. 2) St. Catherine's will always be useful, but as it is, it will not develop into a first class hospital. There is no space. The locality would not matter so much, because if it were really first class, people would come no matter where it is. For a good hospital there must be at least two doctors and trained nuns or nurses. The building is not as important as the staff. If the nuns think that there is not room for two hospitals – (I mean Catholic) – and if they wish to let the Civil Hospital or a Protestant mission develop a good maternity and infant welfare place in the City, then I would much prefer if you would start the new hospital in Peshawar or some good village district. I can say in all sincerity, that all we want is a good field and no antagonism – against Catholics – least of all the F.M.M. Only please let me know so that we can make our plans."

Anna had already told Monsignor Winkley: "I am absolutely ready to do whatever you and the nuns think best."

The new Society had barely begun and its founder was already focusing on the future. How else to prepare candidates for the missions? They had to know where they were going and what they were going to do.

"During this one year of preparation the Candidates will get spiritual and missionary training and begin to learn the language. In the Medical line this is absolutely essential. I wasted a lot of time in the beginning not having an idea of Hindustani. If a place is ready for us (somewhere) in the Punjab by next October - we intend sending *the very first* unit there and the second to the Holy Cross Fathers in Bengal. Two other Missionary Societies have already asked us to supply them with Medical Missionaries. We also intend to do village work, train native girls as nurses, and concentrate on maternity and infant welfare work. I shall be very grateful, dear Monsignor, if you will tell me what your plans are, so that we can prepare accordingly, both as regards staff and financial aid."

Anna was very pleased to receive a letter from Pauline Willis, who had made it possible for her to come to America, and subsequently, to stay.

"My thoughts were very much with you on the 8th and I offered my Holy Communion for you and the new

Society. God prosper it is my current wish, for it has a great work before it. How beautiful to start with five, in memory of the five Sacred Wounds."

She could not resist making several suggestions.

"Have you ever thought of calling it a *'Guild'* of Medical Missionaries, à la old time Catholic guilds of the past? This would show it was not in any sense a religious order with vows ... the name Guild might attract more to it."

Her next suggestion was also preceded by a question.

"Must all train in America? It costs so much to get there, as much almost as the passage to a mission, and is that not money wasted? Can't you have a center here – in Ireland ... to attract Irish doctors, and why not at Cork? Could not Miss Ryan help you arrange for the necessary lectures and some convent there to house you?"

Anna's second full week in community with Joanna Lyons began with another major storm that kept them housebound most of the day. Monday, Feast of the Exaltation of the Holy Cross, was celebrated with High Mass at the Holy Cross Seminary and a meal with the Holy Cross Sisters. Their journal says they arrived "late for dinner because we were lost in the woods," and that they attended the closing session of the Catholic Charities Conference afterwards in order to hear the keynote speaker, Cardinal Hayes. The next day, the Feast of Our Lady of Sorrows, marked another rite of passage. "Began our religious services today." Just the two of them, neither one with any experience in the area of rites and rituals; but they knew that where two – and soon, many more – were gathered, the spirit of Jesus, the spirit of God, would be there with them and within them. Later that day they met Father McCarthy, superior of St. Columban's Seminary, and afterward, began cleaning up the house.

Cleaning was a priority throughout the rest of the week. All day Wednesday, all day Thursday, they swept and scrubbed and polished, and on Friday spent the day painting beds and washing windows.

Father Mathis and Father Kehoe dropped in to see them. The telephone was installed. Mid-week Anna set aside some time to reflect on the enormous step about to be taken. On September 23, according to the wording of the directive in the Constitutions of the new Society, she put into writing the commitment she was making, all the while knowing that for her it would not be for three years but forever.

On Saturday Anna and Dr. Lyons went to Sacred Heart Convent "to see the altar that is being given to us. It was made by one of the Mothers and was used at the convent at its foundation as well as for some time after." They were also given a lamp and some other things. The altar arrived at 1000 Newton Street later that afternoon. On Sunday, Mass at Holy Cross Seminary was followed by dinner with the Holy Cross Sisters. Then it was back to cleaning the house on Monday, Tuesday, Wednesday, and Thursday – for a whole lot had to be done in order to be ready for the big event on September 30, when the Society would be formally and publicly constituted. Here is the journal entry for Saturday, September 26.

> "We are getting the Chapel ready. Mr. Rick of the Foreign Mission Seminary is here making a platform for in front of the altar. Sister Patricia and Sister Olga came this afternoon and all together we worked on the lining of the tabernacle – white satin. Our five names – the five who are beginning the society are written on the cardboard back of the lining."

A box of linens from Sacred Heart Convent arrived at the house and then Anna and Joanna Lyons did a little shopping before welcoming Miss Evelyn Flieger, a nurse, who arrived from New York in the afternoon, and Miss Marie Ulbrich, also a nurse, from Dubuque, Iowa, in the evening. The chronicle records the moment marking the realization of Anna's dream:

> "Dr Joanna Lyons, Miss Evelyn Flieger, R.N. and Miss Marie Ulbrich, R.N. joined Dr. Anna Dengel, who had nothing to offer them except an opportunity to embrace a life of service and sacrifice to God as medical missionaries. The house and purse were empty to begin with, but good friends in many quarters stood by us.

Those first friends made an indelible impression on our hearts and will be gratefully remembered all the days of the Society."

The next day, Sunday, early Mass at the parish Church of Saint Anthony was followed by High Mass at the National Shrine of the Immaculate Conception, a celebration that marked the formal opening of Catholic University. The rest of the day was spent sightseeing and running errands. On Monday, it was all hands on deck in order to finish cleaning the house. Tuesday was spent "giving the finalizing touches to the house and chapel. In the evening Father Mathis came and gave us a little conference and Miss Joan Devine, a lab technician, arrived from Philadelphia. Father Mathis mentioned the ecclesiastical appointments for our society." All were members of the Congregation of the Holy Cross.

Ecclesiastical Superior	Father Michael Mathis
Chaplain	Father Francis Goodall
Confessor	Father Francis McBride
Extraordinary Confessor	Father Louis Kelly

Wednesday, September 30: "Our opening day." All were up at 5:00 a.m. to attend Mass at St. Anthony's parish. Monsignor C. F. Thomas of St. Patrick's, who was the Archbishop's representative to all religious societies of women under his jurisdiction, blessed the house before Mass. A friend of Father Mathis, he had been consulted during the process of formulating the Society's Constitutions and had appointed the two Holy Cross priests to be the community's confessors.

Solemn High Mass began at 10:00 a.m. It was the first Mass in the new house. The Celebrant was Father Louis Kelly, superior of the Holy Cross College. Father Mathis was the Deacon and he gave the sermon. Father Goodall was Master of Ceremonies. A subdeacon and acolytes, candles and incense, and the singing of the Holy Cross choir added solemnity and beauty to the liturgical ritual, transforming its simple setting into a sacred space. Present at the Mass on Opening Day were Doctor Anna Dengel, Doctor Joanna Lyons, Miss Evelyn Flieger, Miss Marie Ulbrich, Miss Joan Devine and a number of visitors, among them, members of the Mathis Club. After Mass visitors toured the house and conversed with one another. Pictures were taken for publicity purposes and coffee, cakes, and sandwiches were served.

> "We thought heaps of people would come. We made endless sandwiches. We had some cocoa drink. Anyhow it all went off quite nicely. But after, when they were all dispersed, we were left alone and we had sandwiches for quite a while."

At the end of the day Anna Dengel noted in the journal: "The Blessed Sacrament is now reserved in our house." She also took time to write down her thoughts on this significant occasion.

> "The responsibility and the vastness of the undertaking came before one, on the one hand; on the other, God's Providence and His Holy Will. The day was the day when the Little Flower, less than a half century ago, went to her heavenly home.
> "It was the feast day of St. Jerome. The Gospel of the day is: 'You are the salt of the earth: but if salt lose its savor, wherewith shall it be salted?' What better Gospel message could we receive on the foundation day of our venture for God and the spread of His Kingdom? May God grant us to be a little of His salt...chiefly by our personal holiness and example... This is our vocation: may Christ live within us; then let Him shine forth.
> "The 'Magnificat' was sung after the High Mass by the choir as the Society is dedicated to Our Lady under the Title '*Causa Nostrae Laetitiae*.' Our redemption, our joy has come through her. Mary, Cause of Our Joy, above all look down on the millions and millions of pagan women!"

Yet another affirmative sign for Anna was the second part of the Gospel for Foundation Day as recorded in Matthew, chapter five, and read aloud at Mass.

> "You are the light of the world. A city set on a hill cannot be hidden; nor does anyone light a lamp and

put it under a basket, but on the lampstand, and it gives light to all in the house. In the same way, let your light shine before others, so that they may see your good works and give glory to God."

One could not ask for more: words of grace, words of encouragement for all that lay ahead. "Salt of the earth" … "Light of the world." Yes, the impossible will be made possible with the help of the woman who gave birth to Jesus and is thereby "Cause of our Joy."

It may have been around this time that Anna Dengel formulated her "Prayer for Our Society." It was written in pencil, in a tablet, as if it had suddenly tumbled forth and come straight from the heart.

We beseech Thee, O Lord –
through the intercession of the Blessed Virgin –
conceived without sin –
to preserve Thy family from all harm.
Extend Thy loving protection over it.
Enlighten and direct every member.
Inspire in all members
the spirit of poverty, chastity, and obedience –
charity, gentleness, simplicity, and unselfishness,
and perseverance.
Grant us to love Thee with our whole heart
and our whole soul
and our neighbor as ourselves.
Give us true sisterly love for each other.
Bless and protect our parents,
brothers and sisters and other relatives –
our friends and benefactors –
both spiritual and temporal.

A new community has to suck out from the
Gospel the elements of its specific *raison
d'etre*: its specific way to glorify God.
'So let your light shine'
sums up our whole purpose, our ultimate aims.
Our love and devotion,
coupled with knowledge and skills,
are the light;
serving the sick in the missions,
the good works that glorify God.

Anna Dengel

CHAPTER TEN

The first day of October marked a dramatic shift in focus for Anna and her cadre of pioneers. The aura of anticipation that had permeated the house on Newton Street was replaced by a shared determination to do whatever was necessary to ensure that this new and untested initiative would soon be fully functioning.

> "The work of the year, namely, the spiritual formation of the candidates for missionary life, started without delay. Rev. Francis P. Goodall, c.s.c., initiated us in the exercises and practices of the spiritual and community life, and he acted as our chaplain. Rev. Father Mathis provided us with instruction in religious and missionary subjects. As our first field of labor was to be in the Punjab, in northern India, Hindustani became essential. The 'missionaries to be' worked earnestly at the melodious main tongue of the 'land of the five rivers.' Last to be mentioned, but by no means the least in importance, is the missionary's training to put hand and mind willingly and cheerfully into anything she may be called upon to do. This is the test of the caliber of the missionary. The care of the sacristy and chapel, cooking, general housework, keeping accounts, secretarial work, photography, dressmaking and miscellaneous jobs – all are necessary to 'carry on.'"

Despite the seriousness of their call and the need to which they were inexplicably drawn, those pioneering women had the ability not to take themselves too seriously. Among Foundation Day memories is the following recalled by Anna at a later time:

"I must tell you we had one more candidate in the beginning. She was a Technician. She stayed only a few days because she just couldn't eat those sandwiches. It was a test of her vocation. That is really true. I always felt very sorry for her. She was a very nice person. She was one of the first but we never count her. She only stayed for a few days. She had died since. She must laugh in heaven."

Anna enjoyed reminiscing about their pioneering days. Humorous moments were frequent. She would say:

"Laughing is said to be conducive to health. If that is the case, we laid up a large store of that precious gift in our first year of medical mission pioneering.

"Sr. Agnes Marie was a good cook and so was Dr. Lyons. I was dispensed from cooking because of more urgent duties. Sr. Agnes Marie and I were on the laundry. Then eventually Sr. Laetitia's turn for the kitchen came. She couldn't cook. She made bread pudding. Every day we had bread pudding – mountains of bread pudding – awful. The conversation at the meal was how wonderful it was."

Paying the bills was a perennial concern.

"We were very, very poor. Dr. Lyons had a little money. She paid the rent of the house. It was especially expensive – one hundred dollars, a month. The house was terribly cold because we had no insulation; it had no weather stripping. It had big spaces under the doors and the wind would blow and we would put newspaper there. We had no rugs. In the winter time we frequently had class in the kitchen. We lit the gas in the oven and opened the door to get warm."

Nevertheless, through all of the ups and downs, a sense of humor prevailed. Years later she would say:

> "I stress especially a sense of humor for missionaries. If
> you don't have one, life would become so stiff and so
> hard and serious. If you see the funny side, it helps."

She was able to do that time and time again.

> "Many funny things happened. That is actually,
> positively true. The first six months, I tell you we
> laughed... We laughed and laughed and laughed,
> because there were so many funny situations. We took
> the work in turns. Dr. Lyons could type, which was
> wonderful and Sr. Agnes Marie could cook; so could
> Dr. Lyons. Sr. Agnes Marie was a good housekeeper. If
> nobody was a good housekeeper, that would have been
> dreadful. I went out to give talks and people helped us.
> I was out a lot. Anyhow, it worked very nicely."

Doctor Dengel continued to reflect on the cross-cultural implications of
this new and unfamiliar way of living a dedicated life. She knew from
experience that beneficial practices within western society were often
counter-productive in a different cultural context. Her handwritten
notes from those early days state:

> "The order of the day as set down is provisional; as a
> matter of fact, the present order of the day is different.
> Even this only applies to the year of preparation.
> In the mission field – work, climate, convenience,
> circumstances will dictate the order of the day. In
> the East, one cannot work as hard as in Europe and
> the U.S.A. No advice will convince people of this.
> Everybody has to learn it by experience."

As Anna was bringing her Society into being on behalf of the women
whose physical needs were a burden on her heart, Monsignor Winkley
was preparing a place in Rawalpindi for Anna and her community to
serve. Here is a copy of the letter he sent to her. Dated September 28, it
arrived shortly after the formal founding of the Society and reflects his
wholehearted support and appreciation for Anna and her new initiative.

"May our good God strengthen, bless, and prosper you in your new and great undertaking. This is my sincere wish and daily prayer, for I know that you are fully convinced that you are doing His Holy Will. I assure you, Doctor Dengel, I have always relied on you, and I have ever been confident that you would be faithful to us and the Punjab Mission. I like your idea that the Society should be international. America is a cosmopolitan place and Missionary enthusiasm, especially Medical, promises, I gather, good results. The principles on which you wish to establish the Medical Mission Society are very good and practical. May God bless and prosper it."

Anna was jubilant on receiving such unconditional affirmation from her superior, mentor, and friend. It meant the world to her that he understood where she was coming from and supported her desire to respond to the suffering of women and children anywhere in the world; that he knew the Rawalpindi region and the Punjabi people would always hold a special place in her heart and that she would do whatever she could to respond to the overwhelming need that had sent her in search of resources to address it more effectively. Monsignor Winkley's letter had also included his own plans for Rawalpindi.

"I think you have done wonderfully well in collecting (under the circumstances) so much as you have done. I perfectly agree with you that the Hospital should be up to date – efficient and for this, as you say, trained people are necessary. Now first let me tell you that the site for the Hospital has been purchased. It is the plot of land that you saw and approved of – the only suitable site near the City, as you know. It has cost a big sum. I have paid over $30,000 for it. Well, you know I have not the money (about $50,000) required to build the Hospital. If you get the $50,000 to build the Hospital, we shall not quarrel whether the Hospital will belong to the Punjab Mission or to the new Medical Mission Society. I am out, as you are, to do good to these people for God."

Monsignor Winkley continues to respond in detail to the points Anna had raised in her letter.

> "I wish your Society to have charge of the Hospital and also to be responsible for the upkeep of it. The Franciscan Nuns will do the nursing. Mother Provincial (Alberte) promises to give two or more trained Nuns, and she is willing for other Nuns to be trained. She agrees to your proposal that the Nuns should receive an allowance such as they receive in Government Hospitals here in India. She feels confident that Mother General will agree to our proposals regarding the Nuns. I and Mother Alberta see your point that the Nuns must be trained – the Hospital cannot be efficient otherwise, and it is an efficient Hospital that is needed and not any other."

The Prefect Apostolic of Kafristan and Kashmir also wrote to the Mother General of the Franciscan Missionaries of Mary in Rome that same week.

> "We propose to build an efficient, up to date, Hospital in Rawalpindi City. The land has been already purchased for it. Will you kindly supply us with Nuns to do the Nursing? It will be necessary that some of them should be trained Nurses, and others could be trained in the Hospital later on. Dr. Dengel is collecting in America money for building the Hospital, and the Medical Mission Society, which is being formed in America, will undertake the upkeep of the Hospital. It is proposed to give the Nuns such allowances as they receive in other Hospitals. The Nuns will receive such spiritual help as they have at St. Catherine's."

This was precisely what Anna had hoped for. He went on to describe part two of her proposal for the region.

> "I have thought for some time that it would be good to have a new Ward built near St. Catherine's Hospital

for Indian and Anglo-Indian women and children, as the accommodation in St. Catherine's Hospital is insufficient. I would like, of course, the Nuns to take charge of this Ward, as they have of the Hospital. If you approve of this addition to St. Catherine's, I shall commence to gather the means for the erection of this Ward without delay."

Anna did indeed approve. What she had envisioned for Rawalpindi had suddenly been set in motion. Now that an overall plan was in place for her Society's first mission assignments, full attention could be given to the many issues associated with establishing a permanent base for potential candidates here at home. She would spend the rest of the year settling into this new way of being in the world yet not really part of it, wrestling with pressing responsibilities, such as, how to financially support her community and at the same time seek funding for its mission in India.

Father Mathis, on the other hand, focused on informing ecclesiastical authorities and other religious and secular agencies of the new entity in town. His first letters went to Bishop Thomas Shahan, Rector of Catholic University, and Archbishop Michael Curley, informing them of the new foundation within the Archdiocese of Baltimore. He had to retool his public relations capacities in order to make the cause more widely known because of the ban on fund-raising within the Archdiocese. Prevented from initiating a full-fledged campaign, he had to turn to personal correspondence and word of mouth to promote the new Society's medical mission.

In November Anna received a letter from Mother Alberte, her FMM friend in Rawalpindi. "How happy I am that your work is now firmly established – may Our Lord bless it. You know, my dear Anna, that you have my whole sympathy and most earnest prayers – and later on whatever help I am able to give you." Then she brought up an issue that had remained unresolved, one that she knew had wounded Anna.

"I was very grieved to learn that our name had been used in disapproval of Monsignor's and your plans for the city. Surely you, my dear Anna, knowing us as you do, could not believe such a thing – believe that we could ever dream of a divided kingdom! It was wicked to put down as coming from us what was in other people's mind. You no doubt have been hurt like Monsignor. I want to repeat what I have always thought and said. If God wills it – we shall be happy to work for you and with you – giving your Society our best. You know how I have always deplored the fact that there were so few capable nurses. I know that only those who fear to lose by it will object to a good hospital being started. There could be no question of our taking the financial side of the hospital. St. Catherine's is proof that things go slowly when so much begging has to be done. No, dear Anna, keep the cares of the rupees. If Mother General can help, I know she will."

Mother Alberte concludes with some reassuring words with regard to their relationship.

"I have kept your 'confidences' so jealously and it has often made me boil a little to hear that things that I so scrupulously guarded were known in quarters where they should not have been. The greatest gossipers were not in the Convent – but that does not matter – we can afford to let people talk if there are no misunderstandings between ourselves."

The next day a congratulatory letter arrived from Father William White. Anna's Rawalpindi confessor wrote: "I cannot say how glad I was to realize that you have now started in real earnest. It will be a consolation to me to think that God used me for this purpose, though in such a peculiar way." The following week Anna wrote to Cardinal Dougherty in Philadelphia to thank him again for his support of the Medical Mission Cause and to once again share her concern about vows.

"The subject of vows in our Society is so important and so complicated. We are studying the problem broached by your Eminence under the following headings:
1. To carry out the work which we have set for ourselves in the Society of Catholic Medical Missionaries, we

must be able to practice the medical profession in its full scope.

2. Is there anything in the practice of medicine, surgery, obstetrics, gynecology, medical jurisprudence, teaching of medical subjects which would in any way be against any of the three vows?

3. Advantages of vows in a Society like ours.

4. Possible disadvantages.

5. Why has Rome so far never allowed persons who make public vows to practice the medical profession in its full scope?

"Our constitutions were made on the supposition that Rome does not allow persons who take public vows to practice medicine in its full scope, with a hope, however, that after some years it might be granted, when we have had a chance to prove ourselves and to others that it is possible to practice medicine in its full scope and keep the vows.

"To sum up, I look on it like this. We must be free to practice every branch of the medical profession, in order to help the people of the East in every medical need – so as not to be hindered in any way, we sacrifice the privilege of making public vows at present: the sooner, however, it is granted, the happier we will be individually and the Society on a much safer basis."

The Cardinal responded by return mail.

"The question of religious vows for your proposed Society was taken up by me in Rome more or less informally, because of the conversation held here in my house, in which you expressed an opinion that it would be easier to find subjects for your work, and also easier to hold the Society together if the members were permitted to take vows. If upon further consideration, you think it possible to establish and hold together your Society without vows, of course, this will simplify matters."

There were many things to attend to before the end of the year. In mid-November, Robert Sargent Shriver of First National in Baltimore, a prominent Catholic layman who had been asked by Father Mathis to handle the documentation for an extension of Anna Dengel's stay in America, wrote to say that "The bureau here advises that Dr. Dengel's Bond left here for Ellis Island November 17th, so everything now must be in good order." Decades later Anna made the notation that "Mr. Shriver went bail for me when there was question of renewing my permit to stay in the U.S.A."

Monsignor Winkley wrote again saying he had not yet received any money from the Medical Mission Board. As for the Hospital in Rawalpindi, he made this request.

> "I should like you to send me a plan of what you think should be built. You know better than I do what would be required for a Medical Hospital. As you say, it would be so nice and satisfactory if we could meet and have a talk over matters, but since this can't be, we must do the best we can by writing. There is one great thing we know: we are both of the same mind and are ready to help one another in the great work which our good God has called us to do. I was very pleased to learn that you are much better in health, and that you also feel so happy in work. I shall ever remember you and the Society at the Altar in the Holy Sacrifice, that our good God may bless you all and that He may grant you special assistance to carry out the great work for which He has chosen you."

Another missionary colleague wrote to Anna before November came to a close. Father John Mullan, parish priest in Rawalpindi, was on leave and visiting the USA after recovering from a nervous breakdown. His enthusiastic report on his visit to Philadelphia notes the impact of Anna's visits there and his appreciation for her gifts and dedicated service.

> "I called on the Cardinal and was granted an audience. It all turned on you and on your work past and future. His Eminence said: 'Tell Dr. Dengel she can count

on my help and sympathy in the good work she has undertaken.' I called on Dr. McKay who was full of inquiries about you. In Mater Misericordia Hospital I went to see the Monsignor. We chatted more than an hour about you and your work and on 100 other topics. You can count on him helping you in your work, even in your absence. Mr. William Simpson would use his great influence to promote your work. Mother Dimmann has a great admiration for you and it is well, for she has great influence and will, if occasion arises, wield it all in your cause. Keep all these good friends and make as many more as you can. In India, you could not make as many in a lifetime."

He added in conclusion:

"While I am on this side just think out anything I may do for you when I reach the other side, especially India. You can count on me supporting you in every way, and if you want to consult me on anything, you can do so confidently. My kindest wishes to you and your three co-workers, your earliest disciples. I shall pray for you and them and for the cause, which you have made your own, that God may bless and cherish it."

In December Michael Mathis, as chaplain of the Catholic Medical Mission House, wrote a formal letter accepting the generous donation of a Christmas Crib with Figures to be imported from Austria. Most likely it was a gift from the Dengel family and it was designated to become the permanent property of the community Chapel. It still is.

On New Year's Eve, a Day of Recollection, Anna had much to be grateful for. She penned this prayer in her journal.

"My dear Lord – I feel very dry and distracted today – and I would particularly like to thank you with all my heart for the graces and blessings received in the last year – above all to have made it possible for me to live and work in Your house and service for my whole life now. You have granted my wishes beyond expectation.

I am very especially grateful to you for having given me such good first companions – making them and me so happy. And you have watched over us – given us food for our souls and our bodies – without any effort on our part. I am also grateful for the many friends you have given to me and to the Medical Mission Cause this last year. Dear Lord, make me grateful for everything. In the coming year I will live only for You and use my time only in Your Service. Special resolutions: to be tidy – a real effort to me; to examine myself every evening. I want to make progress in my two life resolutions, which I have 16 years before me already and have made no real efforts yet. So much depends on them. My Jesus, my dear Mother Mary – help me very specially with these three resolutions. My Angel Guardian, remind me often and help me."

The great thing is to look forward.
What I think is so wonderful
and such a consolation
is that we can always
begin again.

Anna Dengel

CHAPTER ELEVEN

Anna had a lot to think about as a new year dawned, bringing with it responsibilities beyond her lived experience. Many unanswered questions tugged at the heart of her pioneering call. Of primary concern to her now was the nature and status of membership in her Society. She and three other women would soon be asked by the institutional Church to formally commit to a way of life that was still very much in flux. As she attended to other pressing needs, Anna compiled a list of priority concerns that required further reflection.

"Does Canon Law state that religious with simple vows are not allowed to do obstetrical work?

Some religious communities are allowed to do obstetrical work – others are strictly forbidden. Do the former obtain it by special dispensation from Rome or because it is originally in their Constitution?

What is the attitude of the Church toward the problem of:
a) Sisters doing obstetrical work
b) nursing the sick whether men, women, or children without distinction of malady
c) staying day or night alone without a companion in a patient's house
d) reading

Constitutions are fundamental regulations of a Society or the order on which a Society is built.

Rules mean a particular reputation, i.e. history, etc.

According to Canon 538, a vocation requires:

(1) no impediments (2) right intention (3) fitness

Explain these points briefly.

> With a Promise, a dispensation is granted more easily
> than with Vows.

Issues that required serious deliberation were sometimes accompanied by an inspirational reminder.

"The interior life will be just what one's watchfulness of heart is.
What would Jesus ask of me this moment?
It becomes easier through Mary."

Occasionally, especially when on retreat, Anna would scribble a prayer at the beginning, or the end, or even in the middle of some concern with which she was struggling, like the following found in a notebook dating back to those early days.

> "Eternal Spirit of God —
> I adore the brightness of Thy purity —
> the unending keenness of Thy justice —
> and the Might of Thy love.
> In Thee I live and move and am.
> Grant that I may always listen to Thy voice
> and watch for Thy light
> and follow Thy precious inspiration.
> I give myself to Thee and ask Thee
> to watch over me in my weakness."

While Anna was wrestling with the deeper issues of meaning and accountability affected by the canonical requirements of the institutional Church, Michael Mathis was introducing the public to his understanding of this pioneering venture. What distinguished his approach from Anna's may be described in this way.

Michael Mathis, an ordained priest and theologian with a doctoral degree, was a member of the Holy Cross Congregation. As director of their Foreign Mission Seminary in Washington, DC, he taught mission theory to the seminarians prior to their assignment to the Bengal region in India. He was aware of the need for women doctors and nurses in the mission field and knew that Anna Dengel's experimental initiative in which he was participating, if it succeeded, would be an historical first within the institutional Church. Because his own experience was shaped by canonical expectations and ecclesiastical Tradition, his approach to preparing women candidates for mission in the new Society proceeded along lines similar to preparing his seminarians. Content in the classroom reflected the best of traditional and essentially male theory and practice, for at that time there was no understanding that preparing a community of women for mission might differ from that of men. As time went on Mathis envisioned a more traditional religious community that one day would be able to practice medicine without reservation, essentially, a less rigid order of nuns. He began to set this in motion within Anna's community right from the beginning. Early on, the year of mission preparation resembled a year of novitiate with many of the expectations that the canonical word implies.

Anna, on the other hand, envisioned a new way of being in mission, one rooted in a life of dedication in the spirit of religious communities with vows but with more flexibility and freedom. A degree of independence was sine qua non in order to function on a par with peers in the medical professions and to competently address devastating need with integrity. Members had to be fully qualified as doctors, nurses, technicians, or in some other relevant area within the field of medicine and be free to do what needed to be done at any time, for anyone, anywhere. Members of her Society were to practice the full scope of medicine unencumbered by archaic regulations while living in community and cultivating a spiritual life. This model had the potential for canonical recognition, either as religious with vows should canon law change in the future, or as a society of dedicated women approved by the Church. Because canon law forbid nuns to practice medicine in its full scope as Anna's Society was emerging, her desire to be in community and in mission while practicing medicine unrestricted within Catholic Tradition was a viable alternative while awaiting systemic change.

At the heart of both visions was the determination to work tirelessly for a change in canon law to allow the full practice of medicine by those who publicly professed the religious vows of poverty, chastity, and obedience. How the community would finally define itself would be determined at that time. While awaiting change Michael Mathis wanted to ensure that the women in mission with Anna were canonically prepared to make religious vows immediately after Papal approval, so that the Society of Catholic Medical Missionaries, in which he would become more and more involved, would be the first to do so within the Catholic Church. Anna was ambivalent. At times she leaned toward a less rigidly defined identity, but with the stability of vows; at other times she was open to the possibility of evolving into something more. However, she was persistent with regard to canonical recognition and adamant that at the present time the Society she had founded, because of the primacy of its mission, was not a congregation of nuns.

Congratulatory messages continued to arrive as word of Anna's foundation spread on both sides of the Atlantic. One letter, however, was sharply critical of certain aspects of the new Society. It came from a well-known and widely respected veteran missionary doctor and was addressed to Father Mathis. Born into a mission-oriented Episcopalian family in Edinburgh in 1867, Doctor Margaret Lamont had spent most of her life in the mission field, accepting government medical posts wherever her husband was stationed – in Sudan, New Zealand, China, Africa, and in India, which captured her heart. She became a convert and through the years met or was in correspondence with some of the early pioneers of medical missions in the Catholic Church. Agnes McLaren was among them. Dr. Lamont championed the cause of women doctors, especially in India, which resulted in an audience with Pope Benedict in 1920. She wrote articles and a small book that proposed the foundation of a society comprised of three concentric circles devoted to medical missions and dedicated to *Alma Redemptoris Mater*, a Marian title dear to her heart. In her letter Dr. Lamont accused Anna of having used that model for her own foundation and of replacing her beloved Marian image with her own *Causa Nostrae Laetitiae*. Dr. Lamont felt that since she had played a pivotal role in the evolution of the medical mission movement, Anna should have credited her and included her in the founding of her Society. She asked her to do so now, insisting she also modify her organization's structure so that it more closely resembled her own three-circle design on which she felt Anna's foundation was based. Dr. Lamont's lengthy, hand-written letter reveals a woman who felt she had not been sufficiently appreciated for the seminal role she had played through the years at great cost to herself. She was now an "old woman" – those were her words – a widow watching from the sidelines as the movement she had tirelessly championed moved into the future without her. She had made some salient points regarding the value of her lifelong dedication and her manifold contributions, which Anna no doubt would affirm. However, in light of Dr. Lamont's relationship with the Medical Mission Board and her international notoriety, Mathis was understandably wary of her strident reaction to an initiative deserving of support and saw it as a threat to its future. There is no evidence that Anna's plan for a Society had been based on the model of Dr. Lamont, which had a very different and more loosely structured identity. Anna's was a basic structural design for a yet to be tested form of religious community life. There were no circles, so to speak, and no complex global matrix. It was simply a community of professional women dedicated to medical missions within the Catholic Church.

Rev. Michael Mathis sent an immediate response to Dr. Lamont. In a letter dated December 1, 1925, he wrote:

> "The account you gave of the history of Catholic medical missions, both in your letter to me and in your article appearing in the Catholic Herald of India, will be kept in our archives as important testimony in this largely unrecorded history of a great movement. Since becoming interested more practically in medical missions I have again and again gone back in thought and in the spoken word to the one from whom I received my first interest in Catholic medical missions, namely, your own self. When I was asked to write a paper for the last meeting of the Catholic Medical Mission Board, I chose for my subject the history of the organization of the Board, and I tried to pay to you at that time the tribute which I thought you deserved. I am sure Doctor Dengel must be encouraged by your keen interest in her organization which has so many features in common with your own ideas and hopes and plans for our Catholic medical mission work."

He closed by thanking her for all she had done to promote Catholic medical missions, noting that Dr. Dengel's society had no organic connection or dependence on the Congregation of Holy Cross.

That would not be the end of it. Dr. Lamont's efforts to be included in this pioneering initiative escalated as she spread the word through her global network of followers and friends that she had been ill-treated by the Society of Catholic Medical Missionaries in America. She reiterated the details in another lengthy letter to Michael Mathis early in the new year. She said that there was "a feeling abroad that Dr. Dengel has not behaved quite fairly to me," adding that Father Mathis, "as editor of the Bengalese should make my share in the matter plainer." She included a detailed description of how to implement her three-circle design. At the heart of her angst was the conviction that "Dr. AD's Society means the *total extinction* of mine, unless she *merges* mine in hers …."

Early in 1926 another uncomfortable situation arose. It concerned the Society's future medical mission in Rawalpindi. To the utter amazement – and dismay – of the Prefect Apostolic and the Mother Provincial of the FMM's, Anna, in a letter to Monsignor Winkley, reversed her position on several key components of their contractual agreement.

> "Concerning the hospital, I have talked it over with Rev. Father Mathis, our ecclesiastical Superior, and also with our own people who will have to do the work and face the situations as they arise. I told them that the Franciscan Missionaries of Mary have been there for many years, are known and liked and no doubt are looking forward to a useful field of labor in the City.… The last thing in the world I would like to do, would be to do anything contrary to the wishes of the F.M.M., as I worked with them in such harmony and got on so well with them. Naturally I thought that it would work with others as it had with me, forgetting in my inexperience that a Community, no matter how small, is a very different thing from an individual, and we all began to realize that it would not be fair to the F.M.M. nor to us to undertake such a difficult proposition."

According to their previous agreement, Anna's society would have charge of the hospital and be responsible for its upkeep and its financial solvency. The FMM's would do the nursing and would be paid for their services as was customary in government hospitals in India, although in this case their stipend most likely would be an agreed upon allowance. The crux of Anna's concern and the consensus of Mathis and the other members of her society, was this.

"We as lay people would not like to exercise authority of any kind over religious as would be necessary if we had full financial responsibility of the hospital. It would not work. Also we do not feel equal to the task of assuming full responsibility without full control. And we would not like to exercise control over any other organization or Community. Other communities do not do it, much less we who are only beginning. I am very glad if the F.M.M. take over the Pindi Hospital. If they can do it, they should do it. If they can't, they should plainly say so. If they should be unable to undertake it, then we will not back out."

If the Franciscan Missionaries of Mary decided to take responsibility for the new hospital in Rawalpindi, here is what Anna proposed to the Prefect Apostolic for her own Society.

"I would be happy if our first field of labor will be in your Prefecture. You know me, I am naturally attached to Mill-Hill and to the Punjab and I know conditions there. I do not mind to what place we go, provided it is a good field for work."

She insisted: "The money sent to you is for the Pindi hospital and is yours." She also said: "I think we could get enough to make a very humble beginning somewhere else, where there is a good field, for instance, Peshawar or Srinagar."

This was not an easy decision for Anna. She knew the impact it would have on her former colleagues in the Punjab and anticipated their disappointment at having to face such a radical change. However, she was now well aware of her own responsibilities, as well as her inexperience, in this new and pioneering role.

"It would relieve me of a great deal of anxiety to have our beginners in a place where they would not be strangers. But I feel it a duty not to expose the young sapling of our Society to a situation that would be too difficult to cope with. I am sure you fully understand what I mean. I also fully trust that you are convinced of my willingness to work in the Punjab or not, whatever seems to be for the good and in harmony with the already existing good works."

Anna's final words were a plea for a quick decision.

"Please, dear Monsignor, let us know soon what you and the F.M.M. decide. The year of spiritual and missionary training for the members of our first unit will be over at the end of September. They will be ready then to go to the Mission field. Before tackling the foundation of any hospital or dispensary, they will spend a few months at least in some good Indian hospital, so as to learn how things are done and managed in India. But it is not too soon to begin preparations now!"

She concluded her letter on a practical note.

"About the plan, it is no use sending one before things are more definite. Wherever we go, we want to begin very small, so to begin with, not much is required. Of course we want the Blessed Sacrament in the house and all the spiritual helps that an average religious community gets. Ours is very simple. Rev. Father Mullan was here and said Mass in our little chapel nearly every day during his stay in Washington. I think that it was very providential that he came; he will be able to tell you something of our simple beginning and our first recruits. His visit was really a very unexpected and pleasant surprise."

The postscript to her letter indicates that her future correspondence would no longer have to be by hand. "Please excuse my mistakes in the typing technicalities," she says. "I am only beginning to learn these modern arts." When Monsignor Winkley conveyed Anna's decision to Mother Alberte in Rawalpindi, she was most gracious in her reply.

"If Dr. Dengel's Society will come and work in Pindi – and prefer to work without us – we shall never resent it. When asked by Dr. Dengel, we accepted. When not wanted, we are equally satisfied, providing the mission does not lose by it; and it would be a thousand pities to deprive the City of such valuable workers. We shall be perfectly satisfied and happy with any decision you take in the matter."

Monsignor Winkley wrote to Anna, stating quite succinctly: "Now you understand: you are going to staff, run, and take entire charge of the Hospital."

Meanwhile, back in Washington, DC, Doctor Dengel's little community had settled into a routine. "Dr. Dengel taught us Hindustani," Dr. Joanna Lyons recalled.

> "It was work but it was interesting, and many a good laugh was had in class. Speaking of laughing; what a lot of it there was, those first months. Such funny things happened, or perhaps it was easy to make us laugh, for all were young and well and tasting the zest of this new venture. After all, it was something of a sporting proposition for four young women, with no capital and little backing to set out to form a society to meet a need, whose ramifications reached into every land. In one way it looked foolhardy, in another not a bit. The great need of this work and the special preparation, the attraction of each member for it seemed an indication of God's call."

Marie Ulbrich chronicled this memorable moment that occurred in the winter of 1926.

> "One night there was a heavy snow fall. In the morning, the mail man brought a check for $1,000 that looked like a million. Dr. Dengel had to have an outlet for her joy and enthusiasm. She couldn't sing a tune, so she grabbed a broom and swinging it with a mighty sweep made for the front walk. She was thanking the good Lord and thinking of all the bills she could pay and all that could be bought with the rest. Suddenly, she came to, at the end of the long block, across from the post

office. She had swept the front walk of about eight of our neighbors."

High on the list of priorities for the New Year was deciding on what community members would wear. According to their Constitution, "The dress shall be that of a layperson, simple and suitable to the profession and the climate, and a crucifix to symbolize the mission call." There was endless discussion about fabric and style and a showcasing of possibilities before a final decision could be made. According to Anna:

"Then finally we decided to take a kind of uniform. First of all, we made one – just a very simple dress. It was made of this very light cotton, like our slips. Sr. Laetitia put it on and I went with her to see Monsignor Thomas who had to view it. It was the funniest thing. I cannot describe it. The expression on his face said everything. He was an old priest. There was nothing to see. It was just the simplest dress … it was awful.

"The day before [receiving the religious garb] I told them they could wear anything they wished as a last blow-up. I don't know why I had this idea. Sr. Laetitia wasn't a bit interested in clothes and I wasn't interested either, nor was Dr. Lyons. But Sr. Agnes Marie! You should have seen her, how she appeared! And of course she was really the one on whom it would have the best effect. She had a nice dress; it wasn't fancy, just nicely cut out. She had some jewels around her neck and on her ears too. She was all dressed up – absolutely like a lady of the world. But that was beautiful. It showed she really gave up something. We didn't, but she did. I had a little embarrassing moment all the same. We had invited the famous Father Burke of the NCWC to give us a conference and he came. I felt very uncomfortable. We were supposed to be not religious women exactly, but pious women! Sr. Agnes Marie all dressed up! I didn't say a thing; that was the arrangement."

In the end their choice of what they would wear as a community was a grey dress that resembled a uniform. For those who were not doctors, it would be worn with a cape. They agreed to adopt their distinctive garb on the First Friday in March.

On March 5, 1926, at a simple ceremony following Mass, the celebrant, Monsignor Cornelius Thomas, Vicar for Religious, conferred the garb and gave them each a copy of their Constitution. Two of them were given a new name. Evelyn Flieger became Sister Mary Laetitia in honor of the Society's patron, *Causa Nostrae Laetitiae*. Marie Ulbrich added Agnes to become Sister Agnes Marie. While the Holy Cross Choir sang, the women left to symbolically "put aside the old" and returned wearing their new garb. Monsignor Thomas concluded the ceremony with the words, "The four of you stick." It was a charge as well as a blessing that continues to resonate here and now, transmitting energy from the past to help transform the present.

There was a three-day retreat leading up to the Society's feast day on March 25. It was led by Jesuit Father John Lyons, the brother of Joanna Lyons, and the tone of it was rather somber, most likely because it was the season of Lent. According to Anna's notes, the preaching focused on the folly of sin, disobedience, ingratitude; the necessity of grace to do anything meritorious; faults, such as, pride, vanity, self-centeredness, pussilanimosity, pessimism, laziness; and hell as a motive for overcoming temptation and personal sin. There was also reflection on the spirit of the three vows. Personal application, for Anna, seemed to follow along these lines:

> ~ for a solid spiritual life we must have solid motives
> ~ what is needed is solid virtue…God's goodness and *love*

Here is what she resolved to do during the coming year:

> ~ be considerate with everybody and in all things
> ~ be reasonable in all things

There were things she was determined *not* to do:

> ~ act without counsel
> ~ take decisive steps in times of depression
> ~ give in to moods, feelings, sentiments

She wrote: "Don't try to do everything yourself. No danger in my case." Her special resolution for the retreat was "to think first and then speak" and "before speaking, pray." Other resolutions were:

- ~ I will work hard
- ~ I will make an effort every day to be silent when I want to speak
- ~ I will pray much more for our Society than I have done up to now
- ~ I will make a fresh effort to keep my two old–life resolutions
  (1) to follow what I have been told
  (2) to make a little plan …

Above all, she wrote: "I will have unbounded confidence in God all my life. I have full reason to."

In April, Sister Mary Laetitia, who was born in England and trained as a nurse in New York City, left for London to take a six-month course in obstetrics before departing for India. Later that month Mother Alberte wrote to Anna saying that Dr. Wadia was leaving Rawalpindi. She wondered whether Anna might have a physician to replace her. Monsignor Winkley reported that "half the Ward at St. Catherine's is now under construction and the other half will be built as soon as we get the funds together. It will certainly fill a great need." The plan was to designate St. Catherine's as accommodation for European and Anglo-Indian patients under the auspices of the FMM. However, at the end of May their Mother General wrote this to Monsignor Winkley:

> "What I do not quite see is how it will work to have in the same place two hospitals under different managements: one well equipped with plenty of means allowing the latest improvements. The other lacking most of those advantages. Of course it would be different if the two institutions were under the same direction. In that case they would mutually help each other, but in the present circumstances, is it not likely that St. Catherine's will gradually dwindle down?"

In this regard Anna and the FMMs were of one accord, although not in direct communication. Both shared their perspectives with Monsignor

Winkley, who would make the final decisions. Anna wrote to him again about the future of St. Catherine's. She had already said there was insufficient space on the present property for an appropriate addition, but now she focused on a more fundamental concern.

> "The nuns cannot do justice to maternity patients. They are strictly forbidden to have anything to do with confinements proper. Even when it caused the patients and me great inconvenience to be left without *any* assistance *at all*, they could not help in spite of their willingness."

This was Anna's main objection, and there were others. "If they continue the hospital and dispensary as it is, *one* doctor will not be able to do the work. The last two years I had my hands full from morning till night." She had an alternative proposal, a conclusion she had reached after much reflection on what she already had experienced in the field and what she could envision.

> "We are starting the hospital in the city. There is plenty of room and we can supply professional medical aid. I know that there will be opposition to face in starting a native dispensary and hospital in the city because the native practitioners think they will lose. As a matter of fact they cannot do the work really needed for the women."

She went on to say that the Government had already spoken out against multiplying little medical institutions instead of equipping the little ones better, and that there had been talk of the Government building a good women's hospital in the city. "So you see," she wrote, "we have to combine all forces to make ours possible." This would mean, of course, that St. Catherine's Hospital would cease to exist when high level medical services for all became available in the modern city hospital she and Monsignor Winkley were planning to build.

> "The need of a hospital for civilian Europeans and Anglo-Indians is so evident that nobody can object; by

combining it with a native one the opposition will be lessened."

Monsignor Winkley and the FMM leadership could certainly affirm this assessment, but the revamping of St. Catherine's was already well-advanced and those with a major stake in the outcome, namely, the London Committee and the Anglo-Indian community in Pindi, held a different view. Monsignor Winkley had no other choice but to finish what he had started.

"Yes, a separate Ward is being built for Anglo-Indians at the end of the St. Catherine's compound. The Anglo-Indians have been asking for this Ward for some time. They are paying for the building. As you say, the great objection is, the multiplication of small Medical Institutions. Your intention to have a good Hospital, efficient in every way, this is what is wanted."

Anna promised to send a building plan for the projected city hospital soon, acknowledging that, under the circumstances, the arrival date of the first mission team sent by her Society would have to be revised. An earlier letter had proposed the following.

"Our present plan is that one doctor and two nurses will go out in the spring, stay over the summer in a hill station to see the methods of an Indian hospital, learn how to deal with the natives and acquire a speaking knowledge of the language, then begin work in Pindi in the autumn of 1927."

She also asked Monsignor Winkley about his plans for ownership of the site and buildings of the new Rawalpindi hospital in the city, wondering if her Society might hold title to the building and be given a long term lease for the land. His reply was that it would be best to discuss and settle those points face to face at some future time.

In June the community in Washington, DC was gifted with a car. It was old, and cantankerous, and they christened it "Jusuf" because they had been praying to St. Joseph to respond to their need for one. They described the vehicle in turn as neurotic, and temperamental, for it would go forward smoothly for a while, then suddenly shift into reverse, or come to a screeching halt, or do absolutely nothing. Nevertheless, members of the community took a turn at learning to drive. A major concern for all that summer was how to increase their numbers. Doctor Dengel was relieved of some of her household chores so that she might conduct publicity and fund-raising campaigns and meet with various visitors, some of whom came seeking medical missionaries for distant lands. There was only one candidate who actually entered that year, a nurse who stayed long enough to receive the distinctive garb, then left because of poor health. The little community decided to pray the Stations of the Cross for 33 consecutive days specifically for vocations. They added, "if it be the will of God." Apparently, it wasn't, at least not at that particular time.

Pauline Willis and the London Committee searched diligently for Dr. Wadia's replacement at St. Catherine's and eventually were successful. However, Dr. Nolan could not go to India before the fall of 1927. Therefore, arrangements were made for Dr. Joanna Lyons to take over in the fall of 1926, which was just a few months away, and stay until Dr. Nolan arrived. It was a serendipitous agreement, since the opening of the new hospital had been delayed and the Society of Catholic Medical Missionaries needed somewhere for their nascent missionaries to go. It had been a while since Anna and Pauline Willis had been able to accomplish something together. Because they were both so busy, they could only correspond briefly now and then. While Anna was bringing her vision to birth, Pauline was rebuilding her family home after it had burned to the ground. Everything in it had been destroyed, including some papers and personal possessions that had belonged to Anna, who had anticipated returning to England when their tour in America was done.

Mother Alberte was delighted that Dr. Lyons was coming to St. Catherine's to fill in for their newly hired doctor whose arrival was delayed. General renovations were complete and the maternity section was about to be moved into the newly constructed ward provided by Monsignor Winkley. When Anna wrote asking where Dr. Wadia's replacement would reside, Mother Alberte replied that doctors no longer lived in the Convent since Anna had gone, adding, "but the Presentation Convent Cottage is at their disposal. We pay the Doctor 200 Rupees and she manages for herself." Then she quipped, "You amuse me when you say you have found how hard it is to move when under the wing of the Church," reminding Anna of how she once felt the FMMs were much too rigid. Monsignor Winkley was pleased that the interim doctor would be one of the first fruits of Anna's new Society.

> "It will give her some experience in the work, and it will also give her a good opportunity of practicing the language. It will take time, as you say, to build the City Hospital, and also a little while to arrange to commence to build, after I have received the plans."

Back in the USA, there were no classes during August, traditionally vacation time in America. The women at 1000 Newton Street were invited to spend a brief holiday at a place nearby on the Chesapeake Bay, and they did.

September would be remembered for three significant first-time events in the history of the Society: the Solemn Promise and public commitment; the First General Chapter held with ecclesiastical approbation; the first Society doctor sent to the foreign mission field. September 23rd. Years later Anna would refer to this day as the true birthday of the Society. It was preceded by an eight-day retreat under the direction of Rev. Francis J. Walsh, a Benedictine monk, and its theme was "union with God." The commitment ceremony took place in the morning at 1000 Newton Street with the Holy Cross Fathers and seminarians in attendance. The Archbishop's delegate presided, and this is the gist of the sermon that Bishop Thomas Shahan gave.

> "The work of the medical missionary is both old and new...But this work has now taken on an organized form. It has entered the ranks of the regular, duly authorized and highly blessed Religious organizations... Today we welcome the first members of the Catholic Medical Mission Society to make their Solemn Promise for three years. Thereby they become a formal Sisterhood of the Catholic Church."

According to what would be formally adopted at the General Chapter the following day, Dr. Anna Dengel, Dr. Joanna Lyons, Sr. Mary Laetitia Flieger, and Sr. Agnes Marie Ulbrich made a Solemn Promise

to observe the Constitution faithfully, swore to remain in the Society
for three years, and to go any place and do any work assigned by the
Superior of the Society.

> *"I, Anna Dengel, having full knowledge of the objects of the
> Society of Catholic Medical Missionaries, of my own free will
> submit myself to its Constitutions and I solemnly promise,
> with the help of God, to observe them faithfully. I swear
> that I will remain in the Society for three years and that I
> will go without delay into any region or place whither the
> Superior of the Society shall send me and that I will accept
> any employment assigned to me."*

Anna Dengel. September 23, 1926

Each of the women had written out the formula and each in turn
placed it on the missal resting on the Bishop's knee, and signed it, while
kneeling before him. Then the Bishop blessed four crucifixes and gave
one to each of the pioneers of Catholic Medical Missions. The ceremony
concluded with Benediction and the joyous singing of "Holy God, We
Praise Thy Name." A footnote in the society chronicle reads:

> "The crucifixes we had decided upon had not arrived, so
> in all haste we got four wooden ones from a local shop.
> We were lucky to get four the same size. The cords were
> knotted and were rather hard to get over our heads."

The incident was symbolic of a missionary's challenge to make do in
all situations. After the commitment ceremony and before the opening
of the Chapter there was to be dinner for the Bishop and guests. Here
is what transpired.

> "As our accommodation was extremely limited, having
> only one small room available to serve in turn as sacristy,
> parlor and dining room, it was no small order. Our
> one and only candidate then did her best to prepare
> a dinner worthy of the Bishop and other ecclesiastical
> guests. To make room to remove the vestments and to
> set the table, the distinguished visitors were invited to

go on the verandah and have a smoke. They followed the suggestion in all simplicity and graciousness and later did full justice to the dinner, which pleased us very much."

The First General Chapter was convened at 2:00 p.m. with the *Veni Creator* – "Come, Creator Spirit." – and continued into the following day. Participating were the four members of the Society and Father Mathis. Bishop Shahan was present in order to preside over the Elections. Doctor Anna Dengel was unanimously elected Superior of the Society and Dr. Joanna Lyons, the mission Superior. Sr. Agnes Marie Ulbrich would be first assistant and stewardess-treasurer, and Sr. Laetitia Flieger, second assistant and general secretary.

What followed was a process of constitutional revision. The lived experience of that first year led the pioneering members to modify the Constitution in order to make it their own. Underlying the changes that were made was the desire to shape the life of the community after the manner of Religious, while at the same time keeping the freedom necessary to carry on the medical mission apostolate. Consequently, they introduced the uniform garb; replaced the simple pledge with a Solemn Promise and Oath of Fidelity, taken for three years; and mandated a year of renewal before making a commitment for life. The year of preparation for mission became a year of probation and spiritual exercises were brought more in line with the norms of the institutional Church. A new article was added to the Constitution:

"It is in the mind of the Foundress and the first General Chapter that the obligations of the members of the Society take the form of the three usual vows of religion as soon as this is permitted by ecclesiastical authority."

With regard to government, there was clarification and strengthening of the role of the Council. Important decisions were not to be left to the Superior of the Society "alone." With regard to making others more aware of this pioneering mission society, the decision was made to publish a Medical Mission Magazine to make the cause known.

There was also a radical shift in the criteria for membership, which had been limited to those fully qualified in some branch of the medical profession. From now on "the members of the Society are medical and associate." The two categories of membership were clearly defined.

> "The medical members must be graduates of a recognized School of Medicine, or of Dentistry, or of Nursing, or of Pharmacy, or they must have completed a recognized course of Technicians. All the other members are associate members; they are not allowed to do medical work but will devote themselves to the non-medical work of the Society."

In the revised Constitution, doctors were allotted a very significant place in government:

- ~ the Superior of the Society shall be a doctor of medicine
- ~ where there are doctors who are members in any house of the Society, one must be the Superior
- ~ the garb of the doctors distinguished them from other members because they wore no cape

As community members, however, all were equal in obligations and in rights and privilege.

The third in a trilogy of major events occurred later that day as Dr. Joanna Lyons left for her year-long assignment to India amid bells and cheers and a few tears, inaugurating a Society tradition of a joyous and prayerful sendoff for the one en route to the missions. Now there were three remaining at home to stir the embers of the fire and flame that had brought them together to commit themselves to a mission of hope and healing. It was a great way to begin the Society's second year of existence. They may not have increased in numbers, not yet, but their hearts and lives were full to overflowing with gratitude and praise. The ticket for Dr. Lyons had been donated by Monsignor Francis Wartl of Philadelphia, the priest who had accompanied Anna from one rectory to another to solicit church collections when she first arrived in America. The future of the Society and its healing mission were dependent on the generosity of others in order to survive. Both Anna and Michael Mathis were keenly aware of this, and in spite of the dire economic situation prevalent all around them, they had faith in the Spirit of God who had led them to this moment, and in the American people, whose generosity knew no bounds.

Anna wrote again to Monsignor Winkley telling him of Dr. Lyons' departure, saying she had given the plans for the construction of the new city hospital in Rawalpindi to her to give to him, adding:

> "I told her to visit hospitals in Bombay and Delhi, so that she can improve on the plan and see how they manage in other Indian hospitals. The plan only provides for immediate needs but is such that it can be completely converted into hospital space, as it will be a permanent building. I am glad that Dr. Lyons will be on the spot whilst it is being built as it will make it easier for you and also we can have a say in the matter from the medical angle."

In November Anna moved her fledgling Society to new living quarters nearby. The farmhouse on Bunker Hill belonged to the Franciscans. It was a blessing to be able to settle into an environment more favorable to a house of spiritual formation. Communal records describe it this way.

> "The temporary home of the Society is perched on one of the many holy hills in the so-called little Rome of America, Brookland, Washington, D.C. Our nearest neighbor hidden from view by trees is the famous Franciscan Monastery. On three sides we see woods and fields and Maryland's rolling country. Our house is a fine old family residence well adapted to harbor a small community of pioneers who are not afraid of 'odd jobs' which crop up every so often."

On December 8th, feast of the Immaculate Conception, Miss Margaret Godwin, a nurse from Canada, entered the Society.

We cannot dilly-dally.
If we go slow, we are behind.

Anna Dengel

CHAPTER TWELVE

During the winter and well into spring, Anna was preoccupied with generating income and making the cause of medical missions – and her own Society – more widely known. Now that membership had been redefined to include women qualified in areas other than medicine and related health services, she was seeking those who might want to serve and would consider her Society. She gave lectures and informal talks, attended meetings, entertained guests, and networked with various constituencies sympathetic to foreign missions, applying the skills she had cultivated in Philadelphia, New York, and New England barely two years earlier. She had come a long way in a very short time and not only geographically. Recent developments within her Society were a witness to the work of the Spirit. Perhaps if she tried hard enough, more women might decide to affiliate with her and benefactors might help alleviate the stress of meeting their essential needs. She prayed for strength and direction in the midst of existential concerns.

> "O Spirit of Wisdom,
>   preside over all my thoughts, words, and actions
>   from this hour until the moment of my death.
> Sprit of Understanding, enlighten and lead me.
> Spirit of Counsel, direct my inexperience.
> Spirit of Fortitude, strengthen my weakness.
> Spirit of Knowledge, instruct my ignorance.
> Spirit of Piety, make me fervent in good work.
> Spirit of Peace, give me Thy peace.
> Heavenly Spirit, make me persevere
>   in the service of Love
>   and enable me to act on all occasions

> with goodness and beneficence,
> patience, charity, mildness, and fidelity."

Anna also strived to keep up with the latest developments in the field of medicine and read whatever she could on missionary work worldwide. To ensure that she had access to the latest in scientific advances and in mission theory and theology, Michael Mathis sought and received permission from Bishop Fumasoni-Biondi for the Superior of the Society of Catholic Medical Missionaries to read books prohibited by the Index. The purpose of this reading, he explained, was to do "research in the history of medical dissertation in the Catholic Church," which meant reading works by non-Catholic writers on ecclesiastical history. He concluded: "I am enclosing a minimal fee for the secretarial work in connection with the faculties in the event that you think well to grant them." In her research on what kind of literature was available worldwide with regard to Catholic Medical Missions, Anna discovered the following: "over 400 Catholic Mission Magazines printed in different languages and in different countries of the world, but not one Catholic 'Medical' Mission Magazine." In her assessment of the status of medical mission literature, she drew the following conclusion:

> "Recently articles on medical missions have appeared in *Catholic Missions* and in various other Mission periodicals. All this goes to prove that Medical Missions is a subject of growing interest. Are we not right in concluding then that a medical mission magazine fills a gap and that it has a definite mission to fulfill?"

She also surveyed what was available within Protestant circles.

> "As Protestants have done, and are doing, such excellent medical work in mission countries, we also investigated their methods of spreading the message. We obtained the names and addresses of seven distinctly medical mission magazines published by different Protestant denominations. Three are published in London, one in Scotland, one in Stuttgart, one in India, and one in China."

Anna wrote to Archbishop Curley for permission to publish a mission magazine under the auspices of her Society.

> "Before your Grace leaves for Europe I would like to ask permission to start a small Medical Mission magazine. We need it to develop our work. There is not even one Catholic Medical Mission magazine in the whole world, yet. There are several Protestant ones."

The Archbishop's response arrived the next day. "You are hereby given permission to begin a small Medical Mission Magazine." She set out to do just that.

Anna envisioned a periodical that would be of interest to ordinary people as well as missionaries in the field. Driven by human suffering and by memories that continued to sear her soul, she knew that there were others who would feel what she was feeling if only she could help them see what she had seen. She was convinced they would be supportive if they knew they could make a difference in the life of a mother and child. Surely many would welcome an opportunity to participate in a mission of compassion. A magazine could facilitate that by telling the stories and sharing the images of mothers and babies from the East in a way that engendered empathy within families here in the West. From time to time she would also report on the latest scientific developments in the eradication of illnesses that have stalked the poor for centuries. She would explain in a way that all could understand the root causes of commonplace ailments and their systemic linkages to societal norms. She would share a doctor's view of infectious diseases that plague humanity, and at the same time, a missionary's compassion for all God's people. Anna would indeed publish a magazine, one that would reignite her own fire and flame, and it would debut in the Fall.

The Society of Catholic Medical Missionaries began publication of *The Medical Missionary* on September 30th in 1927, the second anniversary of its founding, creating a new category in periodical literature. Dr. Anna Dengel wrote the inaugural editorial.

> "SALAAM! With this beautiful Eastern salutation, which is daily on the lips of many millions of Orientals, we heartily greet our friends old and new."

What a wonderful way to let the world know that everyone everywhere was welcome and respected here.

> "It is with the full significance of good will which is contained in this ancient wish that we send our little magazine into the world as a messenger of the Medical Mission Apostolate. We want it to re-echo the aims and ideals of our vocation, the experience and needs connected with our work, and also our gratitude and appreciation for every kind of cooperation."

Her warm and welcoming words were followed by a brief introduction of the focus of her concern.

> "The Orient is teeming with 'real' flesh and blood. Its millions of people are fermenting and effervescing. The very foundation of the old civilization is being shaken because women have begun to rub their eyes and many from their seclusion look into the great world of the twentieth century. It is the dawn of a new day, bringing with it great demands and opportunities, possibilities, social problems and dangers. The Society of Catholic Medical Missionaries hopes, with the help of God, to provide here and there for the needs and opportunities which are the result of the changing tides of civilization among our Sisters of the East."

Anna was well aware of the women's movement taking shape internationally. She herself was the product of the tenacious actions of a cadre of feminists in Scotland and Great Britain, and she had walked those very streets in New York where American feminists had marched for equal opportunity and the right to vote. The next arena for systemic change would involve those civilizations where women were publicly powerless and socially confined. Anna may not have been a self-identified feminist, but a passion for equity and justice was similarly encoded in her DNA. She said of Indian women in the introduction to her publication:

"They are lovable and intelligent, but enslaved in ignorance and helplessness. They are most devoted mothers, yet they allow the evil spirits of ignorance and superstition to carry away two million babies every year. They are forbearing and enduring to a degree which to us is a puzzle. In the past 'fate' was the final word. But at the faintest glimmer of the possibility of relief, 'hope' takes its place. Real, tangible assistance is welcomed. Considering human nature as it is, to what form of assistance would they usually reach out first? What is more elementary and natural than to wish to safeguard their own lives; to rid themselves of disease and pain; to see their children grow up healthy and happy; to prevent unnecessary suffering for their nearest and dearest."

In many ways Anna was ahead of her times, yet at the same time was limited by the institutional frameworks that prevailed. How to tell traditional Catholics - and a part of her identified as that – to embrace something different from their own experience. She wrote:

"And is it not in keeping with the precepts of the Divine Physician who went about doing good and also with the traditions of our Holy Mother, the Church, to stretch out a helping hand without distinction of race, color and creed. This is how Medical Missionaries often get a first call to the practice of Christian Charity and a sphere of influence which is not so much created by words as by deeds. The Medical Missionary meets people in a variety of circumstances, at home or in the hospital and dispensary, in a professional capacity. On account of the sincere effort to help, he or she is accepted as a friend and allowed a glimpse into the inner circle of joys and sorrows, of religion and custom."

The scope of the Society's mission and its medical ministries would not be limited to women and children, although they continued to provide the impetus for Anna's determination. Her Society would embrace whole families, whatever their cultural context, and the effectiveness of the Society's ministrations depended on the support they received from friends and benefactors back home.

> "Through our publication we can lead our friends to our field of labor and let them see what we see and show them what we find. We aim to make it a popular, non-technical monthly, so as to be of interest to Mission Friends in general. It is, however, part of our plan to issue from time to time a supplement which will be of special interest to the medical and nursing professions and missionaries in the field."

Anna described the Society's pioneering venture in this way: "We embark on our journey hand in hand with our friends...as an expedition of explorers bent on working for the honor and glory of God and the relief of human suffering ...." It was to be a partnership, with those here at home considered as vital as those out in the field. That first edition of *The Medical Missionary* featured a lead story on the life of Dr. Agnes McLaren, to whom it owed its existence. Written by Anna and entitled "Sowing the Seeds," it began with an evocative phrase. "The society did not spring up overnight." Anna was determined that no one forget the contributions of those courageous women who had gone before and prepared the way for those who followed after.

By the end of October, the little community in Washington, DC, that had only three members barely a year ago, now numbered eight. Even that was not enough to meet the needs of the house on the hill. "There is so much to be done that each has to be a mob until reinforcements come to swell the ranks."

In November Holy Cross Father George Sauvage wrote to Father Mathis from Rome.

> "I was very glad to see *The Medical Missionary* and hope that Dr. Dengel will succeed in her work. To my mind, there is a great need of such an organization and there is work to do which can be done only by an Association like hers. I suppose that her Association is recognized by the Archbishop of Baltimore and that she has a written Decree of creation from him."

Sauvage was the one to whom Mathis would turn for guidance regarding issues pertaining to Canon Law. Here was an indirect reminder to delve more deeply into the Society's canonical status in the days ahead. Meanwhile, Anna gave an overview of her Society in the magazine's November issue.

> "God has been good to us! After two years we are four hale and happy members, six candidates full of life and good will, and a little army of friends who also are ready to make sacrifices that 'our neighbor yonder' may be happier in soul and body. May God continue to bless everybody's contribution to our work ... the relief of human suffering and the raising of womanhood in non-Christian countries."

December 8, Feast of the Immaculate Conception, marked the official opening of the newly erected Holy Family Hospital for Women and Children in Rawalpindi; and on December 14, this pioneering institution received an official Blessing. Anna rejoiced in this good news. "Perhaps the most outstanding event of our second year is the building of one wing of our hospital in India. It is ready to receive its first staff and its first patients." Here is the story that Anna told to explain the hospital's name.

> "A Pathan who brought his wife with a retinue of fourteen relatives from the border of Afghanistan is responsible for confirming us in our choice. After his wife had been comfortably settled in bed and an hour's chat with the relatives elapsed, Sister thought that the patient had had sufficient time to gain confidence in her surroundings, so she told the relatives that, apart from visiting hours, only one relative was allowed to stay day and night. The husband having read the sign 'Holy Family Hospital' at the gate, quickly retorted: 'Isn't this the Whole Family Hospital?' He was right in his own way. It, and all our hospitals, are for the *whole* family – father, mother, and child – what you do for one you do for all."

In the December issue of the magazine, Anna Dengel introduced her readers to that area of the world where her Society would soon be immersed in mission and dependent on their support, ending the year by reminiscing on her own Rawalpindi days.

"Protestant effort has produced 252 hospitals for India; Catholic effort, six. The Society of Catholic Medical Missionaries is adding the seventh. How did it come about? Very simply and slowly. St. Catherine's Hospital in Rawalpindi, founded by Dr. Agnes McLaren in 1906, can only accommodate 15 in-patients and it is situated in a district between European quarters and a small native bazaar. The greater number of the in-patients and also a good number of the out-patients came from the thickly populated native city about five miles distant. The well-do-do came in tongas. Some came on foot, but the majority came never or rarely as the distance was prohibitive. They would not mind walking for miles, riding on a donkey, or being jolted about in a bullock cart occasionally, but to come regularly for treatment was too much either for their purse or their strength. Besides many husbands, still strong believers in the purdah system, did not approve of their wives going out repeatedly and so far. To reach them, there was obvious need of bringing help nearer to their doors.

"The native Catholics in the city numbering about 150, also needed care and attention. They were visited regularly once a week by the Franciscan Missionaries of Mary of St. Catherine's. Sometimes the writer went with them or instead of them, especially during the fever season. As soon as the women heard of our arrival, they collected all the patients with minor ailments, these were always numerous; without any ceremony, a dispensary in the open was set up. Those who were very ill, we treated in their homes. Catholics were always glad when we visited them. The poverty, to Westerners, is beyond comprehension. A few *charpoys* (string beds), quilts and cooking utensils are their 'all.'"

As is the norm for Anna's understanding of her global mission, the poor and the wealthy were there together, transcending socio-political separations of culture, religion, and class.

"It has been found by experience that the rich, secluded Mohammedan lady, the caste-bound Hindu woman and the sweeper's wife can all be met on the friendliest terms by helping them in their hour of need and sickness. The trouble is not that they cannot be reached, but that there are so few to reach them.

"One wing of our first hospital is completed. Now we have to furnish the chapel and equip the hospital. This year in the native city of Rawalpindi, where there are about 60,000 inhabitants, mostly Mohammedans, Hindus, and Sikhs, Midnight Mass will be celebrated for the first time in the history of the native town. The chapel of our first hospital, which is barely completed, will be the scene. The poverty will have a touch of Bethlehem and the congregation will be mostly the poorest of the poor, outcasts, untouchables, pariahs, in other words, despised human beings. But Our Lord chose the poor...It is now as it was then."

~ ~ ~

January, 1928. Standing on the threshold of what had been and daring to imagine what might be, Anna stepped boldly and confidently into a brand new year and shared her reflections with her growing constituency.

"New Year's is inventory time. One looks backward and forward. Closing the chronicle of 1927, we thank God for His goodness for having provided not only the necessities but even more, for the carrying on of the Society. Many things are included in this. We have Mass every morning in our own chapel, thanks to the kindness of our neighbors, the Fathers of the Franciscan Monastery. The Holy Cross Fathers from the Foreign Mission Seminary continue to give us our spiritual and missionary training. We have many staunch friends,

who help us to keep body and soul together, to train
and send out our missionaries, and to carry on the work
which we set out to do. The New Year has an important
event in store for us – the beginning of the work of our
Society in the Mission field."

Anna set out to make certain that public relations materials gave an
accurate depiction of the Society's purpose and clearly stated the specifics
of its unique mission and ministries. These were the building blocks on
which to construct a solid foundation that would be understood by all,
not only those outside the Society who were supportive of it, but also
those within. The magazine published the purpose statement in every
one of its issues.

"The purpose of the Society of Catholic Medical
Missionaries is to render medical aid, no disease or
condition being excepted, to Christians and non-
Christians in the officially recognized foreign mission
countries of the world."

Simple. Clear. Memorable.

"The scope of the Medical work extends to mission
hospitals and dispensaries, medical schools and training
schools for nurses, infant welfare centers, plague camps,
leper asylums and caravan dispensaries bringing medical
aid from village to village. Obstetrical work and visiting
the sick in their homes are primary needs in mission
countries."

The field of labor of the Society would not be restricted to any one
particular mission country. The first hospital and dispensary would
be in northern India, in the Mill-Hill Prefecture Apostolic of Kashmir
and Kafristan, among the poor from the villages and "where the
Mohammedan and high caste Hindu women are still strictly secluded
and can only avail themselves of medical aid by women."

The driving force behind Anna's unwavering commitment to bring
healing and hope to those outside her faith tradition is illustrated by the
Gospel parable of the Good Samaritan, which has shaped her Society's

medical mission apostolate from the beginning. She alluded to it often, pointing out its emphasis on compassion and mercy while tending to the wounds of another, particularly the stranger, perhaps even an enemy. In February of 1928, she shared the following with readers of her magazine.

> "In the Orient today there are millions of human beings who are strangers to us, who profess a different religion, many of whom are suffering and lie there helpless and voiceless. There are the blind, the cripples, the incurables, the insane and the lepers. All these are so many wounded by the roadside, stripped of happiness and usually unable to call out for assistance. In order to act like the Samaritan, whom Our Lord gave as an example, we must stoop down and see and examine and pour on the oil and wine of mercy and generosity and make arrangements not only for momentary relief, but see the case through even at the cost of personal fatigue and expense. The Good Samaritan had to walk and pay for the wounded stranger at the Inn. The innkeeper is also to be admired for not refusing to harbor a troublesome guest."

Anna reminded her readers that the parable of the Good Samaritan "will be read to the faithful all over the world on the 19th of August. Let us have ears to hear it!" Her application of that Gospel to our own lives is as relevant now as it was then, proclaiming good news – really good news – to all who are wounded or cast aside. It defined Anna's practical and spiritual approach to medical missions and related ministries. Elements of the parable continue to shape the mission spirituality of her Society today.

> "The parable of the Good Samaritan teaches charity and mercy without alluding to conversion. Medical Mission work is primarily and fundamentally charity done for the love of God and our neighbor."

In March, Anna Dengel established her League of Gratitude. As the name implies, this latest initiative was rooted in what has been and always would be for Anna an overflowing gratitude for God's bountiful blessings that continuously saturate our lives. Members would pledge "to offer thanks to God frequently for the gifts of Faith and Health and ask His blessing on the Medical Mission Apostolate." They would also contribute toward this Apostolate through one of seven so-called Branches:

Eucharistic Branch. Bishops and priests who promise one or more Masses annually for the Medical Missionaries and members of the League.

Our Lady's Branch. Religious Brothers and Sisters who offer prayers for the Medical Missionaries and members of the League.

St. Joseph's Branch. Those who contribute $500 or more to the works of the Society.

St. Luke's Branch. Those who contribute $100, either in one donation or covering a period of years.

St. Anthony's Branch. Those who contribute $50 in one donation or covering a period of years.

Little Flower Branch. Those who contribute annually $1.00 or more to the works of the Society.

Junior Branch. Those students who contribute 10 cents.

In addition to the Masses and Prayers of the Members of the League, Benefactors are remembered daily at Holy Communion and in all the prayers and works of the Medical Missionaries. The League of Gratitude was begun "with ecclesiastical approbation."

The month of August gave members of the Society a reprieve from the intensity of multiple expectations, offering the community a deeper appreciation of its idyllic setting.

> "The Medical Mission hill is a beauty spot in summer;
> the isolation and half wilderness and half civilization

give it a comfortable charm. We are all delighted that the vegetable garden is such a success. Because our compound is more like a field than a lawn, we have to engage a man to cut it occasionally. Sr. Anthony, however, recently hit on a cheaper method. During Dr. Dengel's absence, she invited our neighbor's cows, who did it free and for nothing, and enjoyed it at that."

Anna sent a status report to Archbishop Curley in October and received this reply: "I am glad to know that the little Society is sound financially." Good news indeed. Apparently those intensive fund-raising efforts were starting to take effect.

At the end of October Michael Mathis left for India to visit the Holy Cross mission in Bengal. With the Rawalpindi hospital in the Punjab soon to be fully functioning, it was time for Anna's Society to consider a second foundation. The plan from the very beginning had been to first get established in the western region and then move on to the East. Shortly after his departure, Father Mathis wrote Anna thanking her for sending him a copy of the *The Medical Guardian,* which he received – and enjoyed reading – on his second day at sea. "I bought a movie camera before leaving Washington," he wrote, "and tried it out on typical scenes a missionary meets abroad." Mathis also had a second agenda. Following several days in Paris to do a little sight-seeing, his voyage to India included a stopover in Rome and, serendipitously, an opportunity for some advocacy on behalf of the Society. Several young priests from his community, en route to their first mission assignment in Dacca, were to join with leaders of the Holy Cross Congregation residing in Rome for an audience with Pope Pius XI. Mathis would be part of that delegation, and if the opportunity arose, he would raise the issue of medical missions and the future of the Society. He also wrote: "You may be sure that I shall promote the cause of the Society of Catholic Medical Missionaries when I am in Rome with the Holy Father, Cardinal Van Rossum, and Father Sauvage." Cardinal Van Rossum was head of the Sacred Congregation of Propaganda Fide, the Vatican office responsible for missionary activity worldwide. He wrote again after leaving Rome to report on what had transpired.

"On the very first morning of my four days in Rome, all of us Holy Cross who are leaving for India went to see Monsignor Marcetti. At that general meeting I had a chance to ask Monsignor for a private conference later. This I had the next morning. I talked very plainly to him, and I am glad to tell you that he is entirely with us. On Saturday morning I visited with Father General and Father Sauvage. Cardinal Van Rossum alas was sick in bed. I could not go into details with him, but I think I shall get a letter of encouragement from him to you. At our audience with the Holy Father, there were 24 of us Holy Cross people present, hence, I could not take up with His Holiness either your questions or those affecting Holy Cross in Washington."

Michael Mathis was disappointed that he had been unable to advocate more openly and effectively for "your or shall I say our Society," he wrote in a final report to Anna as his time in Rome drew to a close. Perhaps he would try again on his return trip as Father Savauge had advised.

On December 3, feast of St. Francis Xavier, patron saint of missionaries, the first Catholic Medical Mission House for training medical missionaries opened in Würzburg in Bavaria. It consisted of a new building added to the Institute that had been founded in 1922. In 1925 the pope had given 20,000 marks toward its construction. The Bishop of Würzburg blessed and officially opened the new Institute and the Papal Nuncio delivered the inaugural address. Men and women would now be able to study medicine there in preparation for serving in the missions. When asked about training women physicians for medical mission work in the new facility, Monsignor Christopher Becker shared this perspective.

> "I expected to have a similar establishment for ladies as a sort of a pendant to our institute and to have it put under the direction of Miss Anna Dengel, whom after her return from India, I kept back from entering a strict religious order. However, as the Fathers of the Holy Cross in America, where she went to collect funds, encouraged her to start a religious congregation for lady doctors in the United States, I did not put any obstacles in her way. In the meanwhile, we have not as I told

you, developed that part of our institute with regard
to lady doctors but keep only a few women students
with the Rita Sisters here, though they do belong to
our institute. I could not do all things at the same time
but wanted first to develop the male branch, waiting in
the meantime for a lady to turn up with the necessary
qualities to take into her hands the immediate direction
of the female branch."

He continued, adding his perspective to the evolving history of medical
missionary service within the Catholic Church.

"As regards Miss Anna Dengel's undertaking, she has
gone on quite different lines from our own work. You
know that ours is a purely lay undertaking whereas Dr.
Dengel's institute is made up as a religious one. Which
way will be the better for ladies especially has to be
shown still by practice. I myself am inclined to think
that our way of doing things seems to be the preferable.
First of all you may find a good many ladies willing to
join an institute like ours but you won't find so many
willing to enter a religious congregation."

He concludes his comments, which he had been sharing in a letter to
a Canon Ross.

"These are the main considerations I can lay before you.
Of course, it cannot be said yet which way is best, both
certainly have their drawbacks and also their advantages.
For Miss Dengel's work it speaks that the members of
her congregation being always together by threes won't
feel so lonely. With us it is more the common bond of
all the members of the institute belonging together and
holding up each other wherever they may be scattered in
the wide world. The coming of Miss Dengel to London
may help to clear this matter more and more and the
few thoughts I have explained in this letter may perhaps
help you a little for guidance."

Michael Mathis reached Bengal after visiting friends in Bangalore and Madras and very briefly in Calcutta, arriving in Dacca on the 20th of December, six days after the new arrivals and in time to celebrate Christmas with his Holy Cross community. He wrote the following to Anna as the year was drawing to a close.

> "I was pleased more than I can say to find awaiting me (on my return from the Garo Hills) your letter. I was beginning to get lonesome for a word from you. Thanks for your kind good wishes and the card signed by each one of the medicals. I shall treasure this card and keep it for a marker in my Breviary. Pray for me sometimes too – I need it much more than you."

In a Catholic Mission hospital,
love and sympathy must be a testimony
that there is a God of love
who cares for all His creatures.

Anna Dengel

CHAPTER THIRTEEN

The Society of Catholic Medical Missionaries needed another house, specifically, a Motherhouse, like other communities had, not only for the space it would provide, which was currently in short supply, but also for the ambience. A Motherhouse would signify to all in the house, and to the world beyond it, that this was a place of dedication and determination, that a ministry of hope and healing would come to fruition here.

On January 7 Anna Dengel scribbled a "Prayer to St. Joseph for a Motherhouse" on a sheet of paper.

> "Dear Saint Joseph, Please help us to get a Motherhouse – where and when we need it.
> And help us to get all the temporal necessities to spread God's honor and glory.
> Ask for us a spirit of poverty, and humility.
> Also help our missionaries in India.
> Thanking you, dear good Saint Joseph, for all you have done for us. I am yours very gratefully, Anna Dengel.'"

She made this promise in a postscript:

> "When we have the house and have paid for it we will make a nice shrine to you in Thanksgiving."

She had also included the written instruction: "Put the piece of paper preferably under the statue of Saint Joseph." Then she set out to do all in her power to set the plan in motion.

In February of the following year, Anna would tell the story of her Society's simple beginnings and the challenges of securing adequate housing in her mission magazine.

"Three and a half years ago the Society of Catholic Medical Missionaries, then consisting of two members, set out in search of its first house. We rented a nice seven-room frame house in Brookland, DC, not far from the Catholic University. The fact that the only article of furniture available then was a broom did not worry the prospective occupants.

"During the first days, visitors were received most cordially, but had to be satisfied with a seat on grips [suitcases] and trunks. The first article of furniture – a card table – was used as a pedestal for a statue of St. Joseph, who was then and there installed as patron of the temporal affairs of the Society. After two weeks of camp life in the house, we managed to fix it up sufficiently to invite two other candidates. Under the guidance of Sister Patricia, a modest little chapel was furnished. Having few household effects, the remainder of the house did not absorb very much of our time. During that year the walls of our first house resounded with more laughter than probably any other of our future houses ever will, for the pioneer conditions cannot recur in so many varieties of form at one and the same time again.

"After a year's residence there, we determined to transfer our headquarters to a place where we would have less rent to pay, more available space and a heating plant in working order. Our ambitions were high, and we had no reasonable prospects of attaining them. However, one fine day, very providentially, we heard of an empty house on a hilltop near the Franciscan Monastery, which was offered for lower rental, had almost double the space, a good heating plant, lots of land around, and a beautiful view, besides many other advantages. It did not take us long to make the change.

We soon discovered a short cut through the woods to the Franciscan Monastery, and made our way there every morning – rain, hail, or snow – before 6 a.m., quite thankful to have a church so close by. After a short time, however, the Franciscan Fathers surprised us by asking if we would like to have Mass in our chapel. Needless to say, we were more than delighted to accept. The fact that we had Mass every day in our chapel, that the house was so convenient, isolated and beautifully situated, made it so ideal for us that we would like to plant the Medical Mission House here for good, but alas that is not to be.

"From the beginning we were told that the owners would require the site for themselves sooner or later, and it was only our good fortune that the project of building was not carried out before. Now, however, plans are ripe to begin construction after Easter, which means that we have to move *before* then. Being inevitable, it is no use wasting many words about it. Our task now is to house thirteen Medical Missionaries and to make provision for more to come. To find a rented house of the required dimension, allowing for a chapel, parlor, refectory, study room, work room, office and sleeping accommodations, is almost an impossibility, besides being a great financial drain. The temptation is to concentrate all efforts to answer the summons for Medical Missionaries from India, Nigeria and Uganda in Africa, and Northern China, but we are convinced that it will be for the eventual good of the work to solidify the foundation at home before branching out into new fields.

"For these reasons we looked around for a suitable location for the establishment of a Medical Mission House. In the vicinity of the Catholic University we found a piece of property which could accommodate the members of the Society. The price, including the most urgent improvements, is $25,000. To us it looks an insuperable sum, but yet we do not give up hope! ...

> The establishment of a permanent center in America is
> a step of far-reaching importance for our Society."

After sharing the background narrative of her pioneering community
now on the verge of having to evacuate their little house on the hill,
Anna made a plea for financial support, then left the details to Saint
Joseph and his heavenly brigade. The winter term was in full swing.
The curriculum consisted of conferences on Christian Doctrine and the
spiritual life, and classes on Mission Science and the religions, manners,
and customs of the people in those areas where they would eventually
be assigned. Here is one eyewitness report of an additional subject dear
to their hearts.

> "The musical members are practicing Gregorian chant
> and playing the organ. Some people may wonder why
> Medical Missionaries spend time on acquiring so-called
> accomplishments. For missionaries they are almost a
> necessity. For instance, Sister Agnes Marie is the organist
> of the Holy Family chapel. A busy Benedictine Sister of
> Brookland spent many an hour teaching her, and busy
> Sister Agnes Marie made great efforts to find time for
> practicing while at home, and now she is very glad to
> be able to make the chapel resound with music at High
> Mass and Benediction. The interesting and providential
> thing in a community is that everybody has different
> talents, which are all very helpful. An instance of this is
> *sewing.* One of our candidates is a splendid dressmaker,
> which solves the problem of the uniform for the time
> being."

Anna elaborated on this.

> "In a pioneer Medical Mission House where the range
> of activities is necessarily a wide one, no talent remains
> hidden very long. A great deal of our work is spade
> work, which does not show any immediate results. This
> we take for granted, realizing that the foundation must
> be deep and strong. From the very beginning the spirit
> of the Society has been one of optimism, and now, after

three short years, we look into the future with more hope than ever of extending our work."

Anna was a gifted storyteller. This proved to be a valuable asset in presenting her vision to the public. She would weave together an incident from her experience in India with a wisp of wisdom from her Faith tradition and link them both to the here and now. Listen and you may hear her whisper … "Once upon a time …."

"Somewhere in England I once saw a row of houses called 'variegated sublimity.' The houses looked as funny as the sound of the name given to them, but it just struck me that it would be quite an appropriate name to give to some episodes of one's missionary career. Such a one was for instance my experience in India on the feast of the Epiphany five years ago. The feast of the Magi being considered a missionary feast, we always kept it as solemnly as possible. One of the Mill Hill fathers, the chaplain of the Native Catholics, asked the nuns to prepare for the celebration of Mass in the native city.

"So, three Wise Women, two Franciscan Missionaries of Mary and myself, set out in a tonga, and on the way, halted at the houses of Catholics, to drum the congregation together. Some of the toddling population we took along with us, much to their delight. Arrived in the city, we went to the sweepers' lane, where in among a row of mud huts, there was one single-roomed habitation, in which on week days the Catechism and the three R's were taught, and on Sundays and feast days, the Holy Sacrifice was offered up. There the Star stood still for us! The room being a vacuum as far as the naked eye is concerned, there was not much to do except to get one of the Knights of the Broom busy to sweep it to the best ability of this one and only profession open to him. When the dust raised was settled again, we arranged an altar and the vestments for the priest. As soon as all was ready, the congregation – poor people, mostly sweepers, men, some bright-eyed, others blind, women with babies in their arms, shy little girls and solemn looking little boys – crowded in, until the space was so filled that it was difficult to keep room for the priest to turn freely in front of the improvised altar. The music was a mixture of the low pitched moans and groans of the old people and the high pitched squalls of the infants in arms, with the restless shuffling of the young folk in between.

"Mass under such circumstances has its *pros* and *cons*. I hear some people say: pray, what may the *pros* be? Well, the first is that one is thankful that even the greatest poverty is no obstacle to the celebration of the Holy Sacrifice; and the second is that Our Lord is so wonderfully near in such Bethlehems."

In April the Society of Catholic Medical Missionaries moved into its third house in three years. The spacious property on the corner of 6th and Buchanan Streets, NE, was near the campus of Catholic University. Their new address: Catholic Medical Mission House, Brookland, Washington, D.C. While the community would have been happy to remain where they were, that was no longer an option. "To fit twelve people into a house of our dimensions is not an easy task." The move would prove to be exactly what they needed. Here is how they described their new home to benefactors and friends.

"Since March 12th when the purchase of the house was finally settled, our Sisters have been busy packing and preparing the Medical Mission House to be. The building is only about 30 years old, but having been neglected, it requires a great deal of work to make it habitable. It offers first class practice for pioneering! Although we chose the site more with a view to the future, we had to look for one which had several buildings on it which would accommodate us for a number of years. We were fortunate to have found what we wanted. At present the quiet hill behind the Sisters' College is teeming with life: roofers, tinners, electricians, carpenters, painters and plumbers are all hard at work. The property we purchased is bordered on three sides by the grounds of the Sisters' College, so our new neighbors will be the Sisters from many different parts of the United States. This was one of the attractions of the place, there being no doubt that it will be most congenial and suitable. The Baltimore and Ohio Railroad puffs past a few hundred feet from our grounds and as there is a crossing not very far away, it takes an extra loud breath just as it passes by."

Soon after moving into their new residence, a challenging period in the life of this emerging community began to unfold. Agnes Marie Ulbrich wrote this cryptic note in her journal: "Anna Dengel's health declining." There is no further indication of what that might have meant.

Father Michael Mathis returned from six months of travel abroad, primarily in India. He was enthusiastically welcomed by the community of women now living at their new location. They were eager to hear all about his adventures, especially his visit to their Rawalpindi mission prior to returning home. They not only heard the stories; they were able to see the pictures he had taken with his new camera: images of the Pindi community and their hospital and spectacular scenes of the snow-covered mountains of Murree and the Khyber Pass.

Anna wrote a second prayer to Saint Joseph and tucked the paper under his statue alongside the other one. "I want to thank you with all my heart for having given us the means to buy a Motherhouse. We will build you a nice shrine in thanksgiving. Please help us to pay for all the necessary improvements without having to raise a loan." For all of her intellectual acumen, Anna was at heart quite simple ... and direct. She often went straight to the point. If statues could talk, she might have heard Saint Joseph responding, "It's a deal."

Later that month Anna received a letter from Cardinal Van Rossum. Michael Mathis had been expecting it. Following the Holy Cross Congregation's meetings with Vatican officials in Rome, Father Sauvage asked the Cardinal to send a letter of encouragement to the Holy Cross Foreign Mission Society (the Bengalese) and to Anna's Society of Catholic Medical Missionaries, because such a letter would be very helpful to both groups in seeking financial support. The letter revealed that the Cardinal was in favor of the Society's commitment to medical missions.

"I was very pleased to receive a bound copy of your magazine, *The Medical Missionary*, and I am very grateful for it. More than ever, this is the moment to extend as largely as possible the medical contribution to missionary work, not only for the good of the missionaries themselves who would live longer and do better and more work if they had the proper medical help and care, but also for the conversion of the pagan world…how necessary is your contribution to the great work of extending the Reign of Christ on earth."

As indicated above, the Cardinal's approach to medical missions was primarily as a tool for conversion. He saw its value as beneficial to the universal Church and its personnel. For Anna, it was not about conversions. The purpose of medical missions was to alleviate human suffering in the defenseless and underserved – primarily women and children – and thereby witness to the universal compassion of a loving God. Nevertheless, the approval of Rome meant everything to her. Therefore, she would opt to integrate two distinctly different perspectives, and ultimately, two worldviews regarding the mission of the Church. "I am really satisfied with the development your providential initiative has taken," the Cardinal's letter states, "and I hope that this progress will continue …. The needs in this regard are immensely above the help of which we dispose. Your work will incite many young people to follow your example and to devote themselves to this apostolate. With all my heart I bless your work, and I ask the Divine Redeemer by the intercession of Mary Immaculate to give to this enterprise of supernatural charity the necessary support of divine grace so that the fruits may be more and more abundant."

Michael Mathis was delighted. Those affirming words from such a significant representative of the Vatican led him to write to Father Sauvage regarding their conversations in Rome, thanking him for representing the perspective of the Society in a way that helped the Cardinal to see that it was not so very different from his own. Mathis pointed out once again the importance of being able to make public vows. This issue was at the heart of the Society's identity and its sustainability. Consequently, it would remain a topic of concern until it was finally resolved

During the summer of 1929, Anna went to Canada for six weeks, where she attended the International Convention for Nurses, made a retreat in a Trappistine Monastery, and took several other trips before returning to the United States. In September Michael Mathis received a letter from Holy Cross priest W. J. Doheny, who had been traveling abroad.

"By the merest chance I learned that Dr. Dengel's folks lived only four miles out of Innsbruck. I happened to be in Innsbruck last week and drove out to the family home for a short visit of one hour. It was truly delightful. Happily, one of the Doctor's brothers – a student with the Mill Hill fathers – speaks English very well, so we got along famously. I had a lovely chat with the Doctor's dear father. His eyes just beamed when I told him of all the glorious work that the dear Doctor was doing. I called her the saintly daughter of a saintly father, so from now on she will be called *Die Heilige* in her own family circle."

Father Doheny also visited Edmund Dengel's workshop, "where he designs and makes the most beautiful vestments that one would ever want to see. The workmanship is superb and the prices are very low." He encouraged Mathis to persuade his friends to purchase their vestments from him. He also told his colleague to visit Innsbruck and Hall someday and see for himself that "the view from the Dengel home is superb."

September marked the fourth milestone in the existence of the Society. Anna Dengel expressed her gratitude. "We cannot help but see God's blessing on the little seed sown and offer our thanks for the wonderful dispensation of Providence … our family now numbers sixteen." She renewed her Solemn Promise on September 30, using the same formula she had written for the first time, three years earlier. One month later, on October 24, known forever after as Black Tuesday, an event of historic proportions dominated the headlines. The Stock Market crash on Wall Street marked the onset of The Great Depression, a global reality that would last for more than a decade, affecting everyone. The little community at 6ᵗʰ and Buchanan had depended on the generosity of others in order to survive. Those very same people were now in a similar situation. Through the dark days that followed, Anna and her little community often turned to prayer. In an earlier journal Anna had written words that were appropriate now.

"Blessed Virgin, Mother of God and our Mother:
look down on Thy children who greet Thee and love Thee.
As Thou didst allow Thy heart to be pierced
with the Sword of Sorrow
in order to become the Source of Joy to the world –
obtain for us the grace to willingly and joyfully accept
the little sacrifices of our vocation
and bless our work –
so that we will bring relief and joy to many
who suffer in body and soul.
Our Lady, Cause of Our Joy,
intercede for Thy children to Thy Divine Son. Amen."

Early in December Anna wrote to Cardinal Dougherty, her avid supporter in Philadelphia, who was preparing to leave for a meeting in Rome.

"As Your Eminence kindly said that you would put in a good word for us in Rome in the matter of being permitted of taking vows, I enclose what our Constitutions say now about it and also the reasons why we would like to make public vows."

Shortly before Christmas, the Cardinal responded.

"I spoke several times to His Eminence Cardinal Van Rossum about your desire in reference to religious vows and today I presented to him a written memorandum, copy of which I have enclosed. He is interested and favorable. In due time he will lay the matter before his Congregation of the Propaganda. You will pray for success in your petition."

On December 21, the Feast of Saint Thomas the Apostle of India, a physician and three nurses made their Solemn Promise and took the Mission Oath. Two of them, Sister M. Frances Herb and Sister M. Helen Herb, were biological sisters. It was a hopeful note on which to end a challenging year.

Let us look at the world in the right way.
For us it is a paradise of opportunity
to glorify God,
to work out our sanctification,
and to bring sparks and seeds of Christ's love
here and there, wherever we work, wherever we move about,
wherever our anything and everything go.

Anna Dengel

CHAPTER FOURTEEN

On January 14, 1930, the Society's four newest members boarded the *S.S. Augustus* and sailed to Rome via Naples, where they would spend a week visiting the sacred sites. They also hoped to be able to secure an audience with Pope Pius XI, and they did.

> "Our great day is over. We have had an audience with the Holy Father. Very Reverend Father Sauvage, c.s.c., Procurator General of the Congregation of Holy Cross, escorted us from the Via Cappuccini about 11:45 a.m. Our audience was for 12:30 p.m. Father Sauvage teased us by pretending that he would have to fight to get us four admitted because we wore hats; but there was no difficulty at all. The people in uniform only looked at us with as much interest as we did at them. We went up interminable steps and through two large rooms to a smaller one. This was hung with three huge tapestries, the middle one of which depicted Christ healing the sick. We sat there for some time and were conducted then to a smaller room where we were to see the Holy Father all by ourselves.
>
> "We knelt in a semicircle when the Holy Father entered. He first gave his hand to Father Sauvage to kiss, who then presented the Holy Cross Sisters and explained that they were from America and were going to India. He then presented us, telling the Holy Father that one was a dentist and three nurses. The Holy Father was extremely kind. He spoke in Italian: Father Sauvage translated his words exactly.

"The Holy Father said that it was a joy for him to see the Catholic Medical Missionaries, particularly as his desire is to have and foster public interest in Medical Missions and we were carrying it into effect. He realized fully the great importance of medicine in the Missions. For this reason, he had a special section devoted to Medicine in the Missions at the Great Missionary Exposition held in the Vatican. He was glad to see that in various countries, efforts were made and courses organized to place medicine at the service of the Missions. The Catholic Medical Missionaries therefore were responding to his thought and desire. For, he added, in many cases, souls can be reached only through the bodies. The Holy Father gave us his blessing for the Society and all our benefactors."

The sisters were then taken to meet Cardinal Van Rossum, who was extremely gracious.

"Father Sauvage explained that we were Medical Missionaries. Cardinal Van Rossum seemed very pleased and said that it was the Holy Father's great wish to have real medical people in the Missions. He wished to know and was very glad to hear what the Holy Father had said to us. He said that we had a great work to do and a very large field for it and he wished us every success."

Father Sauvage wrote to Anna, addressing her as "Dear Miss Dengel," and gave a full report on what had occurred at the Vatican. He stressed that the Holy Father had been "extremely kind," repeating the Pope's own words to the members of her Society, that it was "a great joy for him to see the Catholic Medical Missionaries," that he realized fully "the great importance of Medicine in the Missions." Father Sauvage also reported briefly on his meeting with Monsignor Marchetti, who was also very interested in the development of the Society. They discussed "the course to be taken to have it approved," and the Monsignor was "very encouraging and very favorable." Father Sauvage then added some encouraging words and advice of his own.

> "I know that you will be very happy to hear this good news. I have no doubt that you will succeed in your work, because it answers a real great need. Of course, you will have to be patient, perhaps to pass through some trials; but Our Lord will be with you and will give you success so long as you work only for Him."

He repeated what he had mentioned earlier.

> "As I told you, when in Washington, the first thing to be done will be to have your Society canonically erected by Archbishop Curley, with the authorization of the Holy See, into a Diocesan Congregation. I hope that it will be possible to obtain that you may take the vows, without having to change the nature and end of your Society. I need not to add that I shall be happy to help you as much as I possibly can in your efforts and work."

On February 2, the four members of Anna's Society, joined by two Holy Cross Sisters en route to Bengal, set sail from Naples on a two-week voyage to Bombay, and from there, a 54-hour train ride to Rawalpindi.

In the USA, Anna Dengel was out giving lectures in "the Middle West." She spent significant time and energy during the winter of 1930 promoting medical missions. She also published a series of articles in the *The Medical Missionary* based on her experiences in India: "Keeping Warm in a House of Snow" … "Oriental Women I Have Met" … "Plague" … "The Suffering of Children in Non-Christian Lands." This allowed her to continue to be present to the subscribers of her magazine while she was on the road. Because Anna was now inundated with administrative responsibilities, she could not be actively engaged in the practice of medicine herself, but she made sure that others would be. Her Society had recently undertaken supervision of two health centers in the city of Dacca in Bengal, one Hindu and one Muslim. In March Sister Mary Laetitia submitted the following report.

> "We are working in two centers. I have one and Sister Helen has the other. All the people speak Bengali, that is, the midwives and *dhais*, with the exception of a woman sub-assistant surgeon, but as she is very seldom

there that doesn't help us much. You can't imagine the misery and poverty of the homes into which we go. Most of the homes are made of bamboo, some with tin roofs, if the people can afford it; if not, just bamboo. It is more of a latticework than a house. Most of the women lie on the floor on a reed mat; they have nothing; a handful of filthy rags usually, sometimes, however they are clean. The poor little baby lies naked on the mat or on a thin piece of old rag.

"When the rain comes (the storms are awful here), the houses are just flooded. If the poor women are Hindus, they are always put out of the house, in a cow shed, if there is one, or in some awful shanty, rich and poor alike. Nobody will go into the Hindu woman's room for a month here, after the birth of a child, so she has to get right up herself, whenever she wants anything. Sometimes we go and find that even to the third day, no tea or milk or any food has been given. It is no good our preparing anything as they wouldn't eat from our hand.

"The Moslem women are not nearly so badly treated in this respect as they are allowed to stay in the house and other people will enter the room. Sometimes the sheds, hovels rather, in which the babies are born are so low that we cannot stand upright, and they are usually so dark, in the case of the poor people, that after coming in from the bright sun it is impossible to see the patient at once. You can't imagine the heat of such places; if the people are Hindus they often keep a fire in the room to keep the devils off. If they are Moslems and poor the patient is in the only room and all the cooking has to be done there.

"The infant mortality is very high in Dacca, around 25 percent. It's a wonder to me that it isn't 100 percent. We certainly never realized that such poverty could exist. There is one consolation and that is, food is very cheap here, so although the people are so poor, they all get enough to eat, at least one doesn't see many very thin people around."

On March 17, the feast of Saint Patrick, Sister M. Laetitia and Sister Helen came together to start the Maternity and Child Welfare Clinic in Dacca. Holy Cross Bishop Crowley wrote the following letter to Anna Dengel in May.

> "I should have written to you weeks ago to thank you for the exceedingly great favor you have shown Dacca in sending the Mission two of your zealous members. The Magistrate remarked to me the other day that he was particularly pleased to notice the happy and cheerful way in which the Sisters regarded the many difficulties inseparable from pioneer work."

In April Dr. Joanna Lyons reported to Michael Mathis on developments in the Rawalpindi mission in the Punjab.

> "Sister Agnes Marie will bring you many details of things out here. I need only say that everybody is well...the newcomers have taken hold very well of the situation. Money matters are satisfactory. We are building four rooms upstairs to complete the second storey. In the busy season we need more space, and lately a windfall came to us from the settlement of St. Catherine's. We put the money into this addition, lest it slip away from us."

Also in April, Anna received the following news from Cardinal Dougherty.

> "The enclosure is the answer of the Sacred Congregation of Propaganda regarding the matter laid before it last December. The gist is that you are to live as good Religious, but not to take Vows."

This unanticipated setback meant that the Society's leaders would have to work even harder to convince ecclesiastical authorities to accept a new understanding of how one might live a dedicated life.

It was at this time that Sister Agnes Marie, R.N., one of the first four members of the Society and pioneer of the Holy Family Hospital in India, was recalled to the Motherhouse to act as Directress of candidates. At about the same time, a piece appeared in the Society's magazine weighing the pros and cons of opening a training school for Indian nurses at the hospital in Rawalpindi.

> "To train natives is one of the great wishes and aims of our Society. Indian young women certainly have the qualities of mind, heart and body to make splendid nurses. The problem, however, is that it is difficult to find girls with the necessary preliminary education. Also, Indian women are accustomed to get married very young; as the course takes a minimum of three years, many get married before completing it. Ups and downs, in the training of native nurses are inevitable, but in this as in every other Mission task, the only thing is to persevere in spite of difficulties."

On May 14 Anna sailed to Europe. Pauline Willis had been urging her to come and help her revive the moribund London Committee that had meant so much to Dr. McLaren. Anna had also needed to take a long overdue rest, one of extended duration, for she was not at all well. She planned to do that in the Tirol, a setting that was conducive to meeting the needs of her body, her soul, her spirit. Later that year Sister Agnes Marie would enter this note in her journal: "The result of this trip was much work and little rest." The reason? One could count the ways that prevented Anna from simply letting go and sitting still.

While in England Anna was asked to give a lecture on Medical Missions and the work of the Society in the Cathedral Hall in London. Cardinal Bourne presided and stressed the need for hospitals and for Christian charity as a means of spreading the faith. He also spoke of the absolute necessity of vocations and emphasized the work of medical missionaries had his "wholehearted approval and blessing." He invited the Society to start a branch house in England, "the sooner the better."

Following an interlude in the Alpine setting that was and always would be her heart's home, Anna accepted an invitation to attend the annual Catholic University Students' Conference in Holland. "Medical Missions" was the theme of the conference that year. Those few days spent at a mission gathering of students in Holland really impressed Anna. "Seeing their enthusiasm and their earnestness to work, hearing their cheerful songs and observing their natural, unaffected ways is sufficient to make one understand why Holland gives so many and such good missionaries. We already have two Dutch candidates in our Society and we hope that many will follow in their footsteps." Her experiences that summer gave Anna renewed energy and fervor. "There is no doubt about it. Medical Missions is in the air. The ball has been set rolling and there is no telling how much momentum it will gain as it goes on."

On August 29 Anna returned from her trip abroad and was soon caught up in the administrative work of the Society. Nevertheless, her medical missionary experiences in India remained at the forefront of her consciousness. She longed to introduce others to what many considered "another world." For her, the Orient was an integral part of this one world that God had created and entrusted to our care. In the November issue of the magazine, she wrote the following editorial.

"During my stay in India I had dealings with many Mohammedans, men and women. There is a certain vigor and uprightness about them which one admires. The women, especially the more well to do, are strictly secluded, which makes their lives narrow and unhealthy. Their two great interests are their children (especially sons) and their jewels. On the whole the women are very good-natured, extremely patient and enduring and really lovable. They rule in domestic matters and are more conservative than men in clinging to old rules and customs; to reach them and to gain their confidence is not easy; in fact, impossible for men and possible only for women with a sincere desire to help them. Medical Missions by women are recognized as the most welcome portals of entry and the most needed service."

That was the core of her message as she went about the necessary task of raising funds at a time when there was very little money to be had. In an editorial she had written for the magazine as summer drew to a close, Anna gave this report.

"Our Missionaries had the privilege of meeting his Excellency Archbishop Mooney, Apostolic Delegate to

India, on his recent visit to Washington. His Excellency said: 'There should be more of you in India.' The editor [Anna Dengel] then replied: 'If you think so, please tell the bishops and priests to make it known generally.' His Excellency then replied: 'Not because you ask me, but because I consider it a matter of conscience, I will speak about it and have already done so. I am convinced that Medical Mission work in India is necessary. Through it Christianity reaches many who would never in any other way come in contact with it.'"

During the first week of September, several hundred Sisters from the United States and Canada who were involved in hospital-related ministries gathered for the 15th annual convention of the Catholic Hospital Association held at Catholic University in the nation's capital. Emphasis was given to the need for more vocations to the nursing sisterhoods. Anna expanded on their call for more women in medical ministries.

> "If 20,000 sisters engaged in the care of the sick in the United States and Canada bemoan the fewness of their number, what can one say of the Mission fields, with ten times the number of inhabitants, perhaps one hundred times more disease and suffering and just a handful of nursing sisters. Our Lord Himself said 'the Harvest is ripe;' the spread of the Kingdom of God could be hastened if the laborers were more numerous. The harvest is rotting away for want of reapers. Who can reflect upon this without a fervent prayer for more vocations to the nursing sisterhoods in general and for those who work in the Missions in particular."

On September 30th Anna's Society celebrated its fifth anniversary. She reflected on their many blessings since Foundation Day.

> "When we started we were four; now we are four times four. We do not ourselves know whether it is little or much. We are a new religious community with the same fundamental purpose of personal sanctification

225

and the practice of the spiritual and corporal works of mercy as other sisters whose special work is the care of the sick, but our field of labor both in kind and locality being different, our methods must necessarily vary also. We are so organized that we are permitted to practice the medical and nursing professions in their full scope including surgery and obstetrics, both of which are very necessary to help people in the Orient often far removed from other medical aid. Our constitutions, our garb, our training are all planned to achieve the end for which we banded ourselves together. We who lead the life and know its happiness and hear the cry of mission bishops for help are sometimes inclined to wonder why we are not more. But we realize that the beginning is slow and hard and we feel that in spite of it we have every reason to sing a Te Deum of thanksgiving on September 30, our first jubilee of five years of existence."

On that day Sister M. Bernadette, R.N. and Sister M. Christine made their Profession and took the Mission Oath by which the members of the Society promise to go to any mission field where they are sent by the Superior of the Society. With regard to that day, Anna wrote:

"In his sermon the Rev. John Delanney, c.s.c. emphasized three necessary qualities of a Medical Mission Sister: kindness and gentleness in her ministration to the sick, a spirit of sacrifice necessary to give up home and country and take up a life of hardship and responsibility, and a great devotion to her community, as it is through this bond that the work is made possible."

In October Anna received the following request from Father Callistus, Provincial of the Order of Capuchin Friars. He was the Secretary General of Missions in Rome.

"I am asked to hold before interested priests a conference about the question: 'if it is convenient that Mission *Sisters* do midwife work in the Missions.' I should be glad to hear your opinion on the matter, and at the same time

I should be grateful. As a practical missionary I do not hesitate to affirm the question with some restrictions. But as many people are of another opinion, I must come with strong arguments to prove my thesis and therefore I ask your advice."

Anna responded to his request by writing an article entitled, "Should Sisters Do Obstetrical Work in the Missions? General Considerations: Need and Scope of the Work." This detailed overview of the issue would give representative ecclesiastics an opportunity to study the central questions at the heart of the current debate. Of what does the training and the actual work consist? What are the necessary qualifications? Who can do the work? She concluded with a practical example of an attempt at bringing medical aid, including obstetrics, to the missions.

In October Michael Mathis sent a letter to Archbishop Curley. His main points appear below.

"During the summer our Father Sauvage from Rome was here in the United States. At the time I consulted him on several occasions upon the canonical status of the Society of Catholic Medical Missionaries. The reason for these consultations was that he had written me during the past year to enquire if the Holy See had issued a decree of erection for the Society. At the time I wrote him that no such decree was received and that I personally didn't know that this was necessary to establish the Society canonically.

"During the summer, however, Father showed me from Canon 492 that this was a requirement, but that we need not worry about it since many other Societies were established by Bishops and then only later was the decree of erection procured from Rome. Father also assured me that he would be quite willing to act for Your Grace in procuring this decree If that was your pleasure. Of course Your Grace understands that this decree of erection merely gives the Society the canonical status I thought it had by virtue of your approbation of June 12 – 1925 to establish the work in the Archdiocese of Baltimore. It does not take it out of its status as a diocesan society.

"Your Grace will recall that the Constitutions of the new Society have been modeled upon the requirements set down in Canon Law for a society of women who lead a community life after the manner of religious under proper superiors but without the three usual vows of religious life (Canon 673); and by the following Canon (canon 674) the foundation of such a Society follows the rules set down for the foundation of religious institutes as outlined in Canon 492."

Father Mathis had summarized, clearly and succinctly, the intrinsic nature and canonical status of the Society. He went on to ask the Archbishop for permission to send Sister Agnes Marie to the novitiate of the Holy Cross Sisters at Notre Dame in Indiana, so that they might prepare her to train future candidates in her own community. He pointed out that they were willing to accept Sister Agnes Marie, who would eventually adapt what she learned there to the spirit and rules of the Society on her return. The following month Sister Agnes Marie Ulbrich made this note in her journal. "I left the Medical Mission House for Saint Mary's Novitiate in November 1930."

On November 2, All Souls Day, a cable from Doctor Joanna Lyons to the Motherhouse announced the sad news of the death of Rt. Reverend R. R. Winkley, Prefect Apostolic of Kashmir and Kafristan. It was a significant loss to the fledgling Society, especially for Anna. Monsignor Winkley had been her mentor and her friend, supporting and encouraging her, unconditionally, through several significant transitions. She wrote the following IN MEMORIAM so that members and benefactors might know something more about the one "whose prefecture we may call the cradle of our Society."

"Monsignor Winkley was a native of Lancashire, England, and a member of St. Joseph's Foreign Mission Society of Mill Hill. He was assigned to the Punjab as a young priest and was the first Catholic missionary to enter Kashmir. During the war he was elected Prefect Apostolic, his territory comprising one of the most beautiful and interesting parts of the world. Monsignor

Winkley's personality was one that radiated peace and confidence. Perhaps his outstanding qualities were his meekness and imperturbable calm. He was kindness and simplicity itself. No one was afraid to approach him. He was extremely economical, and generous with it all. He was known as a good beggar. The secret of his success was that he was able to convince people that it was a privilege to have an opportunity to lay up treasures in heaven. He also believed in taking good care of one's health and taking proper precautions. Many times he warned the writer not to venture out during the scorching heat of the afternoon. He personally designed the plans and supervised the building of several churches and schools, thereby assuring good workmanship and saving thousands of dollars to the Prefecture. His last work was the Holy Family Hospital, in which he was one of the first patients and in which our Sisters had the privilege of taking care of him in his last illness. God called him to his reward on the feast of All Souls' after more than 40 years of missionary labor. Monsignor Winkley heartily approved of the foundation of a specific society of Medical Missionaries. He took a fatherly interest in our humble beginnings. This was a source of great encouragement to us and we shall always gratefully remember it. . . . *requiescat in pace.*"

On November 11 His Eminence Cardinal Dougherty of Philadelphia, Bishop Thomas J. Shahan, and Monsignor Bernard McKenna visited the community at 6th and Buchanan.

"As His Eminence Cardinal Dougherty encouraged at a decisive moment the starting of a society of medical missionaries, and also as it is mainly through his generosity and that of the people of Philadelphia that the Holy Family hospital in the Punjab became a reality, it was with a feeling of solemn joy and gratitude that we received His Eminence in our little house. Meeting our missionaries, His Eminence enquired of each from whence she came and was surprised to find that we were such a cosmopolitan group. He visited our chapel and gave us his blessing and encouraged us by saying that ours was a splendid work."

News from the Society's missions in India rounded out the year. Sister M. Therese reported from Rawalpindi.

"We have so many patients just now that we have to move around quite a bit. I declare that the next move will have to be out to the summer house. It is like playing a game of checkers. At times a compass would be very useful. A few days ago we had a Mohammedan patient for an abdominal operation, who requested to be put on the operating table with her head turned to Mecca. Of course, we gladly granted this request."

Sister M. Frances, who was in charge of the training of native nurses, wrote of her problems in preparing them for government examinations.

"The long dreaded time of examination for the nurses came at last. One of the examiners came to the hospital. I hope the nurses were successful. Only three were able to take the examination, since the others could not learn Roman Urdu in time."

Sister M. Laetitia shared several of her experiences.

"In Dacca one has to be able to speak two languages: One for the Hindus, who speak Bengali; and one for the Mohammedans, who usually speak Urdu. It is not all plain sailing here; sometimes none of the *dhais* whom we are supposed to train show up for classes. On inquiring the reason, one is told they are building houses for a certain person who hired them, or another time they are making a road, or it is the wedding season and they are getting their sons and daughters married off.

"On our rounds visiting mothers and babies we see much poverty. It is one of the reasons of the high infant mortality here (25%). The houses are made of open work bamboo. Usually the mother lies on the floor on a sack or a bamboo mat. When it rains, which it does very heavily here, the whole room often gets flooded out and the mother and baby have to remain there – there is nothing else to be done. Often we cannot even find a rag, clean or dirty, to cover the baby. The monsoon is almost over. It is still hot, but the cold season is due soon. We cannot grumble about the heat here, except that you can 'pick it up' so to speak, but it is heaven compared to Rawalpindi."

Indeed there were hardships also confronting Society members who were living in America, where they were preparing for medical mission work, or awaiting an assignment, or struggling to keep the home fires burning at an historically challenging time. However, hearing the stories of the pioneers who were paving the way for those who would follow after, and knowing that all were part of a sacred call to hope and healing, was reason enough to be thankful. Another reason was the ongoing generosity of benefactors and friends, especially at Christmas, "a time when one experiences more than ever the happiness and privilege of belonging to a religious family of one heart and one spirit." Among the gifts received that year was "a beautiful Crucifix for the chapel" and "a player piano which was not only hailed with great delight by the musicians of the Society, but made great use of during the holidays." There was also a "Christmas turkey…it weighed seventeen and a half pounds. We did not fail to say three cheers for the donors, not to mention the usual prayer after meals for our benefactors: 'Vouchsafe, O Lord, for Thy Name's sake, to reward with eternal life all those who do us good.'"

The milk of human kindness
should flow very freely and generously in us.

Anna Dengel

CHAPTER FIFTEEN

A sign that interest in Medical Missions was on the rise around the world was the growing number of publications devoted to the subject. In the English language, however, the Society's pioneering magazine was still the only one. Its combination of news items, personal stories, professional articles, and photos focused on medical missions made it a valuable resource for a broad spectrum of society. Producing *The Medical Missionary* was a priority for Anna Dengel, its editorial director, and she worked on it zealously. No matter how busy she might have been or how exhausted she might have felt, she would always take the time to ensure a quality publication. She had brought the magazine into existence and was determined to keep it there. She also wanted to maintain its readability and its friendly tone, so she regularly published accounts of her mission experiences in story form. Three articles based on her days as a doctor in the Punjab – "A Small Harem," "The Sun Shines for All," and "Eaters of Dust" – appeared in the first three issues of 1931.

It was becoming a New Year tradition. For the third time in three years, members of the Society were on their way to India. On January 22, at a farewell ceremony in the Holy Cross chapel, three women renewed their Solemn Promise and their Mission Oath. The seminary choir sang an exquisite rendition under the direction of Mr. A. Benson. Presiding Bishop George Dinnigan, c.s.c. congratulated the newly assigned for their wisdom in embracing the path they had chosen and assured them, in the words of the Curé d'Ars, they were going "like a cannonball straight to God." The following day, Sister M. Christine, Sister Margaret Mary, R.N., and Sister M. Bernadette, R.N. left for the missions. Like the previous group that had gone to India, these women also met with Pope Pius XI during a stopover in Rome. Father Sauvage wrote to Anna:

> "I was able to obtain for them a special audience with the Holy Father. The Holy Father was exceedingly kind, even more than usual. Having heard that they were Medical Missionaries, he said: 'We rejoice that you have consecrated your life to such a noble work, and we hope that your example will be followed by many.' He asked each one about her place of birth, spoke some words of German to Sister Bernadette, and in the end, he gave his blessing to the whole Society, to its Founders and to its Benefactors."

The three women who had met with Pope Pius XI would arrive in Rawalpindi in time to celebrate Holy Family Hospital's third anniversary. More than 1,000 patients had been admitted to the hospital and approximately 20,000 had been taken care of in the dispensary since its opening day. Many more patients had also been treated in their homes and during village visits. The Society's training school for native women added to the celebration.

Anna was delighted. She would weave this good news into her talks when out in the public arena during the days ahead.

> "Every now and then I am invited to give a talk on Medical Missions. In spite of the talks and talks and talks I have given on the subject, I enjoy giving more talks, not because the subject is new, but the audience. And the audience I consider as potential candidates, or friends of Medical Missions. The Holy Father said to our Sisters that it is his great desire and ambition to foster public interest in Medical Missions. The Holy Father realizes that in a work like ours, public interest is absolutely necessary. By explaining the condition of the women of the Orient and the need for medical aid, Catholics cannot help but be interested. It is a case of 'love the neighbor as thyself.' My most heartfelt thanks to all who have in the past so cordially and generously

helped to promote our aims and ideals by giving the opportunity of making them known."

Father Sauvage also wrote to Father Mathis, telling him that the petition to Rome for the canonical erection of Anna's Society had to come from the local Archbishop and include the following documents: a brief historical sketch of the Society; a description of the habit for the members and the novices; a brief summary of the Constitution, especially as to the Novitiate and Training of the novices. He concluded by saying: "Tell me in your next letter if the Medical Missionaries would prefer to be under the Propaganda, as their work is exclusively for the missions."

In February Anna decided to pay a visit to Sister Agnes Marie, who had been in the novitiate of the Holy Cross Sisters in Indiana since November. Sister Agnes Marie wrote the following in her journal: "Doctor visited me. She looked like a walking corpse – pale, tired, and very nervous. She went to the Sanitarium in Rome, Indiana for ten days." Although her health was clearly declining, Anna continued to push on.

The Society's celebration of the Feast of Our Lady, Cause of Our Joy, on March 25 featured "the blessing of our bell." Bishop Thomas Strahan came to 6th and Buchanan, and in a simple ceremony, blessed the new bell that would be used to sound the Angelus at noon and again at 6:00 pm; when the Sisters went off to the missions; and on other special occasions.

Life at the Motherhouse appeared to be orderly and tranquil, but an undercurrent of dissatisfaction hovered beneath the surface. The Society's leadership was at odds. Michael Mathis was not happy, although only those of his inner circle knew that this was so. Anna Dengel was not well, yet she continued doggedly to do what she felt needed to be done to keep the community solvent and ready to respond to need. The tension that existed between them was rooted in two very different ways of understanding what had been envisioned, which meant diverse approaches to shaping the nascent community for missionary service. One was more ecclesiastical, the other more mundane. The struggle to sustain their endeavor amid the increasing tension resulted in an accumulation of discontent in Mathis and far too much stress for Anna.

The strained relationship between the two finally reached a tipping point. Mathis hinted to several of his associates that he might consider relinquishing his responsibilities at the Motherhouse if things did not change. He wanted a more integral relationship with the Society and a more authoritative role. In the process of responding to correspondence from Dr. Joanna Lyons, he confided to her some of his displeasure with Doctor Dengel and the limitations placed on him. What he really wanted was a fulltime position within the Society. A Holy Cross superior whom Mathis knew well was currently stationed in Rawalpindi and he and Doctor Lyons discussed the situation. Joanna Lyons wrote to Mathis:

> "A closer relationship with the Society would be a source
> of many blessings and advantages…No other person,
> it seems to me, is so well able to help it along as you."

Mathis wrote to Doctor Lyons again about having spoken with Anna about their strained relationship and his dissatisfaction with his role.

> "I think you will be glad to hear that we had some very
> frank discussion of every phase of the relations of the
> Society and myself before Doctor went to Europe. I
> disliked very much telling Doctor some things about
> the lack of progress in the Society due to her attitudes
> toward any kind of assistance given the Society by
> myself or Holy Cross and toward the externally foreign
> element in the Society, which latter was an obstacle
> for the recruitment of American subjects. The radical
> point I made was that the Society has little chance
> of the growth which is possible until it has either a
> Community of priests behind it or a priest who is
> capable of doing what a Community would do."

Mathis then told Doctor Lyons about Anna's change of heart.

> "While in Europe Doctor wrote me that she was
> beginning to see that some kind of clerical assistance
> was necessary for the development of the work, and
> that, as far as she was an obstacle to the development

she was willing to take a subordinate place if that proved necessary. Of course there is no question of that. Since Doctor's return we have had some very important discussions. One of them led to Doctor's asking Father General to have me assigned exclusively for the work of the Society. We also discussed the same subject with Father Sauvage. I doubt very much whether my Community would ever consent to this."

Then Father Mathis put into words what he was actually seeking: a more systemic relationship between the Society and his own Holy Cross congregation. He envisioned his role in the future to be the bridge between the two.

"It has thus far been a fundamental policy of the Society of Catholic Medical Missionaries not to be identified with Holy Cross and this has prevented our doing many more things for you than we are doing. I really believe that if in the end we judge it is better to increase the relations of the Society of Catholic Medical Missionaries with our community, this is the opportune time from the point of view of Holy Cross."

In conversations with the leadership of his community, Michael Mathis stressed that he was absolutely convinced of the necessity of an integral association between the Society of Medical Missionaries and a community of priests, if not the Congregation of Holy Cross, then perhaps a community he himself would found, either as a member of Holy Cross, or independently, after leaving his own Congregation. Mathis insisted that priests had to play a definitive role in the evolution of this new Society of Catholic Medical Missionaries, and he had to be one of them. Dr. Joanna Lyons responded:

"So far as I can see, God, by natural (and supernatural) inclination and fitness and by circumstances, has called you to be a leader in regard to medical missions. If He has, moreover, shown you the need and the manner of enlisting priests in the promotion of this work and has put you into contact with even two or three of this mind, it would seem an indication of the will of God to proceed to the formation of an association or even of a community of priests devoted to the promoting of medical missions. As to the attitude of Doctor Dengel, I have never had any communication from her on the subject. My feeling is that we should proceed according to the light we have not too rapidly and then God will show further what is His Will."

Michael Mathis began to implement changes at the Motherhouse. He began with the music. They would master Gregorian chant.

"It is not only the Church's rule to have Plain Chant but it is also the only kind of ecclesiastical singing that makes it possible for even very few singers, say two or three, to produce a genuinely religious and truly artistic service anywhere whether it be in the grandest Cathedral at home or in the poorest bamboo chapel in the jungles of India."

Another change was far more substantive. It had to do with the Purpose of the Society statement that appeared in every issue of *The Medical Missionary* magazine. For the first three years, the purpose was:

"... To render medical aid, no disease or condition being excepted, to Christians and non-Christians in the officially recognized foreign mission countries of the world."

In 1930 a phrase had been added after "Christians and non-Christians." It stated: "and to bring the light and consolation of our Holy Faith to the people under their care." The following had also been added as an introduction to the purpose statement, claiming that the Society "is intended for qualified women...attracted to the religious life ...." and that it "is a religious community." Then in the current year of 1931, there was this substantive change:

"The purpose of the Society is to work for the spread of the Holy Faith and to help the sick in foreign mission countries through the establishment of hospitals and dispensaries, etc."

The purpose of the Society now was to "work for the spread of the Holy Faith." For Mathis, this was primary. The healing mission followed. For Anna the Society's purpose had been and always would be the healing mission. This fundamental shift in the mission of the Society had been published in the magazine that she continued to edit, when well enough to do so. It would circulate around the world. She was deeply distressed. On May 9 Anna was admitted to Georgetown Hospital and remained there for a month, where she was treated for liver dysfunction and given a series of transfusions. On June 2 she sent the following handwritten letter to members of her Society.

"Dear Sisters,
As I may die, I want to have a few words of love and encouragement to you. First I want to say that I am completely resigned to the Holy Will of God, and if he should take me at this early stage of the Society, I know that He will provide for it. Then I would like to emphasize that the purpose of our Society is the glory of God, our sanctification, the salvation of souls and the relief of suffering. The four pillars on which our Society will be able to build is the love of God, the love of our neighbor, devotion to Our Lady – to whom our Society is dedicated in a special way, and obedience.

"Our vocation is difficult; we must lighten the burden by great charity and helpfulness to each other. We can never be nice enough to each other. Little children, love one another. Let us do everything for God and with real charity. Let us not overburden ourselves with work to the extent of detriment to the spiritual life, which must be our first concern. Without it, there would be no meaning in our Society, and it would not fulfill its purpose.

"Let us train natives as much as possible and make great sacrifices if necessary to achieve it. Also be generous financially and otherwise in this special task.

"Let our aim be: 'to do our best' each according to their gifts. Let us be reliable and humble. *Let us have respect for all authority* – for each other and *for our patients*, no matter how degraded or poor.

"Let us be anxious and make efforts to be efficient professionally for the sake of greater charity. It is a duty to look after one's health. It is also a duty to look carefully after all the things of the Society, to be good and prudent stewards of the gifts given to us to distribute.

"Let us be simple in everything. Let us not harbor misunderstanding or bitter feelings. Never go to bed without making peace.

"Let us be faithful to our Constitutions, improve them as experience dictates. Let us love the evangelical counsels – *poverty* so exemplified by Our Lord, so inevitable in our work in the foreign missions, so helpful to salvation – *chastity* so beautiful – and *obedience* absolutely necessary and so meritorious. As far as making vows is concerned, let us aim at it and abide by the decision of the Church.

"Let us not give up the purpose for which we were founded. – Besides the spiritual reasons common to all religious communities, we have the aim of practicing medicine, surgery, obstetrics etc. in their full scope, so as to be able to help the people, especially the women in all their needs.

"Let us keep and often pray for the true spirit of liberty of the children of God. Narrow-minded people and those who have an inferiority complex should not be allowed to make the Solemn Promise. Although we are of different degrees of education, of differing ages and from different countries, we can work together harmoniously for the glory of God and the relief of our patients, if each member has the sole aim of doing everything for God and is truly humble. The truly humble will not say: such and such is preferred to me.

"Let us consider it a great privilege and thank God for it every day to be chosen to spend our lives in His Service and to serve Him in His sick and poor.

"Let us always be very grateful to our Benefactors and pray for them. Also the deceased Benefactors. Let us be specially grateful to Father Mathis who helped us to start the Society and to the Holy Cross for their great help and kindness to us. Also the Holy Cross Sisters for training Sister Agnes Marie.

"Asking Our Lord to let us do a lot of good and to bless each and every member of the Society and asking your pardon and also to pray for me, I am with a Mother's love

"Your servant in J.M.J. Anna Dengel."

On June 4 Anna Dengel had a hysterectomy. On June 27 she returned home and began lecturing as before.

While Anna was recuperating, and then back on the road again soon after her return to the Motherhouse, Father Mathis handled everything, tending to administrative details, corresponding with church authorities, acting as chaplain and spiritual guide, at times introducing changes as he went along. Issues arising in Rawalpindi needed immediate attention. Doctor Lyons wrote to him again regarding the situation there.

"Sister Anthony wrote to me of Doctor Dengel's illness (and incidentally of your goodness to them in this trying time.) As it is probable that she is not attending to mail or business, I shall write about a few matters to you and you can acquaint her with them as seems best to you. We are rather hard up for money but St. Joseph always pulls us out....

"Things are not all serene here in the house. Doctor and the Sisters do not get on so well. Nothing very serious ... the thing is kept going by the irritation of all living in the same house and meeting a great deal. Doctor has spoken to a third party of leaving here and going to work in some other hospital (here in India). It is a great pity, one would think, that this problem of the relations of a doctor with a community seems so difficult. I have experienced it from both sides. The only constructive idea I have to offer is that it would be happier for all if the doctor had a quite separate establishment, rather than to live as an appendage to the community, with separate quarters, her own servants and housekeeping arrangements. Medical work and the Eastern climate and surroundings are trying to the nerves. Enforced daily contact outside of working hours aggravates any little antipathies that may be present."

Another letter from Doctor Lyons to Michael Mathis reported that Doctor Dengel had wired confirming a personnel decision. In her letter to Mathis, Doctor Lyons included several suggestions based on her experience at Holy Family Hospital and at Saint Catherine's.

1st "Our members need a full two years' novitiate, carried on in the manner of religious orders in which the members should not have to work too hard, but should have leisure for spiritual growth."

2nd "No secular person should be intimately associated with the Community, (unless perhaps a very brief guest) to the extent of eating with the members or living in or very close to community quarters. It tends to foster antipathies on one side and sympathy or 'taking sides' or telling tales out of school to outsiders."

3rd "It appears to me that a doctor to get on successfully in one of our institutions must be either (a) a person with a community or (b) a person with a separate housekeeping establishment who makes her own social life and is connected with the Hospital establishment only professionally."

"I have heard from more than one of your goodness during the present trying times in Washington and we all thank you most heartily."

In August Michael Mathis sent a lengthy explanatory letter to his Superior General in France outlining where he was coming from and where he wanted to go.

"The precarious health of Doctor Dengel for the past year or so, the growing necessity to solve many problems of the Society of Catholic Medical Missionaries, problems whose solutions have been delayed largely by my inability to give them the attention required, and my being relieved of superiorship last July by the Provincial Chapter have combined to make me consider anew the obligation I feel to give my life to this work.

"You told me that this is a question for my own conscience to decide with the aid of prayer and direction. I have done both since 1927 when I first realized that it would be difficult for me to do justice to this Society in my present position. My conclusion is that I feel the time has come both from the point of view of the Society of Catholic Medical Missionaries and from that of our own Congregation for me to be relieved, if that is possible, of my present work in order that I may give my time and attention to the development of this new Society. My feeling of obligation arises out of the fact that I have been the co-founder of this Society and I feel a natural obligation to care for something which I helped to bring into existence."

Here, then, was the problem, the source of what had been eroding the Society's initial cohesiveness and subconsciously affecting its founder. Michael Mathis felt – had always felt but now openly admitted – that this was also his Society. Therefore, he had every right to shape it and to chart its course into the future. In his opinion he had as much right as his "co-founder" had, and perhaps a little more, because the issues they were facing now were ecclesiastical and canonical, which was his area of expertise. Let Anna preside over mission hospitals and dispensaries with the women. Mathis, a loyal son of the Church, would emphasize spreading the Faith, a priority for him. With regard to the Society, he had for years publicly declared he had assisted the founder, Anna, in bringing it into existence, like a midwife at a birth. Now everything had changed.

In his very long letter to his superior, Mathis spoke of the necessity of overseeing the moral responsibility of the members of the Society, his

Society, expectations that are difficult to understand by persons with no theological training. He wrote:

> "The obligation to live according to the Evangelical Counsels and yet not be permitted to make public vows has developed in the Society an inferiority complex which manifests itself in two ways: a desire on the part of some to leave the Society and enter a religious institute where public vows can be made, and, secondly, on the part of others, an under-estimation of the medical apostolate itself because of the prohibition Canon Law makes for those engaged in the medical and nursing professions; namely, that they should not make public vows. It is absolutely necessary that this inferiority complex be removed, and it seems to me that this can be done only by explaining the true attitude of Canon Law on the subject and above all by concentrating the attention of the Society on the value and glory of its apostolate. The leadership in such an educational campaign must be taken by a priest, who understands the problem and has the moral authority to convince those concerned.
>
> "For the recruitment of subjects for the Society it is most important for public confidence that a priest be closely and officially associated with this Society. If this is ordinarily found to be necessary for almost every newly founded Community of women, how much more so is it for a pioneer work of the Church, for the first Community of professional medical and nursing women founded in the Catholic Church and for a Society that is different from others in its very organization, a difference that involves fine canonical distinctions and yet a Society in which the members are free to practice the full scope of the Medical and nursing professions?
>
> "As co-founder of the Society I have tried to supply the help which only a priest can render...I now ask to devote myself entirely to this work.

"I have asked Doctor Dengel with your permission
to request the Holy See to appoint me to this post as it
sees fit."

These excerpts from a very long exposition by Michael Mathis reflect
his determination to take control of Anna's Society in order to shape its
development. The following statement within that same report indicates
that he was also aware of the inherent value of an alternative approach.

"The uniqueness of the Society in living a community
life without public vows and yet being free to engage to
the full extent in the medical and nursing professions,
might eventually be its strength both in the Society and
for the public at large."

Michael Mathis had set in motion a new phase in his relationship with
the Society. Things would continue as they were before, or so it would
appear, but that would not be for long.

In August Anna left for Europe. Her plan was to go to the Tirol
and rest, as she was not able to rest while at home in Washington. But
first, she had business to attend to. She went to Paris to see the Superior
General of the Holy Cross in Le Mans in order to do what Michael
Mathis had asked her to do, which was, to request that he be assigned
full time to work for the Society. From there she went to Lyon, and
then on to Lourdes.

"It was my good fortune to be entrusted with a little
task to be accomplished in Lourdes and to be given
the wherewithal to make a pilgrimage to the greatest
shrine of Our Lady in the world. I arrived there at
the end of August. The weather was pleasant and the
setting of the city very pretty. The green fields, the
winding river Gave and the round-topped Pyrenees
make a picturesque frame for the all-important spot
in Lourdes: the Grotto. There stands the statue of the
Immaculate Conception in the exact place where Our
Lady appeared to a little shepherdess of fourteen.
"The lights of numberless candles were flickering
before the Grotto, bouquets adorned the rock and

hundreds of eyes were fixed on the statue. One could not help but wonder what thoughts and petitions were in the hearts and minds of the pilgrims. In the afternoon, after a visit to the basilica, I watched the sick being wheeled to the open space in front of it. What a harrowing procession even to one who is accustomed to see suffering. What faces of agony...What disease hidden to those standing by. What hope must be raised in the hearts of them all, at the moment when the Blessed Sacrament is lifted in Benediction over each and every one of them individually.

"In the morning after Mass and Holy Communion at the Grotto, I followed the example of many others and drank water from the miraculous spring and sometime later witnessed a most impressive sight. Many sick were in their wheel chairs outside the baths and a priest of the pilgrimage prayed aloud with outstretched arms and invoked the help of heaven with such vehement prayers and the sick and the people around repeated the invocations with so much fervor, that I at least, felt that at any moment one of the sick might jump up cured. I never heard such prayer before. There was no miracle, however, that morning.

"I had the privilege of an audience with the bishop of Lourdes. I also met the Vicar General, who is a great linguist. It is he who makes all the arrangements for the pilgrimages which come from many lands. He took me personally to the Medical Bureau with which one thousand four hundred and fifty-six doctors are affiliated. He introduced me to the authorities so that I would have the advantage of studying the whole procedure of the Medical examination of the cases. The process is very thorough.

"May I tell you what of all things that I saw, heard and read during my four days' stay in Lourdes struck me the most? It was a little paragraph of a short biography in a cheap guide book of Lourdes. In it, it said, that Bernadette as a girl of thirteen, spent some months with her foster mother to make herself useful minding sheep. When out with her flock she frequently recited the rosary which she had learned to love from the mother of her foster mother. This old lady recited the rosary twenty-five times a day until she died at the age of eighty-eight. [*Anna had written this sentence in capital letters for emphasis.*]

"One may ask: why did Our Lady choose to appear in Lourdes and show her compassion and mercy there through so many miracles of body and soul? Well, nobody can answer the question, but where in the world are there ladies young or old who say twenty-five rosaries a day and make others love it, too?"

From Lourdes Anna went to her home in the Tirol and remained there for about two weeks before moving on to Vienna to attend a Convention of Women Doctors, and then to Budapest, Würzburg, and London. How good it was to be with Pauline Willis again. On October 3rd she opened a house of the Society in Pauline's cottage in Winchcombe, a town in Gloucestershire, about 151 kilometers (or 94 miles) northwest of London.

Back in the USA Father Mathis was keeping Doctor Lyons in Rawalpindi apprised of ongoing developments.

"I believe that you will understand that it is rather difficult to give a reply to the confidential questions with which we have been preoccupied for so long. Many things were making it very difficult to come to a conclusion regarding my giving up my present work and devoting my time and energies to the Medical Missionaries.

"Perhaps the shortest and easiest way to give you the status quo at the present time is to send you a copy of a letter which is a very important one on the subject. It gives you my decision in the case. The latter while addressed to Father General is being taken personally by Doctor Dengel to Europe where she will see our Father General and for the second time try to get him to release me for the work. Whether he does or not, Doctor will present the case directly to the Pope either for permission or for approbation. Naturally you understand how confidential this matter is."

Then he added: "Doctor Dengel is getting along very well. She was quite ill, but the operation has helped her. The trip to Europe will I hope consolidate these gains."

In September Joanna Lyons responded: "I have heard a number of times this summer of how good you were to all of ours during the trying time of Doctor Dengel's illness. Both Sister Agnes Marie and Sister Anthony could not say enough about how you helped. Thanks again from all of us." Also in September, Michael Mathis wrote to Anna who was in the Tirol at the time.

> "I am not at all surprised that the action taken by Father General regarding your request turned out as it did. It is going to be a great sacrifice for our Congregation and we cannot expect to get it lightly."

Mathis went on to say that he had recently spoken with Cardinal Dougherty and informed him about "what you and I had done regarding my possible release from my present work to give my time to the Society. He didn't have anything to say except to inquire if Washington were the best place for the Mother House." The parting words of Mathis to Anna were: "Make sure to remain in Europe as long as it is necessary, first of all for your health, and secondly, for the good of our work."

In November Anna Dengel returned to Washington from her trip overseas. With her were two candidates. On Thanksgiving Day Sister Agnes Marie Ulbrich returned to Washington, DC, having completed her novitiate. On seeing Doctor Dengel, she noted that "her health was poorer than ever." She made the following observation.

> "Dr. Dengel not looking well. She is still very anemic and tires quickly. She apparently is working on forced energy."

They had several discussions about separating candidates from Society members and decided that this would be done so that a more thorough training could be implemented. On December 8, Feast of the Immaculate Conception, Sister M. Xavier Boeckmann, from Arkansas, made her Solemn Promise and took the Mission Oath, and Miss Freda Baum received the garb of the Society and a new name, Sister Mary Gabriel. Seven candidates and all Society members, led by Doctor Dengel, held a simple ceremony to consecrate the novitiate in the building known as Saint Therese. Standing before a statue of "Our Lady of Light, Spouse of the Holy Ghost," they asked for her protection and guidance on the place where the candidates lived and ate and met for exercises other than chapel prayers. As the year was drawing to a close, Sister Agnes Marie noted: "Funds exceedingly low. After daily expenses were paid, $2.50 left and bills coming in." She also added: "Christmas appeal sent out but there has not been a good response on account of the depression." A week later she revised that, saying: "Donations coming faster." Before the year was over, a program was designed and agreed upon that would involve the whole community in securing the resources needed for the coming year. For the proper development of the Society, the aim was

❖ to get enough money before Easter to maintain this house all summer
❖ to pay Doctor Dengel's passage to England after Easter
❖ to buy the London House and maintain it for the summer
❖ to pay interest on our debt
❖ to pay the installment on the Pindi hospital
❖ to pay the way to India for those ready in the Fall of 1932
❖ to bring Doctor Lyons and Sister Laetitia home

This would require approximately $50,000. They noted:

> "Times are considered very hard. Doctor Dengel is not able to go out begging, so looking at it from a natural point of view, it will require a miracle."

And miracles called for prayer. On Gaudete Sunday in Advent, a crusade of prayers was initiated. All nine members of the Society were to participate and the candidates would do their part. The goal was:

1,000	Masses and communions
1,500	rosaries
100,000	ejaculations
2,000	mortifications
1,000	visits
1,000	acts of work

The prayers began that very day and would continue until Easter.

God has been most wonderfully good to us.
When you feel downhearted or discouraged,
begin to count your blessings.

Anna Dengel

Chapter Sixteen

In 1932 Sister Agnes Marie Ulbrich began to keep a personal journal, not about herself but about Anna Dengel. She recorded what Doctor Dengel did, what she said that was of significance, her travel itinerary, and the status of her health through a lengthy period of decline. The information in this journal, she noted, would very likely not be recorded anywhere else and would therefore serve as an historical record of the Society's founder, whom she held in high esteem. "This is not meant to be a diary," she began, "but only a few notes that may not be entered in the chronicles and may eventually prove useful when writing the history. The early spirit may also be contained in this." That primary resource was marked "STRICTLY CONFIDENTIAL" and NOT TO BE READ UNTIL 25 YEARS AFTER DOCTOR DENGEL'S DEATH. It played a role in the writing of this book.

The year 1932 began with an urgent appeal in *The Medical Missionary* magazine. FOURTEEN NURSES NEEDED. That headline was followed by a description of the need.

> "To increase the work of our hospitals in Rawalpindi in Northern India and in Dacca, Bengal, and to be able to start two new missions, we need the minimum of 14 nurses. There can be no doubt that among the thousands of Catholic nurses there would be 14 who would be glad to put their profession in the service of God in the foreign missions where there is so much suffering, so much ignorance of things spiritual and hygienic, if they knew of the need and of the opportunity of this glorious and heroic service for God. We put it in the hands of

Saint Joseph to find a minimum of 14 nurses to enter
our Society on his feast, March 19."

The Society was receiving more and more requests for medical
missionaries and its resources were far too few. To stimulate interest
in faraway lands, Doctor Dengel continued to contribute evocative
articles to subsequent issues of the magazine: "Our Duty Towards
Lepers in the Twentieth Century" … "Use and Abuse of Opium" …
"Malaria" … "Oriental Women I have Met," subtitled, *"Invisible Ladies
of Peshawar"…* "Contemplative Orders in the Missions," and a tribute
to Mary the mother of Jesus entitled "Cause of Our Joy."

Early in the year Doctor Dengel met with community members
and candidates and spoke very seriously about observance of the rule.
Apparently a rebellion was forming among the candidates, who had
been accustomed to a lot more freedom, such as access to the daily
paper, permission to mingle with visitors, and attendance at community
meetings. Suddenly, things had changed. On her return from completing
her own year-long novitiate with another community, Sister Agnes
Marie was now director of what was to be a proper novitiate at 6th and
Buchanan. She imposed a whole new discipline that curtailed previous
liberties and separated candidates from members. The candidates did
not like it, but as they were told by their Superior General who had been
asked by Sister Agnes Marie to intervene on her behalf, they would have
to learn to adjust. Over the next several months a new rule would be
written and submitted to the upcoming Chapter. Implementation of its
underlying spirit had already begun.

Once again Anna was not feeling well. After several days the decision
was made to have two teeth extracted, which left her incapacitated for
several days more. That did not stop her from going to New York, then
on to Philadelphia, and from there to Annapolis, where she lectured
on medical missions. She returned to a busy week at the Motherhouse.
They were mailing 3,000 letters in an appeal for vocations while the
magazine was going to press, so Anna did not get her usual rest and
was utterly exhausted. She said, "Some mornings I feel like a block of
wood and I can hardly get dressed…." A bright spot was a letter from
Sister Marie Alberte who was en route to Rome for the FMM Chapter
and elections. "You did a wise thing to open a house in England," she
wrote, and concluded her words of encouragement with: "I keep you

always in my poor prayers and love you as much as I can say." Because her hands and feet were swollen, Anna checked in with a doctor, and slowly began to improve   .

Before the end of January, a decision by Doctor Joanna Lyons in Rawalpindi would set off a chain reaction throughout the Society. Michael Mathis responded.

"I have known for some time about your desire to enter a contemplative order and I must say I was not surprised....I am writing to you now on the subject not only as a friend but also as the spiritual director of the Society.

"That you have a right to leave the Society of Catholic Medical Missionaries to fulfill a call to the contemplative life is clearly established in theology. However, before doing so you have sufficient understanding of spiritual things to realize that you ought not to do this until you are free to do so. Just as a person in the world who had a call to religious life might be impeded from fulfilling it immediately by obligations at home, so also I feel quite certain that you, as one of the four pioneer members of the Society and particularly as the first mission superior to have had experience on the field itself, owe the Society your services until such a time as it can reasonably replace you without prejudice to the work itself.

"As the first mission superior it is most important that you be present at the forthcoming General Chapter, because you alone have the vital information regarding these pioneer years of the Society's work on the field. Outside of the presence of Doctor Dengel herself, I cannot see that the presence of anyone else is more necessary than your own because the important matters to be taken up for the welfare of the Society will have to be judged very largely by the experience of the work on the field. As the Provincial Superior of the two houses in India and of the other two that are in prospect, it is essential to have a Doctor of the Society to act both from the professional and missionary standpoint. As you know only yourself and Doctor Dengel are capable of fulfilling this post until we get more Doctors which may be within a few years....Therefore this is a serious reason why you ought to remain in the Society until we can train up a Doctor to take charge at Rawalpindi and act as Provincial Superior for India.

"I am not trying to impede the following out of a vocation to which you have a right to aspire. I give you my word that I shall do everything in my power to help you realize your vocation and that my suggestions that you delay are made only from a conviction that you would be injuring a great work in the Church by leaving too soon.

"Finally, I ask you to consider prayerfully another suggestion. Both Doctor Dengel and myself have for a long time been hoping that it would be possible to associate with our work a branch of contemplatives whose duty would be to pray for the success of the active members of the Society and to keep ever alive among all of its members a deep spiritual life as the basis for our medical mission work. Perhaps in God's providence you will be the one to found this work. Please think it over and pray about it."

At the beginning of February Sister Agnes Marie made the following observation.

"Doctor Dengel is more tired than ever. Now she gets up for Mass and goes to bed again immediately after and has breakfast in bed about 8:45 or 9:00. Many days she has not the energy to make her own bed or to eat her breakfast. She was wondering if she should fight this extreme exhaustion but herself realized that she has not enough energy to fight. She spoke one day of a spirit of being 'natural, friendly, nice and accommodating to each other' which she thought should be cultivated more in the Society."

A few days later it was noted that "Doctor is somewhat better, especially if she rests a lot." At about this time Holy Family Hospital in Rawalpindi was celebrating its fourth anniversary and completing a construction project. The *Medical Missionary* magazine reported:

> "In order to accommodate more patients, a building is in process of erection to house the members of the Society and the native nurses, who up to now occupied hospital space. We had to raise a loan to do this, and are of course anxious to pay it off quickly. This is not a good time to ask for a substantial sum, but as every little bit helps, we mention it confidently to our readers."

In March Anna was sent a copy of a letter written by a Benedictine Archabbot in the Tanganyika Territory of East Africa. It was essentially a plea for immediate action regarding women and medical missions. Anna shared it with Cardinal Dougherty because he was involved with ongoing discussions in Rome. It reported that the death rate of native infants was between 40-60% and stated definitively that "native women abhor the thought of any help by a man." Calling for a more enlightened way of dealing with the critical needs of women and children in East Africa, the report stressed "the necessity of training native women, if possible, the wives of catechists and teachers in midwifery," and to do this immediately, which would require a change in canon law for this reason.

> "This training can only be done by our Mission Sisters, trained themselves as nurses and midwives, because nobody else is likely to gain the native woman's confidence. This is, I dare say, also the considered opinion of most, if not all, missionaries, and on the whole coincides with what is made known as the mind of the Holy See in this matter…It is hard to believe that in the mind of the Church professed Sisters are to be barred from this splendid work of Christian charity, where they, to all intents and purposes, are the only people available and by reason of their vocation as mission Sisters, primarily seem to be called upon to step in…. Professed Sisters are allowed to assist doctors operating

on patients of both sexes in any hospital in Europe. Hundreds of professed Sisters have been nursing soldiers during the war. Nobody found or finds that unseemly or improper. On the contrary, they are admired all over the world for their devotion and heroism."

The document concluded with this plea:

"And now I come to the real purpose of this lengthy letter. I entreat Your Excellency to use your influence in order to bring about a change of opinion on this vital missionary question and to obtain a decision that, at any rate for East African Missions, professed Sisters can be trained as midwives and other maternity work. I have no hesitancy in saying that there are not many other questions more important and of more far-reaching consequences for the missionary than the question of how to save the child."

The movement to assure that women with religious vows might practice all aspects of medicine, and most certainly maternity work in mission territories, was gaining momentum around the world, and Anna's little Society of Catholic Medical Missionaries was right there in the midst of it. During the month of March, Anna received the following letter from a Jesuit Bishop in India.

"I thank you most sincerely for your letter and above all for the assurance that you will be very glad to undertake a Medical Mission in Patna diocese, particularly in the Santal country. This is nothing short of grand from our point of view."

In England there was this Society development: "Recently two nurses joined the family circle of our little house, which brings up the membership to the holy number of seven."

In Washington Michael Mathis heard from Joanna Lyons. In a lengthy letter she made her case for responding immediately to a deeper call. Her primary points were these.

"I prayed about this letter and consulted the priest who is my main adviser and received a letter from Doctor Dengel regarding this matter and I am answering both letters.

"It was in the summer of 1928 that I first felt a call to the contemplative life. I laid the matter for advice before four priests...and one (Monsignor Winkley) disapproved firmly of it. As he was (practically) the Bishop and a good and even holy man, I obeyed him to the extent of renewing the solemn promise for a further three years. In the meantime I have tried earnestly to obey the rules of the Society, to keep my unsettled state from troubling any of the others, to seek the advice of priests and to pray. So at length, by the mercy of God, I have arrived at such a state of conviction and peace in my mind regarding this call of God, as I judge it to be, that I feel able to say this: I shall not fear to render an account to God of this decision; nor do I feel called to renew the solemn promise even for a brief period.

"I thought it best that I should not return to the U.S.A. but slip quietly out of sight and enter in India or elsewhere a contemplative house that is willing to have me. (I am now thirty-nine and have been in another religious Society for more than six years.) If I return I shall be there probably at the time my membership expires, which may be upsetting to some of the new ones. At the General Chapter I think I should be somewhat of a nuisance on account of certain convictions that have grown up in my mind regarding the work. (I may say in passing that none of these convictions had taken definite form in my mind in the summer of 1928, when I began to feel the call referred to above)."

Then Joanna shared how she now felt after several years of medical mission experience in India.

1. I do not think that the full practice of medicine is a suitable work for a religious.

2. The Society is spreading itself too rapidly for the forces available.
3. I think that in the long run the interests of the Church are not advanced by our members holding Government jobs.
4. Some of our members are coming out half baked.
5. It seems to me that the principle of a community employing an outside doctor is unsound and unstable.
6. I have an ill-defined perhaps unreasonable idea that if we aim at producing hospitals of high standards, comfortable and up to date, we shall presently cease to have charitable institutions.

She concluded: "Now you see why I would be a nuisance at the General Chapter." She had stated her position honestly and succinctly, and now it was up to the Society to have to deal with it.

Because Anna had been in Europe the previous summer when the Motherhouse had held its annual retreat, she decided to make a private retreat to prepare herself for the upcoming Chapter and its challenging agenda. She was persuaded to go to a retreat house. Its setting would be more conducive to reflection and give her the time and space to prepare for her 40th birthday on March 16, just four days away. She penned pages of notes during that retreat and once again was very hard on herself for having failed to fulfill a list of unrealistic expectations. She made several new lists, interspersing "do's" and "don'ts" with a series of "ought to" and "have to" resolutions for herself and her Society. As always she experienced genuine anguish for constantly falling so far from perfection, and according to her own self-analysis, for having been spiritually ineffective, quick to react, much too busy, and not very likely to change. Nevertheless, she would definitely keep on trying. She wrote:

> I must be patient
> I must be understanding
> I must be compassionate
> I must be forgiving
> I must be trusting
> I must be thoughtful
> I must be just
> I must be the first in the fulfillment of duties
> I must aim at peace and harmony
> I must work hard and consistently and methodically –

> I fail very much in this
> I must have tenacity but not obstinacy
> I must think more and pray more
> I must specially be more loving
> I must be cheerful and not show my anxieties in public
> I must not get discouraged at difficulties
> I must not be ashamed to beg – I still find it very hard
> I must have more devotion to the Holy Ghost
> Jesus, Mary, and Joseph, help me!

These were just a few of her many articulated resolutions. In one sense Anna's reflective notes were a non-stop cry for mercy and an outpouring of devotion for the God who continued to sustain her through all of her ups and downs.

During those days away from the Motherhouse, Anna had time to reflect on the upcoming Chapter in light of the lived experience of the previous six years.

> "What should be carried forward? What required change? Should there be a less rigid separation from the world, for example, easier rules regarding silence, letters, visits home, making the Promise for only three years, a short novitiate? Can we be as good a missionary by our method? Does our method satisfy the heart? The question is whether the new things which seem to make our life easier do not make it harder by remaining attached to the world by a thread."

There were many more questions.

> "Whether through this freedom of movement which is now in our Society we can glorify God more by doing work which He wants done.
> Whether the work can only be done in this way.
> We are poorer than most nuns.
> We have to work harder than most nuns.
> We have less prayer than most nuns.
> We have less training than most nuns.
> We are not as sheltered as most nuns.

Our work is more responsible than that of most nuns.
　We are not as stable.
　We have less spiritual satisfaction.
Can we really do more good than if we were nuns?
　What is required to join our Society?
Our Society combines community life with a definite
　professional work.
As our Society demands all the things necessary for the
　religious life – except perhaps the intention of binding
　oneself for life (this however is an imperfection of the
　Society) but does not offer the advantage of public
　vows, how can we encourage people to join us? The
　only advantage we offer is to do a certain work in a
　certain way, which seems to be best (but of course
　that remains to be seen).

A certain spirit of liberty should reign in the
Society – that is – members should be well grounded
in the Constitutions, Rules, practices, principles, and
spirit of the Society so that they can adapt them to all
circumstances."

One sentence literally jumps off the page in her reflection on the Society:
　"Every time I am asked – do you take vows? – is like a stab to me."
Anna also had made lists that were more task-oriented. For example,
a list of new mission areas to visit before the upcoming Chapter: the
Holy Land; Asia Minor; Persia; Afghanistan; Turkistan; India; China;
Japan; Africa. Because there was an urgent need for a permanent
house in England, she compared the advantages and disadvantages
of leaving Winchcombe and relocating in London. Pauline's cottage
in Winchcombe was cold but it was cheap. It had room for only a few
individuals and did not have the capacity for Mass or Confession or
other spiritual amenities. A house in London would be more expensive
yet more suitable and would be able to accommodate more people.
The purpose of a house in London would be for women to be admitted
there and spend the first six months of candidacy in residence in
their own country before transitioning to the Society's novitiate in
Washington, DC.

During this time of pre-Chapter reflection and evaluation, Anna had been thinking about opening a Medical Training Center as a follow-up to the novitiate. She may have been inspired by what had been put into place in Würzburg. Here are her reasons for considering this option for her own Society.

1. To train candidates in the practice of charity and conduct required of Medical Missionaries
2. To test their fitness and capabilities for the care of the sick
3. To give them an opportunity to learn hospital management
4. To bring about a certain unity

In a more developed rationale she wrote:

> "Members of the Society come from different parts and different schools, learn different ways and methods. In order to work together smoothly and satisfactorily far away in the mission field a certain unity should exist. This could be brought about by a Medical Training Center at home."

Anna returned to 6ᵗʰ and Buchanan where, four days after her birthday, her health deteriorated again.

> "Some days she is very bad – unable to rise in the morning, complexion perfectly white and not one ounce of energy. Complains of pain in her heart region."

However, on Palm Sunday, she was well enough to give the community a few Holy Week reminders.

> "This week is a very special week of devotion in the Society. It must be a week of greater silence, greater recollection than any other time of the year. Without silence we cannot have recollection. Let us therefore keep silence. Let us enter deeply into the spirit of the Church and ask God to give us a deeper insight into the Passion. On Holy Thursday it is the custom to make our Easter Communion as well as a communion

of thanksgiving and reparation. What a blessing it is to have the Blessed Sacrament. We can hardly move about the house without passing the Chapel. We must make an effort not to get used to it but always remember the Real Presence."

Sister Agnes Marie often met with Anna to talk about getting money. Covering day to day expenses was an ongoing challenge and an existential concern. While the Medical Mission Board was no longer a source of income because Anna was not affiliated with them, the Board's director, Jesuit Father Garesché, had sent generous supplies of medicines and equipment to Holy Family Hospital in Rawalpindi, and for this Anna was grateful. Her relationship with the Board remained one of mutual respect and concern for the missions. When Agnes Marie suggested seeking help from Propagation of the Faith directors, Anna said not to expect very much because "they have little interest in us." Then she shared with Agnes Marie some very painful encounters with POF directors in her fund-raising efforts.

> "While travelling around some of them sat back and scarcely listened to what I had to say – others said if you are having such a hard time why did you start. I have been treated like dirt, worse than dirt, like manure by some of them, but I do not want to say anything against them because they are priests of God. It is hard not to become bitter, but I have always fought against it and attributed it all to ignorance. One has to be a confirmed optimist. Many a time I came home after being treated like this with the resolution that I would never go out again. And after a little while, I would shake it off and go again, often only to get the same treatment again."

Many times she also had the opposite experience, which made it possible for her to go on soliciting.

> "Some of them were remarkably good to me, encouraging me, treating me kindly and even helping me. God surely has been good to us and in spite of it all we have always

had enough to live on. It is a good thing that He makes getting money hard, then one doesn't spend it so freely."

She also made a comment that adds another perspective to her mysterious physical condition.

"Now since there are more to share the burden it will become easier. Wait until I take you with me sometime, and then you'll see the treatment that is often given to missionaries. It was mostly that that took so much out of me all these years and put me in this nervous state."

Anna and Agnes Marie also talked about the Society during those days leading up to the Second General Chapter when the Constitution would be reviewed. Agnes Marie wrote in her journal:

"Doctor Dengel in saying what she thought the members of the Society ought to be, said: 'religious, serious minded, professional, superior women.'"

Anna told Agnes Marie that when she was a lay missionary in India considering the need of medical missionaries and their professional work, she pictured "groups of religious, medical women dotted over the mission world – each group a fire of charity doing medical work." Anna also said that "being missionaries demands one thing in its entirety – 'the religious spirit' – whether vows are taken or not. If it has not this spirit, it cannot endure." She also was struck by a remark she had heard several times from the men who had entrusted their wives to her care. "Do not spoil our women." It was as if they were saying: "We confide our women, who are good, docile, ignorant, to your influence. We are glad if you relieve them of their suffering, but do not make them discontented or independent; do not tear them away from us." Anna understood what "do not spoil our women" meant at that time and in that context. What took root within her then was "a deep realization of what a delicate, difficult task the right emancipation of women is."

April added yet another avid ecclesiastical supporter of the Society to the heavenly court. Bishop Thomas Shahan died. He had graced the opening chapters of the Society's unfolding story, and members would continue to pray that he be "rewarded eternally in heaven."

The following month the Archbishop announced that he had received permission from the Holy See to erect the Society of Catholic Medical Missionaries into a Diocesan Canonical Institute. He enclosed a copy of the Decree, along with a bill for 124 lire and asked for an equivalent check in US dollars and cents. For the record, here are the canonical stages in the evolution of the Society of Catholic Medical Missionaries founded by Anna Dengel.

Foundation of the Society
June 12, 1925
Letter from Archbishop Michael Curley of Baltimore

~ ~ ~

Decretum of Canonical Erection
MAY 18, 1932
*DECRETUM by Archbishop Michael Curley of Baltimore
with permission from Rome*

Anna Dengel gave a little talk to her community on the theme, "Be faithful."

> "If we are faithful to our duty – spiritual and material –
> God will give us all the grace we need. Perseverance in a
> life like ours requires a price and this price is faithfulness
> to the duties of every day."

Anna emphasized again the importance of using time well and then asked for prayers for herself, the General Chapter, and for the proposed house in England. In an article entitled "The First Seven Years" that appeared in the June issue of the magazine, Anna wrote: "There is no particular reason for summing up the events and happenings of the first seven years of the existence of our Society, except that the period of seven pioneer years comprises and completes a certain stage." In recalling its early history, she said:

> "Providence soon provided recruits, a doctor and two
> nurses. In the course of seven years they were followed
> by 26 others. The pioneer members will give you a

glimpse of how they fared since they came together to form the nucleus of a Society which then had nothing to offer to them except an opportunity to service the sick and poor in the missions for the love and glory of God."

On May 1 Anna left Washington to spend a few days in Philadelphia and New York before leaving for England. Sister Agnes Marie made this entry in her journal.

"Before she left Doctor Dengel asked all our friends if they could help towards the purchase of the English house. She also took every cent available from here with the hope that enough for living expenses would come in. Times are very hard and so few people have money to give. We cannot make an appeal until Good Samaritan Sunday and will not get much from that. Donations are few and far between. Sister Eleanor and I went to the hospital convention late and came home early so cut the expenses in half."

Sister Agnes Marie included more details of their financial situation, which was precarious.

"Sisters Eleanor and Leonie have to go to summer school. The course is booked at $60.00 for both. They registered on Saturday and were told that the prices were changed and it would be $80.00 instead. We had scraped every cent together and had 60.00 for them and $4.00 left for food. When they returned with the increased bill Sister Anthony and I decided to tell them to wait until Monday June 27 to pay the bill, which could be done. We put our trust in Saint Joseph and the Monday morning mail. Saturday afternoon Sisters Celestine (an old friend from Pittsburgh) and companion came to stay a few days and see Washington. Sister Celestine walked into the office and handed me two $10.00 bills."

Saint Joseph had done it again. "Providence never fails." The two Sisters went to summer school and, for the moment, another crisis had been averted. However, at the beginning of July, the situation was dire again.

> "We are down to one dollar or so and there is no evidence of money coming in but the usual bills are being presented – butter, milk, gas, electricity, etc. etc. We heard of some priests at the summer school who were looking for someone to do their laundry. Thinking that with a little extra effort we could do it for six weeks and it would be the means of a little cash for bread and butter and also to help pay Sisters Eleanor and Leonie's extra expenses, we asked them to let us do it. It is grand to be poor. We get old bread for very little. For breakfast we usually have cereal, bread and jelly, sometimes butter."

Anna Dengel sailed to England on May 3 and spent several weeks in London looking for a house. In June she and Sister Ann attended the Eucharistic Congress in Ireland. On June 18, an Honorary Degree, Doctor of Medicine, was conferred on Anna Dengel by University College Cork, her alma mater. On her return to England, she became very ill. They sent for an old friend of hers, Doctor Alice Johnson, who diagnosed the problem as due to a local infection. Since Anna's tonsils looked suspicious, the doctor had them removed. Anna spent July recuperating and entering into transactions for a house in Osterley, and in August she left for the Tirol. The community in England moved into their new house on August 24. That same month Michael Mathis was informed that permission had been granted to hold the Society's General Chapter in Rome and that he had been authorized to preside. On September 6, two days before the opening of Chapter, Anna Dengel arrived in Rome.

The Second General Chapter was held September 9-22, 1932 at the Convent of the Sacred Heart, Trinita dei Monti. Delegates were Doctor Anna Dengel, Superior of the Society; Sister Agnes Marie; Doctor Joanna Lyons; Sister Mary Laetitia; and Sister Dorothy. Presiding: Reverend Michael Mathis, Ecclesiastical Superior of the Society. The following decisions were made:

1) The Mission Oath remains the form of public dedication to God
2) The Solemn Promise is to be abolished
3) Private Vows of Poverty, Chastity, and Obedience are made to coincide with the period that is covered by the Oath
4) The adoption of a more religious dress no later than March 1934
5) The formation period is lengthened to two years, comprising a six months postulate, one year novitiate, and six months scholasticate
6) The Motherhouse and all houses of the Society will build up a reserve fund for unseen needs
7) New missions will not be started unless a sufficient number of members are available. The Patna mission among the Santals will begin as soon as possible.
8) The following General Officers of the Society were elected for six years: Doctor Anna Dengel, Superior General; Sister Agnes Marie, First Assistant and Secretary; Sister Anthony, Second Assistant and Treasurer; Sister Agnes Marie, Mistress of Novices.
9) The following provisions of the Constitution are suspended until the next General Chapter:
   -- a year of spiritual renewal before taking the Mission Oath for life
   -- the taking of the Mission Oath for Life – all members will renew the Oath for three year periods

Three of the First Four members - Anna Dengel, Sister Agnes Marie, and Sister M. Laetitia – renewed their Solemn Promise and Mission Oath on September 19 at the tomb of Saint Peter, SACRE GROTTE VATICANE, in Rome. The Holy Sacrifice of the Mass, celebrated by Father Michael Mathis in the Clementine Chapel, marked the official closing of the Society's Second General Chapter.

The following day, September 23, Doctor Anna Dengel and Sister Mary Laetitia were scheduled to depart for India. They left the Sacred Heart Convent of Trinita dei Monti and headed to the city of Naples, where they would have a few hours to spend before embarking. They strolled the stone-paved streets and went up the steep hill to the Church of Saint Januarius, where annually, on September 19, the saint's feast day, a sample of his blood that had been preserved in a vial turned to liquid form and remained in that state for approximately two weeks. Because it had occurred only days before, Anna and Sister Laetitia were able to see the results of this amazing transformation as they knelt before the priest presenting the relic for veneration.

At 4 p.m. they boarded the ship, traveling "Second Economic," a less costly option for those en route to the Orient. This meant four other passengers would share the cabin with them. Anna kept a journal of the ten-day voyage, marveling at the undulating sea of sand with its alternating patterns of light and shadow along the Suez Canal, and then the endless expanse of water as they eased out into the open sea. It was a pleasant journey. They arrived in Bombay on October 3, feast of St. Thérèse, Patroness of the Missions. At the Hostel of Saint Thérèse, a boarding house for business girls established by the Franciscan Missionaries of Mary, they were received "as old friends and refreshed with 'the cup that cheers' under all skies and in all climates." The next day they visited the bazaars for a colorful and chaotic immersion in Indian culture and met with Archbishop Joaquim Lima and Monsignor Francis Goodall, c.s.c., before joining two FMM sisters that evening for the long, hot journey by train to Rawalpindi. The compartment for ladies was crowded, and "the dirt and soot were terrific, otherwise there was nothing to complain of." The final hours of the journey took them through desert "dotted with picturesque formations of mud." Anna concluded her journal with the words: "Needless to say, when we pulled into Rawalpindi Station, my pulse quickened, for there on the platform stood our own sisters waving to me."

Anna remained in Rawalpindi for several weeks and then paid a visit to Dacca. On her way she stopped in Benares and Patna to look over the Patna area. The Society was planning to open a hospital there. From Dacca she traveled to the Garo region to evaluate the possibility of beginning a much-needed medical mission. Then it was back to Rawalpindi. Reports to the Motherhouse expressed concern about Doctor Dengel's health, saying she was "in a very bad state." To this Sister Agnes Marie commented, "I think the fact is that she is as usual but until now, being away, they did not realize how bad she is."

In October the Motherhouse had been informed that Cardinal Van Rossum had died. This meant there was now another advocate interceding for the Society from the other side. Meanwhile, Michael

Mathis had been making inquiries among contemplative communities in an effort to find the right place for Joanna Lyons. He was keeping his promise to support her during her time of transition. She was not at all interested in starting another foundation, this time a contemplative branch, within the Society of Catholic Medical Missionaries. In Rawalpindi her replacement would not arrive until January, so Anna assumed the role of interim physician. Little did she know that this temporary role would last for more than a year.

For the first time Christmas at the Motherhouse would be without its beloved Superior. Anna Dengel was in Pindi, where she felt very much at home. The Society also celebrated Christmas in Dacca in Bengal.

> "Sister Mary Laetitia tells us that she was overwhelmed with bouquets at Christmas. Early on Christmas morning a hospital coolie brought her a bunch of flowers which of course he had picked in the hospital compound. She gave him the royal gift of a rupee, which news spread like wild fire. The result was that the whole morning she received bouquets, all from the same source. Needless to say, the gallant gentlemen did not all receive rupees, but it did not discourage them."

This charming incident reflects a core quality of Anna's Society: the hospitable spirit of a loving God blessing everyone, everywhere.

We cannot overemphasize
the duty of being kind, obliging, friendly, and gracious
if we really want to serve in an apostolic manner.
It should be part of our spirit.
It must become a part of us as well
as a part of the Society.

Anna Dengel

CHAPTER SEVENTEEN

The little community at 6th and Buchanan began the New Year prayerfully and penniless. Well, not quite penniless. "Occasionally, Sister Anthony gets down to four cents or six cents." Their faith in Divine Providence, however, never wavered and their gratitude never diminished.

> "All are well and happy. We always have enough to eat and when a big bill has to be paid God sends the money from somewhere. He is wonderfully good to us. Sometimes when Sister has only a few cents and the cook orders meat for dinner we get together and decide on a way out. The chickens usually lay enough to give each at least one egg for dinner. Somebody gave us a big supply of fish done up in salt and oil – more salt and oil than fish – they were tiny to begin with. It was such an awful recipe that they couldn't be used by the hospital so they bestowed them upon us. They are hard to eat but have furnished the meat dish at more than one non-Friday dinner."

That spirit of trust in God and gratitude for whatever was received permeated the Society. The community in London wrote:

> "We are enjoying our place so much! It is wonderful what the Providence of God has done for us. We buy a practically empty house and then all sorts of things begin to arrive, often just exactly as they are needed. And we are all equipped not only with the necessities of

life but with things which are useful and nice to have. Certainly, the Lord takes great care of His own."

There was also good news from Dacca. The first class of nurses had completed its course under the supervision of the Society's Sisters at the Mitford Hospital and, with one exception, successfully passed the Calcutta examination, equivalent to the American State Board exams. One nurse passed with honors, the highest in Bengal.

The Sisters at home were sustained by these reports from their missions and eager to hear the stories of healing and hope that someday they too would be able to tell. They shared these with friends and benefactors and planned to include Doctor Dengel's recent vivid accounts in the next three issues of the magazine: "To India Again" ... "With Our Sisters in Pindi" ... "A Visit to the Aborigines," for this was precisely what was needed to generate support. Anna had gone to check out the setting of the Society's next mission and she shared her experience with those back home who were aspiring to follow in her footsteps, giving them a glimpse of a people to whom no Catholic medical missionary had ever gone before.

> "Of the 38,000,000 inhabitants of India, there are approximately ten or eleven million aborigines. Among these are the Santals, numbering perhaps one hundred thousand. Santal-land is in the eastern part of the Patna Diocese. The Santals dwell on the tops of the Sevalie Ranges – their *pergunnahs* (districts) transversing these ranges in parallel lines from east to west. A Dravidian people with a Mongolian type of features, toned somewhat by the tropical influences of India, they are short of stature, but well built, and of dark complexion."

The Santal culture was unique, as the following example reveals.

> "The highest numeral in the Santal language is ten, corresponding to the number of their fingers. When a Santal wishes to take a document to court against a written document of the *Mahajan* (money-lender), he brings a wisp of straw, or a cord, knotted with ten knots and then a space and then ten more knots and a space,

and so on, until the desired number has been attained. In a similar manner, the date fixed for any event (for example, a marriage), is computed by knotting a cord with the required number of knots and each day opening one until there are none left."

Back in Washington Father Mathis was working assiduously to alleviate the Society's serious financial situation. He kept Anna apprised of his efforts to liquefy the Society's debt, which proved to be impossible with the nation still reeling from its investment losses. He also struggled to find money for the Society's needs.

> "I thought that to secure the funds that are absolutely necessary for the maintenance of the two houses here in Washington and London that I had better go to see Cardinal Dougherty to find out if I could take up collections in that diocese. My interview with him was the most satisfactory I have ever had with any Bishop concerning an appeal of this sort. He not only dictated immediately a very personal and most urgent letter which I was to present to those priests I visited in the diocese but also he went to the trouble of personally making out a list with his own hand of those priests whom I should see especially. Not satisfied with that he asked me to begin as soon as possible and to leave no stone unturned to secure the funds necessary."

With Anna in Rawalpindi Father Mathis was also responsible for seeing that the magazine went to press. In the March issue the Society's statement of purpose once again appeared in a form that was much more reflective of its originating spirit.

> "The Society of Catholic Medical Missionaries is a religious community founded for the purpose of bringing medical aid to the foreign mission field."

The next few months were busy ones, full of challenges and change. Father Mathis told Anna of reorganization plans within his own Holy Cross Congregation. One in particular would affect the Society directly.

> "The last Chapter definitely decided that there is to be no further development of our Foreign Mission Headquarters and that on the contrary our investments along this line are to be contracted."

That meant there would be no more Bengalese Foreign Mission Seminary where "the Medicals" had participated in classes. This radical shift would go into full effect in July. Meanwhile, Mathis was fully engaged in his role as the one in charge at the Motherhouse during the Superior General's absence. In addition to the daily oversight of the Society's central offices, he was preoccupied with how to implement decisions that had been made at the Society's General Chapter in Rome. Because he had a keen interest in music and in the liturgy – so did Anna – he opted to begin there and would keep Anna informed.

> "It would be good to get started on the new form of prayers and in particular those that require special books, like Prime and Compline. You will be glad to hear that Mr. Benson is very keen on teaching them the Compline for the daily night prayer and never before did the Medicals sing so well as at present."

And again he wrote:

> "Today we had a High Mass at the Medical Mission House and the singing was the best it has ever been. I am surprised to see every part of the Mass properly and artistically rendered. I am sure you would have been proud of your candidates this morning. In fact the training has taken on a more settled and determined aspect. I am very much edified and pleased by the progress made in every way."

Then one day in March, finally, Mathis was able to report to Anna that Archbishop Michael Curley had approved their new Constitutions. Mathis asked: "Now the point is, when are these to be put into effect? The most important item to decide is when those who are ready for taking the Oath and making private vows will do so." Being able to make the religious vows of poverty, chastity, and obedience – albeit privately, not publicly – was a giant step forward. It would begin with those individuals whose year of preparation was coming to an end. This was indeed good news, but the following was not. He reported:

> "I just learned from Sister Dorothy in London that her confessor directed her after the retreat to see the Superior of Carmel there to find out if she could enter that house. It is a serious breach of good judgment for Sister to have taken such a step without consultation with the Superiors of the Community to which she has ecclesiastical obligations and of which she has been honored by a Superiorship."

In the wake of that unexpected development came a recommendation from Anna that the novitiate be moved to London. It would stabilize the foundation in England, she said; save money by not having to send candidates to the USA; provide leadership in a house of the Society that was about to lose its Superior. Move the novitiate to England? Michael Mathis was stunned,

> "Your letter to Sister Agnes Marie requesting my advice about the temporary removal of the novitiate from the Mother House in Washington to London brought such a grave matter to our attention that we thought it best to seek heavenly aid through a Novena to the Holy Ghost which terminated this morning with a High Mass. In the meantime we have discussed the matter in great detail and decided to write separate replies to you."

In a lengthy and forceful letter, Mathis rejected the idea and listed a number of reasons why. The following were among them.

> "The proposal noted above – moving the Mother House novitiate – destroys the most important function of the Mother House which must always remain, wherever it be located, the cradle for the spiritual life of the Society and the exemplar novitiate to train our members to our unique community life. The change proposed empties the cradle and transfers the formation of subjects

elsewhere before the Mother House has even fixed the training of the novitiate. In view of these facts there is no doubt in my mind that the novitiate is one of the most important and in the pioneer days perhaps the most important function of the Mother House. The proposal consequently is a very radical step that should not be taken except in an emergency which warrants the risks taken. Our novitiate formation is still largely in the experimental stage demanding the personal care of you and me as founders of the Society."

He went on to stress a point that was extremely important to him.

"I have been warned by several eminent ecclesiastics and notably by one we both know, the Father General of the Salvatorians, never to permit another priest to come between me and the Society. This could very easily take place if the novitiate were moved to London. Indeed if I could be so easily replaced in the formation of our members there would be serious doubt in my mind as to whether I was so necessary to the Society as to warrant my leaving my present position in Holy Cross."

There was yet another reason why he felt his role was so significant.

"Candidates need a safety valve which is not confession but as secure for them as the confessional secret. Not every priest can fulfill this charge in these pioneer days when we are fixing the formation to be given in our Society."

Then of course there was this issue: the centrality of the liturgy and the unique role of liturgical music.

"As the religious life of the Society is crystallizing into action it is clear that a special feature of our community exercise will be perfect liturgical practices and a love of Plain Chant. The decision of the General Chapter in Rome showed the reactions of this movement by selecting Prime for morning prayer and Compline for night prayer. To perform these community exercises with the proper decorum, especially Compline and High Mass, it will be necessary to make plain chant an important part of our novitiate formation."

Mathis also expounded at length on the importance of academic and professional studies and how these need to be integrated into the formal context of religious life. He explained:

"Sister Agnes Marie and I have discussed this question from almost every angle again and again through the past year and we are both convinced that during the period of intellectual, missionary and professional formation, our members are religious and must live as such if we expect them to do so when they are ready for active work on the field. Hence, we think that there should be normally no more training such as Sister Alma is undergoing in Philadelphia where she must live among non-members and without a proper religious superior over her. No other community, even those that are long organized, would dare do that ... Accordingly, it is our sincere opinion that until our Society has developed proper superiors for these houses of studies located away from the Mother House, the academic and professional studies should be made from the Mother House."

As for the very vital aspect of mission preparation, an area that called for a particular kind of expertise: "I think you will have to depend on me to do this for the time being." And finally:

"Has not our experience already taught us that if our Doctors are to remain faithful to the Society they must love it, must find their happiness in its religious life, and must love its members. How can they ever do this unless they grow up in the Society and learn to love it and be happy and contented in it? As far as I can see this is possible only by a genuine religious life in subjection to religious superiors and such a formation is possible at present only at the Mother House."

It is true, he concluded, that "passage money for European candidates would be saved by moving the novitiate to London" and that "additional English donations would be secured." On the other hand, he reasoned, "we would undoubtedly lose much financial support in the United States when it became known that the real Headquarters of the Society were moved to Europe." Mathis wrote to Sister Dorothy saying that she had to stay and fulfill her responsibilities until she could be replaced.

In July Father Mathis was officially given his release from his Holy Cross duties. He reported this to Anna.

> "On July 13, I was formally given permission to devote all my time to the work of the Society. I am to disassociate myself entirely from the work of The Bengalese."

On hearing this Sister Agnes Marie journaled: "We are all very thankful to God. It may have a few disadvantages but many more advantages. God's blessing is surely on the Society." The Holy Cross leadership also made clear that Mathis was to limit his fund-raising activities to Philadelphia and Washington in order to ensure that he did not use his Bengalese friends to help the new cause. Mathis explained to Anna Dengel:

> "Personally I consider our Congregation very gracious and generous in giving me to the work of the Society because our whole Holy Cross Foreign Mission movement has been built around myself and my going is feared will really hurt our cause. Naturally I could not do anything to interfere with the work to which I have given some of the best efforts of my life."

Then he said to Anna:

> "I am particularly anxious that you write a letter of thanks to both our Father General who granted the permission and Father Provincial who opposed my going to the

very end but who nevertheless very religiously accepted the Superior General's decision. I am anxious that you write Father Burns because he has the impression that you went over his head to ask the permission originally of Father General, despite the fact that I have explained again and again to him that it was not you but I who chose and executed this mode of procedure. After all you merely brought to Father General in a personal interview the letter which I had written requesting that I be permitted to give my energies to the work of the Society. So write a nice letter."

This was quite a bit for Anna to digest while so far away and lacking the means of their having a conversation together. There was also something else that Father Mathis had orchestrated of which, until recently, she had been unaware. In a letter to her in January of that same year he had written:

"I wish you would remind Father Donohue about the request in my letter to him – namely, that he try to induce his Superiors to allow Father Dengel, after his ordination, to come to America and help me with the work of the Society. Father Donohue himself had agreed to come when I needed him to help me with the Medical Missionaries. But now that he is so closely identified with the administration of the Prefecture, I thought that it would be more practical and much easier for Mill Hill to spare Father Dengel."

The man to whom Mathis had referred was Anna's brother Josef. A member of the Mill Hill Congregation, he was going to be ordained in England on July 9, 1933, would say his first Mass in the parish church in Steeg, and would then be assigned to a mission in India. Anna had no idea that Mathis was arranging for him to come and assist him in the work of the Society. She undoubtedly wrote to Mathis about this, but only his response remains.

"Regarding the suggestion that your Brother be appointed by the Mill Hill Superiors to assist me with the work of the Medical Missionaries, you did not quite understand. I did not wish to suggest that your Brother leave the Mill Hill Society but that he'd be appointed for this work just as Monsignor Becker of the Salvatorians, Father Ohm of the Benedictines of St. Ottilien, and Father Garesché of the Jesuits are even now working for Medical Missions in various capacities. I am very serious about this because Father Donohue promised to do everything in his power to come himself and since this cannot be done I want him to make good by procuring your Brother for this task. If he were released to help me I would have him prepare for the work for a year or two at Munster University, taking the Mission courses there. Furthermore I have discussed the subject in a general way with your Brother last summer and I think he is an ideal man for the job, having in addition the youth to be molded better for the work than we old codgers."

His request was out of the question. Nevertheless, he had set in motion a whole lot more than Anna Dengel realized at the time.

As summer began, the community in Washington returned to what had been so successful the previous year. "We are taking wash again from the students at the University. Suddenly our community of about 15 is being increased to 27. It takes a lot of begging of furniture, etc. and of changes about the house." They also rejoiced in some encouraging news. His Eminence Pietro Fumasoni-Biondi had been made a Cardinal and was appointed Prefect of the Sacred Congregation of Propaganda Fide. He had once been Apostolic Delegate to India and had visited the Society in Washington, offering Anna's fledgling community encouragement and advice. It was a very good sign that such an advocate was now at the Vatican. Mathis also mentioned that "It has been arranged with Sister Agnes that I occupy the little cottage at the Medical Mission Headquarters," adding that he would have to delay moving in until sometime later, for he needed to get to Philadelphia and start raising money because "we are low in funds." Mathis expressed a concern about Anna's health, saying: "You cannot judge your own case and the importance of taking care of your own health from the standpoint of the society." He added: "I am very sorry to learn that it will be necessary for you to remain in India for so long a time. There is, as you know, so much to do that really requires your personal attention. You may be sure, however, that Sister Agnes Marie and Sister Anthony and myself will do everything we can to promote the work and to train the candidates during your absence."

In August Anna made a retreat, probably in the scenic mountain area surrounding Murree, and constructed her usual lists of do's and don'ts, for this was her way of processing her religious/spiritual life. Again she was fairly hard on herself, not in a castigating way, but in an attempt at honest assessment. The statements she recorded give some indication of what was foremost in her mind and, in some instances, pressing upon her heart, thereby offering a glimpse of her inner struggle to be whole, and perhaps one might even say, holy. Here are a few of the points she recorded:

❖ lack of religious spirit comes from compromising, half worldly spirit
❖ strict observance of Constitution and Rules – failed so far
❖ too much pampering of health – suffer *silently*
❖ very careless in what I say, often uncharitable, of myself
❖ great lack of quiet and repose
❖ make a definite effort to think before I act
❖ do things quietly and methodically
❖ I must aim at all costs not to miss any spiritual exercise voluntarily
❖ I must not give my views on the impulse of the moment, but pray and think
❖ I must be willing to be hidden and like it, and what is more difficult and repugnant to me, to work in public if required
❖ I must have great confidence in God and His work. So far He has done everything – leave Him everything also for the future
❖ I must be firm and courageous in what I think is good for the Society. In that I must not move *one inch*.

Then as a charge to herself for the difficult days that lay ahead:

- ❖ Do your best and be completely at peace
- ❖ Do not get dejected
- ❖ Do not get elated
- ❖ Work hard, as hard as you possibly can. Life will soon be over.
- ❖ Be as good and kind and helpful to all the Sisters and Candidates as possible
- ❖ Beg Our Lord to give you charity, such charity as He wishes us to have for the Society – inculcate that spirit and pray, pray, pray that it may become the spirit of the Society

In August, back at the Motherhouse, Sister Agnes Marie recorded the following in her journal.

"We were given a big surprise and much pleasure by a visit from Miss Pauline Willis of London. This is the first time that Miss Willis has been in America since 1924, when she brought Dr. Dengel over here for the purpose of raising money for the foreign missions. Since that time, Miss Willis has never ceased her interest in all our projects and problems. When the time came for us to expand and establish a house in London, Miss Willis came to our aid and gave us the use of her house in Winchcombe until we were able to purchase the Mater Christi Medical Mission House. As her stay on this side of the water was unavoidably curtailed, she could only give us one day and night. In that short time, however, she gave us the latest news of our little family in Osterley, besides showing the keenest interest in all the angles of the Medical Mission Apostolate here. Before leaving she said: 'Well, I must hurry back to England now, and raise some money for the Mater Christi House and for the Holy Family Hospital.'"

There was also this notation about Father Mathis in that journal.

"Father is absorbing the Medical Mission spirit. In looking at Saint Gabriel's cottage (which he is to live in after September 15th) and the surroundings which are very jungly, he said: 'To get exercise I am going to stop this nonsense of playing tennis and do something useful.'"

At about this time an expansion of sorts was occurring in Rawalpindi. Here is what Anna reported.

"As the land of the north side of the Holy Family Hospital was about to be sold in small lots, and as one high building has already somewhat hemmed us in on that side, we were obliged to buy the land. While regretting the necessity of the purchase, we were glad to be protected against further intrusion."

In September Michael Mathis sent a handwritten letter to Anna Dengel:

"Regarding my change, I am very happy indeed for the opportunity to give my life for the Society because I feel a moral obligation toward it through the manner of its foundation.

"Some of my clerical friends of course are giving me all kinds of warnings about the hard row I am going to have working for and with a religious community of women, though they admire my courage. I must say that this does not worry me, for there are others of the clergy who have encouraged me very much.

"Personally I do not care to make any kind of written contract or modus vivendi. I have full confidence not only in you but also in the other members of the Society and I hope you have the same in me. I believe in this way we can work out our relationship which is already partially determined by Providence and in the future wherever the work and our personal sanctification lead us."

Anna had been away from the Motherhouse for so long that she was beginning to feel uneasy and eager to return. Mathis reassured her.

"I quite agree with you that you ought to return as soon as you can, for there are so many questions that cannot be

addressed satisfactorily without your personal presence
here at the Mother House in our rapidly developing
number of recruits. However, we must be reasonable
about your stay in India. I am sure it is providential, for
it is quite obvious to me that if an emergency such as
exists there did not come up you would never stay there
as long as you have. The value of this stay in India to
the Society, especially in the beginning, is incalculable,
for it will prevent our becoming too theoretical in our
training and aims and thus help greatly to determine
the solid development of the Society for the future.

"I think this thought will make it easier for you to
be away from the Mother house for the length of time
that the conditions absolutely demand. But you ought
to do whatever you can to shorten this time. But do not
exaggerate in this because if things do not go fairly well
in India you will only suffer and worry when you come
back. So make sure that you yourself are satisfied with
the settlement there."

In the Punjab, and in Bengal, Anna had been faced with some very
hard decisions due to the shortage of personnel and the responsibilities
the Society had undertaken. The abrupt departure of Dr. Lyons and
the delayed arrival of her replacement made it necessary for Anna to
fill in as resident physician in Pindi for a period of time far longer than
had been anticipated. As a result she was able to be on site to evaluate
and oversee other essential needs related to staffing and expansion. It
helped significantly that she had been so familiar with all aspects of
that particular mission. Dacca, on the other hand, had originally been
mission territory of the Holy Cross Society and because of the insistence
of Michael Mathis from the very beginning, the Society established a
second mission there.

Dacca was located in Bengal, an area with a very different culture
and a different language. Having to oversee that mission's development
had taken Doctor Dengel out of her comfort zone. The ministry was
embedded in the local governmental framework and it had become clear
to Anna that this was not the way to implement medical mission in the
Society. That, together with the shortage of personnel and inadequate

funding, had led to the conclusion that something had to be done. Consequently, she began to take steps to disentangle her mission from its operational framework. That did not sit well with local authorities or with Holy Cross personnel and their financial supporters. Father Mathis told Anna that Archbishop Crowley "seemed to blame you for the change" in Dacca that had upset so many people. Mathis was ambivalent about where he stood regarding this new direction in a mission territory of his own Holy Cross community, one that he himself had integrated into the mission of the Society.

> "We probably were overzealous in accepting as much responsibility as we have in Dacca but when this is once accepted, we have to face the music and go through with it, especially if it is successful from the standpoint of missionary work. Otherwise, our society will lose true friends and suffer harm from the ecclesiastical standpoint. I feel, however, that you will see this and that you will manage things as best you can. I can, of course, see why you are anxious to put Pindi on a more solid footing and you will note that I have sided with you in my letter to Bishop Crowley, despite the fact that I see clearly the value of his point of view."

At the end of November Mathis sent Anna a summary of what was happening back home. The London community had been told that their postulants had to arrive in Washington by January 8 or they would be obliged to wait until August to enter the novitiate. Mathis was teaching three classes a week on the spiritual life, religion and scripture, and mission to the novices and candidates; and he was relentlessly pursuing church collections in Philadelphia. Despite the horrific depression, no priest had yet refused him. Nevertheless, he wrote, "You would be surprised at how little I now get even in a big parish. A fortnight ago I preached at seven Masses to the biggest crowds I ever addressed and got only $234.00. The people simply haven't got it." The business here has to do with the question of a permanent Motherhouse, he wrote, "and I am beginning to feel like you have always felt that perhaps Philadelphia is the place we should select." Once the Bengalese had ceased to exist, there was no longer a reason to remain in Washington and it was possible to think more broadly about what would be best for the Society. Because such urgent decisions were pending, which included the medical education of the Sisters, Anna was needed at home. She was to arrive as soon as possible. For this reason, Mathis encouraged her to delay her visits to London and Rome until a later time and return by way of the Orient, where she would get a sense of where their missions might be in the future. One might wonder how Anna processed the directive to hurry home by way of the Orient and a visit to that part of the world. Mathis ended his letter by saying: "You act any way you think best because I do not know what pressing matters are in Europe." Then he added: "Despite the fact that we have our ups and downs, you will be pleased to hear that the Mother House is in a very edifying condition whose regularity I think will give you a pleasant surprise."

We want to pioneer,

to plow, to build, to initiate,

to prepare the way for others.

Anna Dengel

CHAPTER EIGHTEEN

On January 31, 1934 Anna Dengel was back in the USA. She did not return via the Orient. She did not visit England or Rome. Instead, she had gone from Rawalpindi in the Punjab to Karachi on the edge of the Sind desert, where she was warmly welcomed by staunch friends she had known from long ago. They were "at the station in full force" to meet her and their time together was a blessing. Karachi was a seaport city. She had planned to sail from there to Bombay, but all the ship's berths were filled. The long, hot journey by train was anything but restful. The ocean voyage from Bombay to Naples took ten full days, and from Genoa to New York, about a week. The temperature was 14 degrees below zero when Anna arrived in Washington. After fifteen months on assignment in the missions, she was finally home.

Doctor Dengel returned from India "in a perfectly wretched state." Those were the words of Sister Agnes Marie Ulbrich, Anna's self-appointed chronicler, director of novices, and nurse. On arrival Anna had been placed under the care of Doctor Gladys Kain, her physician in the past, who concluded that the source of her condition was chiefly glandular. Sister Agnes Marie noted:

> "When she had her operation at Georgetown hospital in 1931, she was X-rayed. Her lungs showed healed lesions but she never knew she had T.B. She probably had it at that time or at the end of the medical course in Ireland."

She also pointed out: "It wasn't until towards the close of her University studies that her health began to fail. She has never been well since."

During those first weeks back in Washington, Anna had absolutely no energy, could hardly raise a finger, she said. Everything was an effort. She would get up just to receive Holy Communion and then go back to bed. Doctor Kain finally insisted that she not get up at all before noon, and once that routine had been established, there was some improvement. She was able to work on Society business for much of the afternoon. Sister Agnes Marie kept track of her activities.

> "Dr. Dengel has many ideas of developing our work. What she stresses most since she is back from India is outstanding charity to the sick and poor, personal service, making them feel real Christian charity. At present it is too machine-like due to lack of Sisters, which necessitates haste, getting outside nurses, etc."

On February 11, Feast of Our Lady of Lourdes, Sister Monica (Lieselotte Neuhaus) and Sister M. Joseph (Elisabeth Podolski) took the Mission Oath and made First Vows. They were the first members of the Society to make private vows officially according to the revised Constitution. That same day nine postulants received the habit, which was now what their garb was called. Sister M. Thomas De Villars and Sister Elise Wijnen were among them. Holy Cross celebrant, Rev. John Boyle, told the women how fortunate they were to have been called to a Society still in its infancy, "just like the apostles, who were among the first to be called to the new apostolate." It was about this time that Doctor Dengel made this announcement.

> "From now on those who come will not be called pioneers. Until now you will be classed as such and all of you have a special place in my heart because you have a spirit of pioneering and I want you to remain imbued with that spirit."

In March there was some improvement in Doctor Dengel's health, Sister Agnes Marie noted, "but her nervous system is completely shattered, so much so that it influences her outlook on life." What Anna needed was a long rest away from the daily demands of an increasingly complex organization, but "she strenuously opposes it every time it is mentioned." With so much hanging in the balance – major decisions to be made, significant changes on the verge of implementation, and the old ways of doing certain things suddenly in flux – she just could not go away again and forfeit the opportunity to have a say in shaping the Society she had brought into being. One of the issues under serious consideration had to do with opening and running a school, a proposal conceived by Mathis that would involve several of his priest friends in the educational aspect of medical missions. Sister Agnes Marie had heard him talk about this often while Anna was out of the country.

> "The school Father Mathis has had in mind for years brings about many discussions. Doctor Dengel opposing for various reasons or at least as far as the Society taking the obligation of it is concerned. She is afraid of going too deeply into debt. She said the principles should be put down in writing and of always abiding by these:
>
> "Never to assume so much debt that it might become a nightmare. God doesn't want that – then one's mind is always on financial things.
>
> "Grow naturally as a tree grows and not to rush into a big thing before the Society is larger and stronger.
>
> "Never to let oneself be carried away by a boom."

Anna Dengel was adamant about not getting too deeply into debt.

> "It is difficult not to let oneself become infected by that spirit but we must guard against it. The post-war boom, which was followed by the present depression, taught us a lesson. Happily we did not assume impossible debts. Where would we be now if we had? Be conservative but have faith in God and take moderate risks if it seems for the glory of God and the good of the Society. Go slowly."

In regard to the school, when talking about mission science and methods, Doctor Dengel could not see the importance of it as Father Mathis seemed to stress. She said:

> "Life is too short to learn everything. Our mission methods should consist in being thoroughly good religious, by knowing and doing our medical work well and especially by a great natural understanding and

toleration of the people and their customs and all to be permeated with the milk of human kindness."

On March 25, the Feast of the Annunciation, Anna wrote a Prayer of Consecration to Our Lady.

"From the beginning we placed our Society under thy protecting
mantle, and out of gratitude and admiration and love
we hail thee Cause of Our Joy.
Today on the ninth anniversary of the Feast in Our Society,
we want to dedicate ourselves to thee publicly and forever
in a special manner as thy children.
We ask you today with great humility and confidence
to be the Mother of our Society.
Let us imitate thee in thy readiness to do God's will.
Obtain for us to live in peace and harmony,
in prayer and in labor,
in dependence on God's Providence,
in poverty, chastity, and obedience.
As our Society works under thy patronage,
bless it with many good vocations,
with many fields of labor,
and with the means to carry on our work
to bring the light of faith into darkness,
relief to suffering, and joy to sorrow.
Our beloved mother, Cause of Our Joy,
bless us today and always. Amen."

On April 10 Michael Mathis wrote to Father James Donahue, the Superior General of his Congregation, saying:

"Yesterday the veil was given to the members of the Society...our former garb did not externalize for the members and for the public at large the true character of membership in this institute. The character of this membership is of course religious. I feel that we have taken a very important step forward in our work."

Anna's limited energies were focused on promoting the Society's mission. One of the ways she did this was by publishing in the Society's magazine vivid accounts of her recent experiences in India. In an ongoing series entitled "Meanderings of a Missionary," she made it possible for the reader to feel the heat and taste the dust and follow the winding roads into and out of remote villages and even sense some kind of invisible bond with the people living there. She told her readers:

> "Our work last summer in the villages was most satisfactory: the people were so kind to us and our services so much in demand. With more sisters we could accomplish more. Now our hospital work progresses well and takes our entire time."

Perhaps it was the gift of being able to reside in more than one world simultaneously that helped sustain Anna's passion for her mission and gave her the strength, day after exhausting day, to continue on, no matter how miserable she felt. Although she was severely limited during this time of recuperation, she was determined to remain at the center of a Society that was rapidly evolving in ways she could never have foreseen. Individuals elsewhere kept her informed of efforts to precipitate a more active role for women in Catholic medical ministries, and the knowledge that advocates for change were clandestinely making progress surely helped her to hang on.

One day Anna received a copy of a letter that a Dominican priest had sent to the Apostolic Delegation of the East Indies. It said that "a Catholic Bishop had received *vive voce* permission for the Sisters to deliver babies at a maternity hospital in India." He also knew of another group of Sisters working with a religious community of men who "also delivered babies… they work on the principle that since there is no positive prohibition, the permission of the local Ordinary is sufficient." Also, he told of a Monsignor who had great difficulty in obtaining permission. No argument seemed to move the Cardinal, until finally, he said: "When our Blessed Lady went to visit Saint Elizabeth she went to help her bring forth a son, and she stayed until that son was actually born. Do you think that after waiting so long that she was not present to help at its birth? And if this were not unbecoming for the Virgin of Virgins, is it unbecoming for the lesser virgins dedicated to God?" With that, "the Cardinal smiled and consented."

Sister Elizabeth, a physiotherapist, had been assigned to the formation house in England, and before she left the Motherhouse, Anna asked her to give the community several lectures on posture and breathing and similar subjects related to personal well-being. Such topics had seldom if ever been addressed. Doctor Dengel introduced the series. "I have these ideals," she began, "and if we realize these, we are the luckiest people in the world." She made three points.

The first: "Through instruction in our religion, to know God and to know how to serve him. How little the people of the world know. This luxury is received only in religious community and in this way we are especially blessed. We are worth little if we do not appreciate this, thank God for it, and put it into practice. We must be thoroughly religious or we cannot be good missionaries. We never try to hide the hardships of missionary life from you. We must want to pray and to work hard."

The second: "We must know the simple things of health. This I learned because I lost my own health, but if I learned something through it, it was worth it. Food – what is good, what is not good, superfluous, etc. I want you all to become enthusiastic and practice the ordinary laws of health. If we observe these and lose our health, it can't be helped. If we lose it voluntarily, it is too bad."

The third: "Exercise ~ Walk ~ our manual labor, our housework is very good for this. Posture, ventilation. All these things enter into health. A slovenly posture shows an unmortified body and is bad for one. The day of amateur work is over in the missions. We must do our work well. Each one of us must prepare ourselves spiritually, professionally, and physically to do our work well for the glory of God."

Then she thanked Father Mathis for all he had done for the Society throughout the past nine years.

Anna Dengel's own health was becoming a matter of increasing concern. Sister Agnes Marie kept a close watch on how she was feeling and reacting, both physically and emotionally.

> "She is extremely nervous and irritable. Everything even normal things upset her. At times she is quite depressed and gloomy and takes a pessimistic view of things, which is most unlike her."

According to Agnes Marie's journal, Anna refused to rest or to take the medicine prescribed and resisted any suggestion that she withdraw to a sanitarium or some other quiet, more peaceful place to recuperate and heal. Her doctor felt that rest and a relaxing hydrotherapy might be all she would need for a cure. Instead, "She is planning to go to England on a visitation and propaganda tour as soon as the motherhouse question is settled but we are going to try and persuade her not to go." Agnes Marie had also heard Anna say: "Nobody knows how terrible I feel."

It is important to point out that the narrative regarding Anna Dengel's physical well-being during this time is based on the perspective of Sister Agnes Marie Ulbrich, since no other records have surfaced to date. She explains why she kept such a diary.

> "I am writing these things in this book because it is strictly private; such things can hardly be even alluded to in the chronicles. This will not be read until after our deaths and I think it will help the biographer of Doctor Dengel's life to understand, as this explains much of what is written in chronicles, letters, articles, etc."

Agnes Marie also directed a word of advice to an unknown biographer writing at some future time.

> "I know you will have the good sense to keep this as it stands out of the hands of the devils' advocates when her cause is up, for they would only misconstrue it. It can all be laid to poor health. She has many virtues and is a marvelous woman and her behavior of the present moment must be viewed in only one light, 'that of a sick woman.' Trials and difficulties and sufferings there are plenty, but that is a good sign. Every foundation that ever amounted to anything had a difficult beginning. Doctor Dengel is suffering keenly and is making others suffer, but God's methods can't be improved upon. Deo Gratias!"

Agnes Marie Ulbrich wanted a future generation to know that despite everything she perceived and all she had experienced, she believed that one day the institutional Church might consider Anna Dengel to have been a saint.

There were a number of other aspects of Anna's persona recorded in Agnes Marie's journal. "As I think of funny little incidents regarding the Doctor Dengel of the past, I shall jot them down," she noted. For example:

> "When Doctor Dengel had her driving lessons back in 1926 she went down to get her license. She knew neither the traffic laws nor how to drive, but when the cop quizzed her, she answered bravely. 'How long have you been driving?' 'A fort night.' 'What?' said he. 'Four nights?!!' The second question was, 'What would you do in case of an accident?' Spontaneously came the answer: 'Render first aid.' She often laughs about it. Anyhow she got her driver's license, but it was courting suicide to ride with her. She would go through town at 40 m.p.h., pass red lights, etc. and never knew she was doing it. This was when we were still wearing hats, so it wasn't so bad. She went down one day, parked the car, likely four feet from the curb, carefully locked it, and went to do her business. When she finished she couldn't find the car, so she concluded it was stolen (our old Ford!) and notified the police. They came to the house, got all particulars about time, place, where parked, model, etc. and went on the lookout for the stolen Ford!! About 2:00 a.m. they found our precious Ford parked blocks from the location she gave. They rescued it; put it to sleep in a garage for the night, and delivered it the next day. She was pinched more than once, and often Sister Anthony had to pay the fine. Finally, in 1931, she gave up driving the car, as her license had expired."

Sister Agnes Marie had many more stories to tell. Here is one that was fairly recent.

> "When the present habit was being planned, Doctor Dengel worked and experimented and talked and talked. For a long time she was opposed to wearing a veil, but finally agreed. One night, during her insomnia, she picked up a brand new white desk blotter from the desk

next to her bed and began to fold and experiment. The result is the one we decided to keep. 'It must be simple and practical,' said she. 'But it can look complicated.'"

As the sloping hillside at 6th and Buchanan welcomed the flowering trees of May, Agnes Marie was relieved to record that "Doctor Dengel is a little better," and that she was taking an interest in some significant items on her agenda. She spoke privately of her great desire to have our own hospital here or in England and to train our own young Sisters. She thinks that the U.S. hospitals are too machine-like, that efficiency, system, etc. are over-emphasized. "We must also give personal service," Anna said, "take a personal interest in our patients, sit with them when they are sick and not let them suffer alone, sit with them and encourage them to eat when they have no appetite, etc. Our Sisters in the missions are much overworked and cannot do it that way now."

Anna was not completely oblivious to how badly she had been acting. Sister Agnes Marie empathized with her when she expressed remorse.

> "Today she said she realized that all this illness has changed her whole personality. She is not so cheerful or optimistic and is a different woman. She thinks all this is due to having her uterus out and at least one ovary removed. She thinks it is all glandular but instead of becoming stabilized, as normally happens, she is getting worse from day to day. Her nerves are very bad too. Now the slightest noise irritates her; she cannot endure strong light. Her suffering is very great."

Sister Agnes Marie was also aware that the difficulties surfacing in other houses of the Society would have a negative effect on Anna. From time to time she herself needed to put those momentary setbacks within a larger context.

> "God is sending us many trials just now but that is a sure sign that He wants our community to grow and flourish and we are grateful. In London the Superior is leaving this month to be a Carmelite. It is difficult to replace her. Dacca is having troubles because the colonel

wants Sister M. Laetitia as Sister-tutor and she is needed
as superior in Pindi."

The Motherhouse had its own issues. "We are very poor," the chronicler
wrote, which was no surprise to anyone. The following incident has a
familiar storyline, except for the way it ended.

> "Father Mathis was going to Philadelphia for the
> weekend to take up a church collection. He asked Sister
> for $10.00 for the trip. She took every penny out of every
> fund and it made exactly $7.00, so she had to confess she
> didn't have more. To our great delight he came home
> with $250.00. All the pastors who couldn't promise a
> collection he asked for a donation and it totaled 250.00.
> Sister Monica was due to sail for England in 12 days
> and we didn't have a cent for her passage, so that 250.00
> paid it and our bills."

Doctor Dengel's condition continued to get worse, so Doctor Kain put
her on complete bed rest for a minimum of two weeks. She was too
weak to take therapy in a sanitarium, the doctor concluded. She had to
build up her stamina. Sister Agnes Marie agreed:

> "Doctor Dengel is very, very tired. In certain things she
> even suspends her judgment for she says she doubts if
> her judgment is sound because she can view things from
> only one angle, that of a tired, sick woman. Everything
> seems so big to her."

On Pentecost Sunday, Doctor Dengel asked everyone to make a private
half hour of adoration in honor of the Holy Ghost, saying: "In our
pioneer days we need the guidance of the Holy Ghost individually
and also collectively, that we may develop along those lines that God
wishes." Agnes Marie continues journaling.

> "During the month of June, Doctor Dengel said she
> thought her whole trouble was due to her operation,
> but Dr. Kain said no, that the operation was only the
> last straw; that she was overworked and very run down,

but because of several hemorrhages, the surgery had
to be done. She asked if she should just go on and
force herself, but Doctor Kain answered: 'absolutely no.'
Doctor Dengel got more and more discouraged and said
she had no hope of getting well because she has been
dragging on for twenty years. Doctor Kain had been
wanting her to go to a sanitarium for treatment but she
wouldn't go."

In one of their many conversations, Sister Agnes Marie learned a bit
more about her Superior General. For the first time Anna spoke of her
student days, telling what it was like to be an alien – on her own – during
the war, completely cut off from home, without a penny to live on; how
the food was insufficient; how her health had steadily declined. She
became utterly exhausted and agitated before things began to change.
Since then, she admitted to Agnes Marie, her health has never been
good. She acknowledged that she needed a whole year of rest. Then
unexpectedly, in July, the community was given an opportunity to enjoy
a summer vacation. In the words of Agnes Marie:

"We have been given a cottage on the Potomac for the
whole season. It is beautifully situated in a private place
so the Sisters can go swimming. For Doctor it is good
too. She has been there for a month and is very happy.
Her nerves are quiet, but she says they are not better. It
is only because they are not provoked and I think she
is right. There are only two or three Sisters there and
everything is ideal. They came home over a Sunday.
Doctor had to attend to various small business matters
and of course visitors had to turn up. They returned on
Monday. She spent two days in bed. Just that little effort
and excitement completely fatigued her. If she writes
two or three letters, she is finished for the day. She says
she is good for only one thing, 'to do nothing.'"

Meanwhile, Father Mathis was doing what needed to be done. Originally,
his community had released him to assist the Society full time for
one year only, and that year had ended. However, the Holy Cross
Congregation, at its recent Chapter, gave him permission to continue

on. "God is good," said Sister Agnes Marie, echoing the sentiments of the community at the Motherhouse. "There is always a fair day after a cloudy one. Doctor Dengel is much calmer, and everything else at 6th and Buchanan is running more smoothly too."

During the first week of August, Agnes Marie Ulbrich's journal describes how Anna's condition deteriorated to the point where something had to be done about it.

> "Doctor returned from the beach on Sunday. In two days she was worse than ever.... Some months ago I strongly urged Sacred Heart Sanitarium in Milwaukee as we know the Sisters there and it has a good name, but she said she couldn't stand the solitude and pious looking nuns around her. She also thinks it is too far away, but she can do it in 20 hours. I know 50 years from now they will say, 'why didn't the community take care of her,' but that is a difficult thing, because she is the boss....Until now she has driven herself by force but now the end has been reached....she sees how 'completely done up' she is and confesses that she must take a complete year's rest."

According to Agnes Marie, Anna spoke seriously during this time about "giving up all work, the government of the Society, etc., for one year. She says, even if she feels better after a time she will stick it out....There are occasional moments when she is her old self, but they are rare." Agnes Marie was well aware of what her diary was preserving for subsequent generations.

> "In the recent jottings I have spoken very plainly but certainly not in a spirit of uncharitableness or disloyalty or criticism. I write as the thing appears to me at the time and I try to remain unbiased. If I were to dress this up, beautify it, change incidents etc., what would be the use of this book?"

During the first week of September, while community members were at the beach, Anna left Washington. Father Mathis and three of the Sisters, who had to travel to Chicago, took her with them and drove her to Sacred Heart Sanitarium in Milwaukee, Wisconsin. Once settled, she wrote to the houses of the Society to tell them to direct all business to the council at the Motherhouse for six months, maybe even a year, if that proved necessary.

At first Anna was quite happy there, "but as usual," noted Agnes Marie, "she continues to write home what should and should not be done. She is *not* resting. She even gave a talk to a group of ladies for which I scolded her properly. She will not get well that way." Anna had been in Milwaukee less than three weeks when Father Mathis wrote to ask her to contact Cardinal Dougherty and say to him that her present situation will mean a delay in efforts to relocate to Philadelphia and that he should keep that move on hold until she was fully recovered. Mathis also told Anna: "I hear that they are going to sell the seminary," which was the Holy Cross Foreign Mission institute that he had established and where he had labored for years, "but keep this quiet because opposition to the project has arisen." He also said that Father Garesché of the Medical Mission Board had started some kind of community of Sisters to run his New York office, a community very similar to theirs in dress, logo, and mission. Mathis was very upset and said he would keep her informed. All this news was certainly not conducive to Anna's remaining uninvolved or to her healing process.

The doctor in Milwaukee told Agnes Marie that every nerve cell in Doctor Dengel's body was exhausted. The community was quick to respond. "We have started a crusade of prayer for her if it be God's will that she get well," Sister Agnes Marie journaled. "Four Sisters said a thousand rosaries for that intention during the summer. Now the community is saying 1000 rosaries – 1000 litanies – 1000 visits – 500 Masses – 500 Communions – 500 Stations." Then she added:

> "I know of at least three Sisters who offered their lives to
> God for her – that they would gladly give their health
> in exchange for her sickness if God so saw fit."

Anna may have been in Milwaukee physically, but in spirit she remained at the heart of the community she had founded, and they would always be for her a source of strength and support.

One of the women who had been with Anna at the very beginning and then left to follow a different path would also be forever one in spirit with the Society. Doctor Joanna Lyons, one of the First Four pioneers, was now back in India. The September issue of *The Medical Missionary* brought her story up to date.

> "After six years as Doctor-in-charge of our hospital in Rawalpindi, North India, Dr. Joanna Lyons left our Society in order to devote herself to a life of Adoration. A year and a half ago she joined the Franciscan Sisters of Adoration of Cleveland, Ohio, and went to India as one of the pioneer members of their new foundation established in 1933 in the Holy Cross Diocese of Dacca, Bengal. The Monastery where the Blessed Sacrament is exposed all day is in the midst of Hindu shops and temples and only a few minutes from the Mitford Hospital where our sisters spend their days and not rarely their nights in the care of the sick. Let us hope that the combined efforts of prayer and work will bring down God's blessing on the mission." Doctor Lyons – now Sister Miriam – made her first vows on July 2, 1934."

On September 30, the 9th anniversary of the founding of the Society, Father Mathis made Doctor Dengel's health the number one intention at the celebration of Mass. Once again finances were critically low. There were several hundred dollars' worth of bills on the desk with less than one dollar in the house and the bank account at zero. Still they were able to celebrate. One of the postulants received a box of candy in the mail and Father Mathis brought ice cream for supper. Before the end of October, Mathis wrote to Anna again.

> "I have been very busy since leaving you in Milwaukee between my classes here and the spiritual work, the work in Philadelphia and the recent mission exposition in Brooklyn. Last night we had a departure ceremony for Sister M. Lourdes, who sailed to Dacca today on the *S.S. Manhattan* in the company of some cloistered Sisters."

Meanwhile, three novices originally from Germany suddenly realized, after 18 months at the Motherhouse, that this was not a lay organization, and they demanded that the Society immediately pay their passage home. $200! That's what it would cost. "And we don't have $2.00! We are frightfully poor." Still, Sister Agnes Marie managed to scrape together the funds to send them on their way. At the sanitarium Anna was wrestling with the latest major change proposed by Michael Mathis. This time it was the magazine. He redesigned it to be more authoritative and intended to invite scholars to write on mission theory in order to appeal to those with an interest in the institutional church. He also planned to enlarge it. While there would be more pages, however, there would also be fewer issues. Anna was circumspect in her response and in defense of her magazine. "As real facts and not fiction was always the policy of the magazine, it is authoritative in a sense, but not in the sense you mean." She wrote:

> "I am fully in favor of an excellent magazine that improves and increases step by step as our Society grows. My idea was that your cooperation would lead to that. I was not prepared for it, that you wanted to be the Editor. Editorship to my mind means the guiding of the policy and to say yes or no to what is to go in and how it is to go in. As the Superior of the Society I feel it my duty to say that these inherent rights that go with editorship should remain in the hands of the Superior of the Society."

Then Anna offered an alternative.

> "It seems to me that with united effort we could produce a better and bigger magazine – but to my mind it should not be such a production that it would flop all of a sudden when you are busy founding a Society for priests or too busy to attend to it for some other reason. To me it is only safe and sound, if it is so that it does not depend entirely on one person."

Then she added this postscript to her letter.

> "This thought occurred to me: If you have the chance of so much material (4 x 64 pages), why not get out a

yearbook and edit it yourself like Monsignor Becker. It could be general and very scholarly for highly educated people."

In his response Mathis agreed that "by reason of the uncertainty regarding my work in the Society, it would be better not to attempt what the Society could not of itself carry out." However, he did want to go ahead with some of his recommendations for content and expansion, despite the bad financial outlook, because he felt an upgraded publication would be a source of recruitment and a more effective fund-raising tool. He had an additional reason, and that was to counteract the momentum that might emerge from Father Gareshé's movement, which he perceived as a genuine threat.

> "It seems that he is going ahead with his purpose to found a community of sisters for medical missions. Hence, it is necessary to present our apostolate as forcefully as we can especially along the lines in which he cannot so easily compete, namely, the scientific."

With regard to editorship, the explanation Mathis offered was: "My name would give confidence and procure contributions for the review that included general mission problems." Then he added: "Of course not to be officially recognized as the editor will be a little embarrassing, not to myself personally, but rather in my relation with others. I have had to ask my Provincial to edit the magazine because we cannot publish without his permission, and also I have let it be known to interested parties, as prospective contributors." In other words, he had already assumed the role of editor after clearing it with his superior, and before informing Anna, had shared the news with others. Nevertheless, he said, "this is of little consequence and people soon forget." He wanted to go ahead with those changes on which they could agree. He also said to Anna: "There would be no necessity for me to be announced as the editor of the review. My only reason for doing this in the other plan was that this had been definitely decided upon by yourself and myself," to which Anna had written on her copy of the letter she intended to keep on file: "No! (must have been misunderstanding)." She had not agreed to that.

In December Michael Mathis wrote a lengthy letter to Father Sauvage in Rome, asking him to intervene should Father Garesché, director of the Medical Mission Board, seek canonical status for "a community of Sisters similar to our own which he had recently founded." Mathis told of his formative role in the establishment of the Board and in articulating its mission, which is "to collect bandages and medicines for the missionaries, not to be engaged in medical mission work directly as professional medical people." He gave several reasons for objecting to this new community, but the main one was that a group with a similar mission and garb will result in a confusion that will be "an injustice to ourselves."

The December issue of the magazine stated that the first edition of the new *Medical Missionary* would be available in January. There was also an announcement at the Motherhouse. Sister Agnes Marie Ulbrich told the community: "Doctor Anna Dengel will not be home for Christmas."

If you have it in the heart,

it may not be so perfect when it comes out,

but it is part of you.

Anna Dengel

CHAPTER NINETEEN

Michael Mathis submitted a very unsettling proposal to Anna Dengel in January of 1935. There were three sections to the document that stated how he intended to exercise his authority within the Society during the next several years. The primary points of concern to Anna were the following:

- training for religious and community life approved at the last General Chapter to be enforced as strictly as possible
- all who have not made the regular novitiate to do so as soon as possible
- work on the field to be regulated so as not to interfere with the two-fold objective noted above
- canonical and liturgical procedures of community in its enactments and activities to be ensured by arranging all matters with ecclesiastical authorities
- Father Mathis to visit India to assess religious formation and to secure medical mission film for propaganda
- finances to be sought through beginning a Medical Missionary Museum
- the Medical Missionary magazine to be improved
- the character of direction given by Father Mathis to be that of representative of the ecclesiastical superior in the community until the next General Chapter (1938) and his official position to be: delegate of the Ecclesiastical Superior, namely, Archbishop Michael Curley

Mathis stated the reason for this surprising shift in his authority. He needed the proper canonical status for taking initiative in the development of the Society during a period of emergency created both by the illness of Doctor Dengel and by the need for this kind of direction in the community at this time. The government of the Society would go on just as it had been, he explained, except that he would step in when and where he thought it was expedient to do so in order to reach the ends noted in his Proposal.

Mathis presented Anna with this series of recommendations just two days prior to her departure for England with the Sisters en route to India. These substantive changes were rooted in an extraordinary change in his status that called for serious consideration, which was not possible at this time. There were so many things that needed to be done before she left the country again that she barely had time to read the document and no time at all to give it the attention it deserved. She scribbled one word at the end of her copy … unique … and then called for a meeting of the Council.

> "I repeated once more in the presence of Father Mathis and the Council Members that in my opinion Father could do all he proposes to do, without assuming this authority. Father then said that it was necessary. I also mentioned to Father that his assuming the authority of delegate of Ecclesiastical Superior might alter the identity of our Society. He answered: 'It might.'"

The majority voted in favor of its implementation.

Anna left the Motherhouse with the departing Sisters before dawn the following morning. While at sea, she was able to reflect on the deeper implications of the proposal and its impact on the Society.

"When I was on the boat and had time to reflect, two questions occurred to me, namely:

(a) If Father Mathis is the Delegate of our Ecclesiastical Superior, then every member of the Society has a moral obligation by force of our oath and our vows to obey Father Mathis. Has the Council the right to vote on such a fundamental change in our Constitutions, or is that reserved to the Chapter?

(b) What is the experience of the church in the relationship of a priest such as Father proposes to a religious community such as ours?"

On arrival in England Anna went directly to the Society's Mater Christi House where she would remain for a month. One of the first things she did was to write to Father Sauvage, c.s.c. in Rome to ask how he would respond to the questions she had posed. She added the following information:

> "The alternative Father put to us if we did not agree to his proposal to be the delegate of the Ecclesiastical Superior, was, to leave us. As the latter would be a kind of a catastrophe for us at this stage, it would seem that we would act against the best interests of the Society not to accept Father's proposal.
>
> "I can honestly say that we do not want to lose Father. He helped us to start our Society; he has been most wonderfully good and kind and helpful to us. I can also honestly say that we followed his advice whenever it did not seem beyond our power. Father is naturally accustomed to do things in a very big way and we are only in our beginnings, so we have to go slowly and cautiously according to our means.
>
> "I also mentioned to Father in the presence of the Council Members, that as Father proposed this status until the next General Chapter only, that it would have to come to a vote at the next chapter (in 1938) and that if it should be in the negative we expose ourselves to the risk of losing Father then, as surely he will not insist less on his status of Delegate of the Ecclesiastical Superior, than he does now."

Anna then wrote to Father Mathis.

> "It occurred to me that we did not consider one of the most important points, namely that the fact of your being the Delegate of the Ecclesiastical Superior would entail a new moral obligation (that of obedience) binding under the oath and vows for every member of the Society. Looking at it in this light, the question is, has the General Council the right to make such a fundamental change in our Constitution. If we had

had more time, this question would certainly have come
up for clarification and sooner or later, it will anyhow,
so I thought it best to do it in the beginning and ask
Rev. Father Sauvage's advice. He is really the only one
who can advise us satisfactorily – because he knows
canon law, he knows you and he knows our Society. I
explained everything as openly to him as I could and
I told him, that I am quite satisfied if he gives you the
answer instead of me, if he wishes. All I want is: to do
the right thing."

In mid-March Father Sauvage wrote to Father Mathis who had also
written a detailed letter to him.

"I received a few days ago your letter dated March
12, 1935. Allow me to say, first of all, that I have no
intention, nor desire, to meddle with the organization
or government of the Catholic Medical Missionaries.
This is no business of mine. I was rather surprised to
receive Dr. Dengel's letter, and my first impulse was
to answer her that I did not wish to be mixed with the
business of the Society. However, I like the Society very
much. I think that, if well organized and directed, it
may become a very important factor in the work of the
Missions … And I desire to help it as much as I can,
from the outside, so that it may become stronger every
day. For this reason, after great reflection, I decided to
answer the best I could the various points raised by Dr.
Dengel. In fact, I simply stated the principles of Canon
Law about the relations between the Local Ordinaries,
i.e., Ecclesiastical Superiors and a diocesan Institute.
She will probably send you a copy of my letter and you
can judge for yourself."

Then Father Sauvage proceeded to tell Father Mathis what had been on
his mind since their previous meeting in Rome.

"Your letter seems to indicate that there is some
confusion about the vows. I think that you never

understood clearly my position in this matter in regard to the Catholic Medical Missionaries. I have always desired that they could take public vows and become a real religious Congregation. I still hope that it may come in the future. At the time you applied to the Holy See for canonical erection, I advised you not to ask for the public vows. I knew then, that if you asked for them, your petition would not be granted or if your petition would be granted, it would be at the cost of a change in your special end, the suppression of the work which is considered by you as the most important. This is the meaning of my conversation with Cardinal Van Rossum and of his rebuke (in a certain sense) to me. At that time, you misunderstood me completely. Through Cardinal Dougherty's influence (and it was, of course, your right to do so) you had the question presented to the Holy Father personally by Cardinal Van Rossum. The answer was negative and corresponded exactly to the attitude taken by me and to the advice I had given you (which seems to show that Cardinal Van Rossum himself had recognized the wisdom of my advice to you). I fear that this answer may delay what I still hope for: the approbation by the Holy See of your work with public vows. But for the time being, you have been erected and you are a society of women without public vows.

"I see by the article quoted by you (art. 79), that there is a serious confusion about the vows. This article says: 'By the Mission Oath and vow of obedience, members engage themselves to obey ...' Now since you are a Society without vows, i.e. public vows, nothing at all should be said about them in your Constitutions nor should they play any part in the government of the Society. The Society and the members of the Society as such have no vows and cannot have any. It is true that the members of the Society may, if they so wish, make *private* vows; but such vows have nothing to do with the Society; they are a private affair in which only the person who makes them and the confessor are concerned. The Society as such and the Superiors have nothing to do with them and may even not know, and ordinarily will not know, of them."

No doubt this response from Father Sauvage was not what Mathis expected. Nevertheless, he did not waver in his determination to move forward with the implementation of his current proposal.

In the latter part of March, Anna went to the Tirol for an extended period of rest and a restoration of her former energies. She remained in the family home in Hall for a while, for she had found her father's health to be "really quite bad again." When his condition began to improve, she went on to Steeg, where the peace and quiet of the countryside proved to be most restful, even though she missed the stimulation of an urban setting. Society issues followed Anna into her Alpine retreat. A letter from Father Sauvage said that "if Father Mathis be appointed as delegate of the Ecclesiastical Superior it is of primary importance to have on both sides a clear understanding and knowledge of the authority of the Ecclesiastical Superior over a diocesan Institute, according to Canon Law, that is, of his power over the Community and of the limits of his power." Anna immediately wrote to Father Mathis.

> "As Father Sauvage says, there should be on both sides a clear understanding and knowledge of the authority of the Ecclesiastical Superior. As far as our Council goes, it was not understood or at least it was not mentioned by anyone, that in case you were appointed the delegate of the Ecclesiastical Superior you would have all the powers and rights of the Bishop. Therefore I consider our vote null and void."

She also sent a lengthy letter to Sister Agnes Marie, who wrote the following in response.

> "Our Society has a wonderful field and scope but it needs to be developed – as Father Sauvage said, it must be properly organized and directed. I think it is fair to say that it is neither properly organized or directed now. I am unable to do it, you are ill and Father says he has

not been given the power to go ahead. To be frank I think it will be years before you can properly take over the work of directing the Society. It is a very big and responsible work and requires a well body and especially *good* nerves. To undertake it in your present state would never, never do."

The push to take charge and redirect the Society continued to intensify as the following letter from Mathis to Sauvage on April 30 makes clear.

"For the past five years Doctor Dengel, despite an extraordinary personality and genuine goodness, has been unable physically to govern the Society. It is a very pitiful fact. Indeed it is a very serious question as to whether or when Doctor Dengel will ever again be able to have the strength which is necessary in these days of organization to govern the Community without authoritative direction of Ecclesiastical authority. The fact is that the Society has suffered terribly in organization, both as to the formation of subjects and finances. Indeed if it were not for the fact of my personal intervention there would hardly be any religious formation worthy of the name. Dr. Dengel is incapacitated to the point that we cannot bring to her attention any serious responsibility without fear of her actually cracking under the strain.

"It became clearer to me in these two years of my close association in the Community that the Community, or at least Doctor Dengel, would like me to do everything I am now doing but to do this under their direction. In other words that I was not to direct this Community but only advise it and to do everything else I could to support it. I would not object to such an arrangement except that they actually need direction and an authoritative direction because outside of one superior, none of them know enough about religious life to direct this community.

"The reason which urged me for years to persuade my superiors to give me this work was a sense of responsibility toward a community of which I thought I was the co-founder. I saw the lack of organization in the Community and the need of direction and I assumed that this was the work which I was called upon to do."

How to confirm both the validity and the necessity of his Ecclesiastical status within the Society of Catholic Medical Missionaries suddenly became clear to Mathis during the month of May. He had written to Archbishop Michael Curley for permission to confront Father Garesché of the Medical Mission Board regarding his founding of a religious community of medical missionaries that was very similar to the Society. On May 7 the Archbishop responded:

"You have my permission to see His Eminence, the Cardinal Archbishop of New York, relative to this multiplication of medical missionary entities. You hold under me an official position in connection with your own Medical Missionary Organization here in Washington. You are fully responsible for the conduct of the house, consequently when you speak to His Eminence, you are speaking in your official capacity as Superior of the Catholic Medical Mission House in Washington."

That was all that Mathis needed. "I always suspected that this was the Archbishop's view of my position in the Society" he wrote to Anna in June.

"As far as I am concerned my responsibility imposed upon me by the Church, through the Archbishop, and approved by my religious superiors is clear. This responsibility is a great deal more than what I asked for when we discussed the matter with the General Council."

He states that all important subjects would now come to him for direction – true direction and not merely advice – direction which the Society must follow in obedience.

Michael Mathis also wrote to Father Sauvage summarizing his new understanding of his role.

> "Regarding the question of my status in the Society, this has been settled, as far as I am concerned, by the consent of my Provincial to my accepting any delegation the Archbishop wishes to grant me in this respect and by Archbishop Curley's letter of May 7th 1935."

Then he added this historical perspective.

> "The Society was established by reason of a letter I wrote the Archbishop in June 1925 outlining the need for such a Community, my interest and the part my Community was willing to let me play in its organization, and the appropriateness of Doctor Dengel's being the founder of a Medical Mission Community. The permission to found was sent to me by the Archbishop in a letter of June 12, 1925 and I think he has always looked upon me as responsible for the establishment.
>
> "The necessity is obvious. When the highest superior in the Society and all the Superiors without exception have never made a real novitiate, advice is not enough. The Society must be directed or else it will not develop in the right direction. Under these circumstances who on earth in the Community is ever going to force members who are now superiors to make a real novitiate. As you see, this is imperative or else all the new members we are training will be spoiled by superiors who have no religious formation and who ultimately determine the policies of the community."

Mathis concluded with the following:

> "Just what we will do I do not yet know. However, the Archbishop's letter, without our even writing to him on the subject, has made it plain to me what my obligations are. How I will fulfill them is another question."

The following sentence in a lengthy letter to Anna Dengel summarizes his position.

> "By an altogether unlooked for avenue I think our problem of my official status in the Society has been settled."

Anna was about to leave for Holland at the invitation of a priest interested in having the Society open a house there. She sent an immediate response.

> "If it works, as I myself hope it will, then there is no need of long explanations. The one thing that matters is to really do our work and promote our apostolate."

At the end of June Mathis reported to Anna.

> "Our film will shortly be ready. I have had several directors of film corporations see it in parts and they have praised it highly. The President of the Victor Animatograph Corporation, New York, which sounded the film, was so impressed with our rendering of the Gospel story of the Good Samaritan that he offered me a job of writing and directing all the parables of Our Lord."

He also mentioned that it had been difficult work, "taking practically all of the extra time I could spare, with the aid of many other people, for the past five months." However, he hoped that those efforts would generate donations and recruits for the Society.

On the 27th of June Mathis wrote to Anna again, indicating the beginning of a systemic shift in the priorities of the Society.

> "Today I want to bring to your attention an important question for your advice. It is that I think that Sister Eleanore and Sister Leonie should be taken out of Medical School this year and be given a real Novitiate. Despite their many good qualities, I am convinced that

they have not the proper religious formation for our work."

He pointed out that this was the most opportune time to interrupt their medical studies, because they had just completed the mandatory two years of theoretical work. He went on to say:

> "I realize that this is an unfortunate proposal, from the medical standpoint, but in my judgment it is secondary to the religious, without which these Sisters cannot do the work that is expected of them as Medical Missionaries in our Society."

Then he mentioned an additional expectation of the canonical year:

> "Of course for a Novitiate mere instruction is not enough. Sister Agnes Marie would have to give personal attention to the correction of faults and the Sisters would have to be freed from all external responsibilities so that they could devote themselves exclusively to their religious and missionary formation."

In his letter Mathis asked Anna for her advice regarding this decision, but she never responded. On August 20 Mathis wrote again.

> "Regarding the question of Sisters Eleanore and Leonie interrupting their medical studies to make a novitiate, I am sorry that you were unable to give a definite opinion, one way or the other because, if they were to make a novitiate this year, it was important to begin immediately after the annual retreat."

For that reason, Mathis continued:

> "I called Sister Agnes Marie and Sisters Eleanore and Leonie to me after the retreat and gave my decision as the delegate of the Archbishop. I am pleased to say that the Sisters took the difficult decision admirably and are now hard at work in the novitiate."

He told Anna that "they requested no exception be made in their regard and were pleased to go to the novitiate to follow the regular order there." Anna's silence led him to write to her again.

> "As this is the first thing I have done on my own initiative, it is unfortunate that I did not have the opportunity to be sure I was of the same mind as yourself on the question because I am sincerely anxious to be of one mind with you in the exercise of my authority."

While spring in the Alpine village of Steeg was pretty much what Anna had hoped for, her plan to spend a quiet summer never came to fruition. Reconnecting with family members and friends had been a blessing, but the stress of knowing what was transpiring within her Society half a world away began to take its toll. Doctor Alice Johnson traveled from London to visit Anna and reported her findings to Doctor Kain in the USA.

> "Knowing her for so long and watching her, my opinion is that the natural course will lead to a complete break. I am afraid you have it to face."

She reported that she had seen this coming back in 1924 and again in 1929 and that the operation in 1931 may have helped to precipitate it. Nevertheless, toward the end of the summer, Anna began to improve. In fact she was so much better that she thought about going to Mater Christi in Osterley again to spend several quiet months in that environment.

In late August Anna wrote to Father Mathis to ask him what she should do with regard to the renewal of her mission oath and vows on September 30, as her canonical three-year commitment within the Society was coming to an end. On September 15 she wrote again to thank him for the dispensation from having to renew her commitment in a house of the Society and to say: "I did not answer sooner because I was not at all well for a while. I feel better again and I hope that it is the last relapse. I would be so glad if I could return to work soon again." She also expressed a concern for Mathis, reminding him of the need to take care of himself.

"Sister Agnes Marie wrote that you preach so often in one day sometimes and that you work terribly hard. I have such an appreciation of health now and I know that overwork is such an enemy of it, that I cannot help warning you for your own sake and that of the Society."

That said, she went on to address the issue that was foremost in her mind.

"As the result of the Archbishop's appointment, we are obliged to obey you under the obligation of our vow of obedience in all important matters. That deprives us entirely of our liberty and my formative influence in the Society and that really would not matter if you would understand every angle of our Society. The difficulty lies in that.

"We certainly need a priest to guide us in religious matters, to advise us and help us in many others, but unless we are allowed to adapt our Society to the work and ideal for which we were founded, I will not and cannot be satisfied.

"If you would understand our work as well as the religious side of our Society, there would be no difficulty, after all we should only be too glad just to have to obey and be relieved of all responsibility. Ever since you disregarded my personal experience and arguments about a veil for doctors, I feel that the fact that we are under obedience to you is a danger because you do not understand our work.

"You and Sister Agnes Marie seem to think that we can just function like any other Community. If that were the case, I say myself - there would not have been need of starting a new one."

Anna was adamant with regard to the position she was taking on the basis of the reasons she had stated. She was convinced that a line had to be drawn in order to safeguard the essential nature of her Society.

"I do not like to trouble Ecclesiastical Authorities, especially at this stage when so much is experimental and should be kept in a fluid state, but unless you yourself decide not to bind us under the vow of obedience, I would be for asking the Archbishop for it unless a General Chapter would be held. I assure you, dear Father, that I have the best intentions of cooperation and also of submission in matters that are in accordance with the purpose of our Society, but I feel more strongly than ever that the purpose of our foundation must be upheld."

On September 30, 1935, Anna Maria Dengel renewed her Mission Oath privately in the parish Church of Saint Oswald in Steeg in the Tirol.

On October 3, feast of Saint Thérèse, patroness of the missions, Pauline Willis sent a letter to Anna that rattled her to the core.

"Deeply interested I am and always shall be in whatever you do, but ever since we were together in Winchcombe the last time, I have been getting more and more bitterly disappointed in the Society you, and I too, have loved so much. It is entirely and absolutely changed from its first character and plan and this, alas, has been done in America, where they have failed to see what a successful Medical Missionary Vocation should be. The Society has now been turned into *nuns*. To me it is unutterably sad, the ruin of the work, after all the effort to start it. It is just another order of nuns of which there are surely enough, and as you and I and people here in Europe know, nuns as medical missionaries are a failure."

She went on to say that she would continue to support the Society financially with £100 annually as she had promised, but once her five-year commitment ended, she would stop.

"I cannot tell you how sad I feel that the work we loved so, has been ruined, the useful scope changed and a new order of unneeded nuns started. I wonder how you feel about it all."

What precipitated this outburst was an incident that had occurred when Anna was staying in London. She had attended an event in a veil, albeit reluctantly. "I had wanted to go in a hat," she said when writing to Mathis about it, "but Sister M. Elizabeth felt so embarrassed about it to have me seen in a hat, that I did not want to make it hard or unpleasant for her." Anna tried to convey the seriousness of the situation.

> "We are not really *nuns*. Miss Willis herself realizes that we cannot move about anymore. We cannot make any headway in England and Europe, if we shut ourselves up. I often told you this, but you did not believe it. Now you hear it from Miss Willis."

In October Anna sent a lengthy letter to Sister Agnes Marie in which she said the following.

> "A few days ago I received an explosive letter from Miss Willis. I must say it was a blow to me. It was the first time since 1911 when I first began to correspond with Miss Willis, that she showed anger or dissatisfaction with the work in which she showed so much interest and for which she did so much – and with me. However, it seems almost providential, for it gives me a direct occasion to say what is and has been a long time on my mind."

Anna then gives a very lengthy and detailed explanation of where she stands with regard to a religious habit and a veil. Her main points are the following.

> "What Miss Willis says about the handicaps of a religious habit and the rules and regulations that are a necessary concomitant, I agree with in many respects and as you know I have not failed to express my conviction.
> "It seems to me that since Father is with us (before he had no time to think deeply about us) and since you were in the novitiate, you have one goal before you, namely that we be *nuns*. The purpose for which we were founded is: to be *Medical Missionaries*. Therefore

that should be our goal. That includes that we have all the virtues and many of the rules and regulations of religious, but not all."

Anna was unwavering with regard to what was appropriate for doctors in the Society.

"As regards doctors, a religious garb with a *veil*, etc., is directly destructive of the medical mission vocation. I have nothing against a simple religious garb or some sign of belonging to a Community, but a veil is destructive and defeats the purpose for which we were founded. Nobody will look on a nun as a doctor who is equivalent professionally to others, simply because she is isolated from the profession; but for the medical profession one cannot be isolated. If one undertakes the responsibility to deal with human lives, one must conscientiously use all the means available, all the more so, if one does it from the highest motive, namely for the love of God, and as a member of a religious Community mentioned by the Church. If I am a doctor and cannot go to meetings and libraries, cannot get books, meet colleagues, and have no social contact with the world, I cannot say: I do not know this or that, please excuse me, I am not allowed to go out alone, I give bad example in the Community if I would be out later than the others, I cannot do this because I have a veil on, etc. etc.

"Doctors also must have a certain independence as regards time, as regards recreation, professional helps such as books, etc. The cry: *all alike* is impossible to be followed. Nuns have a code and standard of behavior that must be followed irrespective of everything else. Some doctors maybe also would like to have all the pleasant and honored things that go with a habit, but for the sake of a greater good or rather an essential, it must be sacrificed.

"Father said to me: 'You will see how differently people will treat you when you have a religious habit.'

Yes, they treat me as a nun, that is very pleasant, but for the sake that I am looked upon as somebody who means it seriously about providing doctors for the missions and not amateurs, I am willing to sacrifice lots of honors and even take insults.

"A religious habit and the title doctor are incompatible. One cannot change ideas and customs of hundreds of years – at least, I have no intention to swim against the stream. But if one begins something new, one can adapt it to the needs. In Europe there are many new religious Communities, different from the old type, and people accept them.

"Late in the evening before taking the veil, I went once more to Father and told him how I felt about it. Father said: 'Your arguments have not convinced me. If you do not take it, it will be serious.' I did, to prevent a break, but my ideas have not changed. They rest partly on personal experience, partly on what I call intuition for the want of a better expression. I feel that it is not possible for doctors in a religious habit with veil to live up to their vocation as Medical Missionaries. I can produce arguments, personal experience and feeling. Women go more by intuition. It is by no means an infallible guide, but it is a valuable one all the same taken together with others."

Anna was not about to concede to what had now become Society practice.

"This question must be settled before I return. I do not want to face the public anymore in a veil, because it gives the wrong idea of a mission doctor. Now that you all have veils, there is no danger anymore that our Society will be misunderstood, because those who do not wear a veil can take a Sister along on occasions when it is necessary to show that we are a religious Community – and we have photos."

With regard to Father Mathis, the driving force behind the push to make the Society more canonically ecclesiastical, she said: "We need Father to guide us in spiritual matters and advise us in many others too and thank the Lord that we have him, but the medical side he does not understand." Then she forcefully stated words that would forever define her Society.

> "*We* must adapt ourselves to the needs; the needs will not adapt themselves to us. We must never be afraid to change if it is needed."

Anna commended Agnes Marie on having been "a faithful and strong pillar of the Society," adding: "and I hope and pray that you will always remain so – but you have been somewhat blinded by the novitiate." Then, to the woman who has been with her from the very beginning and has remained an ongoing support in her illness, she wrote:

> "It is true the thought and wish and will to preserve the purpose of our Society is much in my mind and everything contrary to it, oppresses me. It may really be part of the cause of my slow recovery, as Miss Willis, strange to say, surmises. I must say – I realize more and more that I am completely unworthy to be the instrument in founding such a Society with such beautiful aims and people and the fact that I am laid low so long by complete inability to work, may be a punishment and a sign that somebody else should take the helm. I am resigned – but as long as I am the Superior, I must say what I think."

Shortly after receiving that letter from Anna, Sister Agnes Marie wrote to Sister Laetitia. Under the heading, *Private and Confidential*, she shared the contents of Doctor Johnson's report following Anna's relapse in the Tirol and the doctor's conclusion: "I think that Dr. D. will never again be all right and she may have a complete break." Agnes Marie said to Sister Laetitia:

> "I told Sister Anthony but no one else. It seems to me that the inner circle, so to speak, should know. When

it happens, if it really does, will be time enough for the others to know. It is too bad. However, I think we can still have hopes because the doctor in Milwaukee said last winter that he thought she would get well."

Then Agnes Marie wrote a very long letter to Anna Dengel. "In some points I agree with you, in others I cannot." She went on to say that wearing a habit and veil had never occurred to her, even after completing her novitiate. The suggestion had come from somewhere else within the Society. However, she began to see its value once she became responsible for preparing women to be missionaries who would live a dedicated life. Many had come to the Society not knowing what they were getting into. Was this organization lay or was it religious? In order to remove this ambivalence and clarify the religious nature of this new and experimental way of living wholly for God, certain practices were added that were more indicative of this calling.

> "To make us nuns, properly so called, has *not* been my aim. To make us good sound religious and medical missionaries has been my aim. That I always understood was my goal."

And that was also the underlying issue that had yet to be resolved in a way that was clearly understood by all. "It seems to me that we want strong religious characters, those who wish to give themselves unreservedly to God," she wrote. With this, all would agree. But what did it really mean to be "religious" within this new Society that had been called a "holy experiment" – that was ready and willing to break new ground within the institutional Church. There was now more than one vision underlying its lived reality and conflicting interpretations of what it might mean to be "religious." The result was significant tension, yet at the same time, there was a solidarity of spirit and a lot of good will. Agnes Marie reassured Anna of her loyalty and support, saying:

> "I do not want to be a cross to you nor to oppose you. All this is somewhat of a trial to me because I am a great lover of peace and harmony. Do not worry. No matter what you, or I or anyone else does, in the end our Society will be exactly what God wants it to be and

of course that is what we all want. The finger of God
is in everything, directing it to its best and right end."

In a letter sent to Anna near the end of November, Father Mathis
revisited systematically "the reasons that have urged me to demand last
February that I either direct this Society in certain well defined limits
agreed upon until the next General Chapter or leave." He repeats what
he had said before and then addresses the concern expressed by Anna.

"You state that the obligation of obedience to me as
the Archbishop's representative and my power to take
initiative deprive the community of its liberty to develop
according to its purposes and you, as the Foundress, of
your formative influence on the Society. The liberty
to develop the Society and your formative influence
on the Society are not absolute powers or rights. They
must submit themselves to the direction of proper
ecclesiastical superiors."

Then he adds the following:

"You must not forget that as far as you and I are concerned
it was I and not you who suggested this Society. Indeed
it required more than a suggestion, much argumentation
to break down a natural repugnance you had and to a
certain degree still retain against a Sisterhood, which is
what we founded. Hence, I wonder if left to your own
initiative, whether you would have done anything more
for the founding of a community than Dr. McLaren or
Dr. Lamont had done before you...I do not think that
you have any just complaint from either the theoretical
or the practical standpoint against the power given me
by the Archbishop."

Mathis challenged Anna. "Your hostility to the veil is based on personal
more than on medical grounds" is how he begins his rebuttal.

"I think I understand you and I do not blame you too
much because your views on the freedom of women

and the incapacity of nuns, extreme though they be, are nevertheless sincere. But these are extreme views and you should not impose them on others, especially not on the community."

With regard to his now authoritative status:

"I have not the least doubt about being able to convince the Archbishop or any other ecclesiastical authority about the true need there is of direction, not mere advice, in the present stage of our society.

"You, as Superior General, have never made a real novitiate, have a certain repugnance to sisterhoods, and do not thoroughly understand the religious life. I could very easily prove this. I give only one example, the establishment of our novitiate. It took years to convince you of the necessity to do this, notwithstanding the fact that such a formation is the A-B-C of religious life. In view of this fact how can you be relied upon by the church to govern this Society properly without authoritative direction, not mere advice."

He had a lot more to say in support of his intervention.

"You lack some important powers of organization. You cannot delegate authority sufficiently to preserve initiative in your subjects in order to get essential things done. Your long illness has made it very difficult not only to keep things going but to make any headway."

He warns her of "the possible harm that could come to the Society by a showdown of our differences."

"Be very careful what you do in this matter with ecclesiastical authority because it may prejudice the society at a time when Rome is looking for a community of *puccah* sisters qualified to do medical work to lead a movement of vast proportions in this direction among Mohammedan and Hindu peoples. I know more than

I am at liberty to reveal. But this much I know: our society is being considered for this project. Therefore, you must not minimize its true religious character. In fact any serious squabbling will not help us. Save it till some other time."

Mathis received a written response from Anna in mid-December in which she again commented on how she perceived his change in status and then sought to initiate a truce.

"As far as your status in the Society is concerned, I feel now that I cannot have any responsibility about it anymore. Although it was not very pleasant, I stated openly what I thought. If I am wrong, all the better."

She felt she too had to repeat a major concern of her own.

"The fact that you do not know medicine or nursing or any type of work in the missions would not matter per se, but it seems to me that you think that we can and should be like nuns in every respect. I know from actual experience in the field that nuns – at least the ones I was with – have rules which take no account of human life in the difficulty others are in. I had the most dangerous and difficult maternity cases to attend unhelped by the nuns, who could not even come into the room. I even had the matter taken up in the Motherhouse in Rome; the answer was clearly in the negative and I had to manage alone and without help. This is only one example. I must say that left an indelible horror in me of petrified rules which are looked upon as the acme of idealism whilst others and the work suffer. I want to preserve our Society from that."

The core of Anna's pioneering pursuit was rooted in the following.

"I also told you the reasons why I wanted a religious community - but I always wanted one which would

not be hindered in the carrying out of the medical and
nursing professions in their full scope."

There may be different ways to embody that vision, but for Anna and
her Society, the fundamental thrust was clear.

> "The whole thing is, do we prefer to conform in all
> respects to the traditional rules and customs of nuns,
> or have we the courage to deviate from them in such
> respects as our work absolutely demands? It is quite
> possible that more things are compatible with wearing a
> veil than I consider fit – but I know how easily anything
> not traditional is looked upon askance and as of a lower
> degree of perfection….I cannot understand that you say
> that I should not minimize our true religious character.
> Are not the purpose and our aims an appropriate
> response in our Constitutions and Rules? and in all
> humility, may I not ask, who composed the major part
> of them?"

There was a certain irony in the present situation. She writes:

> "If even at this stage we do not understand the religious
> life, whose fault is it? It is quite true that I am hesitant
> about the novitiate, because I feared that we would lose
> a certain spirit of our own, and that although we would
> acquire many excellent things, but with them handicaps
> for our work. Besides – there was a practical difficulty."

The difficulty, of course, was the critical need for medical personnel in
the Society's already established missions, a need that now was secondary
to a lengthy period of religious formation in addition to the years of
professional preparation that were a *sine qua non*. In mid-December
Cardinal Dougherty of Philadelphia sent a note to Anna.

> "A short time ago I sent to a most prominent Cardinal
> in Rome a letter in which I urged that Religious women
> doctors be permitted to do obstetrical and all kinds
> of gynecological work. I have just heard from this

Cardinal that he read to the Holy Father my letter; and the Cardinal is of the opinion that this petition will be granted. That it will come sooner or later I have no doubt."

Anna wrote to Mathis again, saying:

"I am much better and I think well enough to be able to return to the Society soon.... I expect to spend Christmas with my family – the first time since 1913 – and probably also the last time. My father is very feeble but not worse than when I came. All wish to be remembered to you and send their best wishes."

Anna was where she needed to be for this particular Christmas, away from the problems she could not solve and the pressures she could not handle, surrounded by memories and meaning. "*Stille Nacht. Heilige Nacht.*" If only for a moment, here was a modicum of calm, an oasis of heavenly peace.

We have only one life,
and we must make the most of it.

Anna Dengel

CHAPTER TWENTY

At Christmas Anna was gifted with an opportunity too good to refuse. "A ticket from New York to New York, via around the world, was presented to me. It gave me a thrill which I cannot put into words." Doctor Margarete Hattemer, a 38-year-old female physician from Germany whose application to the Society had not been accepted, decided to take a worldwide cruise and she invited Anna to accompany her. She knew that Doctor Dengel had not been well, and because she herself spoke very little English, she offered to pay Anna's expenses to be her traveling companion. Anna was ecstatic.

> "To me the trip meant a *Mission* trip, of course, and as such, something very valuable. I had the good fortune of having the pleasant and congenial companionship of a friend. As she is also a Doctor and a Catholic much interested in the life of the Church in every phase and place, we had enough in common to make us almost inseparable during the one hundred and thirty-eight days of our cruise."

This assessment came at the end of the trip, which would turn out to be a multifaceted blessing for Anna.

The days leading up to Anna's departure were filled to the brim, and stressful. She would return to America immediately, for the ship was scheduled to sail from New York early in January. Before embarking she had to obtain permission from the Apostolic Delegate in Washington and also from her Society. Fortunately, Doctor Kain told Sister Agnes Marie that she thought the trip would be beneficial for Anna by giving her something meaningful to do until she could return to work. Father Mathis arranged for her to meet with the Apostolic

Delegate on arrival. "Doctor was here about 21 hours and there were 100 things to do," was how Agnes Marie described Doctor Dengel's return to the Motherhouse after many long months away. When Anna met with the Apostolic Delegate, he told her to "stay home and work at developing the movement," for there were rumors circulating that an announcement from Rome was imminent. When Father Mathis explained that the trip was intended to help Anna get well again, the Delegate said with a smile: "Go with a serene mind and enjoy your trip and get well for the big work before you." Then he added: "Of course you are planning to take a Sister with you." "No," said Anna, but when she explained that her traveling companion was a woman and a doctor and would be looking after her, he gave his approval. As Anna made final preparations to leave, Agnes Marie noted in her journal: "Doctor seemed much better…less easily irritated and more reasonable … She will be back on May 26."

In the evening of the following day, January 9, 1936, Anna and her companion set sail on the *S.S. Reliance*. Anna wore the uniform designed for their Sisters in medical school: a grey dress with a turn down collar, and a hat. She stood at the rail, mesmerized, as the city of New York, a magical metropolis with its myriad lights dancing in the water, vanished into the night. To Anna this would always be "one of *the* sights of the world." When the twinkling was visible only in the stars, the two exhausted women retired for the night. Each had her own cabin in a quiet and airy location not far from one another. This would be their sanctuary, offering rest and restoration throughout the next five months. Anna kept a detailed journal of their itinerary and their experiences, which she would later publish in consecutive issues of *The Medical Missionary* magazine. "The first day of our trip, we explored our home afloat," she writes, and for the rest of the week, curiosity led the two adventurers to investigate what their home away from home had to offer: dining areas, sports facilities, a gymnasium, a bevy of shops. They loved the winter garden flush with lilacs and geraniums and canaries that fluttered about, and those cozy corners inviting them to spend "many happy, delightful tea time hours there, listening to the perfectly marvelous music of the ship's band, made up of twenty-three men, artists from tip to toe." Another favorite haunt was the ship's well-stocked library located just above their cabins. It was full of books "on travel and many other conceivable subjects, and written in several languages." For meals "we chose a small table for two, near a port-hole" and enjoyed a wide variety of foods prepared by the ship's chef "and his forty-three assistants!"

As the ship sailed southward, the weather became warmer, and on the sixth day, it was already hot. The first stop, Trinidad, lay just above the equator. Passengers disembarked in Port of Spain and visited places within and beyond several of the major cities. Prior to every port of call, Anna looked into the social, cultural, and religious history of its people, and in every place they visited, she inquired about medical services for the poor and socially disadvantaged, especially women and children. She was particularly interested in those health-related institutions of the Catholic Church. For her this trip around the world offered an opportunity to learn about local needs and the extent as well as the effectiveness of medical mission initiatives. "I left Trinidad with one big regret," she wrote in her journal. "Time did not permit me to visit a Dominican Sister on the leper island of Chacachacare, with whom I had corresponded for years." It was hard "to be so near and yet so far, with a slender chance of ever returning," and not be able to connect.

During the next six days at sea, the first major event was crossing the equator on January 19. "The foghorn sounded furiously" and there were spirited celebrations. As the ship approached its first port in Brazil, two lecturers, an American and a German who held a position as a professor in Chile, presented a series of travelogues "which contributed so much to a better understanding of the places we saw. Not very far below the equator we passed the delta of the Amazon, the mightiest river of the world. In its course of 2,400 miles, no less than 100 rivers join it." Anna was deeply moved by the "enormous virgin forests and swamps" surrounding it, where "many beautiful birds, insects and wild animals can still enjoy the silence and solitude of these untouched regions." The first stop in South America was Bahia, the oldest city in Brazil, founded in 1542 and its capital for 250 years. Their guide, a Franciscan friar, took them to the famous gilded church, where the entire interior consists of ornately gold-plated wood that is dazzling under the lights. Anna recorded that "a Franciscan Father told us of one place in Brazil where, in bygone days, women loaded their hair with gold dust on certain occasions and shook it into the holy water font in the church. I would like to know where such church collections took place before or since!" Brazilians have a great devotion to Mary, she was told, and on the last day of May, they crown her statue amid large processions and joyful festivities.

On January 24, the ship sailed past Sugar Loaf Mountain and into the harbor of Rio de Janeiro, where the gigantic statue of Christ with outstretched arms towers atop Hunchback Mountain, silently welcoming all. Anna discovered that although there are a number of fine hospitals in Rio, maternity and child welfare still had a long way to go throughout the region. Obstetrical care is insufficient even in the towns and it is nearly nonexistent in rural areas where unqualified midwives are the norm. "While we were in search of things missionary and medical," says Anna, "we did not neglect our general education. We tried to see whatever was to be seen; it all belongs to life and leads to a better understanding of it." Before departing Rio, Anna wrote this in her journal.

> "In the evening, we witnessed an extraordinary spectacle. It was the opening of the carnival season. The Avenida Bronco became alive with a stream of human beings of the most varied types I have ever seen or ever expect to see again; bronzed Europeans, who could scarcely be distinguished from the native Brazilians, Negroes, Mongolians, and an endless variety of figures, heads, eyes, noses, hair, coloring, expressions of mixed races! To have seen so many types of physiognomies I count as one of the outstanding sights of my journey around the world."

The ship stopped briefly at the island of Saint Helena in southern Africa, where Napoleon had been exiled and had once been interred, and then went on to Cape Town. "As the boat glided into the harbor on the morning of February 6, we had a fine panoramic view of the red-roofed city spread out along the bay beneath the Table Mountain, the Lion's Head, and Devil's Peak." On disembarking she and her companion immediately headed to the Cape of Good Hope on what was said to be "the finest marine drive of the world," about one hundred miles long, with tunnels reminiscent of Alpine passes hewn into the rock and foaming waves battering the cliffs.

"At the end of the drive, we had a climb of about twenty minutes to a peak from which we could actually see the tip of Africa just below us. It is washed by two oceans, the Atlantic and the Indian. If rocks could speak, the Cape could tell stirring tales of valiant men who braved storms (it was originally called the Cape of Storms), hardships, disease and life itself for God, country, or mammon."

Their return to Cape Town took them through vineyards where "we halted to taste the wine from the famous cellars" and to admire the gabled houses of ancient Dutch settlements. Anna had read extensively about South Africa. She was aware of its mines filled with diamonds and gold, and of the long and fierce struggles between the local inhabitants and those who had emigrated there. Anna had long been interested in the efforts of missionaries such as her aunt and the Visitation Sisters of her boarding school days who had chosen to serve in this part of the world. She was eager to see for herself the place which she, as a young woman, had considered potential mission territory during her own vocational discernment. "Although our minds were already crowded with new impressions, we could not afford to rest. Every minute was precious."

Immediately on returning to Cape Town, Anna and her companion called on Bishop Henneman, P.S.M., "who received us most kindly. As he already knew of our society, no long explanation of my interests was required. He took us mission-seeing in his Ford." They visited many sites in the city and the suburbs and even beyond, driving to a mission settlement in the bush. On the ride back to the city, they were treated to a clear view of Table Mountain in the setting sun. "And our day was not over yet!" The Bishop took them to meet two physicians affiliated with Würzburg. Anna would learn from them that "Catholic Mission Doctors on an organized basis are still something new and rare. Therefore it is quite natural that many problems remain to be solved."

The next and final stop in South Africa was the beautiful city of Durban, where Anna was able to meet and converse with missionary monks and nuns and learn about their many good works and the area's most virulent diseases. She visited Marianhill, a monastic mission station that consisted of twelve thousand acres, and discovered that it had been founded by a Tirolese priest "of good peasant stock" fifty years earlier and that they now had workshops for everything, offering technical instruction in their tannery, carpentry, shoe, and tailor shops, and their art and stained glass studios. There were also schools of every grade and description, a museum, a Cathedral on the summit of a hill, and a hospital, which Anna was eager to see. They also visited the Sisters of the Precious Blood who had a hospital and a training school for native nurses, where they were served "a delicious luncheon in the beautiful and peaceful atmosphere of their Motherhouse" and were then introduced to some of their numerous and diversified activities. "Everything seemed to have a practical turn, suitable for a primitive people," she noted with regard to elements helpful to a group that, owing to changing circumstances in the world, is "forced to emerge little by little from its own simple civilization." From there, they sped through "the valley of a thousand hills" for "we had to hurry to reach our boat. I stepped off African soil with the firm hope of returning and seeing more of it."

On February 11, the *S.S. Reliance* dropped anchor just outside Majunga, the largest and most rapidly growing town on the west coast of Madagascar. And on that day, at the Vatican in Rome, under the auspices of Pope Pius XI, the Sacred Congregation of Propaganda Fide issued its long-awaited Instruction to Religious Institutes of Women Regarding Assistance to Mothers and Infants in Mission Lands. Entitled *Constans Ac Sedula,* the Instruction not only approved the practice of medicine without reservation, but also encouraged religious communities of women to embrace the full scope of maternal care and medical practices as their mission when congruent with their congregational charism.

Anna rejoiced when the news finally reached her on her journey around the world, saying later that "this pronouncement made me very happy because it will mean much help for poor mothers and children and also because the Church now allows this work to Religious." Indeed, the primitive conditions of a large percentage of the native population in Madagascar bore witness to the need for qualified medical personnel. Malaria, leprosy, and malnourishment were widespread. French military and civil doctors were in charge of medical services in the major centers and supervised native doctors in the outlying districts but their numbers were insufficient. *"La Grande Isle* is what the French call this distant colony, which is actually larger than the mother country," Anna noted. "It is a land of beauty and promise awaiting development."

In graced synchronicity, shortly after the pronouncement from Rome that in effect validated the pioneering efforts of Anna and her Society, the ship sailed to India, the land where her pioneering medical mission dream began. She could hardly contain her excitement as the *S.S. Reliance* slid into its berth in the familiar port of Bombay.

> "February the twenty-first was the great day of our arrival in India. For me it was the third landing and, I hope, not the last. I separated from the party and took the first Punjab mail train in order to spend every available hour with our Sisters in Rawalpindi. As the only way to get goods into India cheaply is to take them along personally, I had a vast amount of luggage containing everything from surgical instruments and baby clothes to pills and bandages for the hospital and belated Christmas gifts of American candy for the Sisters.
>
> "My traveling companion for the greater part of the journey was a nice Mohammedan woman who told me that she had married ten years previously at the age of eleven and that she had been in purdah ever since. She tried to make conversation by telling me something of Mohammedan customs and feasts. It gave me a splendid chance to revive my Hindustani. In Delhi people began to pour into the train. Suddenly a Medical Missionary dressed in white stood in the doorway. It was like an apparition! Sister M. Helen, superior of our house in Dacca, was on her way to Rawalpindi where we had arranged to meet since time did not permit my going to Bengal. To find one another in the crowded train at Delhi and even to be assigned the same compartment was an extremely happy coincidence. The trip was very pleasant for we had much to say.
>
> "After about fifty hours of railroad journeying we arrived at our destination on February twenty-fourth and were met at the station by Sister Mary Laetitia and

Sister Ann and in the hospital by all our other Sisters. I was happy to find them all well. The following day I made rounds in the hospital and chatted with the patients and native nurses. The nursery was crowded. The work has increased much since my last visit. Fortunately there was a little lull at the time of my stay so I had a chance to see more of the Sisters. February twenty-eighth came all too soon. I had to leave in order to be in Bombay in time to meet the boat."

She did arrive in time. "At 7 o'clock that night our *Reliance* sounded the whistle, which said 'goodbye' to Bombay. I said *'Auf Wiedersehen!'*"

Anna's next destination was the island nation of Ceylon [now Sri Lanka], just off the southern coast of India. On March 4 the ship anchored in Colombo. Passengers were taken by car to the ancient inland capital of Kandy. Along the way they saw palm groves, cocoanut, nutmeg, banana, and rubber plantations, and stopped to tour a tea factory and savor a cup of Ceylon's finest. Just outside of Kandy they visited the Paradenya Gardens, considered on a par with other botanical wonders of the world, and a watering hole for elephants. On entering the city they were taken to the Temple of the Tooth, a shrine dedicated to Buddha, where many valuable Buddhist manuscripts were kept and venerated by the country's Buddhist majority. After lunch Anna briefly attended a dance performance, then slipped away and hired a rickshaw to take her to the Cathedral, which she had wanted to see but alas could not because it was closed. She also was unable to visit the Papal Seminary founded by Pope Leo XIII, as time did not permit. The tour group returned to Colombo by train. The hilly terrain offered a view of real mountains in the distance where, hidden that day by a thick cloud cover, the 7,000 foot high Adam's Peak bears witness to a local legend that says Adam chose to live in Ceylon after being evicted from Paradise.

Colombo, capital of "the pearl of the orient," and very cosmopolitan, bustled with curio shops and vendors hawking precious gems, such as emeralds, sapphires, rubies, opals, pearls, and the famous "Ceylon moonstone." Time was allotted for exploring its wares, and as always, Anna took in everything, making notes of moments she did not want to forget in the midst of all the chaos. She was determined to visit the

Franciscan Missionaries of Mary at the General Hospital, which was not on the official schedule, and on the last day, despite a torrential downpour, she managed to secure a rickshaw to take her there. "The nuns received me as an old friend," Anna recorded, much to her delight. There were 75 of them. Many of the Sisters had been there for years and were in charge of nursing and also responsible for several leprosaria. They spoke of the prevalence of malaria throughout the country, which was not a surprise to Anna. However, she was startled to learn that in the previous year one-sixth of the total population had been affected, most notably among those who were the poorest of the poor. On departing, Anna recorded in her journal: "My visit to Ceylon was pleasant in every way, but I was not quite satisfied about it, as I had seen very little of the missions." She had hoped to encounter the Oblates, Jesuits, Benedictine Fathers and Christian Brothers, as well as several Sisterhoods. All had flourishing missions there, but the ship's itinerary prevented her from visiting their sites.

"On March 9 the *S. S. Reliance* laid anchor outside Penang, a picturesque island on the west coast of the Malay Peninsula," wrote Anna. "As it was my plan to separate from the party and travel overland to Siam [now Thailand] in order to have more time there, I took a rickshaw to the Siamese Consulate at once after landing." It was closed. After a brief tour of the bazaar and the town she returned at 9:00 am to acquire a visa, then took a ferry to the railroad station where, luckily, the twice-weekly Bangkok express was scheduled to leave that day. The train was crowded. In her compartment for the 22-hour trip were a Sikh family that spoke Punjabi and with whom she could converse; two Japanese boys; and a Chinese girl. The conductor, an Indian from the Malabar Coast, was Catholic, well-informed, and fluent in English, and seemed to enjoy being "bombarded with questions." Anna learned a lot from him about Malay and its people. Most were Muslim; their women did not observe purdah. The train stopped at the frontier, then continued on through the night, passing forests of rubber plantations and an abundance of rice fields, the staple – and cash crop – of the country. "I had fried rice in the train; it was very tastily flavored and truly delicious."

On arrival in Bangkok Anna checked in with immigration and with the local police to register her presence in the city. "A young police officer who had been educated at the Cathedral School kindly escorted me to the Bishop's house." She was graciously received. "He asked me to go to Xieng-Mai in northern Siam, where he intended to start a medical mission. I agreed at once and made plans accordingly." While in Bangkok Anna was hosted by several religious communities, including the Ursulines. During that day, and the next, she was introduced to their many and varied good works within and beyond the city, including a nursery where the children were the poorest of the poor. Driving through Bangkok, "I was tempted to stop here and there, but I was due at the station at 6:00 p.m. to start out for northern Siam. To my surprise, His Excellency and two Ursuline Nuns – and a police official! – were there to see me off."

Anna boarded the train which, for the next twenty hours, sped past rice fields, canals, and villages, and into rocky, hilly terrain with mountain ranges in the distance and woods everywhere. In mid-afternoon of the following day they arrived in Xieng-Mai, the terminus of the Siamese railway. Anna was met by a priest and a Brother and their "tin Lizzie." What ensued was somewhat precarious. "Father drove at top speed, unconscious of ruts and bumps, so much so that I had visions of finding an early grave on Siamese soil." On arrival at the rectory she was warmly welcomed by three French-speaking priests and then by the Mother Superior at the Ursuline Convent, where, "after a little refreshment, 'Lizzie's' horn tooted, which meant off again." They visited a number of institutions – both Catholic and Protestant – that served the local people in a variety of ways. "American missionaries are said to have been the first to introduce modern medicine into Siam," Anna was told. "What amazed me most of all," she noted, "was the large complex of buildings of the Protestant mission in the outskirts of the city; a very fine church, beautiful school, attractive residences for the teachers, and a very up-to-date hospital. It is admirable and stimulating to see the far-flung medical mission work of the Protestant organizations." Much to her delight, "that evening the Ursuline Nuns admitted me into their family circle at recreation, which was a great treat. With the chapel in the house, and being in a convent, I felt as much at home as if I were in Brookland, D.C."

The next day Anna's journal opens with the observation that "Mass in convents all over the world seems to be early; even far-off Xieng-Mai was no exception. At five o'clock in the morning I was roused for Mass at five-thirty." Immediately after breakfast "Tin Lizzie" returned. Father was determined to show Anna the Leper Asylum situated on an island outside the city. Anna was impressed. "Everything is so well organized. When I had had a bird's eye view of the whole, I was taken to the site of the proposed medical mission....When I said *au revoir* to Father Meunier it was not the conventional expression but a sincere hope, in spite of the hair breadth escapes in the 'Tin Lizzie.'"

Anna made the 467-mile return trip to Bangkok by train in the company of several Ursuline nuns. On arrival the following morning, they insisted on taking Anna to their Motherhouse, where she was "refreshed in soul and body." Reverend Mother offered to send two of the nuns, one of them Siamese, plus another friend of the community, to act as sight-seeing guides for Anna for the day. There was much to see in this "city of temples." A fifth of the city's area is temple ground, Anna explains in her diary. There are at least 300 temples (*wats*) in Bangkok. The so-called Emerald Buddha, Siam's greatest treasure, is housed in the royal temple. Then there is the famous sleeping Buddha; and the majestic Wat Arun, with its towers encrusted with glittering tile and pieces of porcelain. A strong Hindu influence was also evident in Bangkok. There was a lot to take in. "After a while," Anna records, "my thirst was beyond endurance. Fortunately I spied an ambulant soft drinks restaurant. The owner carried coconuts on ice in his little wagon. Here was a perfectly sterile drink of nature's own brewing. The cold, sweetish liquid was nectar to me." After a brief period of quiet reflection in the Assumption Cathedral, Anna left for the harbor, where, because of its shallow depth, large ships had to anchor quite a distance from land. "It took us over two hours in a tender to reach the *S. S. Reliance*. I was glad to see it again after my ten days' absence. The steward hailed me like a long lost friend and presented me with copies of our daily news sheet, the *Globe Trotter,* which he had faithfully kept for me." Anna savored two restful days before disembarking again.

Singapore. This bustling island port, a hub for international exchange, lay just below the equator. During their short stay Anna discovered that in the entire Malay Peninsula, including Penang and Singapore, there was not a single Catholic hospital. However, she noted, in Singapore "the government made excellent provision for the sick and the priests had no difficulty in visiting patients and administering the Sacraments in government hospitals." Before departing she visited the

General Hospital, "which is enormous," and was very impressed with all that it had to offer.

The ship left the Malay Archipelago mid-March and set sail for Indonesia. Its territory consists of approximately 17,000 islands. "Between Singapore and Java the sea was as smooth as oil," Anna noted. "On St. Joseph's Day [March 19] we landed at Tandjong Priok, which is seven miles from the business and residential section of Batavia, the capital of Java." The group toured the famous botanical gardens and other sites in and beyond the city, and in the afternoon Anna went off alone to visit the Ursuline School "where one of our Sisters spent her girlhood days and was still remembered by her old teachers." In the evening she took a rickshaw to Saint Carolus Hospital run by the Dutch Sisters of Saint Charles Borromeo. "After an interesting chat," the Sisters took Anna to a local bazaar along the canal, where indigenous people performed for tourists and lavishly displayed their wares. The next day Anna meandered through the streets and bazaars of Batavia with others from the *Reliance*, then went to call on the local Bishop, a Dutch Jesuit. "He told me that the government had a splendid medical organization. Even the people in the interior are well cared for. As the population of Java is almost exclusively Mohammedan, it is not surprising that there are many Mohammedan doctors." She was told that only those doctors and nurses who have passed examinations in Holland or Java are allowed to practice. Foreign doctors may take their examinations only after two years of study there. After the visit, Anna returned to the ship just moments ahead of a tropical cloudburst and then wrote the following in her diary.

> "On account of my visit to the Bishop I arrived late for dinner which afforded me the spectacle of being served alone by a line of fourteen waiters. They formed a regular procession, each one of whom deposited a different delicacy in a large, deep plate."

The next morning the ship anchored outside Semarang. Passengers were taken ashore in a tender and then driven 145 miles to see the monument of the "Great Buddha," one of the outstanding achievements of Buddhist architecture. Along the way "the scenery was enchanting … nature has certainly lavished her gifts on Java." Anna was told that Java's soil is one of the most fertile on the planet, due to lava deposits. The island is also one of the most densely populated places on the face of the earth. They reached the monument a little before noon.

> "We climbed up steep steps to the top. The heat was great because of the radiation from the stone. At the summit is a large dagoba which contains a statue of Buddha. Four hundred and forty-one smaller images of Buddha are scattered about in smaller latticed dagobas all over the monument. The most interesting part of the whole is the biography of Buddha chiseled into stone along the terraces. The bas-reliefs number nine hundred and eighty-eight, and if they were placed together they would be two miles long. The reliefs show a distinctly Hinduistic influence."

Before returning to Semarang, the group visited a Catholic Church nearby. "At seven we reached our boat and at eight we sailed, to awaken the next morning in Bali."

Early on March 23 motor boats took passengers ashore where cars awaited them. Their first visit was to the bat temple, a Balinese shrine in Koesambe where, at the back of a dark cave, a multitude of black bats hung from the walls and the roof. Bats are considered sacred, and the devout say prayers and leave offerings at the shrine. From there, a drive through the countryside revealed rice fields in all stages of growth on both sides of the road. The favorable climate and fertile land are conducive to yielding crops twice a year, with a crop of peanuts and another of maize in between. Observing the local people en route, Anna surmised that they looked happy and healthy. She also concluded that "to anybody who knew India, the Indian strain in them was quickly apparent." The traveling entourage stopped at a village and all were invited into an enclosure where they were warmly received. Anna described their experience.

> "The main hut had mats on the floor and a few pots here and there. A man, a woman, and a few children emerged from a smaller dwelling. In the back was the family shrine. The people seemed to be very religious. They are Hindus of a kind, largely influenced by a pre-Hindu civilization. Their socio-religious life is so

338

intricate that only an expert who has spent a lifetime in the study of it can give an interpretation of the many ceremonies and customs. Among the more elaborate ceremonies are the cremations, for which they erect enormous structures and celebrate expensively."

An extremely popular activity among the males is cock fighting, which is a source of gambling that the government had recently banned except on special occasions. From there the tour group drove through village after village, ascending five thousand feet above sea level for a spectacular view of the island country, which is only ninety-five miles long and fifty miles wide and at the time was home to a million people.

> "The greatest treat of the day awaited us after lunch under a huge spreading banyan tree: a full *gamelon gong* or native orchestra was assembled to accompany the dancers. The whole performance was worth seeing and hearing. It is impossible to describe the music in words; it is the most vivid expression of emotion and mood that I have ever heard."

Anna marveled at the extraordinarily graceful movements of the *lelong* dancers and their ability to interpret and express the music's many moods. On returning to the ship Anna recorded the following observation: "Bali was the first and only country on our whole cruise where we did not meet a single sign of Christianity. As a matter of fact, missionaries had not been allowed to work there. Recently, however, this has been changed." She also wrote: "All of the Americans on board were eagerly looking forward to seeing Manila. It was the one Oriental city with which they were familiar …."

On March 27 "we sailed into the magnificent Bay of Manila. The Constabulary Band greeted us with the 'Star-Spangled Banner' and other patriotic selections; the orchestra of the *Reliance* returned the compliment. It was hard to say which of the two bands was the more accomplished – both enjoy well-deserved fame." A section of the pier, said to be the finest in Asiatic water, had been converted into "a veritable bazaar where all kinds of Filipino specialties and curios were offered for sale," Anna noted, adding: "I heard later on, that the greater part of the retail trade in Manila is in the hands of women." Another key observation: "One thing was evident from the first moment we landed – we were in a Christian country." And then there was this surprise: all the people Anna met spoke very good English.

On disembarking she and her companion went directly to the Archbishop's house. Maryknoll Father William Fletcher arranged for an audience with His Excellency Michael O'Doherty, who was very optimistic about the future religious situation in the Philippines, pointing out that of the twelve million inhabitants, at least ten million are Catholics. Father Fletcher showed Anna and her companion the Cathedral and then took them to St. Paul's Hospital where the Maryknoll Sisters were in charge. The spacious hospital includes a free dispensary and a large social service department for the benefit of the poor. The next day they drove about Manila in a little pony cart, learning first-hand about the homes and the diets and the illnesses of the poor and the prevalence of certain infectious diseases. "We were told that the crowding is caused not alone by poverty but also by strong family ties which make relatives live together," and that much was being done by health authorities and charitable organizations for those in need. Among the dedicated was Maryknoll Sister Frederica who "is hailed and loved as a mother among the poor." Anna visited several other Catholic institutions before returning to the ship, where she recorded an important discovery regarding Filipino women.

> "The Christian Filipino woman holds a very different position in the family from that given to her sisters in India, and in most other Oriental countries. She is usually the business manager of the household, keeps the keys, does the providing, receives all money earned by any member of the family, including the proceeds from the farm produce, and she supervises the expenditures. It is she who 'balances the budget.' A man who fails to turn in his receipts for his wife's direction injures his standing in the community."

Once on board the *Reliance*, there was only a brief interlude before arriving at the next destination.

"Early in the morning of March 30, we sailed leisurely into the spacious harbor of Hong Kong, which has not only unusual scenic beauty, but presents a picture of seaport life never to be forgotten." This trading center, a free port, had been a Crown colony of England since 1841. Wealthy merchants and the British military live in fine houses with beautiful gardens, while the indigenous population is mostly crowded into an area where many narrow lanes branch off in various directions from four large thoroughfares. Each trade seemed to dominate a lane of its own similar to the guild system of the middle ages. Shoemakers, silk sellers, jewelers, clothing merchants were crammed into narrow cubicles, each in their own designated area, draping their wares out in the open while incredible numbers of people squeezed into their tiny "stores." Business was a family affair. In some places, Anna mused, "the members of the shopkeeper's family seemed as numerous as the customers – and just as much in the way!" Weaving her way through the crowds she discovered that "a dentist was plying his trade on the sidewalk. A sign behind him advertised painless extraction, but the facial contortions of the patient seemed to give proof to the maxim that you cannot believe all you read." From there the group was taken to the top of Victoria peak, the highest point in the area, for a wonderful view of neighboring islands and the deep blue waters of the China Sea, dotted with all kinds of crafts. After a steep descent, and a 25-mile circuit of the island, they stopped at a hotel for refreshments. "In the afternoon," writes Anna, "my friend and I went to the Bishop's House, but he was absent." They were warmly received by the resident priest, who took them to meet the Canossian Sisters, an Italian congregation laboring in the interior of China for more than 70 years. "As we were interested in things medical, Mother sent two Sisters with us to a 'home' in the very midst of Chinatown that carried on works for the elderly, the blind, the children – in fact, for anybody in any need whatsoever. On the way back to our boat we saw once more the teeming Chinese life in the main and side streets … a constant to and fro of humanity"… and a realistic introduction to China and its world.

"Long before we gained sight of Shanghai, we felt the throb of its busy life in the countless boats, junks, sampans, or whatever else they may be called, which dotted the waters all around us. They were like so many tentacles reaching miles out into the ocean and giving unmistakable evidence of the hustle and bustle going on in China's greatest seaport. We had been warned that it would be cold, but it was in the mildness of real spring sunshine that we sailed up the Whangpoo River and drew into port on April 3."

The Cruise Director realized that seeing Shanghai in a few days is a rather hopeless task, so everyone was left to follow his or her own interests. That was just fine with Anna and Doctor Hattemer. "We decided to begin by getting a few first impressions. Our geographical observations were supplemented by history and explanations, and we emerged with a bird's eye view of the whole." After their "general survey," they were drawn to "the world-renowned meteorological and seismological station conducted by the Jesuit Fathers ... The whole was very intricate and technical. All we could do was marvel... we spent the remainder of the available time in the book shop, enjoying among other learned works the beautifully illustrated volumes of Father Doré, S.J. on the superstitions of China." Then they visited the stately institution of the Helpers of the Holy Souls, where the nuns look after the elderly and infirm, and were escorted through a beehive of rooms that serve as an orphanage, a school, and a variety of worksites. They lingered in the nursery. "There we saw rows and rows of little Chinese babies in their tiny beds. Each day, we were told, brought new occupants, and each week saw some flying to heaven in spite of the great care bestowed upon them." Their next stops were at the General and Sacred Heart Hospitals. At the latter the Franciscan Missionaries of Mary were in charge of the nursing. Stories of war and its horrors during the Shanghai bombardment resonated deeply with Anna in light of her own personal experience.

Next on their agenda was a visit to Saint Joseph Home. En route, Anna reflected.

> "The Shanghai waters harbor literally a city of boats, where every phase of life goes on just as on land. From the little we could observe it was quite evident that these boat people were very poor. Their poverty has made them scavengers: they collect everything that is collectable, from garbage for food to bits of rags for shoe soles, and are largely responsible for the cleanness of Shanghai harbor! I cannot imagine who was worse off, the people on land or the thousands and thousands of families whose only home was a junk."

The final stretch of their journey through the city also gave them a glimpse of the more well-to-do. Anna records their reaction on reaching their destination. "Saint Joseph's took our breath away!" Indeed, in a single establishment, there were three thousand residents reflecting a broad spectrum of needs under the care and supervision of twenty-five Sisters of Charity, five resident doctors, and ten employees. At Saint Joseph's there was a place for working girls, for the sick, for the old, for babies, for the blind, crippled, incurable, mentally afflicted, and even for the incarcerated. Every imaginable human misery seemed to be represented there. It was very efficiently maintained and it was evident that much of the work was done by the residents themselves under the direction of the Sisters. The last stop in Shanghai was the Cathedral, "which we were anxious to see." They decided not to return to the ship, but instead to go by train to Peiping via Nanking.

> "We left Chapel station on the evening of April 5, traveling second class, which proved very comfortable. The train was heavily guarded by soldiers. Our trip was uneventful, and we arrived early in the morning in the capital of the Chinese Republic not knowing a word of Chinese nor a single soul. We fared extraordinarily well, however, thanks to the Catholicity of the Church!"

It had been a 350-mile journey by train to Nanking. "Our anchor of hope was a Catholic church where we could find a priest to help us. In vain we looked for an information bureau" – not a priority with only 600 foreign residents among 960,000 inhabitants. An English-speaking official came to the rescue. After a winding and bumpy ride in single-seat carts through teeming crowds, Anna and her companion arrived at the Catholic Church, where they were graciously welcomed and given Holy Communion, refreshments, and an overview of the area in fluent French by the administrator of the diocese. "How can we best see Nanking?" Anna asked. Samuel Wei, a seminarian, offered to be their guide for the day. They would have a taxi at their disposal. The two were ecstatic.

Their first visit was to the Ming tombs. "It was a glorious spring day," Anna noted. "The frostiness of the air blending with the mild sunshine effected that physical well-being which brightens spirits and quickens steps. The memory of the old Mings, the inevitable thought of the rise and fall of dynasties in contrast with the stability of the ever-recurring seasons, lent itself to musings. But time was short and we had to push on." Their next stop was "a leap from the past to the present" – the burial place of Sun-Yat-Sen, Father of the Republic. "It is the most impressive mausoleum I have ever seen. It is said that the so-called principles concerning the people, which Sun-Yat-Sen gave to China, were inspired by Lincoln's 'government of the people, by the people, for the people.'" They also visited the so-called cemetery of martyrs before returning to the city, where they encountered a celebration of Children's Day. "There was speech after speech. For at least two hours we listened and waited in the heat of the noon-day sun… right in the midst of hundreds of children…we did not see even one unruly incident. It was a spectacle that impressed me more deeply than anything else in China." Foot-weary and hungry, the two women were glad when their guide suggested lunch. 'Would you like a European or a Chinese restaurant?' he asked. "Chinese! We chorused." After their meal, thoroughly refreshed, they resumed their trip with a walk through one of the parks and a drive past modern buildings, civic centers, universities and the enormous new municipal hospital that boasted the latest equipment. Scattered throughout the city and its suburbs were a number of health stations that offered medical attention to the general public for a nominal fee.

> "At every nook and corner our guide found something interesting to tell us. That included the tablet at Ricci College, where the memory of Jesuit Fathers Ricci and Schall, two famous missionaries and scientists, had been preserved. We scarcely noticed that the evening twilight had enveloped us. Our kind guardian accompanied us to the railway station, where we bade farewell to him and assured him of our undying gratitude for having made our day in Nanking so full and so memorable. During the few hours that remained until train time, we found fascinating occupation in observing the to and fro of Chinese life at the station." Nanking reminded Anna of Delhi. "Both cities had been capitals off and on, had risen to a pinnacle of splendor and then fallen into decay; both are capitals once more of the most populous nations of the world; both have the old culture and the achievements of present-day science side by

side; both had to undergo the growing pains of modern development."

About midnight the two women departed the dimly lit capital of China.

> "We had only two traveling companions – a Chinese lady of the well-to-do class and her little son. He was very well behaved, indeed. We crossed the Yangtze-Kiang by ferry. The train was taken across in sections very dexterously and speedily. The few hours of night passed quickly. Dawn revealed field after field covered with mounds of earth…the graves of the much-revered ancestors. One cannot help but wonder that a nation of 475 million people visited by so many famines can spare, century after century, so much land for burial grounds. To me it shows that the Chinese value sentiment more than material welfare."

Seeing peasants at work plowing, both women found it incongruous to see bulls and donkeys working together. Occasionally they passed a contingent of heavily laden camels plodding along single file. The train stopped twice, briefly, en route to its destination. Anna tried both times to see something of the local environment, but she and her companion were unable to get very far. En route again, as a diversion, they took a walk through the entire train.

> "Everything was clean and tidy, even in third class. The people had their bundles, their padded teapots and baskets of food stowed around them in little piles. There was something fine and noble about these men and women, most of whom bore on their hands and features traces of the wear and tear of life; there is nothing quite so respectable in this world as the evidence of honest toil. I would have liked to sit down for a while in their company, but there was not a single vacant seat."

At daybreak they arrived in Tientsin, the historic main harbor of North China, and took a taxi to a Catholic Church, where they attended Mass. The pastor was a French missionary, who answered all their questions, then hired two rickshaw drivers, explained where the women wanted to go, and "to make sure that we would not be fleeced," paid the fares himself.

> "Many pleasant surprises were in store for us...the up-to-date girls' school of the Franciscan Missionaries of Mary...the fine buildings of the boys' school conducted by the Marist Brothers...the hospital of the Sisters of Charity where we met Dr. Benjamin, the eminent French physician in charge. He told us that he was very successful in treating appendicitis without operation, and also of a treatment of his own for pneumonia."

The two women learned that there were many other Catholic institutions in Tientsin. They had already decided to make a pilgrimage to a convent in the native city, where several Sisters had been martyred some years ago, and their rickshaw drivers had been instructed to take them there.

> "As we were twisting in and out of the muddy lanes on our way, we suddenly encountered a funeral procession. A real Chinese funeral is something for the twentieth-century Westerner to behold – the quaint and multicolored costumes, fantastic umbrellas, paper decorations, and drums carried by the legion of bearers; ornamented vehicles, laden with dragons and other animals and objects made of paper. These last are supposed to be hints to the deities of the kind of comforts the dead would like in the next world. The procession moved very slowly and came to frequent halts."

When the rickshaws could no longer make headway, their drivers just disappeared. "Abandoned, without warning, we decided to make the most of the situation." The two women worked their way through the crowd until they had reached the house of mourning where they could observe everything. Eventually the coffin was placed in the richly decorated hearse. It took a long time before the colorful mule-drawn cortege was on its way. Anna and her friend were "still bent on our pilgrimage to the Sisters of Charity. How to reach them was the question. My friend joined her hands in prayer to indicate to passersby where we wanted to go. After a while a man stopped and beckoned us to follow him." For about twenty minutes he led the way along narrow muddy lanes with walls on either side until they reached a large courtyard teeming with devotees. "We were at a pagan temple," Anna realized, "and some sort of festival was going on. We entered the temple which was full of people. Joss sticks were burning by the hundreds. The fascination of watching Chinese devotion played havoc with our sense of time. Alas! We never reached the Sisters of Charity!"

The other passengers from the *S. S. Reliance* were due to arrive by train late in the afternoon. The sun was already heading toward the horizon when Anna realized that she and her companion had to return to the station at once if they were to join them in the two-hour journey to Peiping. "We were delighted to see our fellow passengers again and to exchange experiences." It was already dark when the train arrived at Chien Men station in Peiping. Anna was relieved to learn that the hotel to which she and her friend had been assigned was within walking distance to the Church of Saint Michael. They slept soundly that night. "We were extremely tired." She would later record that "the four days ahead of us in Peiping proved still more strenuous than the past few days." To get even a cursory view of the most history-laden city of the Orient is a challenge.

> "Peiping has been a city for three-thousand years, and a capital and an archbishopric for more than five hundred. In addition to the accumulation of landmarks such a past would bring, there were geographical difficulties: cities within cities spread out over a vast area which was enclosed in a massive wall, fourteen miles in circumference and perforated by sixteen gates." She succinctly describes the topography. "A wall separates the city into two main parts, the *Inner* or *Tartar* (Manchu) *City*, and the *Outer* or *Chinese City*. Within the *Inner City* is the *Imperial City*, surrounded by a red brick wall; within this again is the *Old Imperial City*, and in the center of this, like the seed in the core in the pulp in the rind, is the walled and moated so-called *Forbidden City*. The *Tartar City* had been the dwelling

place of members of the royal family and high officials; the *Forbidden City*, the residence of the emperor and his family. The *Chinese City* harbors the most sacred edifice of China, the Temple of Heaven. On a marble altar close by the Temple, the emperors, as lords of heaven, offered sacrifice and prayers to the Supreme Being on New Year's Day. Our guide pointed out to us that the Chinese consider this spot the center of the world. We went from building to building; it seemed endless."

They also visited the Lama Temple whose monks were under the authority of the Dalai Lama of Tibet. Nearby was the temple of Confucius, the sage whose ethical principles have molded China for twenty-four centuries. In the shadow of giant cypresses, "we found one of the most remarkable libraries in the world: the nine Chinese classics all hewn in stone. A Manchu emperor had had all the books burned at the instigation of the enemies of philosophy, but the 'friends of wisdom' were able to rewrite them from memory, because classical education had demanded of students from time immemorial that they learn all the classical books by heart."

On the morning of their second day in Peiping, Anna and Doctor Hattemer called on Archbishop Zanin, the Apostolic Delegate of China, who was deeply interested in the development of medical missions in China. Although he was Italian, he spoke to them fluently in French. "His Excellency already knew of our Society," Anna recorded.

"It was from his lips that I heard the grand and glorious and far-reaching news of the Decree, issued a few weeks previously on February 11, not only allowing but urging Sisters to devote themselves to the care of mothers and children in non-Christian lands – to alleviate their sufferings by bringing all the devotedness of religion and all the available means of science to the task."

Maryknoll Father Frederick Dietz, then secretary of the Chinese Synod Commission, and editor and director of *Lumen News Service*, "presented me with my first copy of this Decree." Anna and her friend went on to visit the Catholic University and were impressed with its many buildings, lingering at the Medical Center where some impressive research was underway in their laboratories. Last stop was the Chapel, beautifully liturgical and Chinese in style. It was Wednesday of Holy Week. "We were fortunate enough to be in time for Tenebrae – a truly Catholic close to our enjoyable visit at this center of Catholic education."

The next day, Holy Thursday, they were taken to Mass at the Cathedral and then on a medical sight-seeing trip by one of the doctors who was a source for unity and strength for medical missions all over China. He reported that "the Chinese Government has a network of hospitals and medical relief stations all over the country, but that the meshes of the net were still very wide." Anna was in her comfort zone, learning all about prevalent diseases and the variety of medical services available to those in need. She spent the final hours of her stay in Peiping at the Summer Palace, just outside the city, drinking in its beauty. Her travel journal captured the experience.

> "China's love for symbolism finds expression everywhere, a wealth of hidden history of religious beliefs. Taoism, with its cosmic mysticism, is said to have supplied the mythical dragon emanating a good influence; and the peacock, emblem of resurrection because it changes the plumage every year; while Hindu-tinged Buddhism furbished Chinese art with the lotus and the ubiquitous mystic knot from the sole of Gautama's foot. The Summer Palace gave the Chinese an opportunity to express their excellent craftsmanship and love of beauty."

It had been exhausting to climb those many steps, "yet the peace that reigned (we were the only visitors), the invigorating air and the exquisite views in every direction were a welcome relaxation after the past few days of meandering between walls." Anna was also eagerly anticipating the next day's rest on board the ship before arriving in Korea.

> "On Easter Sunday morning we sailed into Tchemulpo, one of the main harbors of the Hermit Kingdom. The rising sun spread its glow over sky and water. The bay was literally a mirror. There was perfect stillness above and below – 'Land of Morning Calm,' the Koreans call their country. This characteristic of nature seems to belong to them also – we noticed a serene dignity in

the people we saw and met. They are mostly farmers
who grow cotton, rice, and fruit. Time, however, did
not permit us to go beyond Seoul."

They arrived just in time for 10 o'clock Mass. "The Cathedral was a
welcome sight. There was the same ceremonial, the same solemnity
as hundreds of miles away – it made us feel at home! The chant was
Gregorian, much to our delight. Every inch of the edifice seemed to be
occupied." After Mass Anna called on the Bishop and met the Sisters of
Saint Paul de Chartres, who were thinking about building a hospital. On
a tour of the quaint city, the visitors from abroad chanced upon a Shinto
service in a very simple open hall. Shintoism seems to have surfaced
after the annexation of this primarily Buddhist country by Japan in
1910. "Our fellow passengers went curio hunting in all directions. Some
acquired Korean chests with ornamented brass hinges to store 'the
loot,' gathered here and there on the cruise." Before nightfall, everyone
returned to the ship.

> "Favorably impressed by land and people, we cast a
> last glance over the hill-rimmed capital. The Cathedral
> remained in view longest, but finally it too disappeared.
> However, the memory of that Easter Mass within its wall
> will never vanish. It was a demonstration of the unity
> and growth and the eternal youthfulness of the Church.
> It deepened the conviction of the worthwhileness of
> leaving home and country to extend the Kingdom of
> the children of God."

After one day at sea the *S.S. Reliance* arrived in Japan. Spring had
preceded them. "Cherry blossoms greeted us on all sides." They were
driven to the country estate of a major industrialist – "a paradise of
shaded paths and graceful trees." Flowers were in bloom everywhere.
There was a stream with a waterfall and a bridge; and on the lawn, tables
and chairs were arranged in groups. After being refreshed with green tea
and rice cakes, they were taken on a tour of a typical Japanese home and
introduced to painted paper screens and to the art of flower arranging
for cultivating peace of mind. Next on the tour's itinerary was Beppu,
"the hot spring city," with its facilities for baths with either hot water
or with steam in both the sea and in the hot sand on the shore. "We

visited one of the mud baths. Rows and rows of women lay buried up to the neck in hot mud, only the region of the heart being left uncovered." The local bazaar was filled with wooden curios and celluloid novelties, the latter crafted from camphor trees that are plentiful in Japan. They visited the Catholic rectory, where a Salesian priest had them climb up a mountain to reach the orphanage of the Salesian Sisters, where "they treated us to a demonstration of how to strap a baby on the back, a la Japanese."

This mountainous country consists of four large islands and a number of small ones.

> "One of the latter, although only nineteen miles in circumference, is of great importance on account of its religious significance. It is the Sacred Island of Myajima, which we visited. The main shrine is built on supports surrounded by water, and at high tide the temple itself seems to be afloat. Bronze and stone lanterns in profusion adorn the park and shore walks. On feast days, they are lighted – the effect must be softly solemn, amid the stately pine trees and the reflections in the water."

Anna enjoyed the leisurely walks and pleasant views of the island, admiring the hairstyles and dress of the women, and "the clap-clap of their shoes." On returning to the ship, she wrote: "As far as scenic beauty is concerned, one of the super-treats of the cruise was now in store for us. We were due to enter the Inland Sea."

The ship sailed between the islands of Hondo and Shikoku with picturesque views of the coastline, its blinking lighthouses keeping vigil for the small fishing boats and large freighters seemingly adrift on the water. "Everything appeared so artistic. A painted replica could never do it justice, and yet it was all very much like a picture – so fine, so compact, so perfect!" The ship's destination was Kobe, from which a network of trains extended in all directions to accommodate a densely populated area in a major industrialized section of Japan. Before exploring Kobe, the tour group traveled the short distance to Nara, the ancient capital, and the cradle of Japanese arts and literature. Within it was the largest park in the country – "a natural woodland, with hundreds of tame deer." For Anna it offered "a restful oasis amid the comings and goings from temple to temple, whose names are impossible to remember."

> "I can only recall the Great Eastern Temple, which contains the immense Buddha, weighing five hundred tons, and a bell weighing forty-eight tons. The sight that impressed itself most deeply upon me in Nara was the long lane of stone lanterns under ancient trees. It was in this city too that I saw a very fine Protestant church in Japanese style, and I was told that there was a similar Catholic one, but the hour of departure for Kyoto had struck before I could find it."

Kyoto, a very big city, was the soul of old Japan and a stronghold of Buddhism. For more than a thousand years, it had been the residence of the Mikado, or emperor, the oldest hereditary monarchy in the world. Anna was impressed. "It has no less than three thousand Buddhist and Shinto temples – the most unusual of them all is the Temple of the Thousand Golden Buddhas. Having traveled through India, Ceylon, Siam, Java, China, Korea, and Japan, one cannot help but marvel at the extraordinary influence of Buddhism through the centuries."

Osaka, less than an hour from Kobe by train, was not on the program, but Anna managed to get there anyway.

> "I was glad I had an opportunity to see this commercial metropolis … it is a city of smokestacks such as I had never seen before – and what is more, there was smoke from most of the chimneys! My friend and I drove through the newer sections, which are ultra-modern, and also through the older, which are crowded. To get to the cathedral we drove along a canal which was lined with large warehouses which were veritable beehives of activity."

The Bishop, a member of the Paris Foreign Mission Society, had spent many years in Japan. He was very kind to Anna, telling her that Osaka was a great field for works of mercy, especially among the sick. A guided tour of a major department store was an eye-opener – "a marvel from basement to roof." At the end of the tour, the manager put an

English-speaking guide at Anna's disposal so that she and her friend could see more of the sites that seemed so impressive to her. "Thanks to him we saw a great part of the city." They also visited a restaurant and sampled *Sukyaki*. "The performance of eating what seemed to us stew with chopsticks was hilarious! Our gracious waitress encouraged us, and we did not do so badly at all. When we left, the hostess, her daughter, and two men bade us goodbye with profound bows and smiles."

Anna and her friend had not seen much of Kobe. "The surrounding cities held so much of interest that we had no time left to meander about before we had to leave for Yokohama." They did not spend much time in Yokohama either. "Tokyo, only thirty minutes away by electric train, was the big attraction." Her first and last impression of Tokyo was that of an immense modern capital. "The civilization of 2600 years is deeply rooted. This very fact makes the country interesting to the traveler. One of the dominating sights is the Imperial Palace, where the Mikado lives behind moats and walls protected by soldiers." Anna was also impressed by the very modern hospital of the Franciscan Missionaries of Mary. From there she went on to visit a large sanitarium, where strenuous efforts to fight the "white plague" of tuberculosis and to offer palliative care were paramount, and after that, the very well organized Red Cross hospital. "On the wall we saw a chart with the rules for nurses. They might apply everywhere: 'Be kind, be faithful, be persevering, have self-control, be modest, obey rules, be brave, be alert, do not be extravagant, be gentle, courteous, and well-behaved.'" The relevance of these rules to her own novitiate's code of conduct was not lost on Anna as she copied the words verbatim and tucked them into her diary. In her tour of medical establishments, she would learn Japan had plenty of physicians, and many nurses and midwives. "Tokyo also has two medical schools for women, one of them established fifty years ago. The fact that there are about thirty-six hundred women physicians in Japan proves that there is a field of labor for them."

A highlight for Anna was an audience with the Apostolic Delegate, where she learned from his secretary that the Maryknoll Sisters were planning to start a model tuberculosis hospital. Her final visit was to the Catholic University conducted by German Jesuits and Japanese lay professors, the only Catholic institution of higher learning among twenty government universities. Catholicism was taking root in Japan. Besides a number of educational institutions, there were two leper colonies and fifteen hospitals. "The labors of Saint Francis Xavier and the blood of the Japanese martyrs are bringing forth fruit slowly and steadily," Anna noted in her journal.

The *S. S. Reliance* began its homeward journey across the Pacific Ocean, "where the sky regaled us every night with its evening game of lights and colors on the smooth table of the mighty sea, and left us speechless, just to gaze, to absorb, and to marvel at the incomparable Painter!" Anna's heart was full to overflowing with all that she had experienced – a tapestry of cultures and human conditions, all held in the loving embrace of a God known and unknown, Creator of one and all.

> "We praise God.
> Most people praise Him in one form or other.
> I have seen the Moslems praise God.
> They have 99 names in praise of God.
> We gather all this praise and offer it to God.
> Hallowed be Thy Name."

On May 1, in Honolulu, arriving passengers were greeted with *Alohas* and fragrant *leis*. On May 9 "in San Francisco, the moon hung over the city as we sailed into the harbor; and the sun made it truly a Golden Gate as we left again." Los Angeles and Panama and Cuba brought Anna full circle on May 25 to "the Statue of Liberty once more!" She expressed her gratitude to captain and crew. After five months under their solicitous care, "we took leave with a deep feeling of appreciation for their friendliness and expert services. As for our companions on our floating home: they were no longer casual acquaintances but neighbors. Probably we will never meet them again – but hearts do not bother about probabilities. They only smile and say: *'Auf Wiedersehen!'*"

God loves everybody.

You must not think we are the favorite.

The population of the world is growing tremendously every day.

God loves them all.

Anna Dengel

CHAPTER TWENTY-ONE

Anna returned to her community in Washington on May 26. Michael Mathis was not there. He had left for India on a canonical visitation of Medical Mission Sisters shortly before she arrived. "She weighed 171 pounds and looked extremely well," Agnes Marie noted, then went on to elaborate. "As she is very much overweight she looks pudgy. Five months of inaction with a luxurious diet no doubt accounts for it. She came back with about seven dresses – wool and silk, prints, stripes, which she bought along the route and wore. She said she felt out of place in the grey uniform but wore it when she went to convents, to see Bishops, etc."

Ironically, Anna no longer fit in at her Society's Motherhouse, which was now even more like a traditional convent than it had been before. Agnes Marie kept a close watch on her. "After a few days her old symptoms again appeared: excitability, nervousness, unreasonableness. Perhaps adjustment to community life partly caused the difficulty. For two years she was able to follow her own regime (six months at Sacred Heart, one year in the Tirol and six months on the trip). It must have been hard to return to a regular life." Hard to return to a more regulated life would have been a more accurate assessment. Like forcing a square peg into a round hole and blaming the peg for not fitting.

The following comment reveals how little Anna's community knew of her life beyond the confines of the Motherhouse. "Having lived five or six months in a *most luxurious* atmosphere didn't help to make things easier." One wonders how much the Founder of this community had been able to share with them about the voyage of a lifetime that had meant so much to her and had reinvigorated her in body, soul, and spirit. Her trip around the world had given her a more informed understanding of an already inherent global perspective, now nuanced by multiple experiences of cross-cultural immersion.

Surely she would have talked about what she had learned from those enlightening encounters and its relevance for her Society. Her voyage had opened windows to a much wider world of potential and possibility; but instead of inciting "fire and flame" with regard to what she had experienced, she returned to a place walled off from interaction with secular societies and related political complexities. Participants in her pioneering venture had become immersed in a world of their own as they prepared for a future that seemed light years away. Yes, this was Anna's community, but it may not have felt like it. Her intensity continued to be what it always had been, spontaneous and visceral; and her inner struggle between leading her community according to the mandates of external regulations or following the lead of the Spirit without a map to guide her continued unabated. From time to time her emotional distress disturbed the tranquility of convent routine. Were such outbursts simply inappropriate? Or, as some suggested, were they abnormal. Before long she would become sick again, and no one, not even Anna, would connect an individual's usurping of a vision rooted in a divine mandate as the source of her failure to thrive.

Anna's work ethic and ethnic persona were often at odds with established procedures and communal expectations. "She still insists on putting the O.K. or reverse on everything done or written. If only she could learn to parcel out work and give others responsibility." At the heart of this dilemma was an emerging understanding of what it meant to be nuns, for that was what the Society of Catholic Medical Missionaries was in the process of becoming. *Constans Ac Sedula*, the proclamation by the Sacred Congregation of Propaganda Fide to religious institutes of women, was now the primary guideline for shaping Anna's Society. The ground-breaking Instruction, states:

> "Having studied the question with due care and having secured certain necessary faculties from the Holy Father, this Sacred Congregation, acting in accord with the Sacred Congregation for Religious, considers it opportune to issue the following rules and instructions.
>
> "It is to be desired that new Sisterhoods be founded which shall devote themselves, with due safeguards, to the care of mothers and children in peril of life and health. These hoped-for Congregations are to be

formed in accordance with common law. Furthermore, it would please the Sacred Congregation if, in Religious Congregations already existing, groups of Sisters were to be formed for the aforesaid purpose. No Sister may be obliged by her Superiors to undertake obstetrical work; only those are to engage in this particular form of work who are willing to accept this special charge of mission charity from their superiors."

The Instruction went on to describe what was expected of religious communities of women with regard to this new development.

"These new duties require a proper medical and spiritual preparation. The Sisters must secure certificates as doctors or nurses, but, above all, they must be protected by special spiritual safeguards to be determined by their superiors. The Religious should regard this medical service as an expression of Christian charity whereby they open the way for the graces of the Redemption while striving to ease bodily suffering."

Constans Ac Sedula had been issued by Cardinal Fumasoni-Biondi, Prefect of Propaganda Fide, who was well-known to Anna and her Society. She had written to him prior to her trip around the world, asking him for letters of introduction to missionary bishops. He had told her to stay home and work hard at recruiting candidates for her Society; for he knew the release of the Instruction was imminent. While the long-awaited approval of Rome had been something for which Anna had prayed, at the same time, there was cause for concern, for it meant that now there would be a more restrictive external influence on her Society's unfolding. She had often said:

"From my experience in India I was so convinced of the need and of the charity and mission value of the work, that I just felt it worth the sacrifice of making public vows ...."

Now there was the possibility that the vows might compromise the mission in her nascent Society, which was seeking a new way to integrate with integrity both aspects of God's call.

What Anna had originally wanted was that nuns already in convents be allowed to participate fully and freely in medical mission ministries as physicians and as nurses, ensuring that in due time many more trained and dedicated women would be available for healing work among neglected women and children in remote areas of the world, wherever the need was greatest. She had wanted nuns to join the cause that she had been promoting. She did not have to be one, because restrictions that defined such a calling would severely limit her ministry. However, once the prohibition against the unrestricted practice of medicine had been removed, she could envision other options. For years she had longed for a form of religious life within some kind of community, of that there is no doubt, one in which members would make public vows. In essence, what she wanted was a new form of religious life, a new way of being a nun. For this, however, Rome's position was non-negotiable. Either live within a community as a vowed religious according to canon law with its specified mandates and associated customs, or opt for a form of dedicated life that was distinctively lay.

The Society faced a second dilemma associated with this systemic shift initiated by Rome: the length of time that would be required before a potential member could even begin to undertake medical mission work. There would be, first of all, years of canonical preparation; and then, for those who entered without professional training as a doctor or a nurse, the additional years required to become professionally prepared.

During the summer of 1936 Anna's physical and emotional states were sometimes up and sometimes down. Toward the end of September, just before Michael Mathis returned from his summer-long trip abroad, Agnes Marie journaled:

> "Doctor Dengel finally agreed that she would rest for a certain period every day at noon. Sister Pauline is her nurse now. She is very nervous again and at times can't control herself. She told me today that if she keeps working at the present rate, in six months she will be as bad as ever. She can feel herself slipping."

There was also on the horizon this major point of concern.

> "Father Mathis is expected back soon and that will be difficult for her. He is very energetic and wants to go ahead and keep developing the Society. She feels it is her duty to restrain him (which when done moderately and within reason is right). She wants to manage absolutely everything in detail and he being of a quick nature and confident of his ability, there is likely to be friction. He works hard to keep developing the Society and at times, especially when she doesn't feel well, she puts a bad interpretation on his motives and actions. She is afraid he will arrogate power unto himself, which is possible."

Agnes Marie concluded: "There will be many problems to discuss and policies to formulate, so life will be very hard for Doctor." In addition there was the pressing need for a larger Motherhouse. The present house was much too small and terribly overcrowded. "It is an old wooden structure and all the noise carries. It is simply impossible to have 'no noise' in the house."

Father Michael Mathis returned from India in September and immediately turned his attention to several pressing concerns. He sent a letter to Father Sauvage, Holy Cross canonist in Rome.

> "I am under the impression that a canonical novitiate is necessary for those making public vows. What is the ruling on this point? This of course would affect us when the time came for making public vows and since this will be soon, apparently, dependent upon Rome's approval, it will take some time to have all the older members get a chance for a novitiate."

In a lengthy letter to Archbishop Curley, Mathis made the case for needing to move the Motherhouse to larger quarters now available in Philadelphia, which meant leaving the Archdiocese of Baltimore. He was concerned about how the Archbishop might feel about this. The response was brief and to the point.

"The proper thing to do is the best thing for the Organization. If it will help the Organization of which you have charge to move its Motherhouse and Headquarters to Philadelphia, then move the Headquarters to Philadelphia. Sentiment and emotion have no place in a matter like this."

Anna had heard from Cardinal Dougherty. "I trust that you are now completely recovered. When are you coming to Philadelphia?" He added: "One of the pleasures of my life has been the issuance of the Papal Letter. It is manifestly the finger of God, which brought about the result."

In October Anna and one of the Sisters went to Massachusetts to attend a Mission Exhibit. According to Agnes Marie, Anna also "lectured a number of times and actually came home better than she went." She also wrote the following in her diary at the end of November, commenting not only on Anna and the current climate at the Motherhouse, but also on her understanding of her own vocational call.

"Doctor Dengel is really better. It is unbelievable that after these six years of suffering, really eight years since 1929. She is reasonable – gets excited and tense less easily and 'community life is a pleasure again.' I think the decree had much to do with settling her in life. Now our path is clear – before, at least for her, it was clouded. She wanted the community to do good medical work at all costs. This seemingly could not be done or at least could only be done with great difficulty as religious. Some of us insisted on being religious as that was promised us and was according to the constitutions. What to do! For the nurses and non-medical Sisters it would work but in Doctor Dengel's opinion it couldn't, for the doctors function on semi-lay lines. She would never admit this term but we who lived this life for ten years could call it no other. She herself does not understand religious life well because she never made a novitiate and apparently was too tired to think it out when she had time during her rest periods. Now this is all settled and she and all of us are most happy. Her ideal can be attained of being

360

good medical people, doing obstetrics and surgery and at the same time be religious. Everybody thinks we are lay so we have to re-educate the public. Since she is more reasonable, life with Father Mathis is running more smoothly too. His relationship with the community is less disturbing."

Before the end of November, Michael Mathis wrote a long letter to the Rev. J. Burns, his Provincial at Notre Dame, outlining a plan for the future, which he introduced as "something that concerns our Congregation either as a new field of labor or for an important extension of my permission to work for this Society." He said that the Instruction and his recent trip to Rome had convinced him of the urgent need and opportunity "for priests to promote medical missions in the Church." He wanted permission to found a new congregation of priests whose responsibilities would consist of the following four areas:

- the spiritual training and care of our Sisters
- the preaching of their cause in Churches and schools
- conducting medical schools for Sisters on the mission fields
- procuring finances for the capital expenses of mission hospitals

This was his rationale.

> "Inasmuch as our Society, the first founded in the Church exclusively for medical missions, has become the type proposed by Rome for imitation, and since this Society came into existence under the aegis of Holy Cross, it is but natural that I should ask our Congregation to consider the needs and opportunities of priestly service here presented. The fact that the Foreign Mission Seminary is now producing more missionaries than the Mission of Dacca can absorb created what I would like to think is a providential occasion for our Congregation's taking up this new work. The two communities would of course be independent of each other."

He concluded his proposal with the following request:

> "If it is altogether impossible for our Congregation to take up this new work, then I humbly ask permission to try to found a community of priests for this purpose."

In December he wrote to Father Sauvage in Rome regarding the Society.

> "All permissions have finally been given for our moving our Motherhouse to Philadelphia. We shall retain our house here as a house of studies for our Sisters and of course as a very special relic of our origin."

Then he added this bit of information, which indicates how sure he was of being granted permission by his Holy Cross community to implement his proposal.

> "I am also glad to tell you that our province is considering the prospect of giving more priests to the medical mission work, both from the spiritual and financial angles and also in the building and conduct of a medical school for Sisters in India."

Anna had her own agenda.

> "I hope we will keep to our original idea. The idea was to live for God and to dedicate ourselves to the service of the sick for the love of God, and in order to make charity effective, to be trained. We are a Religious Community. In the beginning we were a pious society.
>
> I can tell you that fundamentally there was no difference between the very first day and now because the aim was to give ourselves to God and to do the work which providentially came our way."

We want to make things meaningful –
not much and much and always much more,
but make it more meaningful!

Anna Dengel

CHAPTER TWENTY-TWO

Shortly after the beginning of the year, Anna Dengel left for New England with one of the younger Sisters on a public-relations and fund-raising venture. Michael Mathis, meanwhile, had been refused permission by his Provincial Superior to implement his proposal, so he wrote to his Superior General and repeated his request.

> "Now that our Congregation gives no hope of doing the work which I am convinced only priests can do and which needs to be done to consolidate medical missions in the Church both spiritually and financially, I am forced to the alternative of seeking your permission to found a special community of priests for this purpose. I do this with great reluctance, not only because I have some idea of the troubles involved, but also for the reason of my unworthiness. I feel that I do not have to emphasize this fact to you because I fear that you have not had much confidence in me, and no doubt rightly so. Despite this fact you have been very kind to me always and particularly in permitting me to give all my time to this Society. For this I am very grateful."

In New England Anna was her old self again, fully engaged and full of energy. According to reports to the Motherhouse, however, the situation was anything but positive. "Sister Francis Patrick couldn't manage her. She wouldn't rest at noon, insisted on giving talks to all who asked, even to grade school children, and usually for an hour, standing." Eventually this took its toll. The tour ended in New York with Anna's pre-scheduled talk to the Medical Mission Board and subsequent conversations with bishops and priests. She returned to the Motherhouse exhausted.

Agnes Marie recorded two incidents that, in her opinion, were symptomatic of something more serious. One day the Sisters were clearing brush from an overgrown area next to their property and someone cut down a small tree, perhaps a dogwood. When Anna saw it, she was very upset. She picked it up, brought it into the refectory while the novices were eating, and in a quivering voice, demanded: "Who cut this tree?" A second incident had occurred shortly after her trip around the world. During the time set aside for the community practice of spiritual reading, the Sisters were listening to a passage from the book, *Soul of the Apostolate*. Suddenly Anna interrupted the reader: "Don't believe that – we do not have to follow that doctrine. Put that book away and don't read it anymore." So spiritual reading was discontinued, Agnes Marie recorded, and Anna "finished up the time with an account of her trip." This had occurred the previous summer. There had been other occasions that some members of Anna's community had considered strange, and Agnes Marie kept track of them. For example:

> "For years Doctor Dengel has had strange notions about food. Already in 1930 she forbade that any white bread come into the house. She sends for literature from the places 'who cure everything by diet' and has had speakers in to lecture to the community. They are real quacks. One said that at their institute they cure acute appendicitis by diet and high colonic flushing. She takes it all seriously. Last spring she again denounced carbohydrates. Potatoes could be served 'only twice' a week. No carb substitutes at other times … meat once a day… Finally she had the Sister in charge of the kitchen write out a menu and bring it to her for her O.K. every morning."

Clearly, Anna held strong opinions that differed radically from those around her, but were those opinions irrational? A recent entry in Agnes Marie's diary raises serious questions indeed, not necessarily about Anna, but about those closest to her who continued to perceive her through a very narrow lens.

"She has ideas which are difficult to understand. For years she has been set in her ideas 'that women were ground down, trampled on, and abused by the male sex, clerics and bishops included' to quote her. Her reasons for not wanting a habit were of the same cast. 'Nuns cannot go to libraries' – nothing could change her mind on this – 'so they are usually narrow and often ignorant. They are considered less intelligent than women of the same strata in the world; on the whole they have inferior and undeveloped minds. People of the world think so and therefore we should not appear as Sisters exteriorly at least. The world would not realize that some of our Sisters are doctors if they wear a habit' – Shortly after we got the habit she went to Europe and before returning wrote that she could not meet her friends in New York wearing a habit. She said she did not know what she would wear."

Doctor Kain also shared a concern that she had kept to herself since 1930. She said it was the first time she suspected that something about Doctor Dengel was not quite right. Agnes Marie recorded her story.

"Doctor Dengel had wanted to meet some outstanding M.D. who was coming to Washington. She wanted to discuss a certain medical topic with him. So Doctor Kain arranged a get-together at the house and invited several other doctors. She invited Doctor Dengel to bring a Sister along but she said it wasn't necessary. So Doctor Steward, an old friend, came out for Doctor Dengel. The medical topic was disposed of quickly. There must have been five or six M.D.s. Doctor Kain said she served refreshments around 11:00 and at 11:30 offered to take Doctor Dengel home, but she wasn't ready to go. From early evening one topic after the other was brought up. Doctor Dengel talked rapidly but interestingly on nearly every topic. She contradicted much of what was said but did it so cleverly that all enjoyed it. When Doctor Kain suggested they leave the dining room table, they were so deep in discussion that they preferred to argue it out right there. That continued until 3:30 a.m. when Doctor Steward brought Doctor Dengel home."

Agnes Marie added this comment. "That was probably one of the times she crawled in through the window or slept at the Heenans." Agnes Marie and several others in charge at the Motherhouse were convinced that the erratic behavior and subsequent physical condition of their Founder was more than inappropriate. It was not normal. They feared that she may have reached the breaking point and felt they had to intervene. Doctor Kain concurred. As they reflected on a course of action, Michael Mathis heard from his Superior General regarding his request.

> "Father Provincial and I found that we were in perfect accord as to the only possible reply to your request and he has asked me to inform you of it. We cannot grant you the permission you ask. The liberty of action necessary for a religious founder would necessarily conflict with the proper observance of the rules and Constitutions of the Institute of which you are now a member."

That was on February 8. On February 12 Anna Dengel was admitted to Sheppard Pratt Hospital, an institution established to treat those who were mentally ill. Anna has gone on record saying that this was not voluntary, that she had been brought there against her will. There is no indication that Mathis was involved in that decision, but as Ecclesiastical Superior of the Society, it is hard to imagine he was unaware of this crisis at the Motherhouse, or had been categorically excluded from affirming a plan of action, since his stamp of approval was sine qua non for just about everything. For most of her incarceration there, Mathis remained on the sidelines, most likely because he had no idea how to handle what would become a very volatile situation.

Sheppard Pratt was a well-known mental health facility in Baltimore that treated the full range of psychiatric disorders. While referred to as an insane asylum by the general population, among professionals it was highly regarded for its successful treatment of those who were emotionally disturbed. Its physicians were the best in the region. It was non-sectarian, with Quaker roots, committed to the full recovery of health and a meaningful quality of life for the people they served. There was a waiting list for admission. After consulting with several of the Sisters, Doctor Kain, Anna's physician, had determined that a referral to Sheppard Pratt was the best course of action given Anna's lengthy history of emotional turmoil and physical instability. When the call came that a bed was available and would be held for twenty-four hours, she met with Anna and patiently, insistently, tried to get her to understand that this was what she needed to do if she ever wanted to be well enough again to fulfill her leadership role. Anna strongly resisted, pleaded for an alternative, wept, argued, and refused to go. Doctor Kain, along with Doctor Lalinsky, a member of Anna's community, finally persuaded her. They drove her to the hospital, stayed with her through the admission process, and then left her there on her own.

It would be two-and-a-half months before Anna would be allowed to leave. Ten-and-a-half weeks of feeling abandoned, feeling betrayed, not understanding why she was there or what she had done to deserve this. She spoke out relentlessly against being confined, restrained, humiliated, cut off from her community, deprived of human companionship, bereft of the Sacraments and of so many spiritually supportive essentials, as well as the basic necessities of what had been, for her, a productive and independent life. The hospital had separate sections, one for those more seriously ill and another for those who were less so and could therefore have more liberty to move about unrestrained. This latter area was, according to Doctor Kain, where Anna was supposed to have been assigned, but it was discovered prior to her release that she had been mistakenly classified in the initial phase of evaluation and admitted to the area reserved for acute psychiatric cases. Anna wrote to Agnes Marie:

> "Here I am, the fourth day, completely confined. I am behind locked doors; I cannot reach you or anybody else by phone. I have sent three wires to ask you to come for me. Whether they have gone or not I do not know. I received only evasive answers. My crucifix, my hair pins were taken from me. I have to leave the door open day and night and hear all the noise tramping up and down...talking, radio, etc. My glasses are taken from

me every night. I am in a place where people are put
for whom all precautions are necessary. It was a great
injustice to bring me here. If I have to go away for a rest,
I want to go to a place where I am not treated like an
insane person."

Then she added this in closing:

"Please give my love to all the sisters and tell them to
pray hard – harder than they ever did for me – for I
was never yet in a more unpleasant situation and that
is to say a lot."

As time went on Agnes Marie received Anna's telegrams, which the
institution sent by ordinary mail, in which she pleaded: "Come without
delay and take me home," and: "I shall not eat or drink until you come
to take me home." Anna tried to telephone, but was not allowed to
do so. Agnes Marie was instructed not to visit her. She was told she
needed a time of separation in order to heal. The Sisters, young and old,
corresponded faithfully, filling their letters with uplifting descriptions of
their daily lives and of the property at 6th and Buchanan as it prepared
to welcome the onset of spring; enclosed poems and penciled sketches
of various aspects of their convent routines; sent "oodles of love" and
a promise of prayers and assurance of their genuine concern. "We will
be over," Agnes Marie promised, "just as soon as the doctors think that
you may have visitors."

In mid-March, after Anna had spent more than a month isolated
from her community, Sister Agnes Marie and Sister Anthony went to
visit her in the midst of a snowstorm. It was bitterly cold. They took the
train, and the trolley, then climbed the hill to the hospital. Anna had
asked to see them and the institution had granted her request. Sister
Anthony chronicled the moment.

"Her story of sorrow was heart rending. Her greatest
grief: that we left her there – that keeping her there is
a real injustice – that it will forever be a stigma on her
name as well as on the Society. What she seems to resent
most is that her freedom is taken from her – that she is
considered morally irresponsible. That seems to crush

her. She said that never in her whole life has she suffered like in the past month, that she can understand people dying of a broken heart. It was hard not to weep."

Anna had sent letter after letter to the leaders of her community from the very first day of her being admitted to Sheppard Pratt, pleading for her release, and then demanding it, and she would continue to do so until that issue was resolved. She was there for her birthday, and throughout Holy Week and Easter, and continued to remain isolated from the life source of her spirit during the days that followed. She had complained at the beginning about the lack of religious services. She sorely missed the sacraments. About a week after she had been admitted, the institution had called the pastor of the local parish to come and visit her, for he was the one who ministered to Catholic patients at Sheppard Pratt. He came, but said that nothing would be gained by coming frequently because she talked about irrelevant things. Although Anna's doctor said that Holy Communion could be brought to her if the priest considered it beneficial, apparently, he did not, or did not wish to do so, for he said he would see her again in two weeks and there is no indication that he had ever returned. Agnes Marie encouraged Anna to "try to endure it and make the best of it. The regulations may seem drastic but you will soon be allowed more liberties if you do as they say. That you are not able to receive more spiritual help is to be regretted but that too will improve if you cooperate." Doctor Kain and Sister Agnes Marie kept contact with Anna's physicians, requesting progress reports regarding the nature of her illness and their opinion on the chances of her achieving a full recovery. They wanted to know when she would be able to leave the hospital and if she would ever be well enough again to resume the responsibilities of her busy, stressful life. The doctors were not hopeful. They agreed that something was seriously wrong but had no conclusive diagnosis and no expectations for a cure. They insisted that her confinement continue indefinitely. Anna kept pressing to be released and threatened to do something the Society would regret if they did not transfer her to some other care facility that was more humane and far more conducive to her achieving peace of mind.

Several days after their visit, Sisters Agnes Marie and Anthony received a letter from Anna that said: "If you do not come immediately I will leave the Society." She wanted them to get her out of that institution.

It nearly worked. Sister Anthony was terribly upset. She couldn't reach Doctor Kain, but persisted in calling the hospital that evening and again the following day and was told she could visit Anna. Agnes Marie went with her and they told Anna that they were in the process of securing her release. Agnes Marie wrote in her journal:

> "Doctor was very happy at the proposal of coming home. Sister Anthony took her direct threat to leave the Society very seriously and promised to take her out. I said, 'Gladly, if the M.D.s will discharge you.' Doctor Elgin advised against it but said he would not keep her if we insisted. So Sister and I signed a paper releasing the hospital from all responsibility."

She was to be released the following day. Doctor Kain agreed to pick her up and bring her back to the Motherhouse. Her room was made ready for her and the Sisters were awaiting her arrival. But as Agnes Marie journaled: "Doctor Kain is stalling. She says it is not safe to bring her home." She would do so only if ecclesiastical authority were notified. Agnes Marie had not said anything about the situation to the Archbishop. "I have not even spoken plainly to Father Mathis," and neither had Doctor Kain. "I think it is a great pity that it has to be taken to the Archbishop. The only way is for Father Mathis to do it because the Archbishop expects that." Agnes Marie also noted that "Father Mathis can't and won't take the responsibility" for this development regarding Doctor Dengel. He was up in Rochester, New York, where he had planned to work for several days and was currently engaged in the production of a film. One of the Sisters had recently written to Anna about that. "Sister Theophane has been busy working on the new movie. Father had brought all the apparatus home so his kitchen has been turned into a veritable studio, from all reports. Even Sister Bernadette is in the 'movie' business now." Alas, the Sisters did not succeed in securing Anna's release. She was devastated. Father Mathis had not come to see her, had not said a word to her. She was in an asylum for the insane and he was making a movie.

The following week was Holy Week. The way of the cross had become a reality for Anna. There was no sure sign of an Easter. On Tuesday one of the Sisters wrote: "You will probably be interested to know that we have completed the work we were doing on the film and

Father Mathis is having new prints made this week. We want to show it in the Novitiate 'auditorium' on the day we celebrate the Annunciation." On Holy Thursday Agnes Marie received a very frank letter from the hospital. Decide one way or the other, she was told, because Doctor Dengel expects to come home and gets upset when it doesn't happen. They strongly advised against it and said: she is very definitely sick and needs treatment and confinement "here or elsewhere." Doctor Kain was unable to get in touch with Father Mathis. "She tried about fifteen times but his cousins were out of town when he arrived so he had to stay elsewhere." He returned on Good Friday evening. In her journal Agnes Marie wrote: "He knew practically nothing about Doctor's illness but now he must be told."

On the Tuesday after Easter, Mathis informed the Archbishop about Anna's condition. The Archbishop replied: "I knew before I received your letter that Doctor Dengel is ill and at Sheppard Pratt hospital. She is a mental case. That is all there is to that." Then he added: "Do not worry about it. Say a prayer...." Agnes Marie was horrified. "How could he have known – we thought nobody but the doctors knew." Then something else occurred to her. "Now the Cardinal of Philadelphia will want to know why we haven't done anything about a house there during his absence. He will have to be told too, but on the other hand, he may know as much or more than we," for such news almost always circulates widely on its own. As if things were not convoluted enough, Anna took it upon herself to write directly to Archbishop Curley in order to secure her release. His response: "I am sending this letter to Father Mathis. There is nothing personally that I can do or responsibility that I can take in the matter of getting you out of the place. I realize that you would be better off in a place where you would have Catholic surroundings." Meanwhile the Sisters of Anna's community – so deeply devoted to the one who had made their vocations possible – continued to write to her and pray for her. In an effort to lift her spirits, Sister Pauline enclosed a line from Francis Thompson's poem, *The Hound of Heaven*. "All that I took from thee I did but take, not for thy harms, but just that thou might seek it in my arms."

On April 12 Father Mathis, Sister Anthony, and Sister Agnes Marie went to see Cardinal Dougherty in Philadelphia. Father Mathis told him that Anna was not well. "I hope it isn't a mental case," the Cardinal responded. Mathis turned to Agnes Marie. "I will let Sister explain, because she understands." She gave a brief report on what the doctors had concluded. "Grief was on his face." The Cardinal was pleased, however, that Pratt doctors were working together with the doctors from Johns Hopkins because he had great confidence in the latter. When asked if he still wanted the community to move to his Archdiocese, he replied: "Buy a place. The congregation must go ahead." His final words were: "Tell Doctor to rest and do everything the doctors say and she will be well soon. Give her my very best wishes." Agnes Marie reported this to Anna on her return. Then she shared sad news from Würzburg: Monsignor Becker had died; and some very good news from Rawalpindi. A regional committee had been formed for maternity and child welfare work and suggested that Holy Family Hospital take over its management. Laetitia had accepted. Agnes Marie knew Anna would agree that this will be "a big help to our work in Pindi as a training and experience provider and a feeder for the hospital" and that "Sister's experience in Dacca will prove valuable."

On April 16 Father Mathis received a letter from Archbishop Curley. He had enclosed the eight-page letter that Anna had sent to him, which, according to Agnes Marie, "had been nicely and logically written. She said her rights as a human being are curtailed – she is being deprived of the sacraments, she has no one to confide in ...." Agnes Marie admitted that those statements were true. "The Archbishop replied that the letter is justified, that he could take *no* responsibility in the case but that he would suggest moving her to Mount Hope. He said he did not think Sheppard Pratt a suitable place because it is Freudian." What prompted this change of heart? Anna would later write an account of this turbulent period and include an explanation.

"I probably would have been kept there a considerable time longer had it not been for a Catholic nurse – Alice Warren (nee Nast) - who saw how unhappy I was and said: 'It is cruel to keep you here because you most certainly do not belong here.' She went to a priest in the parish of Towson (Father Helzenouer, the same priest who had visited me once), and they asked the Archbishop to do something to get me out of this atmosphere where my condition daily grew worse." So now, what to do? Agnes Marie was stymied. It would be impossible to keep Anna's illness confidential in any place close to home. "We can't take her to Mount Hope because everybody would know it, as so many nurses affiliate there." When Dr. Kain sought a second opinion from one of her respected colleagues, he insisted that Anna needed to remain where she was. Meanwhile, Anna had asked for copy books and some needle work. While that would suggest she was settling in, she continued to remain dissatisfied with just about everything. Father Mathis, Sister Anthony, and Sister Agnes Marie came to consult with her about the purchase of an estate in Philadelphia, but she was far too agitated to listen, having just spent several days in a ward with patients who were significantly disturbed. She said she is being punished for no reason whatsoever. "Every time we go over she gets so upset; it takes a lot out of her and us." Later that week she seemed to settle down. "If I am to stay here," she concluded, she would need several longer habits, some more needle work, and some yarn. Sister Anthony responded. "We are sending one dress and will send two more as soon as they are finished. We hope you will like the material. It is the best we could get." Then she added: "Father is going to Philadelphia tomorrow with the movie. Hope you are feeling better." She then assured Anna of the prayers of everyone there.

Doctor Kain continued to look for an alternative institution. Saint Francis in Pittsburgh turned out to be primarily a clearing house where patients are diagnosed and then transferred somewhere else. Providence Retreat in Buffalo was predominantly a mental hospital and experience had shown that for Anna, this would not be an option. That left only one choice, Sacred Heart in Milwaukee. All agreed it was not a suitable place for Anna at this time. It was a sanitarium and not a hospital, a place for recovery and not for a cure, and had very few regulations; but Anna had been there before and had found it acceptable. She would be supervised by the same doctor as in her previous stay, and this would provide continuity in the search for a cause and a cure.

On April 28 Anna was officially discharged from Sheppard Pratt. Doctor Kain gave her a choice between Buffalo or Milwaukee. Anna opted for Milwaukee. She had been begging to return to Sacred Heart Sanitarium in order to escape the stigma associated with Sheppard Pratt. It had been decided she would travel by train. Sister Pauline would accompany her and remain with her until she had settled in. Pauline would board the train in Washington. Anna would join her in Baltimore and they would share a compartment during the trip. However, when Doctor Kain brought Anna to the station, she decided not to go. She would go home instead, and then give a talk in New

York before proceeding to Atlantic City where she would remain to recuperate. "If that wasn't satisfactory, then she would try Milwaukee." Doctor Kain stood firm. Anna said emphatically that she was the Superior General; she did not have to go to Milwaukee. She would order Sister Pauline off the train. The experienced Doctor Kain disregarded what she said. The platform was deserted when the train arrived, and when it pulled out, Anna was on board and still objecting. Apparently, from the very beginning, she had made up her mind that she would go to Washington first, and then to Philadelphia to see the proposed property, but that was not going to happen. After a while she quieted down, and before she got to Chicago, she agreed to stay at Sacred Heart and to cooperate in every way. Concerned about Anna's state of mind and subsequent behavior, Pauline paid an additional $1.50 to secure a private compartment from Chicago to Milwaukee. By then, however, Anna was docile and compliant.

Sacred Heart was radically different from the rigid institution where Anna had been confined. There were absolutely no restrictions. "I talked with Doctor William Roberts," Pauline reported. "He took care of her the last time. He was very surprised that Doctor had been at Sheppard Pratt. He wants all the back records he can get. His aim is to keep people out of mental institutions." Pauline was skeptical about the place for it was a lot like a hotel and meant for patients not seriously ill, who can come and go as they please. Doctor Kain had been adamant about Anna remaining behind closed doors, saying: "It is just her type of patient that can do serious harm." Pauline reported that "Anna seems happy and is so glad to be away from Sheppard Pratt." They walked to a small shopping district located a block away. "Doctor bought many stamps." Anna asked Pauline to stay as long as possible. "This is a very lonely place because you are left so much on your own," Pauline wrote, and then added a postscript. "If possible could you send some money for Doctor? She wants to buy a lot of needlework. I'm afraid I'll be hitch-hiking home."

The following day Pauline sent another report to the Motherhouse. "I know that you will be glad to hear that Doctor is much more comfortable. This morning she got a 'salt rub' and will get one every day. This is certainly a marvelous institution for peace, quiet, and rest, and they have a perfect therapy department for any type of packs, tubs, massage, etc. They have a special treatment for arthritis and they give 'bean packs,' which Doctor says 'would be grand for me.' I don't expect to leave here without some treatment myself, I'm afraid, if Doctor Dengel has her way." She did leave eventually, because of Anna's insistence that "only those who are unable to care for themselves have a nurse," and she was not sick. During the days ahead, Anna wrote to various people to thank them for what they had done for her. The nurse who had facilitated her liberation from Sheppard Pratt responded.

> "My dear husband bought me a new Buick car and I do hope it will be my good fortune to take you riding sometime very soon in it. At least I can see you in D.C. on your return. Take a long rest, Doctor, and when you come home, I plan to see you. Ever your sincere friend, Affectionately, Alice J. Warren"

Every year, for the rest of her life, a grateful Anna would send a greeting to nurse Alice Warren during the Christmas season.

Anna also wrote to Archbishop Michael J. Curley in Baltimore, who sent the following response:

> "I am glad you find yourself happy where you are. A complete rest should put you on your feet again, please God, so that you will be able to continue your work for the missions."

Back at the Motherhouse, Michael Mathis sent the following letter to Rev. George Sauvage in Rome.

> "Please give me your advice concerning a very grave problem. Doctor Dengel has become very ill again, and we are cautioned by the doctors that she should be freed from all responsibilities as the only possible means of a cure, even though there is only a slight possibility that there can be a cure. Our General Chapter is supposed to meet in 1938. Do you think the situation grave enough to warrant a meeting this fall to handle this problem?"

What Michael Mathis was requesting was permission from a canon lawyer to hold the Society's General Chapter a year earlier because there were urgent matters that had to be addressed. The Superior General, who was ill, would not be present, so he, as the Society's Ecclesiastical Superior, would preside.

> "It is not absolutely necessary since I have the authority from the Archbishop to do anything necessary, but I feel it would be more satisfactory for the Sisters to have a voice in this important decision. It will be difficult to make headway unless I take things in hand more directly than I have in the past. I have allowed the Sisters under my authority from the Archbishop, which had no restrictions, to act and to submit to me only important matters for direction. That has worked very well and it could function till the Chapter meets. The difficulty is that in the meantime things will not develop or even important measures cannot be taken unless I initiate them. I have full authority to initiate anything subject to the Archbishop, but it is a question of prudence and the best of good will among the Sisters themselves. There are two important questions that have to be solved immediately, a Motherhouse, which will involve us to the extent of $100,000; and a hospital in India, which will involve us to the same extent. Would you please let me know as soon as you can what your advice would be?"

In a letter dated May 31 Father Sauvage responded.

> "You say that Miss Dengel is sick and that she should be freed from all responsibility for the time being. In that case, the Vicar or First Assistant should take her place as long as necessary."

With regard to the General Chapter:

> "If you wish to have it this year instead of next year, the permission of the Holy See is required, but such permission should not be asked for without the consent

of General Council and of *all* the Bishops in dioceses the Society has houses."

He then added the following cautionary advice.

"You have to be careful as to your own powers. (I think that I have already written to you on this point.) You have only the authority given you by the Archbishop of Baltimore, and the archbishop of Baltimore has authority *only* on the houses situated in his Diocese, none at all in the houses in other Dioceses. So any matter of importance regarding the government or modifications of the Constitutions and affecting the whole Society, must be submitted to *all* the Bishops, who have in this regard an *equal* power. You have also to be careful to respect the authority of the General Council, according to Common Law and the Constitutions."

Early in June Father Mathis paid a visit to Anna on his way to Notre Dame. He told Sister Agnes Marie that "he tried to get the diagnosis out of Doctor Roberts, but he was cagey and quickly changed the subject." While Doctor Roberts thinks patients should never be sent to places like Sheppard Pratt, that opinion was not shared by the institution's director.

Later that week at Notre Dame, Mathis, who had modified his proposal to his superiors, now tried to convince them to allow him to found a community of priests devoted to medical missions while continuing to remain a member of the Holy Cross Congregation. He would wait to make vows in the new congregation until it was approved by Rome. In this way he would always be part of a community with vows. Mathis said he felt called, and qualified, to take this initiative to found a new community of priests, since "I, as a member, did some of the pioneer work in the particular phase of this apostolate, which has since been so signally approved by an important instruction from Rome."

At the end of June Sisters Pauline and Elise came to Chicago to attend the Hospital Convention. They spent the weekend with Doctor Dengel but did not see Doctor Roberts because his son had recently died and he had taken a leave of absence. Pauline reported on what she had observed. Physically, Anna seemed fine, had a bit more control, but "is still excitable and unreasonable. She plans a great deal." Anna talked about visiting Bishops, preparing literature, going to Europe, "so we don't know just what to expect."

Around July 1, Sister Anthony received a special delivery letter from Anna asking for her passport and the boat ticket to Europe left over from her world tour. It was still valid on the *Europa*, due to sail from New York on July 7. Sister Anthony would have sent the documents by return mail, but Agnes Marie kept the key to the safe, and she had Father Mathis wire Doctor Roberts first to see if he approved. His return wire said "no." Even though she was no longer scheduled to speak at the International Nurses Congress in London, Anna had still wanted to go. Doctor Roberts had also reported that while Anna "is very much improved mentally, she is far from being well. We will keep her here until she has made the mental improvement that we think is necessary for her to be able to adjust herself outside of sanitarium routine. I have talked to her very frankly about her mental state and insisted that she must give up all responsibility as has to do with the formulation of policy in administrating the affairs of the community. The Sister's mental condition so influences her mental capacity for decision, and rational thinking is not as it should be; consequently, it would not be fair to the community for the Sister to assume any responsibility of decision at the present time."

On July 7 the Superior General of the Holy Cross Congregation wrote to Michael Mathis regarding his request to found an order of priests.

> "To this request I am regretfully forced to reply in the negative. My reasons for doing so are the same as those contained in my letter of February 8. 'We cannot grant you the permission you ask. The liberty of action necessary for a religious founder would necessarily conflict with the proper observance of the rules and Constitutions of the Institute of which you are now a member.'"

On July 30 Mathis received the following report from Doctor Roberts.

> "You will be pleased to know that Doctor Dengel has made very satisfactory improvement since our last letter;

in fact, she is much improved in every way and we
believe that she is ready for a trial at home."

He concluded his letter by saying: "I hope that you will write her real
soon accordingly."

On August 17 Father Mathis wrote to Anna Dengel denying her
request to return to Washington, DC.

> "Since we are almost twice as crowded here now as we
> were last summer and fall, when you found conditions
> very trying by reason of the physical limitations, there
> was no question in my mind as to the reply I should
> make."

That was his primary reason for not allowing her to return. Then he
added:

> "Your intense interest in everything in the community
> will force you into all kinds of details which even a
> superior of normal health would find it difficult to
> cope with. Not being able to cope with them yourself,
> you will only harass and upset those who, in the
> end, must do it. In this way, you will keep the other
> superiors and subjects in even a tenser state than the
> abnormal conditions here have already created. I am
> really becoming very anxious about the health of Sister
> Agnes Marie and my own is not any too good."

Because Anna insisted on coming home, Mathis went to see the Bishop
who was in charge of the diocese during Archbishop Curley's absence.
He said that Bishop McNamara's words were: "Do not let her come
within 100 miles of the Motherhouse." The Bishop also said: "How can
she be the Superior General of that Society?" What Mathis neglected
to tell him was the second part of Doctor Roberts' report on Anna's
present state.

> "Sister has promised to come home and follow
> instructions that I have given her with the understanding
> that if she does not get along, she will be glad to return

to the Sanitarium for further rest and treatment. Doctor Dengel has unusual insight into her present condition and especially into the condition that led her to being sent to Sheppard Pratt. I talked it over with her from every angle. She is anxious to come back to the community in order that you may all know that she has really succeeded in understanding her problem and that she is now willing to suspend her activities until she is well. I think to insist on her remaining here longer under the present circumstances, with the improvement that she has made, would only aggravate the condition, and I sincerely urge that she be given a trial at home. I hope that you will write her real soon accordingly."

On August 26, Michael Mathis wrote to Anna Dengel again. He began the letter by listing urgent and complex issues facing the fledgling Society: the need for a new and much larger Motherhouse; the decision to move out of Washington; development plans in Pindi; a proposed medical center in Patna; the forth-coming General Chapter that would have to deal with the implications of canonical regulations related to a change in status; and "the undermining of the health of our superiors here." Mathis stated bluntly: "The chief reasons for our inability to solve these problems expeditiously is your state of health. Since I have the responsibility for the Motherhouse, as far as the Church is concerned, I feel in conscience bound to try to remedy this situation." Then he added: "After all, we founded the Society together, and the dearest wish of our hearts is to see it prosper and to remove the cause of anything that is seriously hampering its development." The cause impeding development, according to Michael Mathis, was Anna Dengel. "It has to be a frank letter," he wrote. "You probably know better than I and those at the Motherhouse what is really the matter with your health." He went on to list the following.

"There is no serious doubt any longer that it is a mental condition.

Both you and we have been unwilling to admit this fact, but it is useless and even dangerous to dodge it any longer.

381

"Competent physicians, including Doctor Roberts, have warned us that there are times when you should not exercise responsibility, and some have gone so far as to say that in their judgment the legality of your signature to a document could be questioned.

"The other day Bishop McNamara asked me how it was that under the circumstances you could continue to be the Superior of the Society. He knew about your case. Archbishop Curley knew about your sickness. It would be unfair to you not to be informed about the general public's acquaintance with your condition. We are constantly bumping into outsiders who question your mental state. Some of these are your very best friends. This has been more evident since your propaganda trip for funds after Christmas, but there have been rumors along this line for many years. As far as the Society is concerned, very few know exactly what is wrong, but many suspect. But despite it all, every member of the Society loves you dearly. This is due not only to your good qualities and part as foundress, but also to the faithfulness of Sisters Agnes Marie and Anthony, who have shielded you from the other Sisters during times of depression. These two Sisters have paid a big price in impaired nerves and the misunderstandings they have had to suffer from Sisters to whom they did not reveal your condition.

"This is only a very brief summary of the problem and the situation created by your sickness. The facts are such that they demand a remedy. If we do not do it ourselves, I feel quite sure that the Church will. Have you anything to suggest?"

Anna was wounded to the core. The image of who she was, according to Michael Mathis and apparently to others he had named, differed from her own self-image. Yes, she was flawed and emotionally volatile and a burden to those who were close to her. Yes, she had been seriously ill and had not yet fully recovered. But she was not, as he had implied, a mental case, whose prognosis for a cure was doubtful. She was definitely not someone who had to be removed from office because she was unable to function. Important decisions had to be made. She was well aware of that. She was also conscious of the fact that her opinions often differed from those of Father Mathis, and that they did not share a unified vision of the Society and its fundamental purpose. Nevertheless, she was ready to embrace the implications of the change in canonical status required by the proclamation from Rome so that her medical mission society could carry out its healing mission and expand in response to the need. She was not at all ready, however, to walk away from the mission that God had entrusted to her.

Faced with losing everything – her self-esteem, her reputation, her lifelong quest to provide healing ministries to the sick and to the poor, the very purpose of her existence – Anna turned to the Source that had always sustained her when everything else had failed. Out of the depths of her devastation, a resolution arose that would mark this crucifying moment as a decisive turning point: the inauspicious and graced beginning of her recovery, not only of her physical health and her psychological well-being, but also of her Society. The originating spirit of the community she had founded, cultivated, loved, was now on the verge of slipping away. It was up to her to restore it.

The power of miracles we don't have,
but we do have the power of growing all the time
and peering into the secrets of God.

Anna Dengel

CHAPTER TWENTY-THREE

Nearly a week went by before Anna Dengel wrote to Michael Mathis in response to his devastating letter. "I did not answer it sooner because it is hard to speak when one's heart bleeds." She avoided addressing the issues he had raised and made no proposals regarding the governance of the Society, but instead, she outlined a personal plan for her own immediate future.

"Life is very short!" she wrote. "I naturally had to think how I would spend this interval profitably." That interval was the time she would need to realize a complete recovery. She was anxious to leave Milwaukee, and she felt well enough to do so. What was even more compelling was her awareness that the Sanitarium had a lengthy waiting list. How could she justify staying there when others who were in dire need deserved to be admitted. Doctor Roberts had wanted to discharge her in June, but she had nowhere to go. Denied permission to recuperate with her community in England and barred from returning to the Motherhouse in Washington, DC, she went to see the Mother General of the Holy Cross Sisters and asked if she might make her canonical novitiate with them, as this would be a beneficial way to spend her time apart from the Society while waiting to return. A yearlong novitiate in a religious community was a prerequisite for making public vows. This had to be done within one's own congregation, but for Anna this was not possible, nor desirable, so the Holy Cross Mother General offered to write to Rome for an exemption from this aspect of Canon Law. She also extended an invitation. "Since you are ready to leave the Sanitarium, we will be very glad to have you at Saint Mary's while awaiting the decision." Anna reported all of this to Father Mathis and closed with the words, "with kind regards to you … and asking your blessing, Gratefully in J.M.J." Two days later, on September 2, Anna wrote again to Michael Mathis. This time she responded to those specific points that he had raised.

> "I can truthfully say that your letter has not upset my equilibrium. That does not mean that it has not added some weight to the cross of ill health that Providence has imposed on me these last few years. What pains me also is that a share of it has fallen on others on my account. As regards making arrangements that are best for the community and our work and to lighten the burden of the Sisters, I am the first to wish it and to agree to anything that is deemed best."

She made several suggestions with regard to leadership roles before bringing her comments to a close.

> "I appreciated the frankness of your letter and I know that it is well meant. It is an invitation for me to be frank too. It is the only way to clear up misunderstandings, difficulties of adjustments, and mistakes. However, there is no need to do it just now as it would only alter the contents of this letter."

The next day Sister Pauline arrived in Milwaukee. She had seen a copy of the explosive letter Father Mathis had sent. Worried about the emotional impact it was bound to have on Anna, she decided to go and be with her during this time of transition. Her assignment from Sister Agnes Marie was to keep an eye on Doctor Dengel and report back frequently to the Motherhouse with regard to her health and behavior. "Here I am safe and sound in Milwaukee," Pauline wrote on arrival. "Just as I stepped out of the cab, I met Doctor going to mail letters. She was very glad to see me. She looks very well and says she feels fine. There are three or four other Sisters here so Doctor has had some company."

Once she had settled into "a most gorgeous room on the 5th floor of the new wing" and had a good night's sleep, Pauline reported to Agnes Marie that she and Doctor Dengel had a very frank talk. Anna said that Father was absolutely wrong in saying she was mental because of her *emotional* behavior. Pauline tried to convince her that perceptions held by many as a result of her behavior were factual and bewildering; that she was often irrational; that she needed to see herself as other people saw her. "It seems that she just will not believe there is anything wrong beyond emotional disturbance and says she has *always* acted emotionally and thought rationally."

The next day Sister Pauline had a short talk with Doctor Roberts. He said he strongly advised Doctor to ask for a leave of absence from duty. He also said that "Doctor Dengel should not be put in an institution; if you force her into one, she will get her friends and a lawyer and make plenty of trouble. He said there was a *psychological* condition but you couldn't call it *mental* because *mental* implies insanity and Doctor is not insane. He said it is too difficult to make the distinction to risk using the word *mental*. He approves very much of her making her novitiate." Then Pauline added the following to her report to Agnes Marie. "Doctor is wounded very, very deeply over Father's letter. She is so marvelously resigned to it all, although she feels some parts are so unjust. It is hard not to give way to sympathy and just accede to her wishes." She stressed that Anna is still very upset about having been at Sheppard Pratt and is absolutely convinced that "Father deposed me!" Agnes Marie's response to that was: "How she ever interpreted the letter of Father Mathis as 'a deposition' we cannot understand." Agnes Marie also recorded the following in her journal. "She says with vehemence, 'He deposed me with *one shake* of the pen.' It isn't in his power to do so." Anna had asked Sister Laetitia to come visit her on her return from India; and she did. Laetitia also reported to Agnes Marie that "Doctor feels very unjustly treated and much abused."

Father Mathis wrote to Anna again on September 8. "Your beautiful letter of September 2, written under the most trying circumstances, relieved my mind more than any message I have ever received….Hence, I thank God fervently. Indeed it has given me more hope for your recovery than any single item, although naturally the value of my judgment cannot have any medical importance." He went on to say that "since the Holy Cross Sisters have invited you to Saint Mary's to await Rome's reply, it seems to be the best thing to do just as soon as you can arrange to do it." He suggested that Sister Pauline accompany her and stay for a few days to see Saint Mary's and Notre Dame. He closed with his sincere thanks "for the religious spirit of your letter," assuring her of "my constant remembrance of you and yours in all I do."

On September 14 Doctor Anna Dengel was discharged from Sacred Heart Sanitarium in Milwaukee and moved in with the Holy Cross Sisters in South Bend, Indiana. Sister Pauline went with her to her new location. They were given rooms in the building that was the community's infirmary and also an interim residence for Sisters studying at Saint Mary's College on the campus of Notre Dame. It was an ideal setting for Anna. Once she had settled in, she set about doing the necessary paperwork associated with her desire to make her novitiate there. It was a complex and convoluted process. The Mother General was told by Holy Cross canon lawyer Father George Sauvage in Rome that Anna had to petition the Holy See herself, giving reasons for her unusual request and evidence of Episcopal approval. So on September 30, the twelfth anniversary of the founding of her Society, the society that had been instrumental in preparing the way for the ground-breaking change in Canon Law and the canonical validation of her mission's core ministry, Anna wrote to Pope Pius XI. She sent that request to Archbishop Curley in Baltimore, along with the letter from Father Sauvage, and asked for his approval, then told him to send the enclosures with a letter of his own to the Holy See. Agnes Marie was appalled that Anna had done all of this on her own initiative instead of through the appropriate channel, which was the Society's leadership. To her this was yet another example of the problem that Anna had become. The same day, September 30, Father Mathis visited Doctor Dengel in South Bend. "He said that he hoped there would not be a rift," Anna noted in her own journal. "He said that he would still risk it with me… that he would not take back what he had written; that he would be more careful in the future of what he would say." It is not clear precisely when Pauline returned to the Motherhouse. Most likely she waited until life had settled into a routine for Anna before leaving for Washington, where her presence and her services would be very much in demand.

There were two major concerns clamoring for Anna's attention after she left Milwaukee. The first was to do whatever was required to ensure that she would be able to make her novitiate in South Bend, and she had accomplished that. The second was more elusive. She needed to face an existential issue she could no longer avoid. Something was not quite right with her. She felt she had to discover precisely what that was and then decide how to handle it. It would come to the fore in controversy and erupt in confrontation. Ordinarily, she was fine, when she was in control; but when that which she had envisioned suddenly seemed to be slipping away, she was unable to deal with it rationally. Since reason had always been her strength, she was at a loss to understand the root cause of her behavior. With the possibility of a novitiate and its emphasis on introspection hovering on the horizon, she felt compelled, while she had the time, to search for answers to questions she had never thought to ask. She would seek to solve this most perplexing dilemma with a rational analysis of her own disruptive emotional responses. Why does she act the way she does and what might she do about it?

Anna had already begun the process of critical self-analysis while under the care of Doctor Roberts. Most likely he was the reason why she would delve into the field of psychology and may even have suggested to her what books she should read. He had told her that her deficiencies originated there. "In his report to her community he had said: "Her problem is psychological. Her problem is not mental. She is not insane." Psychology probed the depth of the mind, its emotional associations and related behavioral patterns. Here she might find the key to understanding her own reality. Indeed, in a tiny notebook that fit within the palm of her hand, Anna wrote down titles of books and selected quotations. From David Seabury:

> "Psychologically the great end and aim of life should be
>   to discover reality."
> "Understanding never sets the human being free. It has
>   to be carried down into the depths of the human
>   mind and merge with feeling."
> "Avoid the curse of scattered energies."

No source is attributed to the following:

> "One thing at a time."
> "Take care of the personality assets and the deficits will
>   vanish by themselves."
> "Act as if you are normal and you will be normal."

There was also a scrap of paper on which Anna had written: "a self-reliant yet cooperative personality" – and nothing more.

The most significant resource for Anna appears to be the book, *Calm Your Nerves* by Béran Wolfe. She extracted the following:

> "A philosophical mind is one which is capable of conceiving the whole and the proper valuation of its parts."
>
> "Common sense is the strongest, the soundest, and the most magical of all healing forces."

She concluded that the following statement was applicable to her.

> "A nervous breakdown is not an accident, but an unconscious strategy of life, with a definite beginning in an inferiority complex; a definite, if unconscious goal is the production of a feeling of security and a well-defined technique, conscious and unconscious both, of attaining its goal."

The author then presented two sets of ten statements with regard to a psychological profile. The first set posited reasons for behavioral problems, the second offered solutions. This hit home with Anna. It was something she could understand, affirm, and apply. Handwritten in that tiny notebook, in paragraphs numbered one through ten, were Anna's psychological self-analysis and subsequent strategy for change based on what she had read.

"10"

1. "I have a nervous breakdown. That means I have been swimming against the current of life – not with it. Nature has warned me (by a whole galaxy of symptoms) that I cannot succeed in mulling through my private ideas of the universe."

2. "I am going to look for a better way of living. When I find this better way, the symptoms will disappear of themselves. Fighting against symptoms is a waste of time and energy."

3. "My nervous breakdown is the result of my unconscious attempt to save my face by establishing a painful alibi for my personal

failure. I am unaware of my unconscious strategy because I have had to deceive myself before deceiving others. Now I have become a slave to my strategy of evasion. It demands greater and more painful sacrifices of me than I had bargained for. My nervous breakdown has only apparently effected its purpose. I am the loser by keeping it. *Knowledge of my unconscious* mechanisms is vital to my progress. My mis-education in the past is responsible for my difficulties, but my knowledge in the present opens the way to new developments in the future. What I do today will determine my future happiness. I am going to cease worrying about the past and stop being afraid of the future. My problem is to live fully in the present."

4. "Although I have perceived that my pattern of life was inadequate in the past, I have honestly not felt that I could make any change. My feelings are the result of my unconscious attitudes. They are the result of my fears, my dreams, my mistaken ideas about myself and my past. My unpleasant feelings are originally nature's warning signals. I have lied with the truth 'by' unconsciously constructing them into arguments for not going on. I know now that I myself am responsible for these feelings and I shall now act as if feelings were not arguments. No matter what my feelings are, I am going to do what is right, what logic and science tell me is common sense. I have always said, 'When I feel well – I am going to do the right thing.' This is putting the cart before the horse. I am now going to do the right thing, the common sense thing first. This is an indispensable investment in happiness. When I have made my investment I will feel right – I will be happy."

5. "My nervous breakdown is not an accident but the inevitable product of a muddled strategy of life. Even if it were an accident, it could not be cured by magic. It is ridiculous to believe that injections, gland treatments, rest cures, sedatives can cure me. Neither can hypnosis, auto-suggestion, baths, travel, change of air or diet help me overcome my difficulties. They are only the modern equivalents of the savage's incantation rites. My nervous breakdown is itself due to ignorance of the basic facts of life. It

can be cured only by knowledge of what those facts are and by subsequent training along biologically normal channels. There is nothing wrong with my body – and nothing wrong with my mind. My difficulty lies only with my false goals in life, my bad technique in living. I am going to try to be a better general of my vital forces. Others have succeeded. I also can succeed."

6. "One of my chief difficulties has been the fact that I have been an extremist. My motto has always been 100% or nothing. My critical situation made me fear that I would not realize my fantastic ambitions. In order to save my face, I made a worm of myself. No one could expect social responsibilities of a worm. I am a human being. Being an extremist is a sign of infancy. In a grownup world – everything is approximate. I must make efforts to grow up. One way to grow up is curb my personal ambition for power and security. Another important way of growing up lies in training my courage. The child is egoistic. The man is sure enough of himself to share his power with others. Strength grows from the conquest of obstacles. Failures are inevitable. No growth is possible without risking minor defeats. Running away from tests of my ability, however, leads to inevitable paralysis of my existing faculties. I will take a chance."

7. "My nervous breakdown did not begin yesterday. It is the product of years of unconscious training. The reason that I did not break before this is that I did not meet any critical test of my personality. I am glad that it came now, instead of later. It is inevitable that my progress toward normality will not proceed without difficulties. I will not lose heart by minor setbacks. Relapses are minor incidents in growth. I am going to try to stop complaining about my bad lot and I am going to try specially hard to refrain from beginning every statement with my old neurotic theme-signatures 'if' and 'but.' From now on my life is not going to be based on the formula 'either ... or' but on the new normalizing formula 'both ... and.' No more alibis. I know that I cannot undo the mischief of years of false living in a day. But there are years and years of happiness ahead of me, if I change now. I will be patient and persevering."

8. "During my nervous breakdown I have been seeking a scapegoat to blame for my failures. I, as a person, am now responsible for my future success. There may have been factors in the past that can explain my deviations from the normal. Everyone has discouraging experiences. Everyone misses some of his opportunities. Everyone is sometimes frustrated by the innate perversity of inanimate objects. But all these discouragements, while they can explain my present, cannot compel me to remain in this condition, either in the present or in the future."

9. "All during my nervous breakdown I have been working in the fog of the unconscious. I did not realize the source of my inferiority feelings because I was too young to understand them when they were formed. I did not realize my unconscious goal of superiority and security because these things were never taught me in school. I did not conceive that I have really been spending my life in an unconscious profession: keeping up my 'face.' I still want to keep my 'face' because life without self-esteem would be intolerable. But now I understand that the only real security and the only real satisfaction of life consist in an ideal of 'face' bared in service to my fellow man. To this end I must develop my personality to the widest limit that I am capable of attaining. From today on I am going to approach this problem in the light of my conscious understanding instead of muddling through by the uncertain glimmer of unconscious motivations. My human ability to mobilize my conscious forces is what distinguishes me from a worm or a cow. The good life consists in utilizing the tremendous energy of the unconscious for the attainment of conscious, rational, and socially useful goals."

10. "This is the end of my nervous breakdown. So long as I was ignorant of true facts and right values, I was really not responsible for my pattern of life. Now I know what the facts are. No matter how long I have been running up the wrong street, I have lost nothing but a little time. In fact my unhappiness will make me appreciate the joys of complete living all the more. I know the truth and the truth has made me free. From this moment I am going to be the captain of my own soul, the master of my

destiny. My happiness will be sweeter for knowing that I have attained it on my own responsibility. It is easier to be normal than neurotic. From this day on I am going to take the material that nature has given me and weave it into a beautiful design. I have always been asking of life, 'What do I get out of it?' From now on I am going to become an artist in the fine art of living completely.

"I am going to increase my awareness of the world about me. My nervous breakdown has been a result of the stricture of horizons. I have been dying of spiritual suffocation. I have built a vault around myself to keep out dangers and I have only succeeded in keeping out the sun, the good fresh air, and the smiles and encouragement of my fellow men. All that is human is my province. I have been doing nothing but complaining of my miserable feelings and torturing myself with doubts and fears. From this moment I am going to seek my salvation in outside activities. Nothing has come of my breakdown but pain and more symptoms. From now on I am going to direct my energies to living a life of freedom, of reason, of expression, of altruism. Nothing could be worse than my breakdown. I have nothing to lose, everything to gain!"

Clearly, Anna intended this to be for her eyes only: a guideline for her own encouragement and support. Only now is it coming to light so that it may shed light on her life story and perhaps benefit others.

While she was there in South Bend gaining insight into her own behavior, Anna also learned a whole lot more about Michael Mathis. Some of the problems she had experienced had apparently happened before. Risky and unrealistic schemes led to the closing of the seminary for which he had been responsible. A good priest. A likeable man. But "impossible to work with." This knowledge may well have been the turning point for Anna. She now had time to reflect and design a strategy of action to deal with what she had learned.

While she was awaiting word from Rome, Anna had asked that she be kept informed of Society business, which caused quite a stir in Washington. Individual Sisters wrote to her and she responded. Several of them told her that Father Mathis was planning to take over the Society. On November 10 Sister Agnes Marie noted in her journal:

"Who appears on our doorstep at 4:45 p.m. but Doctor Dengel. She came out on the street car. I must say it was a surprise."

Anna proceeded to meet with many of the Sisters individually. She avoided Father Mathis. "Father asked her to come down to his house but she wrote a note saying she did not wish to see him," Agnes Marie recorded. "It seems one of the reasons for her coming home is to prove to the Sisters that she is normal. She tries very hard and is convincing some of them." One of the main reasons for her arriving so unexpectedly, however, "is to move the Motherhouse to South Bend." This was a totally new idea to everyone. Even though Father Mathis was from South Bend, she wanted him "to have nothing to do with it." She had also come to Washington to seek Ecclesiastical permission for the move before she entered the novitiate. "She also said she would get rid of Father Mathis," said Agnes Marie. She and members of the Council were appalled. "He deposed me just like that," she had said at one of their meetings, as she pounded her fist on the table. "The air is very tense" was how Agnes Marie described it. However, many of the Sisters held a different opinion, and Agnes Marie did record that "when with the community, she is more normal, and the Sisters are saying how much better she is." While at the Motherhouse, Anna spent a lot of time with Sister Pauline, with whom she felt understood and accepted and could freely vent her frustration.

On November 12 an Indult of Exclaustration was issued to Anna Dengel in Rome, thereby clearing the way for her to make her Novitiate. On November 16 Rev. George Sauvage wrote to Michael Mathis saying it had been his idea to ask the Sacred Congregation to give Doctor Dengel an Indult that would allow her to live outside her Community. This would make it possible for her to reside with the Holy Cross Sisters. Father Mathis sent the Indult to Archbishop Curley, who wrote on November 29: "I hereby execute on your behalf an Indult of Exclaustration for one year." He mailed it to Father Mathis who sent it on to Anna. She received in on December 11 and sent a copy to Bishop John Noll, who was now her presiding Bishop. She had already inspected an available estate in the vicinity of South Bend with the intention of moving the Society there, and while it appeared to be suitable, its price was beyond their means. Her final preparations included resigning from the Guild of Saint Luke and Saints Cosmas & Damian in London, which was received "with much regret." The Guild asked her "to consent to election as an Honorary Member of the Guild," and apparently she did. On December 14, 1937, Anna Dengel entered the Novitiate of the Sisters of the Holy Cross in South Bend, Indiana, to begin her canonical year. The following account of what happened after that was handwritten by her.

> "Before entering the novitiate I wrote to the General Council at home requesting them to send me regularly a copy of the minutes of the Council meetings so that I would be kept informed of the major events and decisions. This they were not willing to do. A little later, I heard from three sources that Father Mathis was taking definite steps to take over Supreme authority of the Society – as he had wished ever since he came to us in 1933 when he asked the Archbishop to appoint him Ecclesiastical Superior. The Archbishop actually did not realize all that was behind it. Apparently Father Mathis did not tell him that I had been opposed to that for years. The reason why I was opposed is that Father Mathis never had a real understanding of our Society. He wanted to introduce all kinds of things foreign to the purpose of the Society (such as a girls' college, etc.). He was a very good priest, however, and did not spare himself to help us. He was very kind and had a pleasant personality. It is therefore not surprising that a number of the Sisters were easily influenced by him and sided with him."

"As the Council did not want to keep me informed during my novitiate," Anna Dengel journaled, "and as Father Mathis was to be Ecclesiastical Superior, I became anxious about the fate of the Society and went for advice to the Superior General of Holy Cross," who was in residence nearby. The date was January 13, 1938. "This was the first time that I really opened my heart to anybody about the whole situation." He agreed with Anna that it was best to remove Father Mathis, and because he had been assigned by his superiors to assist her in her community, there would be no need for a canonical investigation. He advised Anna to go to Washington as soon as possible. Anna was immensely relieved and grateful that he also agreed to her request to assign Father Goodall "to take care of us spiritually." She asked the Holy Cross Sisters for permission to return to Washington, and it was granted. Anna's account continues.

"I had heard that the Sisters in Washington were making a novena for 'a special intention,' and by intuition I felt interiorly and irresistibly urged to **ACT**. I told Mother Vincentia, who also seemed to understand. I am leaving for Washington this p.m. with a heavy heart and a light heart at the same time. Heavy because it is really a great pity to have to ask for Father Mathis' withdrawal. It will be hard for him and for us. Light-hearted because I feel that our Society will be able to go on unhindered and unhampered by schemes and side-lines and prospects beyond our strength and that the very difficult and nerve-racking task of keeping Father in check will be eliminated. I am longing for peace and shall appreciate it as a treasure of great price when we have it again. I hope that none of our flock will be lost or go astray in this storm. God of goodness and mercy help us!

"Without notifying anybody in D.C., I went without delay. I arrived on the ninth day, the last day of the 'Special Novena!' On the way to the house, I went to see Father McBride at Holy Cross College, our confessor for years, who was known to me as a prudent and wise priest. I told him also what I was about to do. Then bravely I marched forth, up to our house, and on Puertorico Avenue, not far from Father's house, I met him, greeted him, but said nothing. On arrival at our house, I told the Sisters, who were of course surprised to see me: 'Here is the answer to your novena!'

"I took my place right away, to which no objection was made. I wrote a short letter to Father Mathis, which Sister Laetitia typed for me, telling him to sever his connection with us immediately. Needless to say I wrote a long explanatory letter to the authorities at Notre Dame, expressing my gratitude and appreciation for all that Father Mathis had done for us, but at the same time explaining the impossible situation which had prompted my request to Father Mathis to leave us."

This account by Doctor Anna Dengel had remained concealed in her personal archives at her request, along with the story of the struggle she experienced following the Foundation of her Society. Also kept confidential were her personal medical files, starting in 1925. These describe her during the first two years as an "apparently normal individual possessed with a congenial, sociable, and magnetic personality." Her "mild emotional outbursts" began in 1928. They continued sporadically through the years with no apparent cause. "Looking back now," Anna wrote, "I realize there was a clash of ideas about the Society and authority, which subconsciously reacted on my health." As the Society Anna had brought into existence began to look less and less like what she had envisioned and the development of medical missions grew more and more remote, she internalized her disappointment, giving rise to severe distress. Through it all, she insisted:

> "I have tried to keep on good terms with Father Mathis on account of the fact that he had helped us to start the Society and that we were under obligation to him in many ways; and also because the clash of ideas about the Society and authority – although there – was not sufficiently clear that it could be expressed in words. If I had been home, things would have come to a head sooner. Knowing that Sister Agnes Marie got on well with Father Mathis, I sometimes thought that it was better that I was away."

The excruciating pain of the past year that climaxed in Anna's very nearly losing her Society had pushed her to the limits of her ability to endure, yet her faith never wavered. Her decision to confront the monster within her own persona and transform it to graced potential marked a decisive turning point within her, and her community, and the universal Church. It envisioned a new beginning, a pioneering venture that would feature a healing presence among those who were most in need. For the moment, however, there was work to be done to redeem the past here at home.

> "When I announced the change to the Community,"
> Anna noted, "I did it briefly, telling the Sisters that we
> will always be under a great obligation to Father Mathis.
> I asked the Sisters not to speak about the difficulties of
> the past. Under the circumstances, I could not return
> to the novitiate but had to hold the fort at home and
> resumed my work."

Father Mathis wrote to the Archbishop and asked for a canonical
visitation. Bishop McNamara was appointed to carry it out and arrived
unannounced. The entire process was confidential. He saw all the
professed sisters individually and asked Doctor Dengel and members
of the Council to submit written reports. Anna's consisted of fifty-one
separate items that clearly and succinctly documented her concerns
with regard to Father Mathis from the early days of the Society up to
the present time. Writing in support of Anna Dengel, the Holy Cross
Superior General said: "... I have in mind only God's glory through the
preservation of the little Society which Dr. Dengel, like all founders,
has brought forth in blood and tears." Years later Sister Eleanore Lippits
from Holland recalled:

> "The most interesting thing Bishop McNamara told me
> was that while they put Mother's ability to be Superior
> General in question, he found her the most intelligently
> realistic of all."

Mathis was away while the Archdiocese carried out its investigation.
Before it had even begun, and while Anna Dengel was still in South
Bend, Father Mathis had written to Archbishop Michael Curley to
clarify the Society's canonical status, and his own. The Archbishop
responded in a letter dated January 3, 1938.

> "I am in Bon Secours Hospital and read only a part of
> your letter, which is mighty long, but I take from what
> little I did read that you want your status clarified in
> connection with your relation to the Society of Catholic
> Medical Missionaries.
> "Your Medical Missionaries were formed for the
> purpose of aiding the missions of the Holy Cross Fathers

in India and consequently, so far as I understand the situation, the whole purpose of your Foundation had a very limited scope.

"Your unit is considered a Diocesan unit and consequently is under the control and regulations of the Archbishop of Baltimore. Your position in regard to that Community is that of Ecclesiastical Superior with powers to regulate the actions of the Community and for the members thereof who approach you at any time in connection with their duties, their rules, Constitutions, etc. In other words, until such time as you are recalled from the position you now occupy, you represent in the fullest sense the Archbishop of Baltimore with regards to the little Community over which you have been placed. I hope this is clear."

Father Michael Mathis, the Society's liaison with diocesan Authority, had led the Archbishop to understand that this pioneering Society was his, not Anna's; and that its purpose was to serve medical missions under the auspices of the Holy Cross Congregation, an affiliation that the Congregation had refused to consider from the very beginning.

After two months Bishop McNamara and his consultants reached a decision. The Archbishop asked the Holy Cross Superior General to have Father Mathis removed. His opinion of Anna Dengel: "She is as sensible as anybody I can judge from her letters." This was a complete reversal of what he had said of her less than one year earlier when he considered her mentally unstable. The investigating committee knew far more than they could tell. Only the result was communicated to the Society's members.

Although deeply disappointed, Father Mathis received the decision with a gracious acceptance, saying that his heart "would always be in the Society." Sister Agnes Marie summarized the situation from her perspective.

"In a nutshell it is this. Father is very active and energetic and the kind that must have authority and independence – 'a status,' as he calls it. He has been very good to us. At times his judgment is questionable but he has never forced his ideas on us. However, there was an element of danger in being too close. Doctor Dengel is just as energetic and independent and is the kind that also must have authority. She has to be 'the head' of whatever and wherever she is. Both can't be the superior, so one must go; and as she has had more to do with the founding of the Society, it is natural that he should go and she should run it."

Then she added, "But can she?" On March 19 Anna sent an official letter to Michael Mathis, whose residence was still the little house at the bottom of the hill. She wrote:

"Very Reverend Father Donahue, c.s.c. notified me of the Archbishop's decision. Needless to say – the whole thing is painful beyond words for you and for us. To explain my silence, I would like to say that the main reason for it was not resentment but a conviction that any further conversation about business of the Society would be useless after the opinions expressed by you about me in letter and by word. As this is a closed chapter now, I will do my best to banish ill-feelings and I would be glad if an official parting would be in peace and with mutual forgiveness. In this way – it may be possible that sometime in the future we may be able to have the benefit of your spiritual help and influence in some form or other. On the fact of what we owe to you, it is very much; it makes it all the harder to have this heartbreaking episode in our Society. Asking your blessing for us all, Gratefully in J.M.J"

There was no doubt in anyone's mind that Anna Dengel was now in charge. She allowed Sister Pauline to remain as local Superior for a while "because I thought it would be easier and better for the Community and for me. I changed things after some weeks and combined again the office of Superior General and local Superior." Some months later Sister Pauline departed for England to provide leadership there. At the Motherhouse, at least on the surface, things began to improve. The April edition of *The Medical Missionary* appeared with a new cover design more reflective of Anna's original concept and with a revised purpose statement on the opening page.

> "The Society of Catholic Medical Missionaries is a religious community of women founded in 1925 for the purpose of providing medical care to the sick in the foreign missions. The Motherhouse and Novitiate are located in Brookland, Washington, D.C. At present the Society labors in India where the Sisters conduct hospitals, dispensaries, maternity and child-welfare centers, training schools for native nurses and midwives, and similar health activities. It is the purpose of the Society to send Medical Missionaries to any mission field of the world as soon as its numbers permit."

On May 13, Anna's beloved father, Edmund Wilhelm Dengel, died at the age of 81. Bedridden, he had been failing for some time. He never complained. After death, his family said, he looked like a saint. It was not possible for Anna to attend his funeral and her family understood, saying they knew she would be with them in spirit. They all kissed Papa for her, they said, and told her to take care of herself.

In June Anna received a congratulatory message from Cardinal Prefect Fumasoni-Biondi of Propaganda Fide in Rome. He referred to an article in a Catholic newspaper in Dubuque announcing the successful attainment of the Doctorate in Medicine by Sisters Elise Wijnen, Eleanore Lippits, and Leonie Tummers.

> "I should like to congratulate the three new doctors. Tell them that I ask God to bless them in a very special manner. May he guide them in their very lofty apostolate and may he be their constant strength. I am very happy to note the progress that your most useful institute is making. I am more than convinced of the great help it is and will be for the spread of God's kingdom on earth. May God in His providence augment their number and send you benevolent patrons. While I am most pleased to see your numbers increase, I pray most especially that Our Divine Lord will keep the original spirit of

> charity most alive in your community. May God grant
> a constant growth in both."

His closing words echoed those deep within Anna's heart.

The Society's Third General Chapter was held in Washington, DC, from September 8 – 29 at the Bengalese in Brookland. Rev. George Sauvage, c.s.c. agreed to be advisor and guide. The Archbishop appointed him as his delegate to preside at the election. According to earlier Constitutions, only ex-officio members were to participate in the Chapter, which meant seven members in all. As the delegate from India could not come, a substitute was elected. The Council members rejected Anna's recommendation of a Sister with significant experience, an older member who was a physician, and voted for the Sister in charge of the kitchen who, although "a splendid Sister," in Anna's estimation, was unequipped to contribute. The six delegates voted as a block on just about everything, and because they were the majority, they had their way. "Fortunately, we agreed on most things," Anna later reported. "I was elected again – but the Council elected was such that I would only be a figurehead."

Father Sauvage advised the Society to "revise the Constitutions to fit its present state: that as soon as it has permission to make vows, vows will be made. In that case the Constitutions are ipso facto changed without a new permission." He said that nothing can be changed within the Constitutions without the permission of all the bishops because the Society is diocesan. The Society would then petition the Holy See and include the assent of the bishops before receiving approval to make a constitutional change. He said it was advisable for a mission community to be under the Sacred Congregation of Propaganda rather than under the Sacred Congregation of Religious. He said: "This is rather easy to obtain," and advised that the Society transfer at the time of Papal approbation. He also made a final clarification, which is recorded in the closing comments of the minutes.

> "When the Society makes public vows it will be a
> congregation but is not one now. We are not Sisters
> until we have made vows."

There were several other items of interest from this Third General Chapter.

With regard to members going out alone, Father Sauvage suggested that we should add "in case of necessity" because that would meet with the approval of the authorities in Rome and we could interpret it as we thought advisable.

With regard to the name of the Society, the vote was four to three in favor of not changing the name of the Society officially, but that we shall be commonly known as Medical Mission Sisters.

On the question of music and singing: it was decided that the community should sing Compline on First Class Feasts and their vigils and on Sunday; not otherwise; and that it should be left to the local Council in the missions as to whether or not it shall be sung. If it is sung poorly, the Superior shall stop it until there has been more practice.

The following summarizing statement was included in the Chapter Minutes.

> "Father Sauvage told the members that Rome looked to the Society and that if it did not succeed it was his opinion that another would take its place as Rome realizes the necessity for medical missions. He also emphasized the importance of the instruction of the Propaganda in 1936 concerning the foundation of congregations for medical aid in the missions and expressed the view that in his opinion the Society of Catholic Medical Missionaries was in part at least the occasion for such a momentous decision. He said that no decision has been so important during the last two centuries."

The overall consensus was that this had been a fruitful Chapter. Anna fulfilled her role admirably, according to Agnes Marie.

> "Of all surprises, we received our greatest at the Chapter. Doctor Dengel was calm, reasonable and agreeable. We expected a stormy Chapter but it wasn't. The elections were held towards the middle. On the surface she was as cool before as after. She can control herself when she wants to, which shows an improvement. The points for which she fought so ardently for years, she relinquished without a murmur, e.g., her name as Doctor...that a

doctor need not be the Superior General, etc. Even her re-election as Superior General indefinitely was given up without a fuss. Will wonders ever cease!"

At the end of November, Anna wrote to Archbishop Curley. "A few days ago we signed the agreement to buy an estate in Philadelphia." The decision to move the Motherhouse and to retain the present property as a house of studies for members earning their degrees had been made before Father Mathis departed. This was precisely what Anna needed as she looked toward the future, for her relationship with Cardinal Dougherty was one of support and mutual respect. Nevertheless, it would mean yet another upheaval for the local community for whom the past year had been challenging with the return of their Founder, who had been away for such a long time and did things differently; but that was the missionary's way of life and they would soon adjust. It was not easy for Anna either. She reflected constantly on the purpose of the Society, "a work of charity much needed today," in order to stay strong. "If it were not for that," she mused, "I really would myself give it up and go some place in the missions where I could work quietly and in peace."

Anna knew that she had to reshape the present Council in order to be able to function efficiently for the next six years. "As a possible solution for a more satisfactory functioning of our Society," Sister Laetitia would be asked to resign as First Councilor and go back to the Mitford Hospital in Dacca, replacing Sister Helen, who had to return because of poor health. Sister Agnes Marie would also have to resign as Second Councilor and as Novice Mistress and General Secretary and would be reassigned. These and other recommended changes were submitted to Archbishop Curley for his approval. His response:

> "You are Superior for the moment of the Society. I am authorizing you to make, in God's name, any changes you deem advisable for the best interests of the Community. It would be well to consult on this matter, as on all other matters, Doctor McBride who, I am sure, will give you every possible help, without any consideration of himself or anything else save the needs of the Community, in your work."

Anna met with Father McBride, c.s.c., and he told her in the name of God "to appoint Councilors in the best interests of the Society." Shortly before the end of the year, Doctor Dengel called a meeting of the Council to announce the changes in personnel. The reaction was one of disbelief. Agnes Marie expressed it this way in her journal:

> "God help us! Here we are sitting on top of a volcano all the time and it never stops popping. From minute to minute we do not know what will happen and it has been this way almost from the beginning. If ever during my lifetime we have security, stability, and peace, I won't know how to act."

Anna would have responded that security, stability, and peace – meaning absence of anything that disturbs – are not the characteristics of a missionary. In asking to implement these changes, Anna had told the Archbishop what she thought was the reason for the divergent approaches to community life that were giving rise to so much stress.

> "Father Mathis introduced a spirit not suitable to our Society. When Doctor Lyons left to enter a contemplative community, Father Mathis told the Sisters in the novitiate that she had been misdirected, that she could have been a contemplative in our community."

Anna did not mean to dismiss a quiet, contemplative, prayerful spirit that is at the core of a dedicated life and meant so much to those who had been formed in a cloistered environment such as the novitiate; but rather those systemic practices more suitable to a monastery. The original and perennial spirit of the Society is one that accompanies and sustains active ministry out in the world. Agnes Marie had become acclimated to the more monastic style that permeated the novitiate. She felt that Anna's volcanic eruptions, as she would often refer to them, loud voice, and uncompromising approach were more suitable in the world beyond a religious institution. She could not adjust to her bombastic manner that she felt was at times inappropriate. Her journal would continue to record this as abnormal behavior. Agnes Marie did not really mind being removed from the Council. She felt she had suffered enough through seven years of sparring with Doctor Dengel; but she would miss the novices and her novitiate role. She accepted the changes with grace in the spirit of her calling. Eventually she would discontinue chronicling Anna's behavior, which she been doing assiduously since 1931. She felt she had made her contribution by keeping an historical record of one who, she absolutely believed, would one day be a saint.

> "Sometimes the discussion among ourselves turns to Doctor Dengel and the opinions are so varied. Personally I think she is a holy woman despite all. Someday she will likely be Saint Anna Dengel. I am saving her first uniform and other things. I think God will continue to pursue her until she gives in to Him. Saints are different people. I am glad I don't have to live a second life lest my lot be thrown in again with that of a foundress."

In the process of paying such close attention to one who was so very different from her, Agnes Marie came to realize that her own opinions seldom coincided with those of the one in charge.

In the January 1939 issue of *The Medical Missionary*, Doctor Dengel broke the news of moving the Motherhouse from Washington, DC, considered "the cradle of the Society," to Philadelphia, because of "the need of development and growth."

> "We must push on to send an army of Medical Missionaries to India, Africa, and China – to all the mission world. We must recruit generous souls to serve in the mission field. When mission bishops ask us to come to their aid, we must be able to say, 'Yes" and to answer the summons without delay. We must make every possible effort to carry out the Holy Father's wish to bring aid to mothers and children in mission lands, not in the next generation, but in ours."

Sometime in March, before the community moved to Philadelphia, Doctor Dengel visited Fox Chase, and "sang a *Te Deum* [hymn of praise] all alone on the top of the hill. She had promised to do this in thanksgiving for the gift of the motherhouse."

In the spring Anna spent six weeks in Holland and England tending to issues related to the Society's foundations there. She returned to

Washington on June 1 and in August moved to Philadelphia. In the September issue of the magazine she wrote: "At last we can make the happy announcement that our permanent Motherhouse is a reality." The official opening was scheduled for October 3, the feast of Saint Thérèse of Lisieux, patron saint of the missions.

As the Society's Motherhouse sank its roots into its new location and its members awaited Rome's approval of their Constitution, Anna faced a dilemma. She had never made a novitiate, a prerequisite for making vows. She had relinquished that option in order to preserve her Society, and she did not see how it would be possible to do it now. She had given Cardinal Dougherty a lengthy and detailed report of Society events leading up to this moment and said that all had made their novitiate except Sisters Helen, Anthony, Margaret Mary, and herself. She offered this explanation on her own behalf.

> "I tried to make it a few years ago but had to leave because of circumstances. I would like to make it but at present it does not seem feasible. I realize that a canonical novitiate cannot be made up by anything else, but I have been fortunate in many ways. I grew up in a thoroughly Catholic home and country. I went for several years to a boarding school in a Visitation Convent of the old style. It was as strict as any novitiate. We even had to kneel down to ask pardon when we broke anything. I was in France for two years in a school conducted by secularized nuns. The medical school in Ireland where I was for five years had a Catholic spirit and a Catholic atmosphere. When in India I lived in the Convent. Once, when I wanted to go to a dance to see the Prince of Wales, the Reverend Mother cried till I changed my mind! It is now 26 years since I started out on the Medical Mission career and this time has been a kind of novitiate too. Sometimes I thought it was providential that we did not make a novitiate in the beginning because it gave us a chance to develop a spirit specially needed for our work. I will gladly make a novitiate anywhere, provided I can leave the Society

safely or provided I am told – when the responsibility is not mine."

What may have precipitated this response was the following comment from Archbishop Curley in Baltimore.

> "There is a question, of course, which must be taken into account and which would make our situation almost laughable in Rome. It is that you, a Superior of a Religious Community, never made a complete Novitiate. As a matter of fact, to put it very frankly, you are still, more or less, a Postulant. That is something of which Rome will, of course, take cognizance."

This remark had been deeply troubling to Anna. For years she had longed to profess public vows in the institutional Church. Cardinal Dougherty reassured her, saying: "You do not need a novitiate." Much to Anna's relief, she recorded: "Which closed the matter for me."

In 1940 Father Sauvage instructed Doctor Dengel to write to the Ordinaries of all those places where the Society had a house and ask them to approve the new Constitutions. He then asked her to forward their responses to him. Statements arrived from around the world during February, March, April, and May. Each one was affirmative.

On February 22, 1941 the Society was approved by the Sacred Congregation for Religious in Rome. It had permission to make public vows.

On August 15, 1941, Feast of the Assumption of the Blessed Virgin Mary, Doctor Anna Dengel and members of her pioneering community publicly professed their religious vows of poverty, chastity, and obedience in the Archdiocese of Philadelphia. Dennis Cardinal Dougherty, Anna's advocate from the very beginning, presided at the Liturgy and received their vows.

On August 27, 1941, Anna Maria Dengel officially became a naturalized citizen of the United States of America.

In the end, God's work wins.

Anna Dengel

If You Love

Love is inventive.
If you have real love, you are inventive.
If you love, you will find ways and means
    of doing things, of helping people.
If you love, you try to find out;
    you are interested.
Love is interested and you really want to know.
If you love the people, it will help a great deal.
If you really love, you are patient and long-suffering.
If we love, we will really try to serve and not just work.
Certainly, if you love you accommodate yourself.
If you love, you take the trouble; you are indulgent;
    you close your eyes to things.
Also if you love, you are tireless
    and selfless
    and generous.
If you love, you want to give.
One does not spare oneself if one loves.

Anna Dengel

PART TWO

CHAPTER TWENTY-FOUR

The making of public vows introduced a new and dynamic phase within the Society of Catholic Medical Missionaries, now also known as Medical Mission Sisters. The community had already been addressing its members as Sister. Now it could embrace the term "Mother" for its Founder. Rome, however, would wait until April 8, 1943 to formally declare this pioneering group a "religious congregation," because systemic shifts move slowly in the institutional Church. The same cannot be said of the charismatic Doctor Dengel. She immediately set in motion a long desired, globally oriented era of expansion. Having waited far too long to continue what she had started, she was eager for her community to turn its attention outward to address the needs of others, instead of fixating on the infrastructure of an alternate way of life.

> "We cannot touch the moral and psychic wounds of the world without helping the open, physical wounds. It should make us happy that we can do a little – even though only a little, because we are so few – but something to relieve the horrible suffering and pain in the world."

In 1939 Anna moved the Motherhouse and its Novitiate to Philadelphia, where the overall governing body – the Superior General and her Council – became a Generalate. That same year a branch of the Society took root in the Netherlands with the establishment of a Postulancy in Imstenrade; while on another continent, Holy Family Hospital opened its doors in what had been the Catholic Cathedral in Patna, India. In 1944, it would begin a school of nursing, admitting women irrespective of religion, culture, or caste.

In 1943 the Society founded the Catholic Maternity Institute (CMI) in Santa Fe, New Mexico, to offer neonatal care to women. The following year it introduced the first school for nurse-midwifery operating under private auspices in the USA. This pioneering initiative was the direct result of restrictions imposed on international travel because of World War II. An affiliation with Catholic University of America in Washington, DC made it possible for CMI midwifery students to receive academic credit. Three years later, in partnership with CMI, Catholic University launched the country's first Master's degree with a focus in nurse-midwifery.

Because Medical Mission Sisters could not leave the country, the Society began work at the Catholic Colored Clinic in Atlanta, Georgia in 1944. Twenty years later, at the height of the civil rights movement in America, Dr. Anna Dengel was among the 4000 people gathered to witness the dedication of Holy Family Hospital and Medical Care Center in Atlanta. Committed to healing all people and to treating all equally, the Sisters began to work toward the full integration of that institution with a policy that stated: "No patient is assigned to a room on the basis of race, creed or color."

In the early 1940s, Anna Dengel brought many guests to 8400 Pine Road in order to expose the community to a variety of perspectives. Dorothy Day came to evening recreation to tell about her work and her "philosophy." Other visitors spoke on advocacy, cybernetics, Eastern spirituality, Asian art and other subjects of interest. Anna hosted Bishops from around the world, and when she lectured on Missiology, she would stress that "as Medical Missionaries, the needs and sufferings of humanity must find an echo in our hearts."

In 1945 Anna Dengel published a book entitled *Mission for Samaritans*. Its subtitle summarizes the content as "a survey of opportunities in the field of Catholic Medical Missions," which Anna situates spiritually and theologically within a fundamental call to love.

> "The interpretation and fulfillment of Christ's great commandment of charity lies at the root of all mission activity and therefore at the root of the medical mission apostolate. This commandment teaches us that the love we have for God cannot be separated from the love we owe our neighbor."

In his Foreword to the book, Right Reverend John M. Cooper, Ph.D. of Catholic University writes:

> "We must use our best wisdom and judgment, as well as plain 'horse sense.' We must also use all the resources that science and scientific research have placed at our disposal. The Society founded by Dr. Anna Dengel is a pioneer organization in its field, established to meet old but newly recognized needs with new-won scientific methods, under the age-old Catholic spirit of unselfish love."

In addition to the Divine mandate to "love our neighbor as ourselves," Anna points out an additional motive for undertaking medical missions. It is "the tremendous debt which we, the white race, owe" to the people in other parts of the world because of the "often brutal exploitation of the natives and their countries by colonial powers." She stresses that "our own time also shares the guilt" for the terrible crimes that were committed "against the peoples of other races, utterly disregarding their God-given rights and values." She writes passionately about the necessity of understanding medical missions, not only as a work of compassionate love, but also as a demand of justice, saying that "for past and present guilt, God demands restitution." Her conclusion: "the medical apostolate is indeed one of the most fitting and Christlike ways of doing so."

In November of 1945 Doctor Dengel traveled to India on the *SS Santa Paula*. She disembarked in Karachi, visited Lahore and Patna, and spent Christmas in Rawalpindi, then paid a visit to her brother Joseph, a Mill Hill missionary priest in northern India. He was stationed in Dehra Dun, capital city of the state of Uttarakhand, a picturesque setting on the banks of the Ganges in the foothills of the Himalayas. "Where my brother was living," she discovered, "there was no other priest for hours of travel around." Anna returned to Patna before the end of the year, then in January, 1946, traveled to Calcutta, and Dacca, and Mymensingh, and Toomilah, then back again to Dehra Dun to spend time with her brother. In February of 1946, Doctor Dengel arrived in Kottayam, a district of the state of Kerala in the south of India, a lush and tropical expanse of paddy fields and backwaters and countless rubber plantations. She had come to Kerala as Superior General to visit the Mary Giri Sisters, whose path had become deeply embedded in that of her own community over a period of years. Here is how that happened.

In October of 1937 Anna Dengel received a letter from Father Sebastian Pinakattu, a diocesan priest of the Syro-Malabar Catholic Church, which traces its roots back to Saint Thomas the Apostle and is in full communion with Rome. He had read an article about the Society in a British publication and wrote to Doctor Dengel to tell her of his desire to found a congregation for the medical mission apostolate in the Syro-Malabar Church. He asked her to help him begin a Malabar branch of the Medical Mission Sisters, and although she was very interested, she replied that there were no Sisters available at that time. Encouraged, Father Pinakattu replied that he would look for women willing to undertake missionary work and see that they were trained as nurses prior to their religious formation for the Sisterhood. Anna was enthusiastic about what he had proposed. She had already considered training indigenous women as nurses in preparation for religious life. Father Pinakattu and his Bishop strategized on how they might proceed. As a result, in September, 1939, Anna was asked to choose from among three options as to the nature of the congregation he would found: (1) a Malabar branch of her Society; (2) a group affiliated with her Society; (3) "an independent Congregation," one that would be "trained under you and under the direction of your Sisters." In December Anna wrote that Medical Mission Sisters responded favorably to the proposal for an indigenous congregation dedicated to medical missions. "I assure you that we are very much interested in helping India's daughters to help their own people." However, she refrained from choosing precisely what their relationship might be. Instead, she suggested criteria for the selection of candidates and promised to send Sisters to oversee their formation.

In 1940 Father Pinakattu sent five women to study nursing in Rawalpindi. He meant this to be the first step in starting a Malabar branch of the Medical Mission Sisters. A second group of seven arrived in March of 1941. All of them did well in their studies, despite the fact that the language and culture were different from their own. Doctor Dengel was pleased. "They proved to be very good, pious, kind to the sick, gentle, studious, and refined..." She had sent Sister Pauline to be in charge of their well-being. Father Pinakattu continued to send a group to Rawalpindi every year. By the time the first four graduated, a total of sixteen young women from Malabar had studied nursing there.

In July of 1943, the Society received permission from Cardinal Dougherty in the USA to help bring this new foundation in South India into existence. In November permission was also granted by Cardinal Fumasoni-Biondi of Propaganda Fide. He stated, however, that Bishop Kalacherry would have to apply to the Sacred Congregation for Oriental Churches because the Malabar Church was under its jurisdiction. Once ecclesiastical issues had been addressed, Doctor Dengel wrote to Father Pinakattu to suggest a policy of relationship between his group and her own.

> "I shall ask our sisters to forward to you a copy of our Constitutions. Perhaps His Excellency would allow the Malabar Medical Mission Sisters to adopt them with suitable modifications as to name, patron, religious habit to be worn, exercises of piety, regulations of the houses, etc. As regards the habit, it should be thoroughly Indian and at the same time practical for the work of the care of the sick."

In her opinion the initial candidates should be the Rawalpindi graduates. In November 1943 the first four returned to Kerala to begin religious life. Anna knew that the Bishop wanted to place the new foundation under the patronage of the Immaculate Heart of Mary, so she suggested naming the congregation "Medical Mission Sisters of the Immaculate Heart of Mary, Queen of the Missions." Both the Bishop and Father Pinakattu happily agreed. The Society's magazine announced: "On November 17, 1943 Bishop Kalacherry laid the foundation for a novitiate building upon the hillock, Parummalakinnu, in the presence of a huge crowd of priests, sisters, and laity, both Catholic and non-Catholic, and called it *Mary Giri* (Mary's Mount)." On May 24, 1944, the four pioneers – Mariamma Thomas Vadakkummury, Thresiamma Mathew Chirakadavil, Mary Thomas Neriamparampil, and Rose George Kuthivalachel – began their postulancy. The Bishop named Father Pinakattu their Director; Anna Dengel appointed Sister Pauline Downing to be their novice mistress and Sister Vincent Deegan her assistant. She urged them to convey the underlying spirit of the Society by adapting to local customs whenever possible, and she stressed, even in the liturgy.

> "Keep everything as Indian as you can, the housing, the food, the dress, etc. All these things are quite compatible with religious life. In the training, I think you will have to stress the positive; go more for acquiring virtue, and correct the faults that way. But you will find out yourself."

Anna knew from experience that those distinctive values definitive of her "holy experiment" had to be instilled from the very beginning of the formation process.

Although the new foundation had become a reality, its status, remained uncertain. Would the group become autonomous? Or would it retain an affiliation with Anna Dengel's Society? This had always been Father Pinakattu's intent, but he had begun to waver. In August 1944 Bishop Kalacherry of Changanacherry wrote to the Sacred Congregation for the Oriental Churches and requested permission for the Mary Giri Sisters to be affiliated with the American Medical Mission Sisters. Permission was granted. The formal protocol stated that the new congregation was to be "on the model and under the guidance of the American Medical Mission Sisters, two of whom will preside over the spiritual and religious formation of the community." The expectation was that it would reflect as closely as possible the Society from America. However, Anna Dengel was not happy with the decision to adopt an identical mode of dress and told this to the Bishop.

> "In our Society the Sisters have been taught from the beginning to appreciate the good, the noble and beautiful in the people among whom they work and were warned against any tendency of substituting Western customs and habits, except in cases where they are harmful and wrong. With this ingrained attitude and teaching in our Society, Your Excellency will see that I will not uphold our principles if I would favor a Western habit for the Indian Sisters…if they have the same habit, the responsibility, then I would almost say the stigma, of Westernizing them, will fall on our Society."

Nevertheless, Anna assured the Bishop of her commitment to this undertaking, which would mark the formal beginning of Indian Medical Mission Sisterhood: "the first of its kind in India, Burma, and Ceylon," is how Father Pinakattu expressed it. She wrote:

> "As we are very much interested in helping Indian Sisters and see that the hope of development of Catholic hospitals in India is in native Sisterhood, we would consider it a great privilege to be allowed to undertake the formation of the Indian MMS."

On September 8, 1944 the new institute was erected under the title Medical Mission Sisters of the Immaculate Heart of Mary, Queen of the Missions, popularly known as Mary Giri Sisters. The first four members received a habit identical to that of Anna's Society and a copy of the same Constitutions. They were given new names. Along with the name Mary, they chose to honor the four who were said to have stood at the foot of the cross during the passion of Jesus: Veronica, Salome, Magdalen, and John. From the beginning they had been told that as the first Indian Novices, they would be starting a branch of the Society of Catholic Medical Missionaries (SCMM). However, in 1944, the final decision made by the Apostolic Delegate was they would be a separate community. This new and surprising revelation was extremely upsetting, not only for the pioneering members, but also for the Sisters in charge. "This was not what we wanted," is how the four Malabar candidates expressed it. It was a sensitive issue, as Father Pinakattu's position regarding the community's autonomous status had very definitely changed. He decided to make the Malabar community a separate entity. As Director, he was the one in charge. He took responsibility for all aspects of community life even after Sisters Pauline and Vincent had arrived, resulting in a growing tension between him and the Society. This radical change in status was upsetting to the candidates. Although they respected him and appreciated all he had done for them, they had been promised one thing and were not willing to settle for another. They shared their concerns with Sister Pauline, but she, and the Society, could not do anything about it. By the end of January 1945, several manifestations of a distinction between the two communities began to emerge. These were reflected in modifications to the proposed habit and headpiece for the Malabar community, for

Doctor Dengel had decided that if the two were to be distinct from one another, their mode of dress should differ. She also decided that at First Profession the Malabar Sisters would receive a symbol of the Immaculate Heart of Mary on a silver chain, and not the Society crucifix. By the end of March the second group had completed their studies, and in July, received the habit.

In February 1946, Anna Dengel arrived in Kottayam. It was her first visit to the Malabar community she had nurtured for years. She was joyfully greeted in genuine South Indian fashion with a large welcoming banner at the gate; garlands, bouquets, and dancing; fireworks, and the ringing of bells – the Church bell and all the bells that they were able to garner. She stayed about six weeks. Because this emerging community had to have its own Rule, Anna helped formulate one by integrating elements from Society documents into a new Constitution, which was officially approved by the Bishop in April the following year. While she was with them, the candidates told her of their disappointment in having lost their affiliation with her Society, which had been promised to them. She assured them that once they were full-fledged members, they could try to reverse that decision by approaching the Congregation for Oriental Churches with their concerns.

On September 8 the "first four" made their first profession of vows within the Syrian Rite celebrated by Malabar Bishop Kalacherry. Anna Dengel would have liked to have stayed to be part of that joyous occasion, but she was expected in Rawalpindi, where three of those newly professed Sisters would soon be assigned. She remained about a month in Pindi and was there on April 28 for the ceremonial laying of the foundation stone for the new Holy Family Hospital. From there she went to Lahore, and then on to Patna. On June 2 she sailed to Europe where she spent the summer, first in England, then in Holland for the opening of a combined Novitiate/House of Studies; and finally, in Austria, where the chance to be with family and friends was precisely what she needed. She did not return to the USA until the end of September. In January 1947 she traveled to South America; in November, to Mexico; and dealt with urgent Society issues during the months in between. March 19 marked the opening of Holy Family Hospital in Mandar, India – an 80-bed rural hospital among tribal people. Because a life of service was now a possibility for indigenous women, a novitiate was added. The Society also established a foundation in Makassar, Celebes, Indonesia with a commitment to provide supervision of a 26-bed obstetrics department at Stella Maris Hospital and a 26-bed maternity clinic at St. Melania Maternal and Child Welfare Centers and Midwifery School.

On August 15, 1947, India was granted its independence by the British Empire. With the historic enactment of Partition, its territory was subdivided into two separate nations: India to the south, Pakistan to the north. On the basis of religious and cultural identity, millions of displaced persons – whole populations of Hindus, Sikhs, and Muslims, as well as other ethnic groups – spearheaded the largest mass migration in human history as the uprooted moved from where they had been to where they felt they had to be. If there was ever a need for medical missions, it was there and then, in the turbulence of upheaval and in the lingering aftermath of widespread misery. Sister Alma Julia, on staff at Holy Family Hospital in Pindi at that time, wrote the following account:

> "What can you do in a 100-bed hospital when you wake up in the morning and find 2000 people outside your gates, sometimes half of whom should be hospitalized? The most helpless and the dying, as well as women in labor, were carried into the hospital. The stretcher bearers carried out the dead. Two or more sisters would go outside and make the rounds of the refugees...Military jeeps patrolled the streets. Barbed wire was stretched across the roads leading into the city. Curfew was enforced. But we Sisters were allowed to pass everywhere. It wasn't a matter of bravery. We just knew that we were perfectly safe. For twenty-five years our sisters had been taking care of Moslems, Hindus, and Sikhs in this mission hospital. The people knew we treated all alike – that we had nothing to do with politics."

With the stroke of a pen the Society's infrastructure also became more complex. Patna was in India and Rawalpindi was now in Pakistan.

The Society held its Fourth General Chapter from August 8-25 in Philadelphia and re-elected Anna Dengel as Superior General. A multitude of issues dominated the agenda. Convincingly, Anna spoke of how she envisioned the future of her ever-expanding Society that now consisted of 179 members, which included 53 novices and 18 postulants.

> "We should consciously work hard by every means to develop the Medical Mission Apostolate. I conceive or visualize as making present, as manifesting the love and compassion of Christ all over the world, like Christ sending out messengers, to help where the need is greatest, where the people are poorest ... We should be happy and rejoice over every effort ... Our field is enormous ... With gratitude to God for all that we have been able to accomplish, we may say that the future is promising."

Anna stressed the importance of being grateful for all that had transpired up to the present moment and lifted up the following blessings.

> "We have the approval of Rome, which we should esteem and value very highly. We have not only great scope, but also such a holy, beautiful and interesting vocation. We are getting more solidly organized. Our watchword for the next six years should be: consolidate spiritually and also consolidate the work and of course advance with a holy prudence that draws and does not shun sacrifices. Join with me in a fervent *Deo Gratias* (Thanks be to God) for the past and a fervent *Sursum Corda* (Lift up your hearts) for the future."

During the course of the Chapter, which focused on multiple aspects of efficiency and organization, Anna made clear her heart's desire that members "be really religious to the bone, understand religious life, be formed in it and live it like a second nature." She gave a detailed report on the Society's role in the emergence of an indigenous religious community in Kottayam, which she referred to as "our most constructive work so far." While appreciating all the good that was done in helping to make this happen, in light of present circumstances, it was decided to disassociate from the Mary Giri foundation "in order to avoid any unpleasant breach in relationship." It was a difficult decision, but a necessary one. There was also unanimous agreement to open new postulates and novitiates in the western hemisphere. The decision clearly indicated that "race should not be a barrier in admitting candidates to the Society," a statement deemed necessary due to the turbulence of the times. It was also decided to begin the process of seeking Papal approval, which would liberate the Society from cumbersome Diocesan regulations whenever it was necessary to implement Society-wide change. Before adjourning it was agreed that the next Chapter would occur, not in six years, but in ten. Anna Dengel's words following the Chapter still resonate today.

> "...If, after experiencing all the goodness and care that Divine Providence has lavished on us spiritually and temporally during our pioneer years, we would not have great confidence and trust for the future, we would surely be to blame. We started with nothing and we really were never in want of anything necessary."

After the Chapter Anna Dengel informed the Mary Giri Sisters and Bishop Kalacherry of the Society's decision to discontinue its involvement in the Malabar experiment. Their response was immediate. The Sisters entreated the Society to continue to work with them and a distressed Bishop Kalacherry apologized for being unaware of the tension that had existed. "If only I knew it early I would have prevented it ... even changed the Director." He asked that the Society reconsider. After lengthy negotiations, the Council reversed its decision and appointed Sister Xavier Boeckmann novice mistress for the Malabar Novitiate and assigned Sister Pauline to the now burgeoning novitiate in the USA. The following March, the first Catholic Hospital in the state of Travancore opened in Bharananganam. Immaculate Heart of Mary Hospital, under the auspices of the Mary Giri Sisters, was staffed by those nurses who had trained in Rawalpindi. The Bishop appointed Father Pinakattu the Director of the new hospital. He moved to Bharananganam. The crisis involving the Mary Giri Sisters and the Medical Mission Sisters had been resolved.

Medical Mission Sisters established three foundations of their own in 1948. In Karachi, now Pakistan, the Society assumed management of Saint Therese's Nursing Home, anticipating that one day it would be transformed into a hospital.

Two Sisters from the Mitford Hospital in Dacca went to Mymensingh in East Bengal to prepare for the construction of a small hospital in fulfillment of a promise that had been made to a Holy Cross Bishop.

The opening of a dispensary in Berekum, Ghana, led to the construction of yet another Holy Family Hospital and signified the Society's first mission in Africa.

Before the end of the year, the Dutch Sisters opened an outpatient department and maternity clinic at a hospital in the city of Solo (Surakarta) in central Java, Indonesia.

In the late 1940s, Mother Teresa of Calcutta spent time at Holy Family Hospital in Patna in order to learn how to care for the sick and dying before beginning her own community in India, the Missionaries of Charity. Years later she wrote this about Anna Dengel and the Medical Mission Sisters.

> "Our two congregations are very similar in their works. It is 'love of neighbor in action.' I was influenced during my time in Patna, when I saw how the sisters in the hospital cared for the sick and dying.

> For me it was a living example of what we should be doing for the poorest, and so I learned from them how to do it with love and devotion. It is a wonderful gift of God to be allowed to serve the sick and dying. Mother Dengel has brought this gift of God to the Church."

In March 1949 Anna Dengel went to Europe and remained for several months. She made a pilgrimage to Fatima, visited Pauline Willis in her home outside of London, and then spent the summer in Steeg and in Hall before arriving in Rome in September for the International Conference of Catholic Doctors and an audience with the Director of Propaganda Fide. She had hoped to receive good news with regard to Papal approval, but instead she was told the request had been denied. The Society was not quite ready. In her report to the community, she said:

> "I cannot deny that the answer was a real disappointment to me, but I can also sincerely say, that in a sense I am glad of the postponement. It is a great incentive to

us to dig the foundation deeper, so that the tree and
the branches and the fruit will be stronger, bigger, and
better. So, instead of bemoaning the delay, let us roll
up our sleeves and work on ourselves and the all-round
development of our Society."

She had also looked for a house in Rome, with permission from the
Council, but could not find anything suitable. In October she went
to Karachi, then to Rawalpindi, where she remained for ten days
before moving on to Lahore, Dehra Dun, Mussoorie, Patna, Mandar,
Calcutta, and Bombay. On November 8 she flew to Madras and then
flew to Trivandunum. On arrival in Kottayam, she took a bus to
Bharananganam, where she was able to see for herself all that had been
accomplished by the Mary Giri Sisters. From there she went to Dacca
to alleviate some tensions, then left to spend Christmas in Rome.

The year 1950 was a Jubilee Year for the Church and for the Society.
In a circular letter to the Sisters, Anna Dengel wrote:

"We, the pioneers,
should thank God with all our heart
for having led us
so fatherly,
so motherly,
so wonderfully,
through these twenty-five years.
How many graces and gifts
have we not received
collectively and individually?"

In February Anna Dengel went to Berekum, Ghana. It was the final stop
on her visitation of all the Society's missions. On March 25, feast of the
Annunciation, the community in Philadelphia celebrated the opening
of the new Holy Family Hospital in Rawalpindi as enthusiastically as
did the Sisters in Pakistan. In June Anna was in Rome and went from
there to Vienna for the International Academic Mission Congress.

At the end of September the Society initiated a series of events at
the Motherhouse to celebrate its Silver Jubilee. Hundreds of benefactors
and friends joined the Medical Mission Sisters in giving thanks for

twenty-five graced years of compassionate healing ministries. Anna Dengel invited Michael Mathis to share in the festivities and to celebrate the Foundation Day Liturgy. It was the first time he would be with the Society since 1938. When his car pulled up to the main entrance, Anna hastened to welcome him, warmly and enthusiastically. In an instant, a page was turned and a new chapter began. He stayed three days and agreed to return to give lectures on liturgical prayer, his area of expertise.

Even with all the support from others, the community was poor, as it always had been. It survived on the money it was able to raise through donations solicited by mail; church collections when possible; and the generosity of individual benefactors. Nevertheless, the decision was made to add additional space because of the many applicants who were seeking admission. The magazine put it this way. "Our crowded condition has reached its limit. Money or no money, ground was broken for a large chapel, dormitory, and refectory." It would be a two-storied building "to be completed in six months." And it was. Forty-six women had entered the postulate during the Jubilee year. What helped enormously was the gift of a house in Mountain View, California from Mrs. Paul Fretz. After she transferred ownership of her lovely estate, "Marymeade," to the Society, it was decided to begin a second postulate there.

On May 31, 1951 His Eminence Cardinal Dougherty died. It was a heart-rending loss for Anna and her Society. He had been such an avid supporter of the medical mission cause. In her tribute to him Anna wrote: "Less than a year ago he paid us a last visit. He said he wanted to meet all the Sisters, all 140 of them. We put an armchair in the corner of the library, and there he received every Sister. His memory shall be blessed all the days of our Society."

The issue of canonical status regarding the Mary Giri Sisters surfaced again in 1951. The first four members had never intended to found a new community and were determined to pursue affiliation with Anna Dengel's Society. One of them wrote to Anna saying that they do not like being under the directorship of priests. After Bishop Kalacherry died and his successor had been installed, they asked Bishop Matthew Kavukattu to please remove the Director. He considered it a legitimate request. So did the Apostolic Nuncio, who told the priest: "Now that the Sisters have reached sufficient development, it would be better if they are left to manage their own affairs." Father Pinakattu acquiesced. He wrote to Anna Dengel: "…if the Sisters think that it is good for the Society and its work." Anna certainly did, but not out of any self-interest.

> "As you know from the beginning our desire was and still is to help the community get on its feet irrespective of affiliation to our Society. I can sincerely say that we bestowed the same interest, care, and love on them when it became more or less clear that your idea was that they should be a separate community. No matter what lies in the future, one thing is certain: that you were God's instrument in bringing about the foundation of the community and the community must and always will be grateful to you. The sacrifices you made and are still making will no doubt be a help in the foundation. Very often there are misunderstandings and incompatibilities but in the end God's work wins, even though perhaps in ways different than foreseen."

The process of merging began officially in January of 1952. Anna visited the Sisters briefly to offer encouragement. For nine months the Mary Giri Sisters prayed daily to the Holy Spirit, but when September had arrived and there was still no word, seventeen professed members petitioned Mother Dengel to intervene on their behalf. All she could do then was express her concern.

> "I feel strongly that we must do our best to make the affiliation possible. It would be too hard on Malabar Sisters and us if we would not be one united family."

In February of 1953 the Bishop invited Anna to review the conditions for Affiliation and to help draft a mutually agreeable solution regarding the conditions for Amalgamation set by Rome. The underlying challenge had been the issue of two different Rites. By May that had been resolved. The Malabar province would remain under the Jurisdiction of the Sacred Congregation for Oriental Churches. At the time permission was finally granted, the Malabar community consisted of 38 professed sisters, 16 novices, plus several postulants and aspirants. Mother Anna Dengel returned to Kottayam in November to assist the Sisters in preparing for final vows. The two communities officially became one congregation on November 25 with the arrival of Cardinal Tisserant from Rome. Society records state:

> "It was His Eminence Cardinal Tisserant, the great Patron of the Oriental Churches, who remade history, granting the Sisters permission to be an integral part of SCMM with due respect to their ritual allegiance, by recognizing the Mary Giri Foundation as the Syro-Malabar portion of the Society of Catholic Medical Missionaries."

On November 28, ten Sisters made their Final Profession into the hands of Mother Anna Dengel. The pioneering Malabar initiative was a branch of SCMM at last. Medical Mission Sisters around the world joined with them in rejoicing.

The lush tropical terrain enveloping the Malabar community in southern India must have felt like the Garden of Eden to Anna, who so loved nature. On the other hand, the extensive and panoramic expanse surrounding the Motherhouse in America was every bit as lovely, in its own way. Its many acres in the Fox Chase section of Philadelphia lay at the very edge of the city and spilled over into Montgomery County. Two large forested parks and a farm lay just a recreational walk away, where picnics on feast days gave those preparing for religious life an outlet for pent up energies. The property had an apple orchard, a small lake and a rippling brook, gardens where postulants and novices planted and picked carrots, cucumbers, radishes, rhubarb and multiple ears of corn; a barn with cows that gave milk and cream that the Sisters churned into butter; a bevy of chickens, a pen of pigs, and a tractor always in motion. There was also a lot of wildlife, either resident or just visiting: fox, skunk, deer, raccoon, a flock of wild turkeys foraging for food, just like the community, who fed them now and then. From this enchanted garden of sorts, filled with songbirds and butterflies, Anna Dengel sent healing and hope to the far corners of the world.

In April of 1953 the Alliance of Catholic Women of Philadelphia held their annual Spring Luncheon at Convention Hall. Anna Dengel was the principal speaker. She received an award and the Society was given a $1000 donation. Exhibits at schools and conventions kept the Sisters busy making the cause of medical missions known. In September

Anna left for Pakistan and India. She arrived in New Delhi on October 1 for the official laying of the "dedication stone" at Holy Family Hospital. The Vice President of India presided at the ceremony.

As Superior General, Anna was inundated with requests for doctors, nurses, and medical facilities from Bishops around the world. On New Year's Day in 1954 she reminded the community of all that had been accomplished so far and what was still to be done. She said she saw "a propelling force, like a mighty wind, strongly in the Society's favor." Two major undertakings – Holy Family Hospitals in New Delhi, India and in Dacca, East Pakistan – would be opening that year, and others would soon follow. A lot was going on at the Motherhouse as well. Collective prayer was invigorated by a growing interest in the liturgy, thanks to Father Mathis, and participation in a liturgical movement that signaled what was to come. There was also a consistent cultivation of a more informed world vision due to the Sister Formation Movement and to scholars, artists, and practitioners who came to speak to the community on missiology and social/political issues, deepening an awareness of systemic change inherent in the signs of the times. Some Sisters attended the Institute of Spirituality at Notre Dame. Some delved into Bible study or Liberation Theology. Some, for the greater good of the community, locally and abroad, were educated in fields that at the time were referred to as non-medical. Anna Dengel had always had an insatiable thirst for knowledge relevant to the here and now. This quality emerged in her Society and sank deep roots. In May of 1955 LaSalle College in Philadelphia awarded Doctor Anna Dengel an honorary membership in Alpha Epsilon Delta, a National Premedical Honor Society. In June she received an honorary Doctor of Science degree from Marquette University in Milwaukee. That year she was also honored with the following citation.

1925 – 1955
Thirty Glorious Years
Whereas
Mother Anna Dengel, M.D.
had the dauntless courage to pioneer in an uncultivated area of
the Lord's vineyard, and
Whereas
her zeal bore fruit in the founding of the

Society of Catholic Medical Missionaries,
the first order of its kind in the Church's history, and
Whereas
Mother Dengel's work is internationally and rightfully recognized
as a modern spiritual medical crusade, and
Whereas
this incredible accomplishment would be only a pious dream
but for the profound faith and love that gave spiritual substance
to the extraordinary natural talents of Mother Dengel and
her unerring sense of values both human and divine:
Be it resolved that
**The National Federation of Catholic Physicians Guilds
of the United States**
salutes with prayerful pride a professional equal
and a spiritual superior.
May Mother Dengel and her Sisters of the Medical Missions
continue their magnificent work of the past thirty years
under the guidance and protection of
God and His Blessed Mother.

In September the Sisters in Fox Chase celebrated the Society's 30th Anniversary with a series of events. Father Mathis came and stayed for a week. He lectured on the liturgy, introduced the singing of Vespers in the vernacular, and facilitated a Sunday vigil service with the community. On September 22 an event for the public was held at the Academy of Music. It sold out well in advance. Bishop Fulton J. Sheen was the principal speaker. He had dinner with the community at the Motherhouse before the event began. In his talk he referred to Mother Dengel as "the woman who has done more for the missions than any woman living today." Over two thousand people were in attendance. On September 30th Father Mathis and Mother Dengel informally reminisced on the early years of the Society. In the 30th anniversary issue of *The Medical Missionary,* Mother told how she saw the Society "as a new flower in the garden of the Church."

"A new community has to suck out from the Gospel,
the elements of its specific *raison d'etre*; its specific way
to glorify God ... 'So let your light shine' sums up

our whole purpose, our ultimate aims. Our love and devotion coupled with knowledge and skills are the light, serving the sick in the missions, the good works that glorify God."

Those who were just setting out on the path needed to know what had guided those who had set out before them.

"In our Society we did not have many preconceived notions, or experience, or traditions. We developed as it seemed reasonable and serviceable for our purpose and only laid down what we had already lived. The race for one world is on. It is not won yet by far, but the fact that it is in motion, is the significant factor and the thing to grasp. Be in step with the needs of our own lifetime, into which our responsibility is set by God's Providence."

Postulants, novices, and junior professed Sisters in Philadelphia were blessed with informative sessions with Mother Anna Dengel, who was eager to share with them perspectives on the Church and on the Society's pioneering beginnings.

"In charting the route of our Society, we developed in a very simple way, and that's why it really worked! We just lived and did what common sense and whatever knowledge we had dictated and in that way the spirit of our Society developed. We couldn't be a Congregation, that is, take public vows, because it wasn't permitted. Sisters with public vows were not permitted to do obstetrics and study medicine. Yet we wanted to be a community. I felt the only way would be through a group, through team work. In a way we lived in the manner of religious, we had the evangelical counsels.

'In reality, compared to now, it was all very simple; it was all much less formal, much less organized, not that we are so organized yet. The whole Constitutions were planned for a pious society; that is, an organization in the Church approved and canonically erected and the members live in the manner of religious, and in community; but they don't make public vows. They make private vows, take an oath, make promises. That was how it was when we started in our Constitutions."

The Society Chronicles record her as saying:

"The Ecclesiastical Superior for the Religious Communities of women in the Archdiocese of Baltimore, said that our Society was a noble and holy experiment....During the three years of our existence it never occurred to us that it might fail or that it was just an experiment."

Anna often added humor to serious conversations.

"We were what is called a pious society, and a priest later said to me that he hoped we were pious still."

She made sure that the uninitiated knew it had not been easy.

"We had a hard time being or becoming ourselves as Medical Mission Sisters. The men kept trying to be in charge of us."

Also, she left no doubt, that no matter how hard it had been in the past or might be in the future: "The power of women is much greater than they themselves suspect."

Because in the mid-1950s full-fledged medical missionaries in religious communities were commonplace, Anna wanted to be sure that those who would carry on the work understood how special that was.

"The word 'Medical Mission' was not used in the Church before our Society. The Protestants used it, because they expressed their love of the sick in Medical Missions. For them, it was unthinkable to take care of the sick without professional training. In the Church, devotion was used. It goes a long way, but not the whole way in our times. Our Society was the first to use the expression 'Medical

Mission' and the reason was that we wanted to stress the professional training to the missions. It is a pioneer movement and a new development in our life."

She was quick to credit the forerunners of her own pioneering effort.

"It is to the honor of Protestants that they have been the pioneers and leaders in the health fields in the missions."

At the same time she made certain that those to whom the future was entrusted understood they too were pioneers.

"Every Sister who comes to the Society has to start pioneering in her own life, a pioneer to herself."

Fundamental to the mission was her unwavering conviction that "In a Catholic mission hospital, love and sympathy must be a testimony that there is a God of love who cares for all His creatures; that all [people] of all races, of all conditions, are brothers [and sisters] in Christ." There are so many ways to "show our gratitude and love," she would say. "Fortunately, opportunities surround us like air." Sometimes, her words of wisdom were copied onto cards that were tucked into a Bible or a favorite book of prayer.

"The personal love of Christ applied to our neighbor
would make us more patient, more attentive,
more thoughtful, more concerned,
more sympathetic, more anxious to help,
to do the best for those under our care,
relieve them, cheer them, comfort them,
be kind to those whom they love,
discreet, tactful, respectful,
considerate of their customs,
and never be hard."

Anna Dengel had "a great love for the church" and told the sisters "they should know the church, live with her in her liturgy, and labor and suffer for her extension." She also said in one of her classes:

> "I love the religious life, and as one grows older one realizes that it is so full because it is to love God with sincerity, simplicity, and enlightenment....if you have correct value and estimation of what religious life is... then your religious vocation like a tree well-rooted will stay."

She would say: "I want our Society to be Enlightened, simple, sincere – to love God with simplicity, sincerity, and Enlightenment."

From time to time the question would arise: should the Society's focus be exclusively on the poor. Anna was firm in her conviction.

> "Some people think that it is better to help the poor exclusively. I would prefer to help the poor exclusively. To be sick and poor combined is painful, but the rich are also human beings, and they need care too, especially in the missions. In our hospitals, if we didn't treat the rich, we couldn't help the poor. The only solution is to treat patients according to their means and there is no less charity; and as for the spiritual, they are just as much in need."

In the spring of 1955 a dozen Sisters departed for the missions. In 1956, there were two departure ceremonies for twenty-one more. Plans were set in motion to open a leprosarium in Kokofu in Ghana; and Anna was determined to plant a seed in the Philippines, even as the Council protested, saying: "no more new foundations." There were more than enough already to coordinate and oversee. However, when confronted with overwhelming need, plus a windfall of vocations, Anna found it hard to say no. She insisted: "If you do something, something happens; if you do nothing, nothing happens." That approach had always made sense to her. "We have only one life and we must make the most of it." She often told her community:

> "Our whole life is to be missionary, so we must be completely impregnated with the mission spirit. Mission ideas must influence our whole thinking, our praying and our acting."

And again:

> "We must *be* missionary. It has to come out of us itself. It has to be so developed in us that it will be a manifestation of our interior and of our spirit no matter where we go."

She also said in reference to the Society's many missions:

> "We don't want to make places for ourselves to stay. We want to make the people capable of carrying on the work themselves. That is really our aim."

Anna was a strong advocate for the rights of workers.

> "Another thing we cannot stress too much is fair compensation for those who are employed. It is a sin that cries to heaven. In the missions, we can lead in that way."

She often used the following example.

> "In India, it is not customary to give servants holidays. We give them two weeks holiday. When they don't receive a holiday, it forces them to lie and there are all kinds of tales about relatives who have died. But when you give them their proper holiday, they don't have to lie. I am sure that their parents die, but now only once."

Mother Dengel was eager to share her experiences and her wisdom, not only with the novices and newly professed Sisters, but also with their families. Whenever possible, she would meet and greet them on visiting day, revealing the spirit of hospitality that was inherent within her Society. In 1956, the College of Steubenville in Ohio awarded Anna Dengel the "Poverello Medal" in honor of Saint Francis and "in recognition of her great benefactions for humanity, exemplifying in our age, the Christ-like spirit of charity which filled the life of Francis of Assisi.

In February 1957 Mother Dengel flew to Rome to work with Holy Cross Father Edward Heston on reopening the process of petitioning for Papal approval. He had already agreed to be Canonical advisor for the upcoming Chapter. They were privileged to have an audience with Pope Pius XII. In March Anna received an honorary Doctor of Law degree from Manhattanville College in New York.

In May a cable from London told of the death of Miss Pauline Willis on the 7th of May. She was close to 87 years old. "If we had gone in search of a friend and benefactor from one end of the world to the other, we could not have found a better one than Pauline," said Anna, as she recalled how she, the Society, and so many others on both sides of the Atlantic were deeply indebted to her. "The only thing that mattered to Miss Willis was good works, works, works! 'The good works' were her life. Her works will follow her. We need her prayers more than she needs ours; but still we pray that she and all her family may rest in peace."

In addition to those places already mentioned, other foundations had been established or embellished in several countries on several continents during the decade that followed the 1947 Chapter.

In India the Society began staffing Saint Mary's Hospital in Mussoorie; opened a school of nursing in Mandar, a Novitiate and dispensary in Poona, and hospitals in Patna, Bombay, Kodarma, Thuruthipuram, and Changanacherry.

In Pakistan Medical Mission Sisters were instrumental in establishing the Trained Nurses Association of Pakistan, which began around 1950; and opened a new 60-bed hospital in Karachi.

In Africa the Society took responsibility for the full range of nursing services at Ernest Oppenheimer Hospital in Welkom, South Africa; in collaboration with the government, opened a hospital in the village of Pendjua in the rainforest of Zaire, where two distinct Pygmoid tribes had no access to medical care; and took charge of a government hospital in Kiri in the Belgian Congo. In Ghana Medical Mission Sisters opened a leprosarium in Kokofu, a school of nursing in Berekum, and a hospital in Techiman.

In Venezuela MMS assumed management of Our Lady of Coromoto Hospital in Maracaibo and opened Holy Family Hospital in Caripito.

In Indonesia, a Novitiate for Indonesian girls was started in Lawang on the island of Java and a hospital was opened in Pare Pare.

In the USA a house of studies was established in St. Louis. Many young women were entering the Society to participate in what Mother Anna Dengel called "a labor of love." In her diary Anna clearly expressed "the spirit of the Society," which she cherished wholeheartedly.

"Serve with love.
Serve God in everybody and everything
with real personal love."

The Society's Fifth General Chapter convened on August 5, 1957. In her opening remarks Mother Dengel said to the twenty-six participating Sisters that this Chapter marked the end of an experimental and somewhat flexible period in the Society. From now on things would have to be more definite and precise. She mentioned the growth in membership and in mission development since the previous Chapter. There were now 470 professed Sisters in 36 houses in 10 countries. She stressed the increase in mission development because of so many urgent needs, noting that organizational structures must adjust accordingly. She also spoke of the state of the world and how it continues to influence the work of the Society. The buzzword ricocheting everywhere was: be aware of the signs of the times. The challenge for the Society now, was not only to be aware of the signs, but to learn to interpret them.

Mother Anna Dengel was re-elected Superior General for the next ten years. Two of the Chapter decisions were to establish Pro-Provinces and regions; and to move the Generalate to Rome. It was clearly stated that both these actions should be done as soon as possible. Anna said in her letter to the Sisters on Foundation Day:

"Our Chapter was not revolutionary but evolutionary, which proves that from the beginning we were on the right track and kept on it. We must not forget why we entered religion and that our first duty is to glorify God by our holiness. In this connection we must think of our work, not only what it does for others, but what it does to us. In other words, as work fills such a major part of our lives, we must make it so that our own soul profits by it. It gives us the chance to fulfill our vows and practice every virtue."

Mother left Philadelphia for Rome on September 14. The entire community assembled for a most memorable departure ceremony that some said "resembled a funeral" because so many were in tears. It marked the end of an era for the Fox Chase Motherhouse on 8400 Pine Road in Philadelphia. For Mother Anna Dengel, it meant the beginning of another. She said she was leaving in peace with the conviction that the work of the Society was well on its way. Her parting words were: "Somebody said that it might turn out to be a new holy experiment."

We must lift our hearts to God always,

and if they are there,

we will do our duty joyfully, generously,

and with much love.

Anna Dengel

CHAPTER TWENTY-FIVE

The Society of Catholic Medical Missionaries, encouraged by its founder, decided to adopt a more efficient administrative structure. The Dutch pro-province, already in existence, was joined by an American pro-province and the Syro-Malabar region. This new matrix included the central government offices in the process of moving to Rome. Father Mathis telephoned Anna Dengel. "You outdid Holy Cross who took a hundred years to get to Rome." It probably seemed that long to Anna before the Generalate finally settled in. After an exhaustive search for a place large enough to accommodate its needs, the Medical Mission Sisters purchased a building previously occupied by the Felician Sisters. It became home base for Mother Dengel and the Generalate offices and had ample living space for Sisters visiting from around the world. Meetings to coordinate and discuss issues relating to the Society's worldwide mission began to take place just a stone's throw from the Vatican.

When Pope Pius XII died in October of 1958, his successor, Pope John XXIII, set in motion a groundswell of unprecedented change within the institutional Church, generating many a conversation within Anna Dengel's global Society. Seven years earlier, as Superior General, Anna had already alerted her community to pay attention to the Holy Spirit at work in the world. "We are living in a marvelous time," she would say, "not an easy time, however. The old things have to be understood and sometimes rethought to be valued, and new ways have to be carved out." She wrestled with the deeper issues underlying current events and wanted the members of her Society to do the same.

"The present state of affairs in the world and especially in non-Christian countries is one of revolution, evolution, transition, radical or at least definite change. It is a force like an avalanche that started quietly and small, but has gained such momentum that nobody can hold it back and no well-meaning person would want to hold it back. The old and primitive civilizations now have a passion to rule themselves and a tremendous ambition and zeal to acquire knowledge and skill to provide a respectable standard of living, and to gain the respect of the world at large. In this we can be of acceptable service, if it is unselfish, enlightened, effective, and rendered with kindness and devotion."

In November Anna traveled to the Netherlands to receive an honorary Doctor of Medicine degree from the Roman Catholic University of Nijmegen. On June 11, 1959, the Society of Catholic Medical Missionaries was granted its long-awaited *Decretum Laudis,* or Papal approval, by Pope John XXIII through the Sacred Congregation for Propagation of the Faith. This transformed the Society into a Pontifical Congregation subject directly to the Holy See, thereby fulfilling its desire to be "rooted and founded in the Church." The news reached the Generalate on June 22. Anna was ecstatic. So were Medical Mission Sisters all around the world. Because Papal approval was a sign of the Church's continued protection, it was customary for a Congregation to choose a Cardinal Protector. Anna asked Amleto Cardinal Cicignani, who had long been a friend of the Society. He wholeheartedly accepted. In September he came to the Generalate to explain to Anna the ceremonial details associated with assuming this role. The official ceremony, at which the Holy Cross seminarians sang, was held at the Generalate house on Piazza Cimone on December 3, the feast of Saint Francis Xavier. A large crowd filled the room, eager to hear the Cardinal's words and to share in the celebration that followed.

Anna's travels continued unabated. She attended relevant conferences and carried out visitations to the Society's many mission sites, including those that were added during the years leading up to the Chapter. Four missions were established before the end of the '50s. The Sisters in Philadelphia assumed administration of Saint Vincent's Hospital for expectant and unwed mothers and their babies in 1958. The following year Holy Family hospitals opened in three areas of the world: in Venezuela (Judibana); Malawi, Central Africa (Phalombe); and Myanmar, formerly Burma (Rangoon). Everywhere Anna encouraged the many selfless and devoted members who made medical missions possible, reminding them to "be in step with the needs of our own lifetime, into which our responsibility is set by God's Providence." She often stressed putting emphasis on the quality of their healing services, something too easily overlooked in chaotic situations.

> "We must have, keep, and pray for real sympathy – the milk of human kindness. We have to have it to touch hearts. This often means going out of our way – that extra work and care and trouble – but that is the beauty of our life."

Time and again Anna's teaching to the Sisters all around the world returned to the theme of love. "Our love and devotion, coupled with knowledge and skills, are the light serving the sick in the missions, the good works that glorify God." Her passionate compassion was legendary.

Speaking to supporters about what she had seen on a recent trip through India and Pakistan, she described the many malnourished children with bloated stomachs and vacant eyes, and the unrelieved pain of the women. She paused, reflected, then banged her fist on the table and shouted: "It eats me up!"

On March 10, 1960, Father Michael Mathis died. A large number of Medical Mission Sisters who were in the United States attended the funeral in South Bend, Indiana. On hearing the news, Anna sent a letter to all the Sisters. "He was as ready as anyone could be, blessed with years and a full priestly life," she wrote. "Still the actual news of his death brings up deep emotion with the realization of all he was and did for us. I can sincerely say that I am grateful to God for having given us a priest to help and guide us in the first steps, and that I am very grateful to Father Mathis personally." She reflected on how he had "instilled in us a love for the liturgy" and had helped the Society cultivate a deep appreciation for liturgical music. "Just to live in the Liturgical Year is a joy." Anna Dengel often said: "Good singing can mean so much. Look at it as prayer. Think how you sing to God; do it as an act of worship." Many Sisters have heard Mother say: "When I get to heaven I want to learn to drive, to type, and to sing." Occasionally, those components varied, but always she included learning how to sing. Music was a bond both visionaries shared. What a blessing to have been able to conclude their relationship this side of heaven on such a positive note.

In Rome the Generalate moved to a new location on the Via Aurelia. In the USA Anna Dengel was awarded a medallion that stated "Catholic Woman of Achievement for 1960" by the Women's National Institute of New York City. In September of 1961 Anna was made an honorary citizen of her home town, Steeg, in Lechtal, Austria. The Society added seven more hospitals to its list of medical missions in the 1960s: Vietnam (Qui Nhon); Jordan (Amman); Uganda (Fort Portal); Kenya (Nangina); Ethiopia (Attat); India (Mundakayam); and the Philippines (Bongao). Additional houses were also erected in India, Germany, and the Philippines; and in 1970 a foundation would be established among the Maasai, a semi-nomadic people living in the shadow of Mount Kilimanjaro in Loitokitok in eastern Kenya. In the years leading up to the Sixth General Chapter, Mother Anna Dengel continued to visit her missions around the world. Even after she had turned seventy, she attended events of significance within the Society: for example, the reception of the habit ceremony in Essen, Germany and the opening of the new Holy Family Hospital in Atlanta, USA in 1964; and the 1965 reception and profession ceremonies in Philadelphia. She kept up-to-date on developments within the institutional Church and on current events globally, often referring to relevant issues when communicating with the Sisters.

In January of 1962, Mother Dengel sent a Newsletter to all the Medical Mission Sisters, asking them to pray for the Vatican Council throughout the rest of the year. In August she received another award: an Honorary Fellowship in the American College of Hospital Administrators in Chicago, in recognition of the outstanding role she had played in helping to meet the health needs of impoverished people around the world. The members of her Society would soon take her passion for justice to another level of engagement. As socio-political realities dominated the news, many Medical Mission Sisters became part of the movements for justice and peace on behalf of the disenfranchised in ways that Anna could never have anticipated. The liturgical movement, the women's movement, civil rights and anti-war movements, Liberation Theology and the Bible studies that empowered Base Communities in barrios and favelas around the world led to a shift in consciousness that in time would transform the universal Church by placing it in the midst of the world and not apart from it. By the time the Second Vatican Council was officially convened on October 11 in 1962, a growing number of priests, religious, and laity were ready to embrace Pope John XXIII's call for *Aggiornamento* and a spirit of open-mindedness and change. In 1965 Anna Dengel told members of the Society to be prepared for an emerging future in the spirit of conciliar decisions.

> "We are at the break of a new era after a long dawn... now things are becoming clearer and imperative. It is our responsible task to bring the Society into tune with the mind and decisions of the Council and the teaching of the Holy Father and recent popes."

Anna encouraged all to reflect on the Council's underlying theme of openness to the Spirit in preparation for the upcoming Chapter.

> "First of all we must get together in prayer for this important event in the Society, which occurs at a providential moment when the whole Church is in the process of Aggiornamento, giving clarification and also specific directives to Religious. It is our duty to study and apply them."

It was agreed before the Chapter:

> "The general spirit ... should be laid down in the Constitution, which should be a 'book of life,' containing that which will remain and is not bound to particular circumstances of time or place."

On the Society's 40th anniversary, September 30, nine Bishops who were in Rome for the Council and knew the Society, came to the Generalate to offer their congratulations. After a celebratory Mass and a meal, there were shared stories, and for the Sisters, "a nine-fold blessing from the Bishops."

In mid-1966 Anna Dengel was in Austria, where she was awarded the *"Ehrenring"* – Ring of Honor – from the Austrian government in recognition of her services to humankind. In October, in Innsbruck, she received the honorary title of "Chairman of the Doctors' Guild." In the fall of 1966, Pro-Provincial Chapters took place in preparation for the General Chapter. At that time Mother Anna Dengel was nominated by the Prefect of the Sacred Congregation for Religious to serve on the executive committee for the founding of the International Union of Superiors General to be headquartered in Rome. In January of 1967 Anna stressed in her New Year Circular Letter to the community that the focus of the year would be on issues related to the General Chapter.

> "As regards the General Chapter, my mind, and also yours, no doubt, are full of thoughts and questions, hopes and doubts, desires and ideals, pros and cons, light and blind spots, all ready to go into a melting pot of continuous prayer, of Gospel and Council searching, of weighing, balancing suggestions and proposals received from young and old and in between."

The First Congress of the International Union of Superiors General took place in Rome during the first two weeks of March. Mother Dengel was elected delegate for the English speaking Superiors General in Rome and enjoyed participating in such a significant and stimulating event. On March 16 the Generalate celebrated Anna's 75th birthday. Clergy and friends joined the community for a day of joyful festivities, which included Mass for the first time in the new house. In June Doctor Anna Maria Dengel was awarded the Golden Cross of Honor by the Republic of Austria in the presence of a distinguished gathering in Vienna.

The days leading up to the Chapter were filled with preliminary meetings. Two of the pre-Chapter recommendations were: that the Constitution be rewritten in line with the spirit and thinking of Vatican II; and that the works of the Society be integrated as much as possible in the country of establishment and help develop that country's health care. Recommendations regarding Religious Life included the wish to do away with what is not essential and the suggestion that Community Life be studied and updated. There was also a specific request regarding garb: that the Sisters have the freedom to wear lay clothes. Recommendations concerning Government state clearly the wish for a structure based on the principles of freedom and the primacy of the person; participation and representation; subsidiarity and decentralization; and authority as a service role.

A major topic of concern was the stark decrease in vocations. If the trend continued, many of the Society's missions would be in jeopardy. Some Chapter delegates stressed that new people needed to be given opportunity to do things their own way and the freedom to order their lives accordingly. Mother Dengel made this statement to the Chapter delegates. "If we do not put this 'something new' into operation, there is no chance for the Society." She said in a circular letter sent to all Society members: "We are at the end of an era." She then suggested turning the page "with joyful and comforting thoughts," not with distress, regret, or a sense of loss. "Let us begin the new era," she said, indicating that she herself was ready. Symbolically, a new Generalate building, under construction for quite some time, was solemnly blessed on September 30, with many dignitaries and Medical Mission Sisters in attendance.

On October 11, 1967, the Feast of the Motherhood of Mary, the Sixth General Chapter convened at the Generalate of the Medical Mission Sisters on Via Aurelia in Rome. Mother Anna Dengel set the tone and articulated a sense of direction.

> "It is up to the Chapter to give the shape and form to helpful structures and a way of life conducive to holiness, happiness, and wholesomeness appropriate for our task as Medical Mission Sisters in the world of today."

Those words infused her "holy experiment" with a sense of timelessness, as that which for her had been a new beginning was about to begin again. She reminded the delegates of the core characteristics of their Society.

> "We have love for Our Lady, Cause of Our Joy and for the liturgy, we have the spirit of industry and simplicity, we are joyful and have the gift of finding occasions for a feast with music and song, we can cheerfully rise to the occasion in case of need."

She also emphasized what was for her and for her Society a foundational sine qua non.

> "I would like to express here particularly, gratitude: above all gratitude to God the Creator and Giver of all good gifts, gratitude to all who cooperated with us to serve those in need, and to those in need who give us the opportunity to serve them."

She said to the delegates who represented all 728 community members around the world:

> "I want to thank all the Sisters for all they have done for me and with me, and for what they have been for me."

What had really mattered to Anna resonated through words that came straight from the heart.

> "I had the good fortune to have the confidence and loyalty of the Sisters during my years of office, which lightened the burden and really made it a labor of love."

Her closing words were a benediction.

> "May we live our renewed and adapted life so as to draw down God's continued blessing on the Society and all its members."

The hard work of restructuring for adaptation, enculturation, and renewal continued into November. The originating spirit of the Society was to be the foundational imperative for all aspects of change. Mother Dengel's words from the past held a promise for the future.

> "As Medical Missionaries the needs and sufferings of humanity must find an echo in our hearts. That is why you came to the Society. In our day and age this is of paramount importance. This is our vocation: to make Christ live within us, then let him shine forth."

She shared with Chapter delegates how Medical Mission work was integral to the meaning of the Society.

"Medical Mission work as carried out under the mandate of the Church, is a work of love, justice, and effective concern for those in need of restoration of health and for the promotion and preservation of the health of peoples in developing countries (or in countries of particular need), to enable them to use their God given faculties and endowments as fully as possible for their development, human dignity and happiness."

Before the Chapter came to a close on the morning of November 10, Sister Jane Gates had been elected Superior General. She was the first to assume the role that had been synonymous with that of the Founder since the Society began. On November 12 Gaetano Cardinal Chicognani came to the Generalate, and in the presence of all the Chapter members, presented Mother Anna Dengel with the *"Pro Ecclesia et Pontifice"* (for Church and Pope) medal from the Holy See. Also known as the "Cross of Honor," it is given for distinguished service to the Church and is the highest honor that can be awarded to the laity by the pope. The Cardinal said that "Mother Dengel had never looked for praise – she had no time for it. The only praise she did seek was the *Decretum Laudis*, for the community." Society annals state: "… the occasion seemed to please the Cardinal so much!" The written records also say: "There was a delay in beginning the ceremony since the secretary had forgotten to bring the medal!"

Significant outcomes of the Society's Sixth General Chapter were: a new Constitution; a new government system based on active participation of the members according to the principles of subsidiarity and decentralization; a flexible formation program; freedom to wear lay clothes and to use one's baptismal name; and a new vision of the work of the Society.

Implications for the future, influenced by Vatican II theology and its shift in how the Church would now describe its mission, were: a re-thinking of religious life and the work of the Society; greater participation in decision-making, not only by the Sisters, but also by the people with whom they work and those who benefit from their services; shared responsibility for the community's lifestyle and prayer; stress on health care and community development work; an increase in communication among members throughout the world; and a growing sense of "One World" emerging. The following prayer by Anna Dengel, articulated at an earlier time, reflects the perennial spirit of her Society through decades of evolutionary change.

> "Grant Thy blessing on our Society.
> Keep in us a spirit
> of joyful service,
> of the milk of human kindness,
> of not counting the cost,
> of do and dare for God."

There was a significant shift in responsibilities from Mother Anna Dengel to Sister Jane Gates and the General Council following the 1967 Chapter. The transition was not an easy one for Anna, or for Jane, but in time Anna adjusted, and to some extent, moved on. In between travels she spent time organizing her personal papers as well as official documents and artifacts of historic significance for the Society's archives, thereby ensuring that future historians had access to primary sources. She made certain that sensitive materials relating to her illness and to the crisis in leadership precipitated by Father Michael Mathis remained sealed and inaccessible for twenty-five years after her death. She kept in touch with certain ecclesiastics in the Vatican with whom she had a relationship and went there on a regular basis. During the years leading up to the next General Chapter, which was once again on a six-year cycle, she corresponded with individual Sisters and was kept informed on all aspects of MMS life-in-mission. She also had many visitors. Much of the time conversations dealt with post-Conciliar developments.

In the spring of 1969 Anna became seriously ill and was admitted to Saint Elizabeth Hospital in Essen, Germany. She returned to Rome in September. In January, 1970, she had eye surgery in Essen and did not go back to Rome until January of 1971. At Pentecost in 1973, as Medical Mission Sisters around the world were steeped in preparations for yet another Chapter, Mother Anna Dengel sent them a letter that included the following passage.

> "As the 'Sun is setting' for me, it is a consoling feeling
> that those who helped to build up the Society will under
> Holy Mother Church, continue to 'deliver the goods!'

The future is YOURS. May the past be witness that I
did my part to the best of my ability. The task God gave
me to do brought me joy and hardships. The hardships
were borne with readiness for the love of God and our
Cause. You are as conscious of the needs of the present
day, as I was of the needs of my day.

*Emitte Spiritum Tuum, et renovabis faciem terrae,
Alleluia.*

["Come, Holy Spirit, and renew the face of the
earth."]

With what more suitable prayer could I end my words
to you?"

The Seventh General Chapter was held in the fall of 1973 in Rome at
the Generalate of the Christian Brothers. Mother Dengel was present.
She had written a lengthy reflection entitled "The Course of Events
that Led to the Founding of the Society" and she asked Sister Monica
Neuhaus to read it aloud during a plenary session, so that those who
would shape the Society's future would know something of its past.
Anna said to the assembly: "Through all of these happenings, the hand
of God's Providence has always been clear, for event followed event
without my planning it."

At the heart of the 1973 Chapter was the evolution of a Common
Purpose rooted in a more inclusive understanding of the Society's
healing mission. It affirmed healing as the directional force that unites
all the members and is "the underpinning of all our involvements." In
light of that fundamental assessment, the proposal stated:

"We commit ourselves to hear the call of a suffering and broken
world and become one with it in its struggle toward wholeness and
completion."

"As community we experience that a totality of relationships draws
us beyond our local situations, across national and cultural boundaries
to the People of God and to the community of all [humankind.]"

The Chapter had taken a quantum leap into the heart of the Mission
to which Anna Dengel, and those who followed her, had been called.
Radiating out from medical missions would be a variety of healing
ministries which, in time, would be understood as "a healing presence
at the heart of a wounded world" and "at the heart of the community of

life." The 1973 Chapter embodied the spirit of its Founder in ways that she might never have been able to articulate but would most surely have blessed. Elements of change would always flow from Anna's unwavering vision of and passionate commitment to "a labor of love."

Before the Chapter was adjourned, Mother Anna Dengel was given a lighted candle, which she passed to Sister Jane Gates, who gave it to Sister Godelieve Prové, a Belgian doctor, who had been elected to serve as the third Superior General of the Society.

Throughout 1975 festivities took place to celebrate the Society's Golden Jubilee year. September 30, the 50th anniversary of Foundation Day, was the culminating event and the Founder of this "holy experiment" – that little girl whose father had been told to "take her home to die" – had lived to celebrate it. She cherished the following from the Vatican.

> "To our beloved daughter in Christ,
> Anna M. Dengel, S.C.M.M.,
> in commemoration of the fiftieth anniversary
> of the foundation of the Society of
> Catholic Medical Missionaries,
> we are happy to extend
> as an expression of our paternal benevolence
> in the Lord,
> our special Apostolic Blessing,
> invoking upon all the Sisters of the Congregation
> the grace to continue in their joyful
> ecclesial and religious apostolate
> of bringing Christ's name and his loving kindness
> to those in need."
> *Pope Paul VI, January 24, 1976*

Soon after, in 1976, Anna Dengel had a stroke. In 1979, she had another.

On the morning of April 17, 1980, Medical Mission Sisters in Rome gathered around the bedside of their beloved Founder in silent, prayerful vigil as she slipped peacefully away. People who came to visit "found Mother in her own room, her face very beautiful, almost glowing with peace and serenity, all wrinkles and all signs of age and suffering gone."

The following day, in chapel, they saw her "dressed in her grey habit, blue veil and profession cross." The chronicle continues.

> "Cardinal Rossi, prefect of the Sacred Congregation for the Evangelization of Peoples, celebrated the Eucharist with us in the chapel around Mother, as an expression of the great respect and appreciation of the Church for what Mother has contributed by her life and mission. The stream of visitors continued for four full days."

Medical Mission Sisters from around the world joined those who were already there, so that "with Sisters of so many nationalities, having lived in so many parts of the world, the whole Society was truly represented." They brought with them the memories of all those who had been the beneficiaries of Anna's tireless efforts to bless them with hope and healing, so that it truly can be said: in spirit they also were there.

A Eucharist of Thanksgiving was celebrated on Monday, April 21, in the Church of the *Campo Santo Dei Teutonici* in Vatican City. The décor was deeply symbolic: the Paschal Candle with sprigs of delicate white orchids; eighty-eight tulips from Holland; a small bouquet of red alpine roses from the Tirol; some earth from Anna's mother's grave brought by the son of the late headmaster who had taught little Anna during her first school days in Steeg. The church was filled to overflowing with friends, relatives, and dignitaries from Austria and Rome. The Liturgy transmitted an "all-pervading sense of Easter and life ... around Mother we were all drawn together as one community in faith and prayer." After the Eucharist, all processed out of the church and around the cemetery to the grave. Mother was buried there, in the *Campo Santo dei Teutonici*, a small cemetery within Vatican City, in the shadow of Saint Peter's.

This story ends as it began, with the pairing of two women who would have an everlasting impact on one another's lives and the lives of so many others. Driven by compassion, they shared an insatiable desire to alleviate the suffering of women and children who had no access to professional medical care. Agnes McLaren, M.D. paved the way for Sister-doctors in the Roman Catholic Church. Anna Dengel, M.D. made that vision tangible through a worldwide network of medical services and supportive ministries focused on healing and wholeness.

Doctor McLaren died on April 17. So did Anna Dengel – 67 years later. What an appropriate ending to this chapter in the Book of Life.

Let us look at the world in the right way.
For us it is a paradise of opportunity
to glorify God.

Anna Dengel

"So let your light shine
that they may see your good works
and glorify your Father who is in heaven"
expressed the fundamental idea of our Society.
At first you may not fully understand it,
but if you think more deeply and often,
you will.

Anna Dengel

Photo Album

Mama and Papa, with Anna, Ida,
and baby Hans

Anna (left) and Ida (right) with schoolmates in
Hall

Anna
(right)
with a
friend in
Ireland

Anna (left) with family members and
sewing staff

Ida (left) and Anna in traditional dress in Tirol

Anna (back row, left) and school hockey club in Cork

Anna and her family, 1912: Papa with her siblings (right and rear) and Amalie with her children

(below) Anna with Amalie, Papa, and all her brothers and sisters in 1920

Anna (above) with her father as she leaves her homeland
And (for the two photos below it):
Portraits of Anna as a young woman

Graduation Day, October 25, 1919:
The National University of Ireland in Cork

Passport photo, c. 1920, Cork, Ireland

Doctor Dengel gaining experience in surgery prior to leaving for India

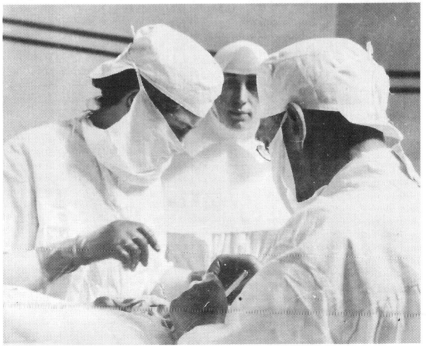

Doctor Dengel in an ad hoc outpatient clinic at St. Catherine's (above) and treating a patient in Baramula (below)

Anna at Saint Catherine of Genoa Hospital for
Native Women and Children in Rawalpindi,
India: 1920-1923
A quiet moment in Pindi (right)
In Kashmiri dress at Baramula (below)

Baramula, Kashmir, India

Doctor Anna Dengel in Rawalpindi:
a cross-cultural immersion that would shape the rest of her life

Anna with Mother Marie Alberte (above) before leaving India; and with Dr. Wadia (right), her replacement

Coming to America, 1924: Pauline Willis and Anna Dengel with ship's Captain and fellow passengers

Foundation Day, Medical Mission Sisters, September 30, 1925, Washington

The first four members of the Society: Dr. Joanna Lyons; Dr. Anna Dengel; Evelyn
Flieger, R.N., and Marie Ulbrich, R.N.

Medical Mission Sisters, First Profession, 1926, Washington

Dr. Anna Dengel and Dr. Joanna Lyons, 1926, Washington

Anna in Washington: going out into the world (left) and (below)

Anna and her family in Steeg in the Tirol: with her sister and niece (above left) and with her parents

Anna at spiritual reading in Washington in the spring of 1932

In Rome with Fr. Michael Mathis (left) for the Society's Second General Chapter in the Fall

Anna with Agnes Marie Ulbrich in 1927 at their second house (above) and with their dog (below)

Society supporters with Anna and members (above); Anna's return to her first mission (below)

Honorary Doctorate
Awarded to
Doctor Anna Maria Dengel
at the
University of Cork Ireland
1932

With two little
friends and in the
habit adopted by the
Chapter in Rome:
1932

Mission Moments

Anna joins the ranks of canonical Religious women after her Society is formally deemed a congregation by Rome in April 1943

Agnes Marie Ulbrich celebrates the Society's Golden Jubilee

Anna Dengel and Michael Mathis 1950

Anna Dengel and Bishop Fulton J. Sheen 1950

Portraits of Mother Anna Dengel, Superior
General of the Medical Mission Sisters

Mother Anna Dengel with nursing and midwifery students in Indonesia (above) and with her Malabar Sisters in India (below)

Anna in Yemen (top photo) and in India

Anna in Murree, 1951 (above) and in the Austrian Tirol in 1960

Agnes McLaren, MD
July 4, 1837 – April 17, 1913

Anna Dengel, MD
March 16, 1892 – April 17, 1980

ANNA DENGEL

HONORARY DEGREES
Doctor of Medicine
University College, Cork
[National University of Ireland]

~

Doctor of Science
Marquette University, Milwaukee

~

Doctor of Law
Manhattanville College, New York

~

Doctor of Medicine
Catholic University of Nijmegen
Netherlands

~

Honorary Fellow
International College of Surgeons
Academic Hood Conferred in Chicago

~

Honorary Fellowship
American College of Hospital Administrators
Academic Hood conferred at
McCormick Stadium, Chicago

AWARDS
Paladin Grand Cross
Catholic Students Mission Crusade, USA

~

Alliance of Catholic Women Award
Archdiocese of Philadelphia

~

Honorary Membership
Alpha Epsilon Delta
National Premedical Honor Society,
LaSalle College, Philadelphia

~

Poverello Medal
College of Steubenville, Ohio

~

Laetare Medal
Saint Luke Guild of Boston

~

Xavier Award
New York Province of the Society of Jesus
(Jesuits)

~

Citation
National Federation of
Catholic Physicians Guild
Presented by Bishop Fulton J. Sheen

~

Honorary Membership
Doctors Guild of Austria

Poverello Medal
College of Steubenville, Ohio

~

Distinguished Daughter of Pennsylvania
Award conferred by the Governor

~

Medallion of Honor
Women's International Exposition
New York City

~

Honorary Membership
Philippine Women's Medical Association
Awarded in Manila

~

Award of Merit
University of Santo Tomas
Manila, Philippines

~

Honorary Citizenship
Bestowed by the Local Council
Steeg, Austria

~

Ehrenring Award
Presented by President of the Tirol
Innsbuck, Austria

~

Ehrenzeichen
The City of Solbad, Hall, Tirol

~

Guild of Catholic Doctors of the Tirol
Certificate of Honorary Membership

~

Golden Cross of Merit
Republic of Austria

~

Medical Women's International Association
Honorary Membership

~

Pro Ecclesia et Pontifice
Papal Award
Conferred by Cardinal Cigognani,
Vatican Secretary of State

~

Anna Dengel was also invited to accept an
Honorary Doctorate from the following
institutions, but had to decline:
Stonehill College, Easton, Massachusetts
University of Portland, Oregon
Villanova University, Pennsylvania
Saint Mary's College, Notre Dame, Indiana
La Salle College, Philadephia

Areas of Medical Mission Sisters Involvement 1925-2016

★Current Involvement   ■ Past Involvement

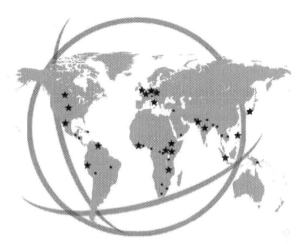

NORTH AMERICA
★Canada
★Mexico
★United States

CENTRAL AMERICA
■ Guatemala
■ Nicaragua
■ St. Lucia

SOUTH AMERICA
■ Bolivia
■ Brazil
★Peru
★Venezuela

EUROPE
★Belgium
★Germany
★Italy

★The Netherlands
■ Switzerland
★United Kingdom

AFRICA
■ Botswana
■ Cameroon
■ Democratic Republic of Congo
★Ethiopia
★Ghana
★Kenya
★Malawi
■ Nigeria
■ Republic of South Africa
■ Rwanda
■ Swaziland
■ Tanzania
★Uganda

MIDDLE EAST
■ Jordan
■ Republic of Yemen

ASIA
■ Afghanistan
■ Bangladesh
■ Bhutan
★India
★Japan
★Indonesia
■ Micronesia
■ Myanmar
★Pakistan
■ Papua New Guinea
★The Philippines
■ Thailand
■ Vietnam

EPILOGUE

I was sixteen when I first met Anna Dengel. My friend and I had come to Philadelphia from northern New Jersey to check out the Medical Mission Sisters, because I wanted to be one. As I waited in the small parlor, Mother Dengel appeared. She greeted me with a gigantic smile and captivating warmth. "I want to be a doctor and a missionary," I said. "You are too young," she responded, then told me to finish my education and come back when I was older. So I did. I returned later that year after I had graduated high school and had turned seventeen. I entered the Society on November 1, 1955.

In 1964 the American Province published a book on the Society entitled *If It Matters*. I had been appointed to its editorial board and was assigned to write the piece on the Society's Founder. I can still recall my feeling of inadequacy. Four of us, and Mother Dengel, sat around a small table as I read aloud what I had written. After I finished, there was silence. Then Mother said something like, "all right, then," and we moved on. The others were amazed. For me it was a rite of passage into legitimacy. I would eventually be named editor of *The Medical Missionary* magazine, the publication so dear to the Founder's heart. I was determined that it would remain an extension of her prophetic and pioneering spirit.

That same year I received a Bachelor of Music degree from Catholic University in Washington, DC, not at all what I had dreamed of when I made my vows as a Medical Mission Sister in 1958. Poised on the threshold of Vatican II, the Society had been part of the movement that anticipated the vernacular in liturgical rites and ritual song. I was in Fox Chase when Father Michael Mathis introduced Vespers in English and we began to experiment with new ways of communal prayer and praise. When provincial leadership decided that someone had to be qualified to lead the community through the liturgical changes that lay ahead, I was asked if I would be willing to do so. I had the right to refuse, I was told, but for me, that would not have been easy, for I felt a responsibility as a member of my community to go wherever I was sent and do the work assigned. Catholic University had a stellar school of music. However, it was more oriented toward the treasures of the past than possibilities for the future. Within months after receiving my degree in sacred music, ecclesiastical authority announced that the language of the liturgy in the USA would be in the vernacular. I picked up a guitar and began to channel songs the Spirit sang to and through me in a language all could comprehend: songs with rhythm and relevance, metaphors and meaning, songs that encouraged me, and in time, would radically transform me, leading me and many into a new era of creativity in the universal Church.

As those songs made their way around the world, Superiors of various religious orders wrote to Mother Dengel to say how much they appreciated them. I saw her in Rome in 1971. She told me she loved my music, was thrilled with the Christmas carols I had sent her prior to their publication, and when she had heard I would be presenting a program to major superiors of women, said she wanted the first ticket! The following year she wrote to me in Philadelphia: "I thank God with you for your gift to carry the message of the Gospel in such an appealing way far and wide. Don't forget me if you have anything new again, as I always appreciate it." In 1975, the Society's Golden Jubilee year, I sent her three unpublished songs celebrating themes dear to her heart. She responded:

> "What a lovely and much appreciated surprise I received yesterday in your Jubilee songs! Thank you very much for the gift of them to me and to the Society!"

One year later I received a lengthy hand-written letter from Sister Monica Neuhaus, her friend and faithful companion. It began:

> "Ever since the day when Mother suffered her stroke, she has asked me specially to write to you – to Australia, she said – and to send you her love and to tell you that she was with you in thought and prayer. Almost daily

she has spoken of you and asked me all over again to write to you."

The bond that had been established between us through the sharing of sacred song led to an intermingling of energy that did not end when her life ended. Such a connection in the realm of spirit transcends finite limitations, keeping a channel for communication potentially open. She was present as I searched through her archives, and I felt her guidance often while I was writing this book. I invited Anna to tell her own story and I am convinced she has. There were moments in her life I would never have revealed to others on my own.

Two questions had spearheaded my initial research: (1) Where was Anna Dengel during the greater part of the 1930's and why do we know so little about her during that span of time? (2) Why do some Holy Cross seminarians in South Bend, Indiana persist in referring to Rev. Michael Mathis, c.s.c., as co-founder of our Society? Finding answers to those questions meant examining documents sealed for decades and shining a light on areas some would prefer had been left in the dark. As the Society evolved, it seems as if the blueprint for this pioneering entity had two separate architects – albeit, working together, but on two different designs – one seeking a whole new framework for meeting the needs of women and children who had no access to professional medical care; the other focused on changing the infrastructure of the institutional Church. Both shared a fundamental vision but differed in their approach, contributing significantly to the evolution of the Church's understanding of mission in diverse ways.

Anna Dengel was Founder, not co-founder, of the Medical Mission Sisters, as this biography makes clear. The contribution of Michael Mathis, however, was significant and lives on in the Society's love for the liturgy and liturgical music. Ironically, I entered the Society to become a physician like Anna Dengel. Instead, I am a theologian known for my contribution to sacred song. Over time the Holy Spirit has revealed that there are multiple ways to be a healing presence in the world. Again, in the words of Anna Dengel: "In the end, God's work wins."

A Labor of Love

Love seeks union: God is in us, around us, with us.
Serve God in everybody and everything
    with real personal love.
If we serve with love, nothing is unbearable.
Our work will surely bear fruit for eternity,
    if we serve our neighbor out of pure love.

Let the love of God, which prompts our service,
    shine through.
Our love of God must not only be affective but effective.
Our love and devotion, with knowledge and skills,
    are the light serving the sick in the missions,
    the good works that glorify God.

Love is measured in sacrifice.
To put love in order, love all alike.
Our love must be centered in God.

Love is a matter of getting into one's bones
    and one's mind.
Love is expressed in a positive way
    in deeds, in sacrifices, and in duty.
To do one's duty sincerely and conscientiously
    is a manifestation of greater love.

A greater love is manifested by generosity.
Love wants to give, does not count the cost.
Nothing is too much for love.
    Joy is a fruit of the labor of love.
If you do it with love, you do it with joy.
    Charity is supernatural love.
It is a vocation of greater love.
It is a labor of love.

Anna Dengel